T0249135

Selected Writings

George Washington

Selected Writings

WITH AN INTRODUCTION BY
Ron Chernow

LIBRARY OF AMERICA PAPERBACK CLASSICS

THE SELECTIONS FOR THIS
LIBRARY OF AMERICA PAPERBACK CLASSIC EDITION
ARE DRAWN FROM
GEORGE WASHINGTON: WRITINGS,
EDITED BY JOHN RHODEHAMEL,
VOLUME 91 IN THE LIBRARY OF AMERICA SERIES,
PUBLISHED WITH SUPPORT FROM
THE JOHN M. OLIN FOUNDATION

Contents

INTRODUCTION
by Ron Chernow

We commonly think of George Washington as the quintessential man of action, robust and red-blooded, not as an accomplished man of letters, but his achievements were inseparable from his excellent command of language. For too long Washington has suffered from an unfair stereotype as a bland and bloodless character, even a bit of a stuffed shirt. More than anything else, his writings refute that unfortunate impression, which has served to distance Washington from posterity. Admittedly, Washington never wrote with the easy grace of a Jefferson, the sparkling wit of a Franklin, or the mental agility of a Hamilton. Nonetheless, in his letters, general orders, and presidential messages, we feel most acutely the full force of his commanding personality. If often reticent in public, he was typically passionate, even vehement, in the private statements that poured endlessly from his quill as he kept up a vast correspondence. To encounter Washington in his papers is to confront a notably hot-blooded and opinionated man, not the taciturn sphinx of American myth.

It is striking that, from his earliest adventures in the French and Indian War, the young Washington grew accustomed to committing his exploits to paper. In 1753, at age twenty-one, he was dispatched by the royal governor in Williamsburg, Virginia, to deliver an ultimatum to the French commandant on the western frontier, demanding his withdrawal from the so-called Ohio Country claimed by England. Washington left a detailed diary of this hazardous journey into the wilderness, recording how he forded streams swollen by rain and snow, parleyed with Indian chieftains, and scouted sites for a fort. He conjured up his mission vividly, describing how he donned "Indian walking Dress" as he trudged through a frigid landscape and was pitched from a hand-made raft into icy waters. He boasted, with considerable justice, that he had "a Constitution hardy enough to encounter and undergo the most severe tryals."

The thrill of reading any collection like this one—or of any biography, for that matter—is to watch the slow, groping evolution of a callow young man or woman into the self-assured personage known to history. Blessed with a sterling capacity for self-criticism, Washington underwent a stunning metamorphosis from an ambitious, often clumsy young officer into an enlightened leader. In the early letters, one can see through his pose of youthful nonchalance, as when he writes breezily, after a particularly bloody encounter with the French, "I heard Bulletts whistle and believe me there was something charming in the sound." All the while, with his "application and diligent study" of his duty, Washington molded himself for future greatness. He revealed a stern, unflinching sense of duty, chiding the men under his command for the "Insolence of the Soldiers, the Indolence, and Inactivity of the Officers." Previewing things to come, he also displayed a keen sense of injustice, protesting that the Crown had denied him and other colonial officers the royal commissions they coveted: "We cant conceive, that being Americans shoud deprive us of the benefits of British Subjects; nor lessen our claim to preferment. . . ." Over the next twenty years, this rage broadened and deepened into a full-blown critique of imperial injustice toward the colonists.

George Washington presents special challenges to any biographer who has tried to capture him in print. The problem has less to do with the supposed remoteness of his personality than from the fact that he led a compartmentalized life, exhibiting different traits in different settings. As a general and politician, Washington was capable of exquisite courtesy and sensitivity toward subordinates, but he presented a much more temperamental side of his personality when he acted as a planter or slaveholder. The present edition richly portrays Washington in his many guises. After his service in the French and Indian War, he married the wealthy widow Martha Dandridge Custis and took up the life of a prosperous tobacco planter. Perhaps as a result of financial insecurity in his youth, he was often testy and quarrelsome in business dealings. In these selections, we see him rebuking his London agent, Robert Cary & Co., for obtaining inferior prices for his tobacco and sending him shoddy goods in return—personal grievances that festered, contributing to his growing disgust with England. We also watch him overseeing the slaves at Mount Vernon and occasionally resorting to harsh measures, as when he sells a slave named Tom—"a Rogue & Runaway"—into Caribbean servitude in exchange for molasses, rum, and other goods.

In the aftermath of the Stamp Act and the Townshend Duties, Washington began to find his political voice and it was an unmistakably militant one. He was never an original or systematic thinker, but he grasped fully the revolutionary ideas circulating in the colonies. For all of his moderation and pointed reluctance to resort to arms, he expressed himself with fervor and eloquence, especially when under the sway of powerful feelings. He denounced the Stamp Act as a "direful attack" upon the liberties of the colonists and spied a larger conspiracy at work: "our lordly Masters in Great Britain will be satisfied with nothing less than the deprivation of American freedom." When violence erupted at Lexington and Concord, Washington wrote a letter throbbing with palpable emotion, lamenting to a friend "that a Brother's Sword has been sheathed in a Brother's breast, and that, the once happy and peaceful plains of America are either to be drenched with Blood, or Inhabited by Slaves. Sad alternative!"

Inevitably, a large portion of this collection is devoted to the eight and a half years that Washington spent as commander-in-chief of the Continental Army. Although this edition includes documents that touch upon every major battle of the war in Washington's theater of command, the selection is not limited to purely military matters. Washington's wartime papers reveal how, in the absence of an executive branch of government, he functioned as a surrogate chief of state. In his general orders, he attempted to forge a sense of national unity, informing his men that "all Distinctions of Colonies will be laid aside; so that one and the same spirit may animate the whole. . . ." In exhorting his men to avoid "profane cursing, swearing & drunkenness," he wasn't simply enforcing military discipline, but shaping the character of a new nation.

The wartime writings throw into high relief just how much Washington grew in stature during the conflict. He was not, by nature or background, inclined to egalitarian feelings when he went to Cambridge, Massachusetts in 1775 to assume command of the New England militias besieging Boston. At first glance, he wrinkled his nose at his new soldiers, dismissing them as "an exceeding dirty & nasty people." It bothered him that the rank and file fraternized openly with their officers. But his letters show how he grew to love these men and admired their extraordinary sacrifices for the patriot cause. During the severe winter at Valley Forge, he wrote an indignant letter to Henry Laurens, president of Congress, rebutting critics of his leadership. "I can assure those Gentlemen, that it is a much easier and less distressing thing, to draw Remonstrances in a comfortable room by a good fire side, than to occupy a cold, bleak hill, and sleep under frost & Snow without Cloaths or Blankets." He went on to say of his soldiers, "I feel superabundantly for them, and from my soul pity those miseries, which it is neither in my power to relieve or prevent." Washington startles us repeatedly with his personal development, as when he responds warmly to Phillis Wheatley, the slave poet who sent him an ode she had written in praise of him. In a gracious note, the Virginia slave owner invited her to his headquarters, adding that "I shall be happy to see a person so favoured by the Muses."

The wartime transformation of George Washington was underscored by two events late in the conflict. On May 22, 1782, he read with horror a letter addressed to him by an officer named Lewis Nicola, suggesting that he reign as America's first monarch. Washington's response—eloquent, succinct, and decisive —scotched the idea instantly. He replied that "no occurrence in the course of the War, has given me more painful sensations than your information of there being such ideas existing in the Army" and he urged Nicola "to banish these thoughts from your Mind. . . ." He then dealt with a potential mutiny of his officers, who feared that they would be demobilized without the pay and pensions promised to them. Washington worried that such a drastic action would plunge the country "into a gulph of Civil horror." In a speech of surpassing eloquence, Washington promised the men that he would lobby Congress for their demands. Striking a personal note, he reminded the officers, "As I have never left your side one moment, but when called from you on public duty, . . . it can *scarcely be supposed*, at this late stage of the War" that he was unconcerned with their welfare. In his "Farewell Address to the Armies," he again sounded a tender, loving note as he bid farewell to "those he holds most dear." This personal bond with his soldiers is one of many delights of these selections.

Washington never left thoughts of Mount Vernon far behind during the war. Despite his apotheosis as the American Cincinnatus, he continued to fret about money, and his writings reflect the peculiar mixture of high drama and mundane concerns that permeated his life. Toward the end of the war, he forewarned his estate manager, Lund Washington, "I shall come home with empty pockets whenever Peace shall take place." His monetary troubles were then exacerbated by the hordes of tourists and curiosity-seekers who descended upon his estate for unannounced visits, prompting Washington to lament bitterly that Mount Vernon resembled "a well resorted tavern." In the years between the war and his presidency, as Washington tried in vain to regain a sense of privacy, a new contemplative tone entered his letters. As he told Lafayette, "I am retireing within myself; & shall be able to view the solitary walk, & tread the paths of private life with heartfelt satisfaction." The warrior, as he mellowed, began to sound more like a sage. On the subject of war, he wrote, "My first wish is, to see this plague to Mankind banished from the Earth; & the Sons & daughters of this World employed in more pleasing & innocent amusements than in preparing implements . . . for the destruction of the human race." This late-blooming Utopian streak in a veteran of two prolonged wars is yet another of the astounding transformations that Washington's writings bring to glowing life.

At many times in his life, Washington had to exercise restraint and tact in his public utterances. Whether serving as commander-in-chief of the Continental Army or as the first president, he functioned as the supreme figure of a fragile national unity and had to be something of a cipher onto which a hopeful nation could project its aspirations. When he decided, late in the Revolutionary War, to publish his opinions on the urgent need for a more solid union of the states, he knew that, having subordinated his views to the civilian control of Congress for eight years, a tremendous gulf existed between his private and public statements. As he confided to Alexander Hamilton, "All my private letters have teemed with these Sentiments. . . ." When he published his valedictory "Circular to

State Governments" on June 8, 1783, he issued his sweeping political views to a wider public for the first time.

At the close of the war, Washington announced his permanent departure from public life, a forlorn hope that could never be fulfilled. His status was too lofty for early retirement, he cared too deeply about the fate of the country, and he was too disturbed by the crises that punctuated the postwar era. In his "Circular to State Governments," he confessed he was "stepping out of the proper line of my duty" as he issued a series of broad-gauged political judgments. He called for an "indissoluble Union of the States under one Federal Head"; recommended a more robust Congress; and warned of "Anarchy and confusion" unless such changes were implemented. When it came to these critical political issues, Washington's sense of urgency only intensified in the coming years.

Whereas other, more intellectual founders often formed their ideas from books, Washington crafted his ideas in the throes of action. As commander-in-chief, he had seen the dangers of a feckless Congress and selfish states and worried after the war about the "disinclination of the individual States to yield competent powers to Congress for the Fœderal Government. . . ." While Jefferson and Madison came to view a strong central government as the gravest threat to individual liberty, Washington clung to the opposite view, warning in 1784 that "a half starved, limping Government, that appears to be always moving upon crutches, & tottering at every step" would ultimately lead to chaos and despotism. Washington's apprehension about the fatal weakness of the federal government mounted until he confided to John Jay in 1786 that the Articles of Confederation had to be amended "or the fabrick must fall." Although Washington agonized over whether to attend the Constitutional Convention, thereby breaking his vow that he had retired from public life, the vigor of his political views, best expressed in his letters, left little doubt that he would attend. By a unanimous vote of the delegates in Philadelphia, he ended up serving as the president of the convention.

As if borne along by an irresistible tide from one major event to the next, Washington found it impossible to turn down the presidency—a position that was his for the asking—despite his extreme misgivings about assuming the post. His letters make clear that he didn't secretly pant for power. In fact, he insisted that the presidency "has no enticing charms, and no fascinating allurements for me." By now the young man who had dreamed of fame and glory had enjoyed more than his fill of recognition. In his private writings, Washington, who knew well his own strengths and limitations, expressed candid doubt that he was qualified for the highest office. On April 16, 1789, when he set out for his first inauguration in New York, he jotted down in his diary that he did so "with a mind oppressed with more anxious and painful sensations than I have words to express."

During the war, Washington made decisions by canvassing the opinions of his generals, and he adopted a similar practice with his cabinet officers. As a result, the process of presidential decision-making appears in his correspondence in fine-grained detail. From the outset, Washington approached decisions with painstaking care, stating, "I consider the successful Administration of the general Government as an object of almost infinite consequence to the present. . . ." To Madison, he touted the importance of governmental precedents, insisting that this first administration must "be fixed on true principles." Guided by his slow but thorough methods, Washington compiled an outstanding record as president and committed amazingly few errors.

Washington hoped to preside over a benign, non-partisan brand of politics and never dreamt that virulent party warfare would emerge during his two terms in office. Still greater was his shock that the rancor sprang from within his own cabinet, with Treasury Secretary Hamilton and Secretary of State Jefferson spearheading factions that hardened into two parties. Instead of siding with one man or the other, Washington tried to maintain a tenuous balance and arbitrate their vicious feud. This collection offers a comprehensive account of his failed mediation efforts. As Washington assured Jefferson, "I have a great—a sincere esteem and regard for you both, and ardently wish that some line could be marked out by which both of you could walk." With both of his remarkable lieutenants, he pleaded that "instead of wounding suspicions, & irritable charges, there may be liberal allowances—mutual forbearances —and temporising yieldings on *all sides*." As it turned out,

Washington was waging a losing battle and in his "Farewell Address" he felt the need to promulgate one final warning against partisanship: "The alternate domination of one faction over another, sharpened by the spirit of revenge natural to party dissension . . . is itself a frightful despotism." In the end, Washington found it impossible to sustain this delicate balancing act and identified his administration more openly with the Hamiltonian party, known as the Federalists.

Washington has long been such a sacred figure in American life that many readers will be taken aback to discover just how much abuse he endured as president. Feeding the partisan mayhem was an opposition press often instigated by his own Secretary of State. Editorial writers pounded Washington mercilessly, accusing him of everything from plotting to restore the monarchy to acting as a British double agent throughout the Revolutionary War. He was the first, but hardly the last, president to complain that "every act of the Executive is misrepresented, and tortured with a view to make it appear odious. . . ." He protested that "a set of infamous scribblers" had characterized his actions "in such exaggerated and indecent terms as could scarcely be applied to a Nero; a notorious defaulter; or even to a common pick-pocket." This deeply felt outrage was largely confined to his private letters.

Until his death in 1799, Washington remained anxious and watchful about the uncertain fate of his country. He was never able to retreat fully into the privacy that remained a tantalizing but futile fantasy for him. The writing on display in this volume resonates with the passion and intelligence, the dignity and paternal concern that more than justify Washington's claim to being the Father of his Country. In this volume, the man of letters takes his rightful place beside the man of action.

Selected Writings

Journey to the French Commandant

On Wednesday the 31st. of October 1753 I was Commission'd & appointed by the Honble. Robert Dinwiddie Esqr. Governor &ca. of Virginia

To visit & deliver a Letter to the Commandant of the French Forces on the Ohio, & set out on the intended Journey the same Day. The next I arriv'd at Fredericksburg, & engag'd Mr. Jacob Vanbraam, Interpreter, & proceeded with him to Alexandria where we provided Necessaries. From thence we went to Winchester & got Baggage Horses &ca. & from there we pursued the new Road to Wills Creek, where we arriv'd the 14th: of November.

Here I engag'd Mr. Gist to Pilot us out, & also hired four others as Servitors (vizt.) Barnaby Currin, & John McGuier (Indian Traders) Henry Steward, & William Jenkins; & in Company with those Persons I left the Inhabitants the Day following. The excessive Rains & vast Quantity of Snow that had fallen prevented our reaching Mr. Frazer's, an Indian Trader at the Mouth of Turtle Creek, on Monongehela, 'til Thursday.

22d: We were inform'd here, that Expresses were sent a few Day's ago to the Traders down the River to acquaint them with the General's Death, & return of Major Part of the French Army into Winter Quarters. The Waters were quite impassable, without Swimming our Horses, which oblig'd us to get the loan of a Canoe from Mr. Frazer, & to send Barnaby Currin & Henry Steward down Monongehela, with our Baggage to meet us at the Forks of Ohio, about 10 Miles to cross Allegany.

As I got down before the Canoe, I spent some Time in viewing the Rivers, & the Land in the Fork, which I think extreamly well situated for a Fort; as it has the absolute Command of both Rivers. The Land at the Point is 20 or 25 Feet above the common Surface of the Water; & a considerable Bottom of flat well timber'd Land all around it, very convenient for Building. The Rivers are each a quarter of a Mile, or more, across, & run here very nigh at Right Angles; Allegany bearing N: E: & Monongehela S: E: The former of these two is a very rapid swift running Water the other deep & still, with scarce any perceptable Fall. About two Miles from this, on the S: E: Side of the River, at the Place where the Ohio Company intended to erect a Fort; lives Singess, King of the Delawars; We call'd upon him to invite him to Council at the Logstown.

As I had taken a good deal of Notice Yesterday of the Situation at the Forks; my Curiosity led me to examine this more particularly; & my Judgement to think it greatly inferior, either for Defence or Advantages, especially the latter; For a Fort at the Forks wou'd be equally well situated on Ohio, & have the entire Command of Monongehela, which runs up to our Settlements & is extreamly well design'd for Water Carriage, as it is of a deep still Nature; besides a Fort at the Fork might be built at a much less Expence, than at the other Place. Nature has well contriv'd the lower Place for Water Defence, but the Hill whereon it must stand, being a quarter of a Mile in Length, & then descending gradually on the Land Side, will render it difficult & very expensive making a sufficient Fortification there. The whole Flat upon the Hill must be taken in, or the Side next the Descent made extreamly high; or else the Hill cut away: otherwise the Enemy will raise Batteries within that Distance, without being expos'd to a single Shot from the Fort.

Singess attended us to Logstown, where we arriv'd between Sunsetting & Dark, the 25th: Day after I left Williamsburg. We travel'd over some extream good & bad Land to get to this Place. As soon as I came into Town, I went to Monacatoocha (as the Half King was out at his hunting Cabbin on little Bever Creek, about 15 Miles off) & inform'd him, by John Davison Interpreter that I was sent a Messenger to the French General, & was ordered to call upon the Sachems of the Six Nations, to acquaint them with it. I gave him a String of Wampum, & a twist of Tobacco, & desir'd him to send for the Half King; which he promis'd to do by a Runner in the Morning, & for other Sachems. I invited him & the other Great Men present to my Tent, where they stay'd an Hour & return'd.

According to the best Observations I cou'd make, Mr. Gist's new Settlement (which we pass'd by) bears about W: N: W: 70 Miles from Wills Creek, Shanapins, or the Forks N: B: W: or N: N: W: about 50 Miles from that; & from thence to the

Logstown, the Course is nearly West, about 18 or 20 Miles; so that the whole Distance, as we went & computed it, is at least 135 or 40 Miles from our back Settlements.

25th: Came to Town four of ten French Men that Deserted from a Company at the Cuscusas, which lies at the Mouth of this River; I got the following Account from them. They were sent from New Orlians with 100 Men, & 8 Canoe load of Provisions, to this Place; where they expected to have met the same Number of Men, from the Forts this Side Lake Erie to convoy them, & the Horses up, but were not arriv'd when they ran off. I enquir'd into the Situation of the French on the Mississippi, their Number, & what Forts they had Built: They inform'd me that there were four small Forts between New Orlians, & the Black Islands, Garrison'd with about 30 or 40 Men, & a few small Pieces of Cannon in each. That at New Orlians, which is near the Mouth of the Mississippi, there is 35 Companies of 40 Men each, with a pretty strong Fort, mounting 8 large Carriage Guns; & at the Black Islands there is several Companies, & a Fort with 6 Guns. The Black Islands is about 130 Leagues above the Mouth of the Ohio, which is 150 above New Orlians: They also acquainted me, that there was a small Palisadoed Fort on the Ohio, at the Mouth of the Obaish, about 60 Leagues from the Mississippi: the Obaish heads near the West End of Lake Erie, & affords the Communication between the French on Mississippi, & those on the Lakes. These Deserters came up from the lower Shawnesse Town, with one Brown an Indian Trader, & were going to Philadelphia.

About 3 o'Clock this Evening the Half King came to Town; I went up & invited him & Davison privately to my Tent, & desir'd him to relate some of the Particulars of his Journey to the French Commandant, & reception there, & to give me an Account of the Way & Distance. He told me that the nearest & levelest Way was now impassable, by reason of the many large miry Savannas; that we must be oblig'd to go by Venango, & shou'd not get to the near Fort under 5 or 6 Nights Sleep, good Traveling. When he went to the Fort he said he was receiv'd in a very stern Manner by the late Commander, who ask'd him very abruptly, what he had come about, & to declare his Business; which he says he did in the following Speech.

FATHERS I am come to tell you your own Speeches, what your own Mouths have declar'd. FATHERS You in former Days set a Silver Bason before us wherein there was the Leg of a Beaver, and desir'd of all Nations to come & eat of it; to eat in Peace & Plenty, & not to be Churlish to one another; & that if any such Person shou'd be found to be a Disturber; I here lay down by the Edge of the Dish a rod, which you must Scourge them with; & if Me your Father shou'd get Foolish in my old Days, I desire you may use it upon me as well as others.

NOW FATHERS it is you that is the Disturber in this Land, by coming & building your Towns, and taking it away unknown to us & by Force. FATHERS We kindled a Fire a long Time ago at a Place call'd Morail, where we desir'd you to stay, & not to come & intrude upon our Land. I now desire you may dispatch to that Place; for be it known to you Fathers, this is our Land, & not yours. FATHERS I desire you may hear me in Civilness; if not, We must handle that rod which was laid down for the Use of the obstropulous. If you had come in a peaceable Manner like our Brothers the English, We shou'd not have been against your trading with us as they do, but to come Fathers, & build great Houses upon our Land, & to take it by Force, is what we cannot submit to.

FATHERS Both you & the English are White. We live in a Country between, therefore the Land does not belong either to one or the other; but the GREAT BEING above allow'd it to be a Place of residence for us; so Fathers, I desire you to withdraw, as I have done our Brothers the English, for I will keep you at Arm's length. I lay this down as a Tryal for both, to see which will have the greatest regard to it, & that Side we will stand by, & make equal Sharers with us: Our Brothers the English have heard this, & I come now to tell it to you, for I am not affraid to discharge you off this Land. This, he said, was the Substance of what he said to the General, who made this Reply.

NOW MY CHILD I have heard your Speech. You spoke first, but it is my Time to speak now. Where is my Wampum that you took away, with the Marks of Towns in it? This Wampum I do not know, which you have discharg'd me off the Land with; but you need not put yourself to the Trouble of Speaking for I will not hear you: I am not affraid of Flies or Musquito's; for Indians are such as those; I tell you down that River I will go, & will build upon it according to my Command: If the River was ever so block'd up, I have Forces sufficient to burst it open, & tread under my Feet all that stand in Opposition together with their Alliances; for my Force is as the Sand upon the Sea Shoar: therefore here is your Wampum, I fling it at you. Child, you talk foolish; you say this Land belongs to you, but there is not the Black of my Nail yours, I saw that Land sooner than you did, before the Shawnesse & you were at War: Lead was the Man that went down, & took Possession of that River; it is my Land, & I will have it let who will stand up for, or say against it. I'll buy & sell with the English (mockingly). If People will be rul'd by me they may expect Kindness but not else.

The Half King told me, he enquir'd of the General after two English Men that were made Prisoners, & receiv'd this Answer.

CHILD You think it is a very great Hardship that I made Prisoners of those two People at Venango, don't you concern yourself with it we took & carried them to Canada to get Intelligence of what the English were doing in Virginia.

He inform'd me that they had built two Forts, one on Lake Erie, & another on French Creek, near a small Lake about 15 Miles asunder, & a large Waggon Road between; they are both built after the same Model, but different in the Size; that on the Lake the largest; he gave me a Plan of them of his own drawing. The Indians enquir'd very particularly after their Brothers in Carolina Goal. They also ask'd what sort of a Boy it was that was taken from the South Branch; for they had, by some Indians heard, that a Party of French Indians had carried a White Boy by the Cuscusa Town, towards the Lakes.

26th: We met in council at the Long House, about 9 o'Clock, where I spoke to them as follows,

> BROTHERS I have call'd you together in Council, by Order of your Brother the Governor of Virginia, to acquaint you that I am sent with all possible Dispatch to visit & deliver a Letter to the French Commandant of very great Importance to your Brothers the English: & I dare say to you their Friends & Allies. I was desir'd Brothers, by your Brother the Governor, to call upon you, the Sachems of the Six Nations, to inform you of it, & to ask your Advice & Assistance to proceed the nearest & best Road to the French. You see Brothers I have got thus far on my Journey. His Honour likewise desir'd me to apply to you for some of your young Men to conduct and provide Provisions for us on our Way: & to be a Safeguard against those French Indians, that have taken up the Hatchet against us. I have spoke this particularly to you Brothers, because His Hon. our Governor, treats you as good Friends & Allies, & holds you in great Esteem. To confirm what I have said I give you this String of Wampum.

After they had considered some Time on the above, the Half King got up & spoke.

> NOW MY BROTHERS. In Regard to what my Brother the Governor has desir'd of me, I return you this Answer. I rely upon you as a Brother ought to do, as you say we are Brothers, & one People. We shall put Heart in Hand, & speak to our Fathers the French, concerning the Speech they made to me, & you may depend that we will endeavour to be your Guard.
>
> BROTHER, as you have ask'd my Advice, I hope you will be ruled by it, & stay 'til I can provide a Company to go with you. The French Speech Belt is not here, I have it to go for to my hunting Cabbin likewise the People I have order'd are not yet come, nor can 'til the third Night from this, 'till which Time Brother I must beg you to stay. I intend to send a Guard of Mingoes, Shawnesse, &

Delawar's, that our Brothers may see the Love and Loyalty We bear them.

As I had Orders to make all possible Dispatch, & waiting here very contrary to my Inclinations; I thank'd him in the most suitable Manner I cou'd, & told that my Business requir'd the greatest Expedition, & wou'd not admit of that Delay: He was not well pleas'd that I shou'd offer to go before the Time he had appointed, & told me that he cou'd not consent to our going without a Guard, for fear some Accident shou'd befall us, & draw a reflection upon him—besides says he, this is a Matter of no small Moment, & must not be enter'd into without due Consideration, for I now intend to deliver up the French Speech Belt, & make the Shawnesse & Delawars do the same, & accordingly gave Orders to King Singess, who was present, to attend on Wednesday Night with the Wampum, & two Men of their Nation to be in readiness to set off with us next Morning. As I found it impossible to get off without affronting them in the most egregious Manner, I consented to stay.

I gave them back a String of Wampum that I met with at Mr. Frazer's, which they had sent with a Speech to his Honour the Governor, to inform him, that three Nations of French Indians, (vizt.) Chippaway's, Ottaway's, & Arundacks, had taken up the Hatchet against the English, & desired them to repeat it over again; which they postpon'd doing 'til they met in full Council with the Shawnesse, & Delawar Chiefs.

27th: Runners were dispatch'd very early for the Shawness Chiefs, the Half King set out himself to fetch the French Speech Belt from his hunting Cabbin.

28th: He return'd this Evening, & came with Monacatoocha & two other Sachems to my Tent, & beg'd (as they had comply'd with his Honour the Governor's Request in providing Men, &ca.) to know what Business we were going to the French about? This was a Question I all along expected, & had provided as satisfactory Answers as I cou'd, which allay'd their Curiosity a little. Monacatoocha Informed me, that an Indian from Venango brought News a few Days ago; that the French had call'd all the Mingo's, Delawar's &ca. together at that Place,

& told them that they intended to have been down the River this Fall, but the Waters were geting Cold, & the Winter advancing, which obliged them to go into Quarters; but they might assuredly expect them in the Spring, with a far greater Number; & desired that they might be quite Passive, & not intermeddle, unless they had a mind to draw all their Force upon them; for that they expected to fight the English three Years, (as they suppos'd there would be some Attempts made to stop them) in which Time they shou'd Conquer, but if they shou'd prove equally strong, that they & the English wou'd join to cut them off, & divide the Land between them: that though they had lost their General, & some few of their Soldiers, yet there was Men enough to reinforce, & make them Masters of the Ohio. This Speech, he said, was deliver'd to them by an Captn. Joncaire, their Interpreter in Chief, living at Venango, & a Man of Note in the Army.

29th: The Half King and Monacatoocha came very early & beg'd me to stay one Day more, for notwithstanding they had used all the Diligence in their Power, the Shawnesse Chiefs had not brought the Wampum they order'd, but wou'd certainly be in to Night, if not they wou'd delay me no longer, but send it after us as soon as they arriv'd: When I found them so pressing in their request; & knew that returning of Wampum, was the abolishing of Agreements; & giving this up was shaking of all Dependence upon the French, I consented to stay, as I believ'd an Offence offer'd at this Crisis, might have been attended with greater ill Consequence than another Day's Delay.

They also inform'd me that Singess cou'd not get in his Men, & was prevented from coming himself by His Wife's Sickness, (I believe by fear of the French) but that the Wampum of that Nation was lodg'd with Custaloga, one of their Chiefs at Venango. In the Evening they came again, & acquainted me that the Shawnesse were not yet come, but it shou'd not retard the Prosecution of our Journey. He deliver'd in my Hearing the Speeches that were to be made to the French by Jeskakake, one of their old Chiefs, which was giving up the Belt the late Commandant had ask'd for, & repeating near the same Speech he himself had done before. He also deliver'd a String of Wampum to this Chief, which was sent by King Singess to be given to Custaloga, with Orders to repair to, & deliver up the French Wampum. He likewise gave a very large String of black & white Wampum, which was to be sent immediately up to the Six Nations, if the French refus'd to quit the Land at this Warning, which was the third & last Time, & was the right of this Jeskakake to deliver.

30th: Last Night the great Men assembled to their Council House to consult further about this Journey, & who were to go; the result of which was, that only three of their Chiefs, with one of their best Hunters shou'd be our Convoy: the reason they gave for not sending more, after what had been propos'd in Council the 26th. was, that a greater Number might give the French Suspicion of some bad Design, & cause them to be treated rudely; but I rather think they cou'd not get their Hunters in.

We set out about 9 o'Clock, with the Half King, Jeskakake, White Thunder, & the Hunter; & travel'd on the road to Venango, where we arriv'd the 4th: of December, without any Thing remarkably happening, but a continued Series of bad Weather. This is an old Indian Town, situated on the Mouth of French Creek on Ohio, & lies near No. about 60 Miles from the Logstown, but more than 70 the Way we were oblig'd to come. We found the French Colours hoisted at a House where they drove Mr. John Frazer an English Subject from: I immediately repair'd to it, to know where the Commander resided: There was three Officers, one of which, Capt. Joncaire, inform'd me, that he had the Command of the Ohio, but that there was a General Officer at the next Fort, which he advis'd me to for an Answer.

He invited us to Sup with them, & treated with the greatest Complaisance. The Wine, as they dos'd themselves pretty plentifully with it, soon banish'd the restraint which at first appear'd in their Conversation, & gave license to their Tongues to reveal their Sentiments more freely. They told me it was their absolute Design to take Possession of the Ohio, & by G—— they wou'd do it, for tho' they were sensible, that the English cou'd raise two Men for their one; yet they knew their Motions were too slow & dilatory to prevent any Undertaking of theirs. They pretended to have an undoubted right to the river from a Discovery made by one La Sol 60 Years ago, & the use of this

Expedition is to prevent our Settling on the River or Waters of it, as they have heard of some Families moving out in order thereto.

From the best Intelligence I cou'd get, there has been 1,500 Men this Side Oswago Lake, but upon the Death of the General, all were recall'd to about 6 or 7 Hundred, which were left to Garrison four Forts, 150 or thereabouts in each, the first of which is on French Creek, near a small Lake, about 60 Miles from Venango near N: N: W: the next lies on Lake Erie, where the greatest Part of their Stores are kept about 15 Miles from the other; from that it is 120 Miles from the Carrying Place, at the Fall of Lake Erie, where there is a small Fort, which they lodge their Goods at, in bringing them from Morail, the Place that all their Stores come from; the next Fort lies about 20 Miles from this, on Oswago Lake; between this Fort & Morail there are three others; the first of which is near the English Fort Oswago. From the Fort on Lake Erie to Morail is about 600 Miles, which they say if good Weather, requires no more than 4 Weeks Voyage, if they go in Barks or large Vessells that they can cross the Lake; but if they come in Canoes, it will require five or six Weeks for they are oblig'd to keep under the Shoar.

5th: Rain'd successively all Day, which prevented our traveling. Capt. Joncaire sent for the half King, as he had but just heard that he came with me: He affected to be much Concern'd that I did not make free to bring him in before; I excused it in the best Manner I was capable, & told him I did not think their Company agreeable, as I had heard him say a good deal in dispraise of Indians in General. But another Motive prevented my bringing them into his Company: I knew that he was Interpreter, & a Person of very great Influence among the Indians, & had lately used all possible means to draw them over to their Interest; therefore I was desirous of giving no more Opportunity than cou'd be avoided. When they came in there was great Pleasure express'd at seeing them, he wonder'd how they cou'd be so near without coming to visit him, made several trifling Presents, & applied Liquors so fast, that they were soon render'd incapable of the Business they came about notwithstanding the Caution that was given.

6th: The Half King came to my Tent quite Sober, & insisted very much that I shou'd stay & hear what he had to say to the French. I fain wou'd have prevented his speaking any Thing 'til he came to the Commandant, but cou'd not prevail. He told me that at this Place Council Fire was kindled, where all their Business with these People were to be transacted, & that the Management of the Indian Affairs was left solely to Monsieur Joncaire. As I was desirous of knowing the Issue of this, I agreed to stay, but sent our Horses a little Way up French Creek, to raft over & Camp, which I knew wou'd make it near Night.

About 10 oClock they met in Council, the King spoke much the same as he had done to the General, & offer'd the French Speech Belt which had before been demanded, with the Marks of four Towns in it, which Monsieur Joncaire refused to receive; but desired him to carry it to the Fort to the Commander.

7th: Monsieur La Force, Commissary of the French Stores, & three other Soldiers came over to accompany us up. We found it extreamly difficult getting the Indians off to Day; as every Stratagem had been used to prevent their going up with me. I had last Night left John Davison (the Indian Interpreter that I brought from Logstown with me) strictly charg'd not to be out of their Company, as I cou'd not get them over to my Tent (they having some Business with Custaloga, to know the reason why he did not deliver up the French Belt, which he had in keeping,) but was oblig'd to send Mr. Gist over to Day to fetch them, which he did with great Perswasion.

At 11 o'Clock we set out for the Fort, & was prevented from arriving there 'till the 11th: by excessive rains, Snows, & bad traveling, through many Mires & Swamps, which we were oblig'd to pass to avoid crossing the Creek, which was impassible either by Fording or Rafting, the Water was so high & rapid. We pass'd over much good Land since we left Venango, & through several extensive & very rich Meadows, one of which was near 4 Miles in length, & considerably wide in some Places.

12th: I prepar'd early to wait upon the Commander, & was receiv'd & conducted to him by the 2d. Officer in Command; I acquainted him with my Business, & offer'd my Commission

& Letter, both of which he desir'd me to keep 'til the Arrival of Monsieur Riparti, Capt. at the next Fort, who was sent for & expected every Hour.

This Commander is a Knight of the Military Order of St: Lewis, & named Legadieur St. Piere, he is an elderly Gentleman, & has much the Air of a Soldier; he was sent over to take the Command immediately upon the Death of the late General, & arriv'd here about 7 Days before me. At 2 o'Clock the Gentleman that was sent for arriv'd, when I offer'd the Letters &ca. again, which they receiv'd, & adjourn'd into a private Appartment for the Captain to translate, who understood a little English, after he had done it, the Captain desir'd I wou'd walk in & bring my Interpreter to peruse & correct it, which I did.

13th: The chief Officer retired to hold a Council of War, which gave me an Opportunity of taking the Dimensions of the Fort, & making what Observations I cou'd. It is situated on the South or West Fork of French Creek, near the Water, & is almost surrounded by the Creek, & a small Branch of it which forms a Kind of an Island, as may be seen by a Plan I have here annexed, it is built exactly in that Manner & of that Dimensions. 4 Houses compose the Sides; the Bastions are made of Piles drove into the Ground, & about 12 Feet above sharpe at Top, with Port Holes cut for Cannon & Small Arms to fire through; there are Eight 6 lb. Pieces Mounted, two in each Bastion, & one of 4 lb. before the Gate: In the Bastions are a Guard House, Chapel, Doctor's Lodgings, & the Commander's private Store, round which is laid Platforms for the Cannon & Men to stand on: there is several Barracks without the Fort for the Soldiers dwelling, cover'd some with Bark, & some with Boards, & made chiefly of Logs, there is also several other Houses such as Stables, Smiths Shop &ca: all of which I have laid down exactly as they stand, & shall refer to the Plan for Explanation.

I cou'd get no certain Account of the Number of Men here; but according to the best Judgement I cou'd form, there is an Hundred exclusive of Officers, which are pretty many. I also gave Orders to the People that were with me, to take an exact Account of the Canoes that were haled up, to convey their Forces down in the Spring, which they did, and told 50 of

Birch Bark, & 170 of Pine; besides many others that were block'd out, in Readiness to make.

14th: As the Snow increased very fast, & our Horses daily got weaker, I sent them off unloaded, under the Care of Barnaby Currin & two others, to make all convenient Dispatch to Venango, & there wait our Arrival, if there was a Prospect of the Rivers Freezing, if not, then to continue down to Shanapin's Town at the Forks of Ohio, & there wait 'till we came to cross Allegany; intending my Self to go down by Water, as I had the Offer of a Canoe or two.

As I found many Plots concerted to retard the Indians Business, & prevent their returning with me, I endeavour'd all in my Power to frustrate their Schemes, & hurry them on to execute their intended Design. They accordingly pressed for admittance this Evening, which at length was granted them privately with the Commander, & one or two other Officers. The Half King told me that he offer'd the Wampum to the Commander, who evaded taking it, & made many fair Promises of Love & Friendship; said he wanted to live in Peace & trade amicably with them; as a Proof of which, he wou'd send some Goods immediately down to the Logstown for them, but I rather think the Design of that is to bring away all of our stragling traders that they may meet with; as I privately understood they intended to carry an Officer, &ca. with them; & what rather confirms this Opinion, I was enquiring of the Commander by what Authority he had taken & made Prisoners of several of our English Subjects. He told me the Country belong'd to them, that no English Man had a right to trade upon them Waters; & that he had Orders to make every Person Prisoner that attempted it on the Ohio or the Waters of it.

I enquir'd of Capt. Riparti about the Boy that was carried by, as it was done while the Command devolved upon him, between the Death of the late General & the Arrival of the Present. He acknowledg'd that a Boy had been carried past, & that the Indians had two or three white Scalps, (I was told by some of the Indians at Venango 8) but pretended to have forgot the Name of the Place that the Boy came from, & all the Particulars, tho' he Question'd him for some Hours as they were carrying him past. I likewise enquired where & what they had done with John Trotter, & James McClocklan, two Pensylvania Traders, which they had taken with all their Goods: they told me that they had been sent to Canada, but were now return'd Home.

This Evening I receiv'd an Answer to His Honour the Governor's Letter from the Commandant.

15th: The Commander order'd a plentiful Store of Liquor, Provisions & ca. to be put on board our Canoe, & appear'd to be extreamly complaisant, though he was ploting every Scheme that the Devil & Man cou'd invent, to set our Indians at Variance with us, to prevent their going 'till after our Departure. Presents, rewards, & every Thing that cou'd be suggested by him or his Officers was not neglected to do. I can't say that ever in my Life I suffer'd so much Anxiety as I did in this affair: I saw that every Stratagem that the most fruitful Brain cou'd invent: was practis'd to get the Half King won to their Interest, & that leaving of him here, was giving them the Opportunity they aimed at: I went to the Half King and press'd him in the strongest Terms to go. He told me the Commander wou'd not discharge him 'till the Morning; I then went to the Commander & desired him to do their Business, & complain'd of ill Treatment; for keeping them, as they were Part of my Company was detaining me, which he promis'd not to do, but to forward my Journey as much as he cou'd: He protested he did not keep them but was innocent of the Cause of their Stay; though I soon found it out. He had promis'd them a Present of Guns, &ca. if they wou'd wait 'till the Morning. As I was very much press'd by the Indians to wait this Day for them; I consented on a Promise that Nothing shou'd hinder them in the Morning.

16th: The French were not slack in their Inventions to keep the Indians this Day also; but as they were obligated, according to promise, to give the Present: they then endeavour'd to try the Power of Liquor; which I doubt not wou'd have prevail'd at any other Time than this, but I tax'd the King so close upon his Word that he refrain'd, & set off with us as he had engag'd. We had a tedious & very fatiguing Passage down the Creek, several Times we had like to have stove against Rocks, & many Times were oblig'd all Hands to get out, & remain in the Water Half an Hour or more, getting her over the Shoals: on one Place the Ice had lodg'd & made it impassable by Water; therefore we were oblig'd to carry our Canoe across a neck Land a quarter of a Mile over. We did not reach Venango 'till the 22d: where we met with our Horses. This Creek is extreamly crooked, I dare say the Distance between the Fort & Venango can't be less than 130 Miles to follow the Meanders.

23d: When I got Things ready to set off I sent for the Half King, to know whether they intended to go with us, or by Water. He told me that the White Thunder had hurt himself much, & was Sick & unable to walk, therefore he was oblig'd to carry him down in a Canoe: As I found he intended to stay a Day or two here, & knew that Monsieur Joncaire wou'd employ every Scheme to set him against the English, as he had before done; I told him I hoped he wou'd guard against his Flattery, & let no fine Speeches Influence Him in their Favour: He desired I might not be concern'd, for he knew the French too well, for any Thing to engage him in their Behalf, & though he cou'd not go down with us, he wou'd endeavour to meet at the Forks with Joseph Campbell, to deliver a Speech for me to carry to his Honour the Governor. He told me he wou'd order the young Hunter to attend us, & get Provision &ca. if wanted. Our Horses were now so weak & feeble, & the Baggage heavy; as we were oblig'd to provide all the Necessaries the Journey wou'd require, that we doubted much their performing it; therefore my Self & others (except the Drivers which were oblig'd to ride) gave up our Horses for Packs, to assist along with the Baggage; & put my Self into an Indian walking Dress, & continue'd with them three Day's, 'till I found there was no Probability of their getting in, in any reasonable Time; the Horses grew less able to travel every Day. The Cold increas'd very fast, & the Roads were geting much worse by a deep Snow continually Freezing; And as I was uneasy to get back to make a report of my Proceedings to his Honour the Governor; I determin'd to prosecute my Journey the nearest way through the Woods on Foot. Accordingly I left Mr. Vanbraam in Charge of our Baggage, with Money and Directions to provide Necessaries from Place to Place for themselves & Horses & to make the most convenient Dispatch in. I took my necessary Papers, pull'd off my Cloths; tied My Self up in a Match Coat; & with my Pack at my back, with my Papers & Provisions in it, & a Gun, set out with Mr. Gist, fitted in the same Manner, on Wednesday the 26th.

The Day following, just after we had pass'd a Place call'd the Murdering Town where we intended to quit the Path & steer across the Country for Shanapins Town, we fell in with a Party of French Indians, which had laid in wait for us, one of them fired at Mr. Gist or me, not 15 Steps, but fortunately missed. We took this Fellow into Custody, & kept him 'till about 9 o'Clock at Night, & then let him go, & then walked all the remaining Part of the Night without making any Stop; that we might get the start, so far as to be out of the reach of their Pursuit next Day, as were well assur'd they wou'd follow upon our Tract as soon as it was Light: The next Day we continued traveling 'till it was quite Dark, & got to the River about two Miles above Shanapins; we expected to have found the River Froze, but it was not, only about 50 Yards from each Shoar; the Ice I suppose had broke up above, for it was driving in vast Quantities.

There was no way for us to get over but upon a Raft, which we set about with but one poor Hatchet, & got finish'd just after Sunsetting, after a whole days Work: We got it launch'd, & on board of it, & sett off; but before we got half over, we were jamed in the Ice in such a Manner, that we expected every Moment our Raft wou'd sink, & we Perish; I put out my seting Pole, to try to stop the Raft, that the Ice might pass by, when the Rapidity of the Stream through it with so much Violence against the Pole, that it Jirk'd me into 10 Feet Water, but I fortunately saved my Self by catching hold of one of the Raft Logs. Notwithstanding all our Efforts we cou'd not get the Raft to either Shoar, but were oblig'd, as we were pretty near an Island, to quit our Raft & wade to it. The Cold was so extream severe, that Mr. Gist got all his Fingers, & some of his Toes Froze, & the Water was shut up so hard, that We found no Difficulty in getting off the Island on the Ice in the Morning, & went to Mr. Frazers. We met here with 20 Warriors that had been going to the Southward to War, but coming to a Place upon the Head of the Great Cunnaway, where they found People kill'd & Scalpt, all but one Woman with very Light Hair, they turn'd about; & ran back, for fear of the Inhabitants rising & takeing them as the Authors of the Murder:

They report that the People were lying about the House, & some of them much torn & eat by Hogs; by the Marks that were left, they say they were French Indians of the Ottaway Nation, &ca. that did it.

As we intended to take Horse here, & it requir'd some Time to hunt them; I went up about 3 Miles to the Mouth of Yaughyaughgane to visit Queen Aliquippa, who had express'd great Concern that we pass'd her in going to the Fort. I made her a Present of a Match Coat; & a Bottle of rum, which was thought much the best Present of the two.

Tuesday 1st: Day of Jany: We left Mr. Frazers House, & arriv'd at Mr. Gists at Monangahela the 2d. where I bought Horse Saddle &ca. The 6th: We met 17 Horses loaded with Materials & Stores for a Fort at the Forks; & the Day after, a Family or two going out to settle; this Day we arriv'd at Wills Creek, after as fatiguing a Journey as it is possible to conceive, rendered so by excessive bad Weather: From the first Day of December 'till the 15th. there was but one Day, but what it rain'd or snow'd incessantly & throughout the whole Journey we met with nothing but one continued Series of cold wet Weather; which occasioned very uncumfortable Lodgings, especially after we had left our Tent; which was some Screen from the Inclemency of it.

On the 11th. I got to Belvoir, where I stop'd one Day to take necessary rest; & then set out for, & arrived at Williamsburg, the 16th. & waited upon His Honour the Governor with the Letter I had brought from the French Commandant, & to give an Account of the Proceedures of my Journey. Which I beg leave to do by offering the Foregoing, as it contains the most remarkable Occurrences that happen'd to me.

I hope it will be sufficient to satisfy your Honour with my Proceedings; for that was my Aim in undertaking the Journey: & chief Study throughout the Prosecution of it.

With the Assurance, & Hope of doing it, I with infinite Pleasure subscribe my Self Yr. Honour's most Obedt. & very Hble. Servant.

January 16–17, 1754

AN AMBITIOUS YOUTH

To Richard Corbin

Dear Sir:

In a conversation at Green Spring you gave me some room to hope for a commission above that of a Major, and to be ranked among the chief officers of this expedition. The command of the whole forces is what I neither look for, expect, nor desire; for I must be impartial enough to confess, it is a charge too great for my youth and inexperience to be intrusted with. Knowing this, I have too sincere a love for my country, to undertake that which may tend to the prejudice of it. But if I could entertain hopes that you thought me worthy of the post of Lieutenant-colonel, and would favour me so far as to mention it at the appointment of officers, I could not but entertain a true sense of the kindness.

I flatter myself that under a skilful commander, or man of sense, (which I most sincerely wish to serve under,) with my own application and diligent study of my duty, I shall be able to conduct my steps without censure, and in time, render myself worthy of the promotion that I shall be favoured with now.

January 28, 1754

INDIAN AFFAIRS

To Robert Dinwiddie

Honble Sir,   25th April 1754 Wills Creek

Captain Trents Ensign Mr Ward this Day arrived from the Forks of Monongehele, and brings the disagreeable account that the Fort on the Seventeenth Instant was surrender'd at the summons of Captain Contrecour to a Body of French consisting of upwards of one Thousand Men, who came from Venago with Eighteen pieces of Cannon, Sixty Battoes, and three Hundred Canoes: they gave him liberty to bring off all his men and working Tools, which he accordingly did the same Day.

Immediately upon this Information I called a Council of War to advise on proper measures to be taken in this Exigence; a Copy of whose resolves, with the proceedings I herewith inclose by the Bearer, who I have continued Express to your Honour for more minute Intelligence.

Mr Ward has the Summons with him, and a speech from the Half King which I also inclose with the Wampum: He is accompanied by one of the Indians that is mentioned therein, who were sent to see where we were, what was our strength, and to know the time to expect us out; the other Young man I have prevailed upon to return to the Half King with the following Speech.

"Sachems Warriours of the Six united Nations; Shanoahs and Delawares, our Friends and Brethren:

"I received by the Bucks Brother your speech, who came to us with the two young men five sleeps after leaveing you; We return you thanks from Hearts glowing with Affection for your steadfast adherence to us, for your kind speech, and for your wise Councils, and directions to the Bucks Brother.

The Young man will inform you where he met a small part of our army advancing towards you, Clearing the Roads for a great Number of our Warriours that are immediately to follow with our Great Guns, our Ammunition, and our Provisions.

I could not delay to let you know our Hearts and therefore have sent back one of the Young Men with this speech to acquaint you with them; while I have sent the other according to your desire to the Governour of Virginea with the Bucks Brother to deliver your speech and Wampum, And to be an Eye witness of the preparations we are makeing, to come in haste to support you, whose Interest is as dear to us as our Lives. We resent the usage of the treacherous French, and our Conduct henceforth will plainly shew to you how much we have it at Heart.

I cannot be easye without seeing you, before our

Forces meet at the Fork of the Roads, and therefore have the greatest inclination that you and Esscruniata or one of you meet me on the Road as soon as possible to assist us in Council. To Assure you of the good will we bare you; and to confirm the truth of what has been said, I herewith present you this string of Wampum that you may thereby remember how much I am Your Brother and Friend

Go: Washington
als
Connotaucarious

To the Half King
Esscruneata & the Belt of Wampum

I hope my proceedings in these affairs will be Satisfactory to Your Honour, as I have to the Utmost of my knowledge consulted the Interest of the Expedition and good of my Country: whose Rights, while they are asserted in so just a Cause I will defend to the last remains of Life. Hitherto the difficulty I have met with in Marching has been greater than I expect to encounter on Ohio where probably I may be surround'd by the Enemy; and this occasion'd by those who had they acted as becometh every good Subject, would have exerted their Utmost abilitys to forward our just designs Out of Twenty four Waggons that were impress'd at Winchester, we got but Ten after waiting a week, and some of those so illy provided with Teams that we could not travel with them without the Soldiers assisting them up the Hills. when it was known they had better Teams at home. I doubt not but in some points I may have strained the Law, but I hope as my sole motive was to Expedite the March, I shall be supported in it should my authority be Questioned which at present I dont Apprehend will, unless some busy body intermeddles.

Your Honour will see by the resolves in Council that I am destin'd to Monongehele with all the diligent dispatch in My power. We will endeavour to make the Road sufficiently good for the heaviest Artillery to pass and when we Arrive at Red Stone Creek Fortifie ourselves as strongly as the short time will allow off. I doubt not but to maintain a possession there till we are Reinforced (If it seasonably Arrives) unless the waters rising admit their Cannon to be convey'd up in Canoes and then I flatter myself we shall not be so wanting for Intelligence but to get timely notice of it and make a good Retreat.

I hope your Honour will see the absolute Necessity there is for haveing as soon as our Forces are collected a Number of Cannon (some of heavy Mettle) with Mortors Granadoes &c. to attack the French, and put us on an equal footing with them.

Perhaps it may also be thought adviseable to Invite the Cherokees, Cawtabas, and Chicasaws to March to our Assistance (as we are informed that Six Hundred Chippoways & Ottaways are Marching down Sciodo Creek to join the French that are coming up Ohio). In that case I would beg leave to recommend their being Orderd to this Place first that a peace may be concluded between them and the Six Nations for I am informed by several hands that as there is no good harmony subsisting betwixt them that by comeing first to Ohio it may create great discords and turn much to our disadvantage.

As I had oppertunitys to the Governour's of Maryland and Pensylvania I wrote to both acquainting them with these advices, and inclosed the Summons and Indian speech, which I hope your Honour will not think me too forward in doing: I consider'd that the Assembly of Maryland was to sit in five days time, and the Pensylvania Assembly now Sitting and that by giveing them timely notice something might be done which would turn to the advantage of this Expedition which now requires all the Force we can Muster.

By the best information I can get I much doubt whether any of the Indians will be in to treat in May. I am with all due respect and regard Your Honours most Obt & Very Humle Servt

Query Whether the Indian Women and Children if they settle amongst us are to be maintained at our Expence or not, they will Expect it.

WOUNDED PRIDE

To Robert Dinwiddie

Youghiogany
Sir,   May 18, 1754.

I am heartily concerned, that the officers have such real cause to complain of the Committee's resolves; and still more to find my inclinations prone to second their just grievances.

I have endeavoured, as far as I was able, to see in the best light I could the trifling advantages that may accrue; yet nothing prevents their throwing down their commissions, (with gratitude and thanks to your Honor, whose good intentions of serving us we are all well assured of,) but the approaching danger, which has too far engaged their honor to recede till other officers are sent in their room, or an alteration made regarding their pay, during which time they will assist with their best endeavours voluntarily, that is, without receiving the gratuity allowed by the resolves of the Committee.

Giving up my commission is quite contrary to my intention. Nay, I ask it as a greater favor, than any amongst the many I have received from your Honor, to confirm it to me. But let me serve voluntarily; then I will, with the greatest pleasure in life, devote my services to the expedition without any other reward, than the satisfaction of serving my country; but to be slaving dangerously for the shadow of pay, through woods, rocks, mountains,—I would rather prefer the great toil of a daily laborer, and dig for a maintenance, provided I were reduced to the necessity, than serve upon such ignoble terms; for I really do not see why the lives of his Majesty's subjects in Virginia should be of less value, than of those in other parts of his American dominions; especially when it is well known, that we must undergo double their hardship.

I could enumerate a thousand difficulties that we have met with, and must expect to meet with, more than other officers who have almost double our pay; but as I know you reflect on these things, and are sensible of the hardships we must necessarily encounter, it would be needless to enlarge.

Besides, as I have expatiated fully (and, perhaps, too warmly) in a letter to Colonel Fairfax, who, I suppose, will accompany you to Winchester, upon the motives that occasion these my resolves, I shall not trouble you with them; for the subject leads me too far when I engage in it.

Another thing resolved by the Committee is, that only one sergeant and one corporal be allowed to a company; with whom it is as much impossible to do the necessary duty, as it is to conquer kingdoms with my handful of men.

Upon the whole, I find so many clogs upon the expedition, that I quite despair of success; nevertheless, I humbly beg it, as a particular favor, that your Honor will continue me in the post I now enjoy, the duty whereof I will most cheerfully execute as a volunteer, but by no means upon the present pay.

I hope what I have said will not be taken amiss; for I really believe, were it as much in your power, as it is your inclination, we should be treated as gentlemen and officers, and not have annexed to the most trifling pay, that ever was given to English officers, the glorious allowance of soldier's diet—a pound of pork, with bread in proportion, per day. Be the consequence what it will, I am determined not to leave the regiment, but to be amongst the last men that quit the Ohio, even if I serve as a private volunteer, which I greatly prefer to the establishment we are now upon. I am, &c.

FIRST CONFLICT

To Robert Dinwiddie

                        From our Camp at the Great Meadows
Honble Sir   29th of May 1754
    To answer your Honour's Letter of the 25th by Mr Birney—I shall begin with assuring you, that nothing was farther from my intention than to recede, thô I then pressd and still desire that my Services may be voluntary rather than on the present Pay—I am much concernd that your Honour should seem to charge me with ingratitude for your generous, and my undeserved favours, for I assure you Honble Sir, nothing is a greater stranger to my Breast, or a Sin that my Soul more abhor's than

that black and detestable one Ingratitude. I retain a true Sense of your kindnesses, and want nothing but oppertunity to give testimony of my willingness to oblige as far as my Life or fortune will extend.

I cou'd not object to the Pay before I knew it. I dare say your Honour remembers the first Estimation allowd a Lieutt Colo. 15/ and Majr 12/6 which I then complaind very much off; till your Honour assurd me that we were to be furnish'd with proper necessary's and offerd that as a reason why the pay was Less than British: after this when you were so kind to preferr me to the Comn I now have, and at the same time acquainted me that I was to have but 12/6—This, with some other Reason's induced me to acquaint Colo. Fairfax with my intention of Resigning, which he must well remember as it happd at Belhaven; and was there that he disswaded me from it and promised to represent the trifling pay to your Honour, who would endeavour (as I at the same time told him that the Speaker thought the Officr's pay too small) to have it enlarg'd.

As to the Number's that applied for Commission's and to whom we were preffer'd; I believe, had those Gentlemen been as knowing of this Country, and as Sensible of the difficulties that would attend a Campaign here as I then was—I concive your Honour wd not have been so troublesomly sollicited as you were; yet, I do not offer this as a reason for quitting the Service. for my own part I can answer, I have a Constitution hardy enough to encounter and undergo the most severe tryals, and I flatter myself resolution to Face what any Man durst, as shall be prov'd when it comes to the Test, which I believe we are upon the Border's off.

There is nothing Sir (I believe) more certain than that the Officer's on the Canada Expedition had British pay allowd, whilst they were in the Service, Lieutt Wagr Captn Trent, and several other's whom I have conversed with on tht Head, and were engagd in it, affirm it for truth: therefore Honble Sir, as this can't be allow'd; suffer me to serve a Volunteer which I assure you will be the next reward to British pay, for As my Services, so far as I have knowledge will equal those of the best Officer, I make it a point of Honr to serve for less and accept a medium.

Nevertheless, I have communicated your Honour's Sentiments to them; and as far as I could put on the Hipocrite, set forth the advantages that may accrue, and advis'd them to accept the Terms, as a refusal might reflect dishonour upon their Character; leaving it to the World to assign what reason's they please for quitting the Service—I am very sensible of the pernicious consequence that will attend their resigning, as they have by this gain'd some experience of the Military Art, have a tolerable knowledge of the Country, being sent most of them out at different times with partys: and now are accustom'd to the hardships and fatiegue of Living as we do, which I believe were it truely stated, wd prevent your Honour from many troublesome Sollicitations from others for Comns. This last motive, has, and will induce me to do what I can to reconcile matter's; thô I really believe there is some tht will not remain long witht an alteration.

They have promis'd to consider of it, and give your Honour an answer. I was not ignorant of the allowe which Colo. Fry has for his Table, but being a dependt there myself deprives me of the pleasure of inviting an Officer or Friend, which to me wd be more agreeable than the Nick Nacks I shall meet with there.

And here I cannot forbear answering one thing more in your Honrs Letter on this head; which (too) is more fully express'd in a paragraph of Colo. Fairfax's to me as follows "If on the British Establishment Officer's are allowd more Pay, the Regimentals they are oblig'd annually to furnish, their necessary Table and other Incidents being considerd, little or no savings will be their Portion"—I believe it is well known we have been at the expence of Regimentals (and it is still better known, that Regimentals, and every other necessary that we were under an indispensable necessity of purchasing for this Expedition, were not to be bought for less Virga curry, than British Officer's cd get for sterling money; which they ought to have been, to put us upon a parity in this respect, then Colo. Fairfax observes that their Table and other Incident charges prevents them frm saving much: if they dont save much, they have the enjoyment of their Pay which we neither have in one sense nor the other: We are debarr'd the pleasure of good Living, which Sir (I dare say with me you will concur) to one who has always been used to it; must go somewhat hard to be confin'd to a little salt provision and Water: and do duty, hard, laborious duty that is almost inconsistent with that of a Soldier, and yet have the same Reductions as if we were allowd luxuriously: My Pay accordg to the British Establisht & common exchange is near 22/ pr Day, in the Rm of that the Committee (for I can't in the least imagine yr Hr had any hd in it) has provided 12/6 so long as the Service requires me, whereas, one half of the other is ascertain'd to the British Officer's forever: now if we shd be fortunate enough to drive the French from Ohio—as far as your Honour wd please have them sent to—in any short time, our Pay will not be sufficient to discharge our first expences.

I would not have your Honour imagine from this, that I have said all these things to have the Pay encreas'd—but to justify myself, and shew your Honour that our complaints are not frivolous, but are founded upon strict Reason: for my own part, it is a matter almost indefferent whether I serve for full pay, or as a generous Volunteer; indeed, did my circumstances corrispond with my Inclination, I shd not hesitate a moment to prefer the Latter: for the motives that lead me here were pure and Noble I had no view of acquisition but that of Honour, by serving faithfully my King and Country.

As your Honour has recommended Mr Willis you may depend I shall with pleasure do all that I can for him.

But above all Sir, you may depend I shall take all possible means of procureing intelligence, and guarding against surprises, and be assur'd nothing but very unequal number's shall engage me to submit or Retreat.

Now Sir, as I have answer'd your Honour's Letter I shall beg leave to acqt you with what has happen'd since I wrote by Mr Gist; I then acquainted you that I had detach'd a party of 75 Men to meet with 50 of the French who we had Intelligence were upon their March towards us to Reconnoitre &ca. Abt 9 Oclock the same Night, I receivd an express from the Half King who was Incampd with several of His People abt 6 Miles of, that he had seen the Tract of two French Men xing the Road and believ'd the whole body were lying not far off, as he had an acct of that number passing Mr Gist—I set out with 40 Men before 10, and was from that time till near Sun rise before we reach'd the Indian's Camp, havg Marched in small path, & heavy Rain, and a Night as Dark as it is possible to concieve—

we were frequently tumbling one over another, and often so lost that 15 or 20 Minutes search would not find the path again.

When we came to the Half King I council'd with him, and got his assent to go hand in hand and strike the French. accordingly, himself, Monacatoocha, and a few other Indians set out with us, and when we came to the place where the Tracts were, the Half King sent Two Indians to follow their Tract and discover their lodgment which they did abt half a mile from the Road in a very obscure place surrounded with Rocks. I thereupon in conjunction with the Half King & Monacatoocha, formd a disposion to attack them on all sides, which we accordingly did and after an Engagement of abt 15 Minutes we killd 10, wounded one and took 21 Prisoner's, amongst those that were killd was Monsieur De Jumonville the Commander, Principl Officers taken is Monsieur Druillong and Monsr Laforc, who your Honour has often heard me speak of as a bold Enterprising Man, and a person of gt subtilty and cunning with these are two Cadets—These Officers pretend they were coming on an Embassy, but the absurdity of this pretext is too glaring as your Honour will see by the Instructions and summons inclos'd: There Instructions were to reconnoitre the Country, Roads, Creeks &ca to Potomack; which they were abt to do, These Enterpriseing Men were purposely choose out to get intelligence, which they were to send Back by some brisk dispatches with mention of the Day that they were to serve the Summon's; which could be through no other view, than to get sufficient Reinforcements to fall upon us imediately after. This with several other Reasons induc'd all the Officers to beleive firmly that they were sent as spys rather than any thing else, and has occasiond my sending them as prisoners, tho they expected (or at least had some faint hope of being continued as ambassadors) They finding where we were Incamp'd, instead of coming up in a Publick manner sought out one of the most secret Retirements; fitter for a Deserter than an Ambassador to incamp in—stayd there two or 3 days sent Spies to Reconnoitre our Camp as we are told, tho they deny it—Their whole Body movd back near 2 Miles, sent off two runnors to acquaint Contracoeur with our Strength, and where we were Incamp'd &ca now 36 Men wd almost have been a Retinue for a Princely

Ambassador, instead of Petit, why did they, if there design's were open stay so long within 5 Miles of us witht delivering his Ambassy, or acquainting me with it; his waiting cd be with no other design than to get Detachts to enforce the Summons as soon as it was given, they had no occasion to send out Spy's; for the Name of Ambassador is Sacred among all Nations; but it was by the Tract of these Spy's they were discoverd, and we got Intilligence of them—They wd not have retird two Miles back witht delivering the Summons and sought a sculking place (which to do them justice was done with gt Judgment) but for some especial Reason: Besides The Summon's is so insolent, & savour's so much of Gascoigny that if two Men only had come openly to deliver it. It was too great Indulgence to have sent them back.

The Sense of the Half King on this Subject is, that they have bad Hearts, and that this is a mere pretence, they never designd to have come to us but in a hostile manner, and if we were so foolish as to let them go again, he never would assist us in taking another of them. Besides, looseing La Force I really think wd tend more to our disservice than 50 other Men, as he is a person whose active Spirit, leads him into all parlys, and brought him acquainted with all parts, add to this a perfect use of the Indian Tongue, and gt influence with the Indian He Ingenuously enough confessd that as soon as he saw the commission & Instructions that he believd and then said he expected some such tendency tho he pretends to say he does not believe the Commander had any other but a good design.

In this Engagement we had only one Man killd, and two or three wounded, among which was Lieutt Waggener slightly—a most miraculous escape, as Our Right Wing was much exposd to their Fire and receivd it all.

The Half King receiv'd your Honour's speech very kind: but desird me to inform you that he could not leave his People at this time, thinking them in great Danger—He is now gone to the xing for their Familys to bring to our Camp & desird I wd send some Men and Horses to assist them up; which I have accordingly done—sent 30 Men & upwards of 20 Horses. He say's if your Honr has any thing to say you may communicate by me &ca; and that if you have a present for them it may be kept to another occasion, after sending up some things for their imediate use, He has declar'd to send these Frenchmens Scalps with a Hatchet to all the Nations of Indian's in union with them, and did that very day give a Hatchet and a large Belt of Wampum to a Delaware Man to carry to Shingiss: he promis'd me to send down the River for all the Mingo's & Shawnesse to our camp, where I expect him to Morrow with 30 or 40 Men with their wives & Children, to confirm what he has said here, he has sent your Honour a String of Wampum.

As these Runnors went of to the Fort on Sunday last, I shall expect every hour to be attackd and by unequal number's, which I must withstand if there is 5 to 1 or else I fear the Consequence will be we shall loose the Indians if we suffer ourselves to be drove Back, I dispatchd an express imediately to Colo. Fry with this Intelligence desiring him to send me Reinforcements with all imaginable dispatch.

Your Honour may depend I will not be surprizd, let them come what hour they will—and this is as much as I can promise —but my best endeavour's shall not be wanting to deserve more, I doubt not but if you hear I am beaten, but you will at the same hear that we have done our duty in fighting as long there was a possibility of hope.

I have sent Lieutt West accompanied with Mr Sprilldorph & a Guard of 20 Men to conduct the Prisoners in, and I believe the Officer's have acquainted him what answer to return yr Honour.

Monsiur La-Force, and Monsieur Druillong beg to be recommend to your Honour's Notice, and I have promis'd they will meet with all the favour that's due to Imprison'd Officer's: I have shew'd all the respect I cou'd to them here, and have given some necessary cloathing by which I have disfurnish'd myself, for having brought no more than two or three Shirts from Wills Ck that we might be light I was ill provided to furnish them I am Yr Honour's most Obt Hble Servt

NB I have neither seen nor heard any particular acct of the Twigtwees since I came on these Water's, we have already began a Palisadod Fort and hope to have it up tomorrow I must beg leave to acqt yr honr tht Captn Vanbraam & Monsr Peyrouney has behav'd extreamely well since they came out—& I hope will meet wth yr Honrs favr.

"SOMETHING CHARMING IN THE SOUND"

To John Augustine Washington

Dr John

Since my last we have arrived at this place, where 3 days agoe
we had an engagemt wth the French that is, between a party of
theirs & Ours; Most of our men were out upon other detachments, so that I had scarcely 40 men under my Command,
and about 10, or a doz. Indians, nevertheless we obtained a
most signal Victory. The Battle lasted abt 10, or 15 minutes,
sharp firing on both sides, when the French gave ground &
run, but to no great purpose; there were 12 killed, among
which was Monsr De Jumonville the Commandr, & taken 21
prisoners with whom are Monsieurs La Force, Druillong, together with 2 Cadets. I have sent them to his Honr the Governor at Winchester conducted by Lieut. West & a guard of 20
men. We had but one man killed, 2 or 3 wounded and a great
many more within an Inch of being shott; among the wounded
on our side was Lieut. Waggoner, but no danger will ensue.

We expect every Hour to be attacked by a superior Force,
but shall if they stay one day longer be prepared for them; We
have already got Intrenchments & are about a Pallisado'd Fort,
which will I hope be finished today. The Mingo's have struck
the French & I hope will give a good blow before they have
done, I expect 40 odd of them here to night, wch with our
Fort and some reinforcements from Colo. Fry, will enable us
to exert our Noble Courage with Spirit. I am Yr Affe Bror

I fortunately escaped without a wound, tho' the right Wing
where I stood was exposed to & received all the Enemy's fire
and was the part where the man was killed & the rest wounded.
I can with truth assure you, I heard Bulletts whistle and believe
me there was something charming in the sound.

May 31, 1754

BRADDOCK'S EXPEDITION

To John Augustine Washington

To Mr Jno. Auge Washington
Dear Jack

Immediately upon our leavg the C. at Geors. Ck the 14th Inst. (from whe I wrote to yo.) I was siezd wt violt Fevers & Pns in my hd wch cond wtout the lt Intermisn till the 23 follg when I was reliev'd by the Genls absolty ordering the Phyns to give me Doctr Jas Powder; wch is the most excelt mede in the W.) for it gave me immee ease, and removed my Fevrs & othr Compts in 4 Days time. My illness was too violent to suffer me to ride, therefore I was indebted to a coverd Waggon for some part of my Transpn; but even in this I cd not conte for the joltg was so gt that I was left upon the Road with a Guard and necessys, to wait the Arrl of Colo. Dunbars Detacht, whh was 2 days M. behind. The Genl giving me his wd and honr that I shd be brought up before he reachd the French Fort; this promise, and the Doctrs threats that if I perseverd it woud endanger my Life, determind my halting for the above Detacht.

As I expect the Comn betn this & Wills Ck will soon be too dangerous for single persons to pass, it will possibly stop the Interce of Lettrs in any measure; therefore I shall attempt (and will go through if I have strength,) to give you an acct of our proceedings, of our Situation, & of our prospects at present; which I desire yo. may come to Colo. Fairfax &ca my Corrispts; for I am too weak to write more than this Lettr. In the Lr wch I wrote fm Georges Ck I acqd you that unless the numr of Wagns were retrenchd & the carryg Hs incrd that we never shd be able to see Duquisne: This in 2 Days afterwards, wch was abt the time they got to the little Meadows with some of their F. Waggon's and strongest Teams, they themselves were convinced off, for they found that beside the almost imposy of gettg the Wagns along at all; that they had often a Rear of 3 or 4 Miles of Waggons; & tht the Soldrs Guarding these were so disunitd that if we had been attackd either in Front, Center or Rear that part so attackd, must have been cut of & totally defeatd before they coud be properly sustaind by any other Corps.

At the little Meadws there was a 2d Council calld, for there had been one wherein it was representd to all the Offrs of the difft Corps the gt necessity there was for Hs. & how laudable it wd be to retrench their Baggage and offer the Spare Hs. for the Publick Service. In order to encourage this I gave up my best Horse (wch I have nevr hd of since) & took no more baggage than half my Portmanteau cd easily contn. It was also sd tht the numbr was to be lessend, but this was only from 210 or 12, to 200 wch had no perceptable difference.

The Genl before they met in Council askd my prive Opinn concerng the Expn; I urgd it in the warmest terms I was master off, to push on; if we even did it with a chosn Detacht for that purpose, with the Artillery and such other things as were absolutely necessary; leavg the [   ] and other Convoys with the Remainder of the Army, to follw by slow and regular Marches, which they might do safely while we were advanced in Front. As one Reason to support this Opinion, I inform'd tht if we cd credt our Intelligence, the French were weak at the Forks but hourly expectd reinfts wch to my certain knowledge coud not arrive with Provns or any supplys durg the continuance of the Droughth—as the Buffaloe River down wch is their only commn to Venango, must be as Dry as we now fd the gt xing of the Yaughe; wch may be passd dry shod.

This was a Scheme that took, & it was detd that the Genl, with 1200 Chosen Men and Officers of all the differt Corps, with the following Field Officer's (vizt Sr Petr Halkett who acts as Brigadier, Lt Colo. Gage Lt C: Burton, and Majr Sparke, with such a certain number of Waggons as the Train wd absolutely require, shoud March as soon as things coud be got in readiness for them; which was compleated, and we on our March by the 19th, leavg Colo. Dunbar & Majr Chapman with the residue of the Regts, Companys most of the Women and in short every thing behind; except such Provision's & other necessarys as we took, and carried upon Horses.

We set out with less than 30 Carriages (Inclg all those that transported the Howetzers, 12 prs, 6 prs, &ca) & all of those strongly Horsed; which was a prospect that conveyd the most infinite delight to me, tho' I was excessively ill at the time. But this prospect was soon over turned, & all my Sanguine hopes brought very low when I found, that instead of pushing on with vigour, without regarding a little rough Road, they were halting to Level every Mold Hill, & to erect Bridges over every brook; by which means we were 4 Days gettg 12 Miles; where I was left by the Doctrs Advice, and the Genls absolute Orders, otherwise I woud not have been prevaild upon to remain behind, my own Detachmt as I then imagin'd, and believd I shall now find it not very easy to join my own Corps again, which is 25 Miles advanced before us; tho' I had the Genls word & Honr pledgd in the most Solemn manner, that I shd be bt up before he arrived at Duquisne. They have had frequent Alarms and several Men Scalp'd, but this is only done to retard the March; and harass the Men if they are to be turnd out every time a small party of them attack the Guards at Night; (for I am certain they have not sufficient strength to make head against the whole.

I have been now 6 Days with Colo. Dunbars Corps, who are in a misserable Condition for want of Horses; not havg now one half enough for their Wagns so that the only method he has of proceeding is to March on himself with as many Waggon's as those will draw, and then Halt till the Remainder are brought up which requires two Days more; and I believe, shortly he will not be able to stir at all; but there has been vile management in regard to Horses; and while I am mentiong this, I must not forget to desire, that you'll acqt Colo. G. Fx that I have made the most strict enquiry after his Man & Horses, but can hear nothing of either; at least nothing that can be credited. I was told that the Fellow was taken ill upon the Road while he was with Sr Jno. St Clairs Detachmt, and [   ] the certainty of this I cant answer for, but I believe there is nothing more certn than that he is not with any part of the Army. And unless the Horses stray and make home themselves I believe there is 1000 to 1 whether he ever sees them again: for I gave up a horse only one Day, & never coud see or hear of him afterwards: My strength wont admit me to say more, tho I have not said half what I intended cong our Affrs here. Business, I shall not think of but depd solely upon yr mant of all my affrs, & doubt not but they will be well conducted— You may thank my Fds for the Lettrs I have recd; wch has not been *one* from *any Mortal* since I left Fairfax, except yourself and Mr Dalton. It is a piece of regard & kindness which I shd endr to acknowe was I able, and sufferd to write. All your Letters to me I wd have you send to Mr Cocks of Winchester or to Govr Innis at Fort Cumberd, & then you may be certn of their comg safe to hand; otherwise I cant say as much. Make my Complimts to all who think me worthy of their Enquirys. I am

Gt xing on the Yaughe June 28th 1755

P.S. Added afterwards, to the foregoing Letter as follows

A Great Misfortune that attended me in my Sickness was, looseing the use of my Servant, for poor Jno. was taken abt the same time that I was, with near the same disorder; and was confind as long; so that we did not see each other for several Days. He is also tolerably well recoverd. We are now advand almost as far as the gt Meadows; and I shall set out tomorrow morning for my own Corps, with an Escort of 100 Men which is to guard some Provision's up; so that my Fears and doubts on that head are quite removd.

I had a Letter Yesterday from Orme, who writes me word that they have passd the Yaughyangane for the last time, that they have sent out Partys to scour the Country thereabouts, and have Reason to believe that the French are greatly alarmd at their approach.

2d July 1755

DEFEAT ON THE MONONGAHELA

To Robert Dinwiddie

To The Honble Robt Dinwiddie Esqr.
Honble Sir

As I am favour with an oppertunity, I shoud think myself inexcusable, was I to omit givg you some acct of our late Engagemt with the French on the Monongahela the 9th Inst.

We continued our March from Fort Cumberland to Frazer's (which is within 7 Miles of Duquisne) witht meetg with any extraordinary event, havg only a stragler or two picked Up by the French Indians. When we came to this place, we were attackd, (very unexpectedly I must own) by abt 300 French and Indns; Our number's consisted of abt 1300 well armd Men, chiefly regular's, who were immediately struck with such a deadly Panick, that nothing but confusion and disobedience of order's prevaild amongst them: The Officer's in genl behavd with incomparable bravery, for which they greatly sufferd, there being near 60 killd and woundd A large Proportion out of the number we had! The Virginians behavd like Men, and died like Soldier's; for I believe out of 3 Companys that were there that Day, scarce 30 were left alive: Captn Peyrouny and all his Officer's down to a Corporal, were killd; Captn Polson shard almost as hard a Fate, for only one of his Escap'd: In short the dastardly behaviour of the English Soldier's exposd all those who were inclin'd to do their duty, to almost certain Death; and at length, in despight of every effort to the contrary, broke & run as Sheep before the Hounds, leavg the Artillery, Ammunition, Provision, and every individual thing we had with us a prey to the Enemy; and when we endeavourd to rally them in hopes of regaining our invaluable loss, it was with as much success as if we had attempted to have stopd the wild Bears of the Mountains.

The Genl was wounded behind the Shoulder, & into the Breast; of wch he died three days after; his two Aids de Camp were both wounded, but are in a fair way of Recovering; Colo. Burton and Sir Jno. St Clair are also wounded, and I hope will get over it; Sir Peter Halket, with many other brave Officers were killd in the Field: I luckily escapd witht a wound, tho I had four Bullets through my Coat and two Horses shot under me: It is supposed that we left 300 or more dead in the Field; abt that number we brought off wounded; and it is imagin'd (I believe with great justice too) that two thirds of both those number's receiv'd their shott from our own cowardly dogs of Soldier's, who gatherd themselves into a body contrary to orders 10 or 12 deep, woud then level, Fire, & shoot down the Men before them.

I Tremble at the consequences that this defeat may have upon our back setlers, who I suppose will all leave their habitation's unless their are proper measures taken for their security.

Colo. Dunbar, who commands at present, intends so soon as his Men are recruited at this place, to continue his March to Philia into *Winter* Quarter's; so that there will be no Men left here unless it is the poor remains of the Virginia Troops; who now are, & will be too small to guard our Frontiers. As Captn Orme is writg to yr honour I doubt not but he will give you a circumstantial acct of all things, which will make it needless for me to add more than that I am Honble Sir Yr most Obt & most Hble Servt

Fort Cumberland July 18th 1755

"A CIRCUMSTANTIAL ACCT OF MY DEATH"

To John Augustine Washington

To Mr Jno. Auge Washington

Dear Jack

As I have heard since my arrivl at this place, a circumstantial acct of my death and dying Speech, I take this early oppertunity of contradicting both, and of assuring you that I [   ] of the livg by the miraculous care of Providence, that protected me beyond all human expectation; I had 4 Bullets through my Coat, and two Horses shot under and yet escaped unhurt.

We have been most scandalously beaten by a trifling body of men; but fatiegue, and the want of time, prevents me from [   ]ing any of the [   ] till I have the happiness of seeing you at home; which I now most ardently wishd for, since we are drove in thus far. A Weak, and Feeble State of Health, obliges me to halt here for 2 or 3 days, to recover a little strength, that I may thereby be enabled to proceed homewards with more ease; You may expect to see me there on Saturday or Sunday Se'night, which is as soon as I can well be down as I shall take my Bullskin Plantation's in my way. Pray give my Compts to all my Fds. I am Dr Jack Yr most Affecte Brothr

Fort Cumberld 18th July 1755

To Robert Dinwiddie

Honble Sir   Winchester Saturday Octr the 11th 1755
   As I think it my indispensible duty to inform you particularly
of my proceedings, and to give the most plain and authentic
acct from time to time of our situation, I must acquaint your
Honour that immediately after giving the necessary Orders at
Fredericksburg and dispatching expresses to hurry the Recruits
from Alexandria, I rid post to this place passing by Lord Fairfax's who was not at home, but here; where I arrivd Yesterday
abt Noon, and found every thing in the greatest hurry and
confusion by the back Inhabitants flocking in, and those of the
Town removing out, which I have prevented as far as it was in
my power.
   I was desirous of proceeding immediatelly at the head of
some Militia to put a stop to the Ravages of the Enemy believing their Numbers to be few, but was told by Colo. Martin who
had attempted to raise the Militia for the same purpose that it
was impossible to get above 20 or 25 Men, they having absolutely refus'd to stir, choosing as they say to die with their Wives
and Family's—Finding this expedient was likely to prove abortive, I sent of expresses to hurry on the Recruits from below,
and the Militia from Fairfax, Prince William, &ca which Lord
Fairfax had ordered—and also hired Spies to go out and see to
discover the Numbers of the Enemy, and to encourage the
Rangers who we were told, are blocked up by the Indians in
small fortresses—but if I may offer my opinion—I believe they
are more encompassd by fear than by the Enemy: I have also
Impressd Waggons and sent them to Conogogee for Flour,
Musket Shott, and Flints; Powder, and a trifling quantity of
Paper bought at extravagent prices for Cartridges, I expect
from below. Six or eight Smiths are now at Work repairing the
few Arms that are here, which is all that we have to depend upon.
A man was hired the 24th of last Month to do the whole but
neglected, and was just moving off in Wagns to Pennsylvania; I

pressd his Waggon's, and compelld him by Force to assist in this Work.

In all things I meet with the greatest opposition no orders are obey'd but what a Party of Soldier's or my own drawn Sword Enforces; without this a single horse for the most urgent occasion cannot be had, to such a pitch has the insolence of these People arrivd by having every point hitherto submitted to them; however, I have given up none where his Majestys Service requires the Contrary, and where my proceedings are justified by my Instruction's, nor will I, unless they execute what they threaten i, e, "to blow out my brains."

I have invited the poor distressed People (who were drove from there Habitation's) to Lodge their Familys in some place of security, and to join our Partys in Scouring the Woods where the Enemy lie; and beleive some will chearfully assist. I also have, & shall continue to take every previous Step to forward the March of the Recruits &ca so soon as they arrive here, and your Honour may depend that nothing that is in my power to do, shall be wanting for the good of the Service.

I woud again hint the necessity of putting the Militia under better Regulation had I not mention'd it twice before, and a third time may seem Impertinent. but I must once more beg leave to declare, (for here I am more immediately concern'd), that unless the Assembly will Enact a Law, to enforce the Military Law in all its Parts, that I must with great regret decline the Honour that has been so generously intended me. and for this only reason I do it—The foreknowledge I have of failing in every point that might justly be expected from a person invested with full power to exert his Authority. I see the growing Insolence of the Soldiers, the Indolence, and Inactivity of the Officers, who are all sensible how confin'd their punishments are, in regard to what they ought to be. In fine, I can plainly see that under our present Establishment we shall become a Nusance; an insupportable charge to our Country, and never answer any one expectation of the Assembly: And here, I must assume the Freedom to express some surprise, that we alone shou'd be so tenacious of Liberty as not to invest a power, where Interest, and Politicks so unanswerably demand it; and from whence so much good must consequently ensue: do we not see that every Nation under the Sun find their accd therein;

and without it no Order, no regularity can be observ'd Why
then shoud it be expected from us (who are all young and un-
experienced) to govern, and keep up a proper spirit of Discipline witht Laws, when the best, and most experienc'd can
scarcely do it with—then if we consult our Interest—I am sure
it is loudly calld for, For I can confidantly assert that the money
expended in Recruiting, Cloathing, Arming, Maintaining, and
Subsisting Soldiers who have deserted, has cost the Country
an immense Sum, which might have been prevented were we
under Restraints, that woud terrifie the Soldrs from such practices: One thing more on this head I will recommend, and
then quit the subject, and that is, to have the Inhabitants liable
to certain heavy Fines, or Corporal Punishments for Entertaining of Deserters; and a Reward for takg them up; if this was
done, it woud be next to an impossibility for a Soldier to Escape
—but on the contrary as things now stand, they are not only
seduc'd to run away, but are also harbour'd and assisted with
every necessary means to make their escape.

Sunday Noon

Last night at 8 o'clock, arrivd an express just spent with fatigue and fear, reporting that a Party of Indians were seen at
the Plantation of one Isaac Julian's abt 12 Miles off, and that the
Inhabitants were flying in the most promiscuous manner from
their dwellings—I immediately order'd the Town Guards to be
strengthned, Perkins's Lieut. to be in readiness with his Company, some Recruits (who had only arrivd abt half an hour
before) to be Arm'd, and sent two men will acquainted with
the woods to go up that road and lay wait, to see if they coud
discover the Numbers & Motion of the Indian's, that we might
have timely notice of their approach. This Morning before we
coud parade the Men to March upon the last Alarm, arriv'd a
Second Express ten times more terrified than the former; with
information that the Indians had got within four Miles of the
Town and were killing and destroying all before them. for that
he—himself—had heard constant Firing, and the Shrieks of the
unhappy Murder'd—upon this I immediately collected what
Force I cou'd, which consisted only of 22 Men recruited for
the Ranger's, and 19 of the Militia and Marchd therewith directly to the place where these horrid Murders were said to be
committed—when we got there, who shoud we find occasioning

all this disturbance, but 3 drunken Soldiers of the Light Horse carousing, firing their Pistols, and uttering the most unheard off Imprecation's, these we took and marchd Prisoner's to Town where we met the Men I sent out last Night, and learnt that the Party of Indian's discovered by Isaac Julian, provd to be a Mulatto and Negro seen hunting of Cattle by his Son, who alarmd the Father, and the Father the neighbourhd. These Circumstances are related only to shew, what a panick prevails among the People, how much they are alarmd at the most usual, and customary Cry's—and yet how impossible it is to get them to act in any respect for their common safety's; an Instance of this then appeard—Colo. Fairfax who arrivd in Town while we were upon the Scout, immediately sent to a Noble Captain (not far off) to repair with his Company forthwith to Winchester: with coolness and moderation, this great Captn answerd, that his Wife, Family, and Corn was at stake, so were those of his Soldrs therefore it was not possible for him to come, such is the Example of the Officer's! Such the behaviour of the Men! And such the unhappy Circumstances on which our Country depends!

Monday Morning

The Men I hired to bring Intelligence from the Branch, return'd last Night with Letter's from Captn Ashby and the other Partys up there, by which we learn that the Indians are gone off. Scouts having been dispersd upon those Water's for several days witht discovering tracts, or other Signs of the Enemy. I am also inform'd that it is believ'd their numbers amounted to 150—that 70 or near it of our People are killd, and missing, and that several houses and Plantations are destroy'd, but not so great havock made as was at first represented—The Ranger's, and a small party of Militia ordered up there by Lord Fairfax I am given to understand intend to March down on Wednesday next, who will be immediately followd by all the Inhabitants of those parts that had gather'd under their protection: I have therefore sent Preemptory Order's to the Contrary, but what obedience will be paid to it—a little time will reveal. I have order'd those Men who were recruited for the Ranger's to join their Respective Company's, and there is also a party of 20 Militia marchd with them, under the Command of Captn Hardin.

Captn Waggener is this Instant arrivd with 30 Rects which he marched from Alexandria in less than three days a great march indeed! Majr Lewis and his Rects from Fredericksburg is expected in Tomorrow, when with these, and 22 Men of Captn Bells now here I shall proceed by quick Marches to Fort Cumberland in order to strengthen the Garrison there. Besides these, I think it absolutely necessary that there shoud be two or 3 Companys exclusive of Ranger's to Guard the Potomack Water's, till such times as our Regiment is compleated; and indeed the Ranger's and volunteer Companys in Augusta, with some of their Militia shoud be properly disposd of on those Frontier's for fear of an Attack upon that Quarter: This thô is submitted to your honour's Judgement, & waits your Order's for execution if it shoud be thought expedient. Captn Waggener inform'd me, that it was with difficulty he passd the Ridge for the Crowds of People who were flying, as if every moment was death. he endeavourd, but in Vain to stop them, they firmly believg that Winchester was taken, and in Flames— I have sent expresses down the several Roads in hopes of bringing back the Inhabitants who are really frighted out of their Senses.

I dispatchd an express immediately upon my arrival to this place with a Copy of the Inclosd to Andw Montour, who I heard was at a place calld long Island with 300 Indians, to see if I coud engage him and them to join us. The Letter favours a little of flattery & &ca but this I hope is justifiable on such occasion's—I also wrote to Gist acquaintg him of the favour your Honour intended him, and desir'd he woud repair home in order to raise his Company of Scouts.

I shall defer writing to the Speaker and Committee upon any other head than that of Commissary, still hoping to be down by the time I mention'd in my last (provided no new disturbances happens) having some points to settle that I am uneasy and urgent abt—I have been oblig'd to do dutys quite foreign from my own, but that I shall never hesitate abt when other's do; and the good of the Service requires the Contrary— In a journey from Fort Cumberld to Fort Dinwiddie, which I made purposely to see the Situation of our Frontier's, how the Rangers were Posted, and how Troops might be disposd off for the defence of the Country, I purchased 650 fine Beeves to be deliverd at Fort Cumberland by the First day of Novr next, at 10/ pr hundd except a few that I was obligd to give Eleven Shilgs for, and have my own Bonds now out for performance of Covenants—this being the Commissarys business, who I am sorry to say has hitherto been of no use, but disservice to me, in neglecting my Orders, and leaving this place witht Flour, and Fredericksburg witht any Provision's for the Rects tho their was timely notice given: I must beg that if Mr Dick will not act, that some Person may be appointed that will, for if things remain in this uncertain Situation, the Season will pass witht havg any Provision made for the Winters or Summer's Campaign: whoever acts as Comy shoud be sent up immediately abt Salting the Provision's &ca, it will be difficult I believe to provide a quantity of Pork—I enquir'd as I rode thrô Hampshire, Augusta, &ca and cou'd not hear of much for Sale.

Most of the new appointed Officer's have been extreamly difficient in their Duty's by not repairing to their Rendezvouses according to appointment: Captn McKenzie, Lieutt King & Ensigns Milner and Dean, who were orderd to send their Recruits to Alexandria by the first of Octr were not arrived when Captn Waggener left that place: nor have we heard any thing of Captn Harrison whose Recruits shoud have been at Fredericksburg by the same time; and Captn Bell only sent his here on Saturday last—If these Practices are allowd off, we may as well quit altogether for no duty can ever be carried on, if there is not the greatest punctuality observ'd, one thing always depending so immediately upon Another.

I have appointed Captn George Mercer (whose seniority intitled him to it) my Aid de Camp, and Mr Kirkpatrick of Alexandria my Secretary, a young Man bred to business, of good character, well recommended, and a person whose Abilitys coud not be doubted—I hope your Honour will be kind enough to dispatch Colo. Stephen, with order's to repair here immediately, and excuse the Prolixity of this; I was willing to give a circumstantial acct of our Situation &ca that you may be the Better enabled to judge what Orders are necessary to give. I am Honble Sir Yr most Obt Servt
Winchester Octr 14th 1755

Majr Lewis is just arriv'd, and on Thursday I shall begin my March to Fort Cumberland allowg the Rects 1 day to Refresh themselves.

FRUSTRATION WITH THE BRITISH ARMY

To Robert Dinwiddie

Honble Sir   Philadelphia March 10th 1757
  We may I think with great Propriety and Justice represent.
  That—The Virginia Regiment was the first in arms of any Troops upon the Continent, in the prest War. That—The three Years which they have Servd has been one continued Scene of Action. That—whilst other Troops have an agreeable recess in Winter Quarters, the Nature of the Service in which we are engagd, and the smallness of Our Numbers so unequal to the Task, keep us constantly in Motion—That nevertheless, all these Services have hitherto been performd with great Spirit and cheerfulness but That continuing in a Service precarious and uncertain: hazarding Life Fortune & health to the chances of War, for the present, and a bare Subsistance, is matter for serious, and melancholy reflection: It tends to promote langour and Indifference: It sickens that laudable and generous Emulation so necessary among Troops: It is nipping in the bud our rising hopes. Hopes that we have been led to cherish: It is discouraging to Merit, and, I can't help repeating, that it is in the highest degree dispiriting to the Officers, more especially those, who, having thrown themselves out of other employments are now to look forward and see, that they are wasting the Prime of their Lives and Constitutions in a Service the most uncertain, and Precarious: In which they can expect to be continued no longer than hard blows, and continual Dangers require their Aid. and when those Causes Cease, are then dismissd, perhaps in a State of disability and Indigence from wounds, &ca.
  These are reflections that must have due weight in every Breast, but the Idiots and Madman's, and have made Our Officers

anxiously Solicituous to know their Fate—at once—and the full extent of their Dependances, that they may regulate their conduct accordingly.

We cant conceive, that being Americans shoud deprive us of the benefits of British Subjects; nor lessen our claim to preferment: and we are very certain, that no Body of regular Troops ever before Servd 3 Bloody Campaigns without attracting Royal Notice.

As to those Idle Arguments which are often times us'd—namely, You are Defending your own properties; I look upon to be whimsical & absurd; We are Defending the Kings Dominions, and althô the Inhabitants of Gt Britain are removd from (this) Danger, they are yet, equally with Us, concernd and Interested in the Fate of the Country, and there can be no Sufficient reason given why we, who spend our blood and Treasure in Defence of the Country are not entitled to equal prefermt.

Some boast of long Service as a claim to Promotion—meaning I suppose, the length of time they have pocketed a Commission—I apprehend it is the service done, not the Service engag'd in, that merits reward; and that their is, as equitable a right to expect something for three years hard & bloody Service, as for 10 spent at St James's &ca where real Service, or a field of Battle never was seen.

If it shou'd be said, the Troops of Virginia are Irregulars, and cannot expect more notice than other Provincials, I must beg leave to differ, and observe in turn, that we want nothing but Commissions from His Majesty to make us as regular a Corps as any upon the Continent—Because, we were regularly Enlisted attested and bound, during the King's or Colony's Pleasure—We have been regularly Regimented and trained, and have done as regular Duty for upwards of 3 Years as any regiment in His Majesty's Service—We are regularly and uniformly Cloathd; Officers & Soldiers—We have been at all the expence that regulars are in providing equipage for the Camp—and in few words I may say, we labour under every disadvantage, and enjoy not one benefit which regulars do.

How different from Us, the Establishment of all other Provincials is, may easily be discernd by considering, that they are raizd for a Season—assembled in the spring and are dismissd in

the Fall. consequently are totally ignorant of regular Service—
They know their Dependance, and had nothing to expect;
therefore coud not be dissappointed. They are never cloathd,
and are at little expence, as they act as Irregulars and paid ex-
orbitantly. There remains one reason more, which of itself, is
fully sufficient to obviate scrupples: & that is—we have been in
constant Pay, & on constant Duty since the commencement of
these Broils, which none others have.

And we flatter ourselves, it will evidently appear, that the
Advantages gaind by the Enemy, and the Ravages committed
on our Frontiers are not owing to the Inactivity of the V. Regt
In proof of which, we appeal to the many bloody Skirmishes
with the Enemy last Campagn to our Behar at Monogahela, &
Services in the Campaign of 1754; To the number of Officers
& Men killd in Battle, &ca &ca.

Recountg these Services is highly disagreeable to us—as it is
repugnant to the Modesty becoming the Brave, but we are
compelld thereto by the little Notice taken of Us—It being
the General Opinion, that our Services are slighted, or have
not been properly represented to His Majesty: otherwise the
best of Kings woud have graciously taken Notice of Us in turn,
while there are now Six Battalions raizd in America, and not an
Officer of the Virginia Regiment Provided for. notwithstanding many of them had distinguishd themselves in the Service
before Orders were Issued for raizing one of the Battalions
above mentiond. Whereas, the disregarding the faithful services of any Body of His Majesty's Subjects, tends to discourage Merit and lessen that generous Emulation, spirit, and
laudable ambition so necessary to prevail in an Army and which
Contributes so much to the Success of Enterprize.

I, in behalf of the Officers of the Virginia Regt beg, that
your Honour will be pleas'd to take their Case into particular
Consideration, and as they think themselves particularly entitled to your Honours Patronage, give them Reason by your
earnest endeavours with His Lordship, to hope for a Soldiers
reward, and redress their Grievances in whatever manner shall
seem to your Honour most conducive to their Interest, and
His Majesty's Service—We are all Sensible, that nothing but
earnest application can obtain promotion, while there are so
many dependants; & we now hope, as justice and equity are

clear on our side, and as this seems to be the Crisis of our Fate that no stone will be unturnd to bring this abt. I am Honble Sir Yr most Obedt Hble Servt

Farewell Address to the Virginia Regiment

To Captain Robert Steward and Gentlemen Officers of the Virginia Regiment.

My dear Gentlemen.   New Kent County 10th Janry 1759

If I had words that could express the deep sense I entertain of your most obliging & affectionate address to me, I should endeavour to shew you that *gratitude* is not the smallest engredient of a character you have been pleased to celebrate; rather, give me leave to add, as the effect of your partiality & politeness, than of my deserving.

That I have for some years (under uncommon difficulties, which few were thoroughly acquainted with) been able to conduct myself so much to your satisfaction, affords me the greatest pleasure I am capable of feeling; as I almost despared of attaining that end—so hard a matter is it to please, when one is acting under disagreeable restraints! But your having, nevertheless, so fully, so affectionately & so publicly declared your approbation of my conduct, during my command of the Virginia Troops, I must esteem an honor that will constitute the greatest happiness of my life, and afford in my latest hours the most pleasing reflections. I had nothing to boast, but a steady honesty—this I made the invariable rule of my actions; and I find my reward in it.

I am bound, Gentlemen, in honor, by inclination & by every affectionate tye, to promote the reputation & interest of a Corps I was once a member of; though the Fates have disjoined me from it now, I beseech you to command, with equal confidence & a greater degree of freedom than ever, my best services. Your Address is in the hands of the Governor, and will be presented by him to the Council. I hope (but cannot ascertain it) that matters may be settled agreeable to your wishes. On me, depend for my best endeavours to accomplish this end.

I should dwell longer on this subject, and be more particular in my answer, did your address lye before me. Permit me then to conclude with the following acknowledgments: first, that I always thought it, as it really was, the greatest honor of my life to command Gentlemen, who made me happy in their company & easy by their conduct: secondly, that had every thing contributed as fully as your obliging endeavours did to render me satisfied, I never should have been otherwise, or have had cause to know the pangs I have felt at parting with a Regiment, that has shared my toils, and experienced every hardship & danger, which I have encountered. But this brings on *reflections* that fill me with grief & I must strive to forget them; in thanking you, Gentlemen, with uncommon sincerity & true affection for the honor you have done me—for if I have acquired any reputation, it is from you I derive it. I thank you also for the love & regard you have all along shewn me. It is in this, I am rewarded. It is herein I glory. And lastly I must thank you for your kind wishes. To assure you, that I feel every generous return of mutual regard—that I wish you every honor as a collective Body & every felicity in your private Characters, is, Gentlemen, I hope unnecessary—Shew me how I can demonstrate it, and you never shall find me otherwise than your Most obedient, most obliged and most affectionate

CLAIMING AN ESTATE

To Robert Cary & Company

Gentn   Williamsburg May 1. 1759.
The Inclosd is the Ministers Certificate of my Marriage with Mrs Martha Custis—properly as I am told—Authenticated, you will therefore for the future please to address all your Letters which relate to the Affairs of the late Danl Parke Custis Esqr. to me. as by Marriage I am entitled to a third part of that Estate, and Invested likewise with the care of the other two thirds

by a Decree of our Genl Court which I obtaind in order to Strengthen the Power I before had in consequence of my Wifes Administration.

I have many Letters of yours in my possession unanswerd, but at present this serves only to advise you of the above Change and at the sametime to acquaint you that I shall continue to make you the same Consignments of Tobo as usual, and will endeavour to encrease it in proportion as I find myself and the Estate benefitted thereby.

The Scarcity of the last Years Crop; and the high prices of Tobo consequent thereupon woud in any other Case, have inducd me to sell the Estates Crop (which indeed is only 16 Hhds) in the Country but for a present, & I hope small advantage only I did not care to break the Chain of Corrispondance that has so long Subsisted, and therefore have, according to your desire, given Captn Talman an offer of the whole.

On the other side is an Invoice of some Goods which I beg of you to send me by the first Ship bound either to Potomack or Rappahannock, as I am in immediate want of them, Let them be Insurd, and in case of accidents reshipd witht Delay. Direct for me at Mount Vernon Potomack River Virginia; the former is the name of my Seat the other the River on which 'tis Situated. I am Gentn Yr Most Obedt Hble Servt

SCIENTIFIC FARMING

Diary Entry

For an Experimt.

Take 7 Pots (Earthen) or 7 Boxes of equal size and number them.

Then put in No. 1 pld. Earth taken out of the Field below, which is intend. for Wheat—in No. 2, 3, 4, 5, 6 and 7 equal proportion's of the same Earth—to No. 2 put Cow dung—to 3 Marle, 4 with Mud from the Marshes & bottoms adjoining the [   ] Field, to 5 Mud taken out of the River immediately, to 6 the same Mud lain to Mellow sum time, and to 7 the Mud taken from the Shoreside at low Water where it appears to be unmixd with Clay. Of each an equal quantity—and at the proper Season of Sowing Oats put in each of these Pots or boxes 6 Grains of the largest and heaviest Oats planted at proper distances—and watch their growth and different changes till Harvest.

N.B. To preserve them from Accidents put them in the Garden and let the Pots be buried up to their brims.

May 22, 1760

"WITHOUT THE LEAST SUSPICION,
PROVOCATION, OR DIFFERENCE WITH ANY BODY"

Reward for Runaway Slaves

Fairfax County (*Virginia*) *August* 11, 1761. Ran away from a Plantation of the Subscriber's, on *Dogue Run* in *Fairfax*, on Sunday the 9th Instant, the following Negroes, *viz.*

Peros, 35 or 40 Years of Age, a well-set Fellow, of about 5 Feet 8 Inches high, yellowish Complexion, with a very full round Face, and full black Beard, his Speech is something slow and broken, but not in so great a Degree as to render him remarkable. He had on when he went away, a dark colour'd Cloth Coat, a white Linen Waistcoat, white Breeches and white Stockings.

Jack, 30 Years (or thereabouts) old, a slim, black, well made Fellow, of near 6 Feet high, a small Face, with Cuts down each Cheek, being his Country Marks, his Feet are large (or long) for he requires a great Shoe: The Cloathing he went off in cannot be well ascertained, but it is thought in his common working Dress, such as Cotton Waistcoat (of which he had a new One) and Breeches, and Osnabrig Shirt.

Neptune, aged 25 or 30, well set, and of about 5 Feet 8 or 9 Inches high, thin jaw'd, his Teeth stragling and fil'd sharp, his Back, if rightly remember'd, has many small Marks or Dots running from both Shoulders down to his Waistband, and his Head was close shaved: Had on a Cotton Waistcoat, black or dark colour'd Breeches, and an Osnabrig Shirt.

Cupid, 23 or 25 Years old, a black well made Fellow, 5 Feet 8 or 9 Inches high, round and full faced, with broad Teeth before, the Skin of his Face is coarse, and inclined to be pimpley, he has no other distinguishable Mark that can be recollected; he carried with him his common working Cloaths, and an old Osnabrigs Coat made Frockwise.

The two last of these Negroes were bought from an *African* Ship in *August* 1759, and talk very broken and unintelligible *English*; the second one, *Jack*, is Countryman to those, and speaks pretty good *English*, having been several Years in the Country. The other, *Peros*, speaks much better than either, indeed has little of his Country Dialect left, and is esteemed a sensible judicious Negro.

As they went off without the least Suspicion, Provocation, or Difference with any Body, or the least angry Word or Abuse from their Overseers, tis supposed they will hardly lurk about in the Neighbourhood, but steer some direct Course (which cannot even be guessed at) in Hopes of an Escape: Or, perhaps, as the Negro *Peros* has lived many Years about *Williamsburg*, and *King William* County, and *Jack* in *Middlesex*, they may possibly bend their Course to one of those Places.

Whoever apprehends the said Negroes, so that the Subscriber may readily get them, shall have, if taken up in this County, Forty Shillings Reward, beside what the Law allows; and if at any greater Distance, or out of the Colony, a proportionable Recompence paid them, by

GEORGE WASHINGTON.

N.B. If they should be taken separately, the Reward will be proportioned.

"THE STAMP ACT . . . A DIREFUL ATTACK"

To Robert Cary & Company

Gentn   Mount Vernon 20th September 1765.

It cannot reasonably be imagined that I felt any pleasing Sensations upon the receipt of your Letter of the 13th of February covering accts of Sales for 153 Hhds of Master Custis's Tobo and 115 of mine.

That the Sales are pitifully low, needs no words to demonstrate —and that they are worse than many of my Acquaintance upon this River—Potomack—have got in the Out Posts, & from Mr Russel and other Merchants of London for common Aronoko Tobo, is a truth equally as certain—Nay not so good as I myself have got from Mr Gildart of Liverpool for light Rent Tobaccos (shipd him at the same time I did to you) of the meanest sort; such as you once complaind of as the worst of Maryland & not Saleable—Can it be otherwise than a little mortifying then to find, that we, who raise none but Sweetscented Tobacco, and endeavour I may venture to add, to be careful in the manage-ment of it, however we fail in the execution, & who by a close and fixed corrispondance with you, contribute so largely to the dispatch of your Ships in this Country shoud meet with such unprofitable returns? Surely I may answer No! Notwithstand-ing, you will again receive my own Crops this year, & 67 Hhds of Master Custis's; but Gentlemen you must excuse me for adding (As I cannot readily conceive that our Tobacco's are so much depreciated in quality as not only to sell much below other Marks of good repute, but actually for less, as I before observd, than the commonest kinds do) that justice to myself & ward will render it absolutely necessary for me to change my corrispondance unless I experience an alteration for the better.

I might take notice upon this occasion also, that my Tobo Netts a good deal less than Master Custis's, & why it shoud do so, I am really at a loss to discover: his 153 Hhds averaging £7.7.7 and my 115 only £5.17.6—perhaps it may be urged that some of mine was Potomack Tobacco, I grant it, but take these out and the Yorks then average £6.6.5 only—If you had al-lowed him the benefit of the Bonded Duties I shoud not have wonderd at the difference, but this I perceive is not done, and certain I am, my Tobacco ought not to have been inferior to his—in any respect—the Lands being the same, & my direc-tions for making it good equally as express.

Tobacco I well perceive for a year or two past, had fallen in its value—from what causes I shall not take upon me to determine —and I am not so extravagent as to believe that my own and Master Custis's Crops shoud fetch their usual prices when other good Tobacco met with abatements; but I am really self-ish enough to expect that we ought to come in for a part of the good prices that are going, from a belief that our Tobacco is of a quality not so much inferior to some that still sells well, and that so considerable a Consignment—when confined in a manner to one House, as ours is—woud lay claim to the best endeavours of the Merchant in the Sales, and in the return of Goods, for many Articles of which I pay exceeding heavily. another thing I cannot easily Account for, unless it is on a Presumption that they are bought at very long credits which by no means ought to be the case; for where a Person has money in a Merchants hands he shoud doubtless have all the benefits that can result from that money—and in like manner where he pays Interest for the use of the Merchants shoud he be entitled to the same advantages, otherwise it might well be asked for what purpose is it that Interest is paid? Once upon my urging a complaint of this nature you wrote me, that the Goods ought to be sent back, and they shoud be returnd upon the Shopkeepers hands in cases of Imposition; but a moments reflection points out the Inconveniencies of such a measure unless (the Imposition be grossly abusive, or that) we coud afford to have a years stock before hand; how otherwise can a Person who Imports bear requisites only submit to lay a year out of any particular Article of Cloathing, or necessary for Family use, and have recourse to such a tedious & uncertain way of relief as this, when possibly a Tradesman woud deny the Goods & consequently refuse them—It is not to be done—we are obliged to acquiesce to the present loss & hope for future redress.

These Gentlemen are my Sentiments, fully, and candidly expressd, without any design—believe me—of giving you offence; but as the selling of our Tobacco's well, & purchasing of Our Goods upon the best Terms, are matters of the utmost consequence to our well doing, it behooves me to be plain and sincere in my declaration's on these points—previous to any change of measures—that I may stand acquitted of the Imputation of fickleness if I am at last forced to a discontinuance of my corrispondance with your House.

Twenty Hhds of my Tobacco from this River makes up Forty eight which I have in Boyes; the remainder (which is trifling) shall be sent by the first Ship that gives liberty; and as I have not been able to discover any advantages we obtain by our

Tobaccos lying so long upon hand, unsold, I shoud be glad to have the present Crops (& so of others if more be sent) disposd of to the first good Chapmen, & the Sales returnd, unless there is a very probable certainty of a rise of price to warrant the keeping of it.

By this conveyance you will receive Invoices of Goods wanted for our Plantation's on York; and those for this River, will no longer I hope be sent in by Boyes for when they come into that River we really suffer by the strange mistakes that continually happen—Last year several parcels of Goods designd for York River were sent to this place and others for me left down there & in going backwards & forwards some were lost (things too of no inconsiderable value, for one of the parcels was a Bale of Linnen) and this year all my Plaid hose for this River came in a package to Mr Valentine & I have them to send for 150 Miles—These mistakes & Inconveniencies woud necessarily be avoided if the Goods were to come by Ships to the respective Rivers; and they woud also escape those frequent damages which is the consequence of shifting them from one Vessel to another, and transporting them from place to place— Oppertunities of doing this cannot be wanting as many Vessels comes to this River annually (from London) some of which lye at my Door.

It appears pretty evident to me from the prices I have generally got for my Tobacco in London, & from some other concomitant Circumstances, that it only suits the Interest of a few particular Gentlemen to continue their consignments of this commodity to that place, while others shoud endeavour to substitute some other Article in place of Tobacco, and try their success therewith. In order thereto you woud do me a singular favour in advising of the general price one might expect for good Hemp in your Port watered & prepared according to Act of Parliament, with an estimate of the freight, & all other Incident charges pr Tonn that I may form some Idea of the profits resulting from the growth—I shoud be very glad to know at the sametime how rough & undressd Flax has generally, and may probably sell; for this year I have made an Essay in both, and altho. I suffer pretty considerably by the attempt, owing principally to the severity of the Drought, &

my inexperience in the management I am not altogether discouraged from a further prosecution of the Scheme provided I find the Sales with you are not clogd with too much difficulty and expence.

The Stamp Act, imposed on the Colonies by the Parliament of Great Britain engrosses the conversation of the speculative part of the Colonists, who look upon this unconstitutional method of Taxation as a direful attack upon their Liberties, & loudly exclaim against the violation—What may be the result of this (I think I may add) ill Judgd measure, and the late restrictions of our Trade and other Acts to Burthen us, I will not undertake to determine; but this I think may be said—that the advantages accruing to the Mother Country will fall far short of the expectation's of the Ministry; for certain it is, that the whole produce of our labour hitherto has centred in Great Britain—what more can they desire? and that all Taxes which contribute to lessen our Importation of British Goods must be hurtful to the Manufacturers of them, and to the Common Weal—The Eyes of our People (already beginning to open) will perceive, that many of the Luxuries which we have heretofore lavished our Substance to Great Britain for can well be dispensed with whilst the Necessaries of Life are to be procurd (for the most part) within ourselves—This consequently will introduce frugality; and be a necessary stimulation to Industry —Great Britain may then load her Exports with as Heavy Taxes as She pleases but where will the consumption be? I am apt to think no Law or usage can compel us to barter our money or Staple Commodities for their Manufacturies, if we can be supplied within ourselve upon the better Terms—nor will her Traders dispose of them without a valuable consideration and surety of Pay—where then lyes the utility of these Measures?

As to the Stamp Act taken in a single and distinct view; one, & the first bad consequence attending of it I take to be this— our Courts of Judicature will be shut up, it being morally impossible under our present Circumstances that the Act of Parliament can be complied with, were we ever so willing to enforce the execution; for not to say, which alone woud be sufficient, that there is not money to pay the Stamps there are many other Cogent Reasons to prevent it and if a stop be put to our Judicial proceedings it may be left to yourselves, who have such large demands upon the Colonies, to determine, who is to suffer most in this event—the Merchant, or the Planter.

I am very much obliged to you for your kind advice of corrisponding with Mr Dandridge—it is a piece of respect due to so near a Relation of my Wifes, & therefore I give you the trouble of the Inclosed; but I have not the least expectation of deriving any advantages from it for thô he has no nearer relatives than her, there are some to whom I believe he has given stronger proofs of his Inclinations of serving—but to you my thanks are equaly due, & I return them with cordiality for the goodness of your Intentions. I am Gentn Yr Most Obedt humble Servt

SELLING A SLAVE

To Joseph Thompson

Sir,   Mount Vernon July 2d 1766.
With this Letter comes a Negro (Tom) which I beg the favour of you to sell, in any of the Islands you may go to, for whatever he will fetch, & bring me in return for him

One Hhd of best Molasses
One Ditto of best Rum
One Barrl of Lymes—if good & Cheap
One Pot of Tamarinds—contg about 10 lbs.
Two small Do of mixed Sweetmeats—abt 5 lb. each
And the residue, much or little, in good old Spirits

That this Fellow is both a Rogue & Runaway (tho. he was by no means remarkable for the former, and never practised the latter till of late) I shall not pretend to deny—But that he is exceeding healthy, strong, and good at the Hoe, the whole neighbourhood can testifie & particularly Mr Johnson and his Son, who have both had him under them as foreman of the gang; which gives me reason to hope he may, with your good management, sell well, if kept clean & trim'd up a little when offerd to Sale.

I shall very chearfully allow you the customary Commissions

on this affair, and must beg the favour of you (least he should attempt his escape) to keep him handcuff'd till you get to Sea—or in the Bay—after which I doubt not but you may make him very useful to you.

I wish you a pleasant and prosperous Passage, and a safe & speedy return, being Sir, Yr Very Hble Servt

THOUGHTS ON NON-IMPORTATION AGREEMENTS

To George Mason

Dear sir,   Mount Vernon 5th April 1769.

Herewith you will receive a letter and sundry papers which were forwarded to me a day or two ago by Doctor Ross of Bladensburg. I transmit them with the greater pleasure, as my own desire of knowing your sentiments upon a matter of this importance exactly coincides with the Doctrs inclinations.

At a time when our lordly Masters in Great Britain will be satisfied with nothing less than the deprivation of American freedom, it seems highly necessary that something shou'd be done to avert the stroke and maintain the liberty which we have derived from our Ancestors; but the manner of doing it to answer the purpose effectually is the point in question.

That no man shou'd scruple, or hesitate a moment to use a—ms in defence of so valuable a blessing, on which all the good and evil of life depends; is clearly my opinion; Yet A—ms I wou'd beg leave to add, should be the last resource; the denier resort. Addresses to the Throne, and remonstrances to parliament, we have already, it is said, proved the inefficacy of; how far then their attention to our rights & priviledges is to be awakened or alarmed by starving their Trade & manufactures, remains to be tryed.

The northern Colonies, it appears, are endeavouring to adopt this scheme—In my opinion it is a good one; & must be attended with salutary effects, provided it can be carried pretty generally into execution; but how far it is practicable to do so, I will not take upon me to determine. That there will be difficulties attending the execution of it every where, from clashing interests, & selfish designing men (ever attentive to their own gain, & watchful of every turn that can assist their lucrative views, in preference to any other consideration) cannot be denied; but in the Tobacco Colonies where the Trade is so diffused, and in a manner wholly conducted by Factors for their principals at home, these difficulties are certainly enhanced, but I think not insurmountably increased, if the Gentlemen in their several counties wou'd be at some pains to explain matters to the people, & stimulate them to a cordial agreement to purchase none but certain innumerated articles out of any of the Stores after such a period, nor import nor purchase any themselves. This, if it did not effectually withdraw the Factors from their Importations, wou'd at least make them extremely cautious in doing it, as the prohibited Goods could be vended to none but the non-associater, or those who wou'd pay no regard to their association; both of whom ought to be stigmatized, and made the objects of publick reproach.

The more I consider a Scheme of this sort, the more ardently I wish success to it, because I think there are private, as well as public advantages to result from it—the former certain, however precarious the other may prove; for in respect to the latter I have always thought that by virtue of the same power (for here alone the authority derives) which assume's the right of Taxation, they may attempt at least to restrain our manufactories; especially those of a public nature; the same equity & justice prevailing in the one case as the other, it being no greater hardship to forbid my manufacturing, than it is to order me to buy Goods of them loaded with Duties, for the express purpose of raising a revenue. But as a measure of this sort will be an additional exertion of arbitrary power, we cannot be worsted I think in putting it to the Test. On the other hand, that the Colonies are considerably indebted to Great Britain, is a truth universally acknowledged. That many families are reduced, almost, if not quite, to penury & want, from the low ebb of their fortunes, and Estates daily selling for the discharge of Debts, the public papers furnish but too many melancholy proofs of. And that a scheme of this sort will contribute more effectually than any other I can devise to immerge the Country from the distress it at present labours under, I do most firmly believe, if it can be generally adopted. And I can see but one set of people (the Merchants excepted) who will not, or ought not, to wish well to the Scheme; and that is those who live genteely & hospitably, on clear Estates. Such as these were they, not to consider the valuable object in view, & the good of others, might think it hard to be curtail'd in their living & enjoyments; for as to the penurious man, he saves his money, & he saves his credit; having the best plea for doing that, which before perhaps he had the most violent struggles to refrain from doing. The extravagant & expensive man has the same good plea to retrench his Expences—He is thereby furnished with a pretext to live within bounds, and embraces it—prudence dictated œconomy to him before, but his resolution was too weak to put it in practice; for how can I, *says he*, who have lived in such & such a manner change my method? I am ashamed to do it: and besides, such an alteration in the System of my living, will create suspicions of a decay in my fortune, & such a thought the world must not harbour; I will e'en continue my course: till at last the course discontinues the Estate, a sale of it being the consequence of his perseverance in error. This I am satisfied is the way that many who have set out in the wrong tract, have reasoned, till ruin stares them in the face. And in respect to the poor & needy man, he is only left in the same situation he was found; better I might say, because as he judges from comparison, his condition is amended in proportion as it approaches nearer to those above him.

Upon the whole therefore, I think the Scheme a good one, and that it ought to be tryed here, with such alterations as the exigency of our circumstances render absolutely necessary; but how, & in what manner to begin the work, is a matter worthy of consideration; and whether it can be attempted with propriety, or efficacy (further than a communication of sentiments to one another) before May, when the Court & Assembly will meet together in Williamsburg, and a uniform plan can be concerted, and sent into the different counties to operate at the same time, & in the same manner every where, is a thing I am somewhat in doubt upon, & shou'd be glad to know your opinion of. I am Dr Sir Your most Obt humble Servant

"IS THERE ANYTHING TO BE EXPECTED
FROM PETITIONING AFTER THIS?"

To Bryan Fairfax

DEAR SIR,   Mount Vernon, 4 July, 1774.

John has just delivered to me your favor of yesterday, which I shall be obliged to answer in a more concise manner, than I could wish, as I am very much engaged in raising one of the additions to my house, which I think (perhaps it is fancy) goes on better whilst I am present, than in my absence from the workmen.

I own to you, Sir, I wished much to hear of your making an open declaration of taking a poll for this county, upon Colonel West's publicly declining last Sunday; and I should have written to you on the subject, but for information then received from several gentlemen in the churchyard, of your having refused to do so, for the reasons assigned in your letter; upon which, as I think the country never stood more in need of men of abilities and liberal sentiments than now, I entreated several gentlemen at our church yesterday to press Colonel Mason to take a poll, as I really think Major Broadwater, though a good man, might do as well in the discharge of his domestic concerns, as in the capacity of a legislator. And therefore I again express my wish, that either you or Colonel Mason would offer. I can be of little assistance to either, because I early laid it down as a maxim not to propose myself, and solicit for a second.

As to your political sentiments, I would heartily join you in them, so far as relates to a humble and dutiful petition to the throne, provided there was the most distant hope of success. But have we not tried this already? Have we not addressed the Lords, and remonstrated to the Commons? And to what end? Did they deign to look at our petitions? Does it not appear, as clear as the sun in its meridian brightness, that there is a regular, systematic plan formed to fix the right and practice of taxation upon us? Does not the uniform conduct of Parliament for some years past confirm this? Do not all the debates, especially those just brought to us, in the House of Commons on the side of government, expressly declare that America must be taxed in aid of the British funds, and that she has no longer resources within herself? Is there any thing to be expected from petitioning after this? Is not the attack upon the liberty and property of the people of Boston, before restitution of the loss to the India Company was demanded, a plain and self-evident proof of what they are aiming at? Do not the subsequent bills (now I dare say acts), for depriving the Massachusetts Bay of its charter, and for transporting offenders into other colonies or to Great Britain for trial, where it is impossible from the nature of the thing that justice can be obtained, convince us that the administration is determined to stick at nothing to carry its point? Ought we not, then, to put our virtue and fortitude to the severest test?

With you I think it a folly to attempt more than we can execute, as that will not only bring disgrace upon us, but weaken our cause; yet I think we may do more than is generally believed, in respect to the non-importation scheme. As to the withholding of our remittances, that is another point, in which I own I have my doubts on several accounts, but principally on that of justice; for I think, whilst we are accusing others of injustice, we should be just ourselves; and how this can be, whilst we owe a considerable debt, and refuse payment of it to Great Britain, is to me inconceivable. Nothing but the last extremity, I think, can justify it. Whether this is now come, is the question.

I began with telling you, that I was to write a short letter. My paper informs me I have done otherwise. I shall hope to see you to-morrow, at the meeting of the county in Alexandria, when these points are to be considered. I am, dear Sir, your most obedient and humble servant.

"A VITAL WOUND"

To Robert McKenzie

Dear Sir,   Philadelphia 9th October 1774
    Your letter of the 13th ulto from Boston, gave me pleasure, as I learnt thereby that you were well, and might be expected

at Mount Vernon in your way to or from James river, in the course of the winter.

When I have said this, permit me with the freedom of a friend, (for you know I always esteemed you) to express my sorry at Fortunes placing you in a service that must fix curses to latest posterity upon the diabolical contrivers; and if success (which by the by is impossible) accompanies it, execrations upon all those who have been instrumental in the execution.

I do not mean by this to insinuate that an officer is not to discharge his duty, even when chance, not choice, has placed him in a disagreeable situation; but I conceive when you condemn the conduct of the Massachusetts People, you reason from effects, not causes; otherwise you would not wonder at a people who are every day receiving fresh proofs of a Systematic ascertion of an arbitrary power, deeply planned to overturn the Laws & Constitution of their country, & to violate the most essential & valuable rights of mankind; being irritated, & with difficulty restrained from acts of the greatest violence and intemperance. For my own part I confess to you candidly that I view things in a very different point of light to the one in which you seem to consider them, and though you are led to believe by venal men (for such I must take the liberty of calling those new fangled counsellors which fly to & surround you, & all others who for honorary or pecuniary gratifications will lend their aid to overturn the constitution, & introduce a system of arbitrary Government,) altho' you are taught, I say, by discoursing with such men, to believe that the people of Massachusetts are rebellious, setting up for independency, & what not; give me leave, my good friend, to tell you that you are abused—grossly abused; and this I advance with a degree of confidence, & boldness which may claim your belief; having better opportunities of knowing the real sentiments of the people you are among, from the Leaders of them, in opposition to the present measures of administration, than you have from those whose business it is not to disclose truths, but to misrepresent facts in order to justify as much as possible to the world, their own conduct; for give me leave to add, & I think I can announce it as a fact, that it is not the wish, or the interest of the Government, or any other upon this Continent, separately, or collectively, to set up for Independence; but this you may at the same time rely on, that none of them will ever submit to the loss of those valuable rights & priviledges which are essential to the happiness of every free State, and without which, Life, Liberty & property are rendered totally insecure.

These Sir, being certain consequences which must naturally result from the late acts of Parliament relative to America in general, & the Government of Massachusetts Bay in particular, is it to be wonder'd at, I repeat, that men who wish to avert the impendg blow, should attempt to oppose it in its progress, or perhaps for their defence, if it cannot be diverted? Surely I may be allowed to answer in the negative; & give me leave to add, as my opinion, that more blood will be spilt on this occasion (if the Ministry are determined to push matters to extremity) than history has ever yet furnished instances of in the annals of North America; and such a vital wound given to the peace of this great Country, as time itself cannot cure or eradicate the remembrance of. But I have done. I was involuntarily lead into a short discussion of this subject by your remarks on the conduct of the Boston people; & your opinion of their wishes to set up for independency. I am well satisfyed, as I can be of my existence, that no such thing is desired by any thinking man in all North America; on the contrary, that it is the ardent wish of the warmest advocates for liberty, that peace & tranquility, upon Constitutional grounds, may be restored, & the horrors of civil discord prevented.

I am very glad to hear that my friend Stewart was well when you left London. I have not had a letter from him these five years, nor heard of him, I think for two—I wish you had mentioned his employment. Poor Mercer! I often hear from him; much cause has he, I fear, to lament his having fallen into the accursed state of attendance & dependance. I remain with very great esteem Dr Sir Your most Obedt Servt

NEWS OF LEXINGTON AND CONCORD

To George William Fairfax

Dear Sir, Philadelphia May 31st 1775.

Since my last (dated about the first of April) I have received from Mr Craven Peyton the Sum of £193.6.10 (as you may see by the inclosed Account) with which, and the Balance of the former Money, I now remit you the following Bills; to wit, one drawn by Mr Thomas Contee on Mr Mollison, for £40 Sterling, and another drawn by Lyonel Bradstreet on Mr William Tippell of London for the like Sum (indorsed by Mr Contee; the strongest assurances being given me, that they are both good) Mr Contee is Mr Mollison's principal Factor, or Agent, in Maryland, and is besides a Man of property himself; but notwithstanding this, the times are so ticklish, that there is no such thing as answering for the payment of Bills. You must therefore, either take the chance of receiving bad ones, or suffer your Money to lay dead.

I have also, since my coming to this place, purchased a Bill from Messieurs Willing and Morris of £161.5.10 Sterling, which will, I believe, for I have not a state of our Account with me, about Balance it. With the Copy of Mr Peyton's Account, you will receive a List of the Rents which he collected since last settlement; and these, as I have not been favoured with a Line from you, since your Letter of June, is all I recollect at present worth communicating relative to your business.

Before this Letter can reach you, you must, undoubtedly, have received an Account of the engagement in the Massachusetts Bay between the Ministerial Troops (for we do not, nor cannot yet prevail upon ourselves to call them the King's Troops) and the Provincials of that Government; But as you may not have heard how that affair began, I inclose you the several Affidavits that were taken after the action.

General Gage acknowledges, that the detachment under Lieutenant Colonel Smith was sent out to destroy private property; or, in other Words, to destroy a Magazine which self preservation obliged the Inhabitants to establish. And he also confesses, in effect at least, that his Men made a very precipitate retreat from Concord, notwithstanding the reinforcement under Lord Piercy; the last of which may serve to convince Lord Sandwich (and others of the same sentiment) that the Americans will fight for their Liberties and property, however pusilanimous, in his Lordship's Eye, they may appear in other respects.

From the best accounts I have been able to collect of that affair; indeed from every one, I believe the fact, stripped of all colouring, to be plainly this, that if the retreat had not been as precipitate as it was (and God knows it could not well have been more so) the Ministerial Troops must have surrendered, or been totally cut off: For they had not arrived in Charlestown (under cover of their Ships) half an hour, before a powerful body of Men from Marblehead and Salem were at their heels, and must, if they had happened to have been up one hour sooner, inevitably intercepted their retreat to Charlestown. Unhappy it is though to reflect, that a Brother's Sword has been sheathed in a Brother's breast, and that, the once happy and peaceful plains of America are either to be drenched with Blood, or Inhabited by Slaves. Sad alternative! But can a virtuous Man hesitate in his choice? I am, With sincere Regard and Affectionate compliments to Mrs Fairfax, Dear Sir, Your Most obt servant,

"I DO NOT THINK MYSELF EQUAL
TO THE COMMAND"

Address to the Continental Congress

The President informed Colo. Washington that the Congress had yesterday, Unanimously made choice of him to be General & Commander in Chief of the American Forces, and requested he would accept of that Appointment; whereupon Colo. Washington, standing in his place, Spake as follows.

"Mr. President, Tho' I am truly sensible of the high Honour done me in this Appointment, yet I feel great distress, from a consciousness that my abilities & Military experience may not be equal to the extensive & important Trust: However, as the Congress desire it I will enter upon the momentous duty, &

exert every power I Possess In their service & for the Support of the glorious Cause: I beg they will accept my most cordial thanks for this distinguished testimony of their Approbation.

"But lest some unlucky event should happen unfavourable to my reputation, I beg it may be rememberd by every Gentn in the room, that I this day declare with the utmost sincerity, I do not think my self equal to the Command I am honoured with.

"As to pay, Sir, I beg leave to Assure the Congress that as no pecuniary consideration could have tempted me to have accepted this Arduous emploiment at the expence of my domestk ease & happiness I do not wish to make any proffit from it: I will keep an exact Account of my expences; those I doubt not they will discharge & that is all I desire."

June 16, 1775

"A KIND OF DESTINY"

To Martha Washington

My Dearest,   Philadelphia June 18th 1775.

I am now set down to write to you on a subject which fills me with inexpressable concern—and this concern is greatly aggravated and Increased when I reflect on the uneasiness I know it will give you—It has been determined in Congress, that the whole Army raised for the defence of the American Cause shall be put under my care, and that it is necessary for me to proceed immediately to Boston to take upon me the Command of it. You may beleive me my dear Patcy, when I assure you, in the most solemn manner, that, so far from seeking this appointment I have used every endeavour in my power to avoid it, not only from my unwillingness to part with you and the Family, but from a consciousness of its being a trust too great for my Capacity and that I should enjoy more real happiness and felicity in one month with you, at home, than I have the most distant prospect of reaping abroad, if my stay was to be Seven times Seven years. But, as it has been a kind of destiny that has thrown me upon this Service, I shall hope that my undertaking of it, is designd to answer some good purpose —You might, and I suppose did perceive, from the Tenor of my letters, that I was apprehensive I could not avoid this appointment, as I did not even pretend to intimate when I should return—that was the case—it was utterly out of my power to refuse this appointment without exposing my Character to such censures as would have reflected dishonour upon myself, and given pain to my friends—this I am sure could not, and ought not to be pleasing to you, & must have lessend me considerably in my own esteem. I shall rely therefore, confidently, on that Providence which has heretofore preservd, & been bountiful to me, not doubting but that I shall return safe to you in the fall—I shall feel no pain from the Toil, or the danger of the Campaign—My unhappiness will flow, from the uneasiness I know you will feel at being left alone—I therefore beg of you to summon your whole fortitude & Resolution, and pass your time as agreeably as possible—nothing will give me so much sincere satisfaction as to hear this, and to hear it from your own Pen.

If it should be your desire to remove into Alexandria (as you once mentioned upon an occasion of this sort) I am quite pleased that you should put it in practice, & Lund Washington may be directed, by you, to build a Kitchen and other Houses there proper for your reception—if on the other hand you should rather Incline to spend good part of your time among your Friends below, I wish you to do so—In short, my earnest, & ardent desire is, that you would pursue any Plan that is most likely to produce content, and a tolerable degree of Tranquility as it must add greatly to my uneasy feelings to hear that you are dissatisfied, and complaining at what I really could not avoid.

As Life is always uncertain, and common prudence dictates to every Man the necessity of settling his temporal Concerns whilst it is in his power—and whilst the Mind is calm and undisturbed, I have, since I came to this place (for I had not time to do it before I left home) got Colo. Pendleton to Draft a Will for me by the directions which I gave him, which Will I now Inclose—The Provision made for you, in case of my death, will, I hope, be agreeable; I have Included the Money for which I sold my own Land (to Doctr Mercer) in the Sum given you, as also all other Debts. What I owe myself is very trifling—Cary's Debt excepted, and that would not have been much if the Bank stock had been applied without such difficulties as he made in the Transference.

I shall add nothing more at present as I have several Letters to write, but to desire you will remember me to Milly & all Friends, and to assure you that I am with most unfeigned regard, My dear Patcy Yr Affecte

P.S. Since writing the above I have receivd your Letter of the 15th and have got two suits of what I was told was the prettiest Muslin. I wish it may please you—it cost 50/. a suit that is 20/. a yard.

"IMBARKED ON A WIDE OCEAN"

To John Augustine Washington

Dear Brother,   Philadelphia June 20th 1775.
I am now to bid adieu to you, & to every kind of domestick ease, for a while. I am Imbarked on a wide Ocean, boundless in its prospect & from whence, perhaps, no safe harbour is to be found. I have been called upon by the unanimous Voice of the Colonies to take the Command of the Continental Army—an honour I neither sought after, nor desired, as I am thoroughly convinced; that it requires greater Abilities, and much more experience, than I am Master of, to conduct a business so extensive in its nature, and arduous in the execution, but the partiallity of the Congress, joind to a political motive, really left me without a Choice; and I am now Commissioned a Generl & Commander in Chief of all the Forces now raisd, or to be raisd, for the defence of the United Colonies—That I may discharge the Trust to the Satisfaction of my Imployers, is my first wish—that I shall aim to do it, there remains as little doubt of—how far I may succeed is another point—but this I am sure of, that in the worse event, I shall have the consolation of knowing (if I act to the best of my judgment) that the blame

ought to lodge upon the appointers, not the appointed, as it was by no means a thing of my own seeking, or proceeding from any hint of my friends.

I am at liberty to inform you, that the Congress, in a Committee (which will I dare say be agreed to when reported) have converted to a Continental Currency—have ordered two Million of Dollars to be struck for payment of the Troops &ca and have voted 15,000 Men as a Continental Army—which number will be augmented, as the strength of the British Troops will be greater than was expected at the time of passing that vote. Genl Ward—Genl Lee—Genl Schuyler—and Genl Putnam—are appointed Major Genls under me—the Brigadier Genls are not yet appointed. Majr Gates Adjutant Genl—I expect to set out to morrow for Boston & hope to be joind there in a little time by Ten Companies of Rifle men from this Provence, Maryland, & Virginia—for other Articles of Intelligence, I shall refer you to the Papers, as the Printers are diligent in collecting every thing that is stirring.

I shall hope that my Friends will visit, & endeavour to keep up the Spirits of my Wife as much as they can, as my departure will, I know, be a cutting stroke upon her; and on this acct alone, I have many very disagreeable Sensations—I hope you & my Sister, (although the distance is great) will find as much leisure this Summer, as to spend a little time at Mt Vernon. My sincere regards attend you both as also the little ones and I am Dr Sir Yr most Affecte Brother

AN AFFECTIONATE LEAVE-TAKING

To Martha Washington

My dearest,   Phila. June 23d 1775.
As I am within a few Minutes of leaving this City, I could not think of departing from it without dropping you a line; especially as I do not know whether it may be in my power to write again till I get to the Camp at Boston—I go fully trusting in that Providence, which has been more bountiful to me than I deserve, & in full confidence of a happy meeting with you

sometime in the Fall—I have not time to add more, as I am surrounded with Company to take leave of me—I retain an unalterable affection for you, which neither time or distance can change, my best love to Jack & Nelly, & regard for the rest of the Family concludes me with the utmost truth & sincerety Yr entire

MAKING AN ARMY

General Orders

Head Quarters, Cambridge, July 4th 1775.
Parole. Abington.   Countersign, Bedford.
Exact returns to be made by the proper Officers of all the Provisions, Ordnance, Ordnance stores, Powder, Lead, working Tools of all kinds, Tents, Camp Kettles, and all other Stores under their respective care, belonging to the Armies at Roxbury and Cambridge. The commanding Officer of each Regiment to make a return of the number of blankets wanted to compleat every Man with one at least.

The Hon: Artemus Ward, Charles Lee, Philip Schuyler, and Israel Putnam Esquires, are appointed Major Generals of the American Army and due Obedience is to be paid them as such. The Continental Congress not having compleated the appointments of the other officers in said army, nor had sufficient time to prepare and forward their Commissions; every Officer is to continue to do duty in the Rank and Station he at present holds untill further orders.

Thomas Mifflin Esqr. is appointed by the General one of his Aid-de-Camps. Joseph Reed Esqr. is in like manner appointed Secretary to the General, and they are in future to be consider'd and regarded as such.

The Continental Congress having now taken all the Troops of the several Colonies, which have been raised, or which may be hereafter raised, for the support and defence of the Liberties of America; into their Pay and Service: They are now the Troops of the United Provinces of North America; and it is hoped that all Distinctions of Colonies will be laid aside; so that one and the same spirit may animate the whole, and the only Contest be, who shall render, on this great and trying occasion, the most essential service to the great and common cause in which we are all engaged.

It is required and expected that exact discipline be observed, and due Subordination prevail thro' the whole Army, as a Failure in these most essential points must necessarily produce extreme Hazard, Disorder and Confusion; and end in shameful disappointment and disgrace.

The General most earnestly requires, and expects, a due observance of those articles of war, established for the Government of the army, which forbid profane cursing, swearing & drunkeness; And in like manner requires & expects, of all Officers, and Soldiers, not engaged on actual duty, a punctual attendance on divine service, to implore the blessings of heaven upon the means used for our safety and defence.

All Officers are required and expected to pay diligent Attention, to keep their Men neat and clean—to visit them often at their quarters, and inculcate upon them the necessity of cleanliness, as essential to their health and service. They are particularly to see, that they have Straw to lay on, if to be had, and to make it known if they are destitute of this article. They are also to take care that Necessarys be provided in the Camps and frequently filled up to prevent their being offensive and unhealthy. Proper Notice will be taken of such Officers and Men, as distinguish themselves by their attention to these necessary duties.

The commanding Officer of each Regiment is to take particular care that not more than two Men of a Company be absent on furlough at the same time, unless in very extraordinary cases.

Col. Gardner is to be buried to morrow at 3, OClock, P: M. with the military Honors due to so brave and gallant an Officer, who fought, bled and died in the Cause of his country and mankind. His own Regiment, except the company at Malden, to attend on this mournful occasion. The places of those Companies in the Lines on Prospect Hill, to be supplied by Col. Glovers regiment 'till the funeral is over.

No Person is to be allowed to go to Fresh-water pond a fishing or on any other occasion as there may be danger of introducing the small pox into the army.

It is strictly required and commanded that there be no firing of Cannon or small Arms from any of the Lines, or elsewhere, except in case of necessary, immediate defence, or special order given for that purpose.

All Prisoners taken, Deserters coming in, Persons coming out of Boston, who can give any Intelligence; any Captures of any kind from the Enemy, are to be immediately reported and brought up to Head Quarters in Cambridge. Capt. Griffin is appointed Aid-de-Camp to General Lee and to be regarded as such.

The Guard for the security of the stores at Watertown, is to be increased to thirty men immediately.

A serjeant and six men to be set as a Guard to the Hospital, and are to apply to Doctor Rand.

Complaint having been made against John White Quarter Master of Col. Nixon's Regmt for misdemeanors in drawing out Provisions for more Men than the Regiment consisted of; A Court Martial consisting of one Captain and four Subalterns is ordered to be held on said White, who are to enquire, determine and report.

After Orders. 10 OClock

The General desires that some Carpenters be immediately set to work at Brattle's Stables, to fix up Stalls for eight Horses, and more if the Room will admit, with suitable racks, mangers &c.

"AN EXCEEDING DANGEROUS SITUATION"

To Richard Henry Lee

Dear Sir,   Camp at Cambridge July 10th 1775.
    I was exceeding glad to receive a Letter from you, as I always shall be whenever it is convenient, though perhaps my hurry, till such time as matters are drawn a little out of the Chaos they appear in at present, will not suffer me to write you such full and satisfactory answers, or give such clear, and precise accts of our Situation & views, as I could wish, or you might expect.

    After a journey, a good deal retarded, principally by the

desire the different Townships through which I traveld, express'd of shewing respect to the Genl of your armies; I arrivd here on this day week; since which I have been labouring with as much assiduity by fair, and threatning means to obtain returns of our strength in this Camp and Roxbury, & their Dependencies, as a man could do, and never have been able to accomplish the matter till this day—now, I will not answer for the correctness of them, although I have sent several of the Regimental returns back more than once to have mistakes rectified. I do not doubt but the Congress will think me very remiss in not writing to them sooner but you may rely on it yourself, and I beg you to assure them, that it has never been in my power till this day, to comply with their orders. could I have conceivd, that which ought, and in a regular Army would have been done in an hour, would employ eight days, I should have sent an Express off the 2d Morning after I arrivd with a genl acct of things. but expecting in the Morning to receive the Returns in the Evening, and in the Evening surely to find them in the Morning (& at last getting them full of Imperfections) I have been drilled on from day to day, till I am ashamed to look back at the time which has elapsed since my arrival here.

You will perceive by the returns, that, we have but about 16,000. effective men in all this department, whereas by the accts which I receivd from even the first Officers in Command, I had no doubt of finding between 18. and 20,000—out of these there are only 14000 fit for duty—So soon as I was able to get this state of the army, & came to the knowledge of our Weakness, I immediately summond a Council of War, the result of which you will see, as it is Inclosed to the Congress. Between you and me I think we are in an exceeding dangerous Situation, as our Numbers are not much larger than we suppose, from the best accts we are able to get, those of the Enemy to be; theirs situated in such a manner as to be drawn to any point of attack without our having an hours previous notice of it (if the Genl will keep his own Council) whereas we are obliged to be guarded at all points, & know not where, with precission, to look for them—I should not, I think, have made choice of the present Posts in the first Instance altho. I beleive, the Communication between the Town and Country could not have been so well cut off without; but, as much labour has been bestowed in throwing up lines—making redoubts &ca—as Cambridge Roxbury and Watertown must be immediately exposed to the Mercy of the Enemy were we to retreat a little further in the Country—as it would give general dissatisfaction to this Colony—dispirit our own People, and Incourage the Enemy, to remove at this time to another place we have for these reasons resolved in Council to maintain our ground if we can—Our Lines on Winter & Prospect Hills, & those of the Enemy on Bunkers Hill, are in full view of each other, a Mile distant, our advanc'd guard much nearer, & the centries almost near enough to converse—At Roxbury & Boston Neck it is the same between these, we are obliged to guard sevl other Places at which the Enemy may Land. The Enemy have strongly fortified, or will in a few days, their Camp on Bunkers Hill; after which, & their new Landed Troops have got a little refreshd, we shall look for a visit, if they mean, as we are told they do, to come out of their Lines—their great Command of Artillery, & adequate Stores of Powder &ca gives them advantages which we have only to lament the want of—The abuses in this army, I fear, are considerable. and the new modelling of it, in the Face of an Enemy, from whom we every hour expect an attack exceedingly difficult, & dangerous—if things therefore should not turn out as the Congress would wish I hope they will make proper allowances—I can only promise & assure them, that, my whole time is devoted to their Service, & that as far as my judgment goes, they shall have no cause to complain. I need not tell you that this Letter is written in much haste. The fact will sufficiently appear from the face of it; I thought a hasty Letter would please you better than no Letter, & therefore I shall offer no further appology, but assure you that with sincere regard for my fellow Labourers with you. Doctr Shippens Family &ca. I am Dr Sir Yr Most Affecte Servt

TREATMENT OF PRISONERS OF WAR

To Thomas Gage

Sir   Cambridge August 11th 1775
I understand that the Officers engaged in the Cause of Liberty, and their Country, who by the Fortune of War, have fallen into your Hands have been thrown indiscriminately, into a common Gaol appropriated for Felons—That no Consideration has been had for those of the most respectable Rank, when languishing with Wounds and Sickness. That some have been even amputated, in this unworthy Situation.

Let your Opinion, Sir, of the Principle which actuates them be what it may, they suppose they act from the noblest of all Principles, a Love of Freedom, and their Country. But political Opinions I conceive are foreign to this Point, the Obligations arising from the Rights of Humanity, & Claims of Rank, are universally binding and extensive, except in Case of Retaliation. These, I should have hoped, would have dictated a more tender Treatment of those Individuals, whom Chance or War had put in your Power—Nor can I forbear suggesting, its fatal Tendency to widen that unhappy Breach, which you, and those Ministers under whom you act, have repeatedly declared you wish'd to see forever closed.

My Duty now makes it necessary to apprize you, that for the future I shall regulate my Conduct towards those Gentlemen who are or may be in our Possession, exactly by the Rule which you shall observe, towards those of ours, who may be in your Custody. If Severity, & Hardship mark the Line of your Conduct, (painful as it may be to me) your Prisoners will feel its Effects: But if Kindness & Humanity are shewn to ours, I shall with Pleasure consider those in our Hands, only as unfortunate, and they shall receive the Treatment to which the unfortunate are ever intitled.

I beg to be favoured with an Answer as soon as possible. And am, Sir, Your most Obedt & very Hbble Servt

To Thomas Gage

Sir   Head Quarters Cambridge Augt 19th 1775.
  I address'd you on the 11th Instant in Terms which gave the
fairest Scope, for the Exercise of that Humanity & Politeness,
which were supposed to form a Part of your Character—I remonstrated with you, on the unworthy Treatment shewn to
the Officers, and Citizens of America, whom the Fortune of
War, Chance, or a mistaken Confidence had thrown into your
Hands. Whether British, or American Mercy, Fortitude, &
Patience are most preeminent; whether our virtuous Citizens
whom the Hand of Tyranny has forced into Arms, to defend
their Wives, their Children, & their Property; or the mercenary
Instruments of lawless Domination, Avarice, and Revenge best
deserve the Appellation of Rebels, and the Punishment of that
Cord, which your affected Clemency has forborne to inflict;
Whether the Authority under which I act is usurp'd, or founded
on the genuine Principles of Liberty, were altogether foreign
to my Subject. I purposely avoided all political Disquisition;
nor shall I now avail myself of those Advantages, which the
sacred Cause of my Country, of Liberty, and human Nature
give me over you. Much less shall I stoop to Retort, & Invective. But the Intelligence, you say, you have received from our
Army requires a Reply. I have taken Time, Sir, to make a strict
Inquiry, and find it has not the least Foundation in Truth. Not
only your Officers, and Soldiers have been treated with a Tenderness due to Fellow Citizens, & Brethren; but even those
execrable Parricides, whose Counsels & Aid have deluged their
Country with Blood, have been protected from the Fury of a
justly enraged Poeple. Far from compelling, or even permitting
their Assistance, I am embarassed with the Numbers who
crowd to our Camp animated with the purest Principles of
Virtue, & Love of their Country.
  You advise me to give free Operation to Truth, to punish
Misrepresentation & Falshood. If Experience stamps Value
upon Counsel, yours must have a Weight which few can claim.

You best can tell, how far the Convulsion which has brought such Ruin on both Countries, and shaken the mighty Empire of Brittain to its Foundation, may be traced to those malignant Causes.

You affect, Sir, to despise all Rank not derived from the same Source with your own. I cannot conceive any more honourable, than that which flows from the uncorrupted Choice of a brave and free Poeple—The purest Source & original Fountain of all Power. Far from making it a Plea for Cruelty, a Mind of true Magnanimity, & enlarged Ideas would comprehend & respect it.

What may have been the ministerial Views which precipitated the present Crisis, Lexington—Concord, & Charlestown can best declare—May that God to whom you then appealed, judge between America & you! Under his Providence, those who influence the Councils of America, and all the other Inhabitants of these united Colonies, at the Hazard of their Lives, are resolved to hand down to Posterity those just & invaluable Privileges which they received from their Ancestors.

I shall now, Sir, close my Correspondence with you, perhaps forever. If your Officers who are our Prisoners receive a Treatment from me, different from what I wish'd to shew them, they, & you, will remember the Occasion of it. I am Sir, Your very Hbble Servant

"AN EXCEEDING DIRTY & NASTY PEOPLE"

To Lund Washington

Dear Lund,   Camp at Cambridge Augt 20th 1775.
Your Letter by Captn Prince came to my hands last Night— I was glad to learn by it that all are well. the acct given of the behaviour of the Scotchmen at Port Tobacco & Piscataway surprizd & vexed me—Why did they Imbark in the cause? what do they say for themselves? what does other say of them? are they admitted into Company? or kicked out of it? what does their Countrymen urge in justification of them? they are fertile in invention, and will offer excuses where excuses can be

made. I cannot say but I am curious to learn the reasons why men, who had subscribed, & bound themselves to each other, & their Country, to stand forth in defence of it, should lay down their arms the first moment they were called upon.

Although I never hear of the Mill under the direction of Simpson, without a degree of warmth & vexation at his extreame stupidity, yet, if you can spare money from other Purposes, I could wish to have it sent to him, that it may, if possible, be set agoing before the Works get ruined & spoilt, & my whole money perhaps totally lost. If I am really to loose Barraud's debt to me, it will be a pretty severe stroke upon the back of Adams, & the expence I am led into by that confounded fellow Simpson, and necessarily so in Seating my Lands under the Management of Cleveland.

Spinning should go forward with all possible dispatch, as we shall have nothing else to depend upon if these disputes continue another year—I can hardly think that Lord Dunmore can act so low, & unmanly a part, as to think of siezing Mrs Washington by way of revenge upon me; howevr as I suppose she is, before this time gone over to Mr Calverts, & will soon after retug, go down to New Kent, she will be out of his reach for 2 or 3 Months to come, in which time matters may, & probably will, take such a turn as to render her removal either absolutely necessary, or quite useless—I am nevertheless exceedingly thankful to the Gentlemen of Alexandria for their friendly attention to this point & desire you will if there is any sort of reason to suspect a thing of this kind provide a Kitchen for her in Alexandria, or some other place of safety elsewhere for her and my Papers.

The People of this Government have obtain a Character which they by no means deserved—their Officers generally speaking are the most indifferent kind of People I ever saw. I have already broke one Colo. and five Captain's for Cowardice, & for drawing more Pay & Provision's than they had Men in their Companies. there is two more Colos. now under arrest, & to be tried for the same Offences—in short they are by no means such Troops, in any respect, as you are led to believe of them from the Accts which are published, but I need not make myself Enemies among them, by this declaration, although it is consistent with truth. I daresay the Men would fight very well (if properly Officered) although they are an exceeding dirty & nasty people. had they been properly conducted at Bunkers Hill (on the 17th of June) or those that were there properly supported, the Regulars would have met with a shameful defeat; & a much more considerable loss than they did, which is now known to be exactly 1057 Killed & Wounded—it was for their behaviour on that occasion that the above Officers were broke, for I never spared one that was accused of Cowardice but brot 'em to immediate Tryal.

Our Lines of Defence are now compleated, as near so at least as can be—we now wish them to come out, as soon as they please, but they (that is the Enemy) discover no Inclination to quit their own Works of Defence; & as it is almost impossible for us to get to them, we do nothing but watch each other's motion's all day at the distance of about a Mile; every now and then picking of a stragler when we can catch them without their Intrenchments; in return, they often Attempt to Cannonade our Lines to no other purpose than the waste of a considerable quantity of Powder to themselves which we should be very glad to get.

What does Doctr Craik say to the behaviour of his Countrymen, & Townspeople? remember me kindly to him, & tell him that I should be very glad to see him here if there was any thing worth his acceptance; but the Massachusets People suffer nothing to go by them that they can lay hands upon.

I wish the money could be had from Hill, & the Bills of Exchange (except Colo. Fairfax's, which ought to be sent to him immediately) turnd into Cash; you might then, I should think, be able to furnish Simpson with about £300; but you are to recollect that I have got Cleveland & the hired People with him to pay also. I would not have you buy a single bushel of Wheat till you can see with some kind of certainty what Market the Flour is to go to—& if you cannot find sufficient Imployment in repairing the Mill works, & other things of this kind for Mr Roberts and Thomas Alferd, they must be closely Imployed in making Cask, or working at the Carpenters or other business otherwise they must be discharged, for it is not reasonable, as all Mill business will probably be at an end for a while, that I am to pay them £100 a year to be Idle. I should think Roberts himself must see, & be sensible of the reasonableness of this request, as I believe few Millers will find Imploymt if our Ports are shut up, & the Wheat kept in the Straw, or otherwise for greater Security.

I will write to Mr Milnor to forward you a good Country Boulting Cloth for Simpson which endeavour to have contrived to him by the first safe conveyance. I wish you would quicken Lanphire & Sears about the Dining Room Chimney Piece (to be executed as mentioned in one of my last Letters) as I could wish to have that end of the House compleatly finished before I return. I wish you had done the end of the New Kitchen next the Garden as also the old Kitchen with rusticated Boards; however, as it is not, I would have the Corners done so in the manner of our New Church. (those two especially which Fronts the Quarter.) What have you done with the Well? is that walled up? have you any accts of the Painter? how does he behave at Fredericksburg?

I much approve of your Sowing Wheat in clean ground, although you should be late in doing it, & if for no other purpose than a tryal—It is a growing I find, as well as a new practice, that of overseers keeping Horses, & for what purpose, unless it be to make fat Horses at my expence, I know not, as it is no saving of my own Horses—I do not like the custom, & wish you would break it—but do as you will, as I cannot pretend to interfere at this distance. Remember me kindly to all the Neighbours who enquire after Yr Affecte friend & Servt

"COME THEN, MY BRETHREN, UNITE WITH US"

To the Inhabitants of Canada

Friends and Brethren,

The unnatural Contest between the English Colonies and Great-Britain, has now risen to such a Heighth, that Arms alone must decide it. The Colonies, confiding in the Justice of their Cause, and the Purity of their Intentions, have reluctantly appealed to that Being, in whose Hands are all human Events. He has hitherto smiled upon their virtuous Efforts—The Hand of Tyranny has been arrested in its Ravages, and the British Arms which have shone with so much Splendor in every Part of the Globe, are now tarnished with Disgrace and Disappointment.— Generals of approved Experience, who boasted of subduing this great Continent, find themselves circumscribed within the Limits of a single City and its Suburbs, suffering all the Shame and Distress of a Siege. While the trueborn Sons of America, animated by the genuine Principles of Liberty and Love of their Country, with increasing Union, Firmness and Discipline repel every Attack, and despise every Danger.

Above all, we rejoice, that our Enemies have been deceived with Regard to you—They have perswaded themselves, they have even dared to say, that the Canadians were not capable of distinguishing between the Blessings of Liberty, and the Wretchedness of Slavery; that gratifying the Vanity of a little Circle of Nobility—would blind the Eyes of the People of Canada.—By such Artifices they hoped to bend you to their Views, but they have been deceived, instead of finding in you that Poverty of Soul, and Baseness of Spirit, they see with a Chagrin equal to our Joy, that you are enlightned, generous, and virtuous—that you will not renounce your own Rights, or serve as Instruments to deprive your Fellow Subjects of theirs.—Come then, my Brethren, unite with us in an indissoluble Union, let us run together to the same Goal.—We have taken up Arms in Defence of our Liberty, our Property, our Wives, and our Children, we are determined to preserve them, or die. We look forward with Pleasure to that Day not far remote (we hope) when the Inhabitants of America shall have one Sentiment, and the full Enjoyment of the Blessings of a free Government.

Incited by these Motives, and encouraged by the Advice of many Friends of Liberty among you, the Grand American Congress have sent an Army into your Province, under the Command of General Schuyler; not to plunder, but to protect you; to animate, and bring forth into Action those Sentiments of Freedom you have disclosed, and which the Tools of Despotism would extinguish through the whole Creation.—To cooperate with this Design, and to frustrate those cruel and perfidious Schemes, which would deluge our Frontiers with the Blood of Women and Children; I have detached Colonel Arnold into your Country, with a Part of the Army under my Command—I have enjoined upon him, and I am certain that he will consider himself, and act as in the Country of his Patrons, and best Friends. Necessaries and Accommodations of every Kind which you may furnish, he will thankfully receive, and render the full Value.—I invite you therefore as Friends and Brethren, to provide him with such Supplies as your Country affords; and I pledge myself not only for your Safety and Security, but for ample Compensation. Let no Man desert his Habitation—Let no one flee as before an Enemy. The Cause of America, and of Liberty, is the Cause of every virtuous American Citizen; whatever may be his Religion or his Descent, the United Colonies know no Distinction but such as Slavery, Corruption and arbitrary Domination may create. Come then, ye generous Citizens, range yourselves under the Standard of general Liberty—against which all the Force and Artifice of Tyranny will never be able to prevail.

c. September 14, 1775

HIGH HOPES FOR QUEBEC

To Benedict Arnold

Dear Sir,   Cambridge 5 Decr 1775

Your Letter of the 8 Ultimo with a Postscript of the 14 from Point Levi, I have had the pleasure to receive—It is not in the power of any man to command success, but you have done more—you have deserved it, & before this I hope, have met with the Laurels which are due to your Toils, in the possession of Quebec—My thanks are due, & sincerely offered to you, for your Enterprizing & persevering spirit—To your brave followers I likewise present them.

I was not unmindful of you or them in the Establishment of a new army—One out of 26 Regiments, (likely Genl Putnams) you are appointed to the Command of, and I have Ordered all the Officers with you, to the one or the other of these Regiments, in the Rank they now bear, that in case they chuse to continue in service, & no appointment take place, where they now are, no disappointment may follow—Nothing very material has happened in this Camp since you left it—Finding we were not likely to do much in the Land way, I fitted out several Privateers rather Armed Vessells in behalf of the Continent, with which we have taken several prizes, to the amount it is supposed of £15,000 Sterling—One of them a valuable Store Ship (but no powder in it) containing a fine Brass mortar 13 Inch—2000 Stand of Arms—Shot &c. &c.

I have no doubt but a juncture of your detachment with the Army under Genl Montgomerie, is effected before this: If so, you will put yourself under his Command and will I am persuaded give him all the Assistance in your power, to finish the Glorious work you begun—That the Almighty may preserve & prosper you in it, is the sincere & fervent prayer of Dr Sir &c.

P.S. You could not be more Surprized than I was, at Enos return with the Division under his Command. I immediately put him under Arrest & had him tried for Quitting the Detachmt without your Orders—He is acquitted on the Score of provision.

A FRESH START

General Orders

Head Quarters, Cambridge, January 1st 1776
Parole The Congress.   Countersign, America.

This day giving commencement to the new-army, which, in every point of View is entirely Continental; The General flatters himself, that a laudable Spirit of emulation, will now take place, and pervade the whole of it; without such a Spirit, few Officers have ever arrived to any degree of Reputation, nor did any Army ever become formidable: His Excellency hopes that the Importance of the great Cause we are engaged in, will be deeply impressed upon every Man's mind, and wishes it to be considered, that an Army without Order, Regularity & Discipline, is no better than a Commission'd Mob; Let us therefore, when every thing dear and valuable to Freemen is at stake; when our unnatural Parent is threat'ning of us with destruction from every quarter, endeavour by all the Skill and Discipline in our power, to acquire that knowledge, and conduct, which is necessary in War—Our men are brave and good; Men who with pleasure it is observed, are addicted to fewer Vices than are commonly found in Armies; but it is Subordination & Discipline (the Life and Soul of an Army) which next under providence, is to make us formidable to our enemies, honorable in ourselves, and respected in the world; and herein is to be shewn the Goodness of the Officer.

In vain is it for a General to issue Orders, if Orders are not attended to, equally vain is it for a few Officers to exert themselves, if the same spirit does not animate the whole; it is therefore expected, (it is not insisted upon) that each Brigadier, will be attentive to the discipline of his Brigade, to the exercise of, and the Conduct observed in it, calling the Colonels, and Field Officers of every regiment, to severe Account for Neglect, or Disobedience of orders—The same attention is to be paid by the Field Officers to the respective Companies of their regiments —by the Captains to their Subalterns, and so on: And that the plea of Ignorance, which is no excuse for the Neglect of Orders (but rather an Aggravation) may not be offer'd, It is order'd, and directed, that not only every regiment, but every Company, do keep an Orderly-book, to which frequent recourse is to be had, it being expected that all standing orders be rigidly obeyed, until alter'd or countermanded—It is also expected, that all Orders which are necessary to be communicated to the Men, be regularly read, and carefully explained to them. As it is the first wish of the General to have the business of the Army conducted without punishment, to accomplish which, he assures every Officer, & Soldier, that as far as it is in his power, he will reward such as particularly distinguish themselves; at the same time, he declares that he will punish every kind of neglect, or misbehaviour, in an exemplary mannor.

As the great Variety of occurrences, and the multiplicity of business, in which the General is necessarily engaged, may withdraw his attention from many objects & things, which might be improved to Advantage; He takes this Opportunity of declaring, that he will thank any Officer, of whatsoever Rank, for any useful hints, or profitable Informations, but to avoid trivial matters; as his time is very much engrossed, he requires that it may be introduced through the channel of a

General Officer, who is to weigh the importance before he communicates it.

All standing Orders heretofore issued for the Government of the late Army, of which every Regiment has, or ought to have Copies; are to be strictly complied with, until changed, or countermanded.

Every Regiment now upon the new establishment, is to give in signed by the Colonel, or commanding Officer, an exact List of the Commissioned Officers, in order that they may receive Commissions—particular Care to be taken that no person is included as an Officer, but such as have been appointed by proper authority; any Attempt of that kind in the new-Army, will bring severe punishment upon the author: The General will, upon any Vacancies that may happen, receive recommendations, and give them proper Consideration, but the Congress alone are competent to the appointment.

An exact Return of the strength of each Regiment, is to be given in, as soon as possible, distinguishing the Number of militia, and such of the old Regiments, as have joined for a Month only, from the established men of the regiment.

This being the day of the Commencement of the new-establishment, The General pardons all the Offences of the old, and commands all Prisoners (except Prisoners of war) to be immediately released.

TROOP TURNOVER IMPERILS
THE SIEGE OF BOSTON

To Joseph Reed

Dear Sir,   Cambridge 4th Jany 1776

Since my last, I have recd your obliging favours of the 19th & 23d Ulto & thank you for the Articles of Intelligence therein containd; as I also do for the Buttons which accompanied the last Letter, althô I had got a sett, better I think, made at Concord.

I am exceeding glad to find, that things wear a better face in Virginia than they did sometime ago; but I do not think that any thing less than the life, or liberty, will free the Colony from the effects, of Lord Dunmores Resentments and Villainies.

We are at length favour'd with a sight of his Majesty's most gracious Speech, breathing sentiments of tenderness & compassion for his deluded American Subjects; the Eccho is not yet come to hand; but we know what it must be; and as Lord North said, & we ought to have believed (& acted accordingly) we now know the ultimatum of British Justice. the Speech I send you—a volume of them was sent out by the Boston Gentry—And, farcical enough, we gave great Joy to them (the red Coats I mean) without knowing or intending it, for on that day, the day which gave being to the New Army (but before the Proclamation came to hand) we had hoisted the Union Flag in compliment to the United Colonies, but behold! it was receiv'd in Boston as a token of the deep Impression the Speech had made upon Us, and as a signal of Submission—so we learn by a person out of Boston last Night—by this time I presume they begin to think it strange that we have not made a formal surrender of our Lines. Admiral Shuldam is arriv'd at Boston. the 55th and greatest part, if not all, the 17th Regiment, are also got in there—the rest of the 5 Regiments from Ireland were intended for Hallifax & Quebec; those for the first are arrived there, the others we know not where they are got to.

It is easier to conceive, than to describe the Situation of My Mind for sometime past, & my feelings under our present Circumstances; search the vast volumes of history through, & I much question whether a case similar to ours is to be found. to wit, to maintain a Post against the flower of the British Troops for Six Months together without ———— and at the end of them to have one Army disbanded and another to raise within the same distance of a Reinforced Enemy—it is too much to attempt—what may be the final Issue of the last Manouvre time only can tell—I wish this Month was well over our heads—The same desire of retiring into a Chimney Corner siez'd the Troops of New Hampshire, Rhode Island, & Massachusets (so soon as their time expired) as had Work'd upon those of Connecticut, notwithstanding many of them made a tender of their Services to continue till the Lines could be sufficiently strengthned—We are now left with a good deal less than half rais'd Regiments, and about 5000 Militia who only stand Ingaged to the middle of this Month; when, according to custom, they will depart, let the necessity of their stay be never so urgent. thus it is that for more than two Months past I have scarcely immerged from one difficulty before I have plunged into another—how it will end God in his great goodness will direct, I am thankful for his protection to this time. We are told that we shall soon get the Army compleated, but I have been told so many things which have never come to pass, that I distrust every thing.

I fear your Fleet has been so long in Fitting, and the destination of it so well known, that the end will be defeated, if the Vessels escape. how is the arrival of French Troops in the west Indies, & the hostile appearance there, to be reconciled with that part of the Kings Speech wherein he assures Parliament, "that, as well from the Assurances I have receivd, as from the general appearance of Affairs in Europe, I see no probability that the Measures which you may adopt will be interrupted by disputes with any foreign Power."

I hope the Congress will not think of adjourning at so Important, & critical a Juncture as this. I wish they would keep a watchful eye to New York—from Captn Searss Acct (now here) much is to be apprehended from that Quarter. A Fleet is now fitting out at Boston consisting of 5 Transports & two Bomb Vessels under Convoy of the Scarborough & Fowey Men of War—300 some say, others more, Troops are on board, with Flat bottom'd Boats—It is whisperd, as if designedly, that they are intended for New Port, but it is generally beleiv'd that they are bound either to long Island, or Virginia—the other Transports are taking In Water & a good deal of Bisquet is Baking—some say for the Shipping to lay in Nantasket Road to be out of the way of Ice, whilst others think a more Important move is in Agitation—all however is conjecture—I heartily wish you, Mrs Reed & Family the Complts of the Season, in wch the Ladies here, & Family, join—Be assured that I am with Sincere Affecte & Regard

"TO BRING MEN WELL ACQUAINTED WITH THE DUTIES OF A SOLDIER, REQUIRES TIME"

To John Hancock

Sir, Cambridge Feby 9th 1776.

The purport of this Letter, will be directed to a single object —through you I mean to lay it before Congress, and at the same time that I beg their serious attention to the subject, to ask pardon for intruding an opinion, not only unasked, but in some measure repugnant to their Resolves.

The disadvantages attending the limited Inlistment of Troops, is too apparent to those who are eye witnesses of them to render any animadversions necessary; but to Gentlemen at a distance, whose attention is engross'd by a thousand important objects, the case may be otherwise.

That this cause precipitated the fate of the brave, and much to be lamented Genl Montgomerie, & brought on the defeat which followed thereupon, I have not the most distant doubt of; for had he not been apprehensive of the Troops leaving him at so important a crisis, but continued the Blockade of Quebec, a Capitulation, from the best Accts I have been able to collect, must inevitably have followed. And, that we were not obliged at one time to dispute these Lines under disadvantageous Circumstances (proceeding from the same cause, to wit, the Troops disbanding of themselves before the Militia could be got in) is to me a matter of wonder & astonishment; and proves, that General Howe was either unacquainted with our Situation, or restraind by his Instructions from putting any thing to a hazard till his re-inforcements should arrive.

The Instance of General Montgomery—I mention it because it is a striking one—for a number of others might be adduced; proves that instead of having Men to take advantage of Circumstances, you are in a manner compell'd, Right or Wrong, to make Circumstances yield to a Secondary consideration—Since the first of December I have been devising every means in my power to secure these Incampments, and though I am sensible that we never have, since that period, been able to act upon the Offensive, and at times not in a condition to defend, yet the cost of Marching home one set of Men—bringing in another—the havock & waste occasioned by the first—the repairs necessary for the Second, with a thousand incidental charges and Inconveniencies which have arisen, & which it is scarce possible either to recollect or describe, amounts to near as much as the keeping up a respectable body of Troops the whole time —ready for any emergency—would have done.

To this may be added that you never can have a well Disciplined Army.

To bring Men well acquainted with the Duties of a Soldier, requires time—to bring them under proper discipline & Subordination, not only requires time, but is a Work of great difficulty; and in this Army, where there is so little distinction between the Officers and Soldiers, requires an uncommon degree of attention—To expect then the same Service from Raw, and undisciplined Recruits as from Veteran Soldiers is to expect what never did, and perhaps never will happen—Men who are familiarizd to danger meet it without shrinking; whereas those who have never seen Service often apprehend danger where no danger is—Three things prompt Men to a regular discharge of their Duty in time of Action, Natural bravery—hope of reward —and fear of punishment—The two first are common to the untutor'd, and the Disciplin'd Soldier; but the latter, most obviously distinguishes the one from the other. A Coward, when taught to believe, that if he breaks his Ranks, & abandons his Colours, will be punished with Death by his own party, will take his chance against the Enemy; but the Man who thinks little of the one, and is fearful of the other, acts from present feelings, regardless of consequences.

Again, Men of a days standing will not look forward, and from experience we find, that as the time approaches for their discharge they grow careless of their Arms, Ammunition, Camp Utensils, &ca; nay even the Barracks themselves have felt uncommon Marks of Wanton depredation, and lays us under fresh trouble, and additional expence, in providing for every fresh sett; when we find it next to impossible to procure such Articles as are absolutely necessary in the first Instance— To this may be added the Seasoning which new Recruits must have to a Camp—& the loss, consequent thereupon. But this is not all, Men ingaged for a short, limited time only, have the

Officers too much in their power; for to obtain a degree of popularity, in order to induce a second Inlistment, a kind of familiarity takes place which brings on a relaxation of Discipline —unlicensed furloughs—and other Indulgences incompatable with order and good government; by which means, the latter part of the time for which the Soldier was engaged, is spent in undoing what you were aiming to inculcate in the first.

To go into an enumeration of all the Evils we have experienced in this late great change of the Army—and the expence incidental to it—to say nothing of the hazard we have run, and must run, between the discharging of one Army and Inlistment of another (unless an Inormous expence of Militia is incurrd) would greatly exceed the bounds of a Letter; what I have already taken the liberty of saying, will serve to convey a general Idea of the matter, & therefore I Shall, with all due deference, take the freedom to give it as my opinion, that if the Congress have any reason to believe that there will be occasion for Troops another year, and consequently of another Inlistment, they would save money, & have infinitely better Troops if they were, even at a bounty of twenty, thirty, or more Dollars to engage the Men already Inlisted (till Jany next) & such others as may be wanted to compleat to the Establishment, for and during the War. I will not undertake to say that the Men can be had upon these terms, but I am satisfied that it will never do to let the matter alone, as it was last year, till the time of Service was near expiring—The hazard is too great in the first place—In the next, the trouble and perplexity of disbanding one Army and raising another at the same Instant, & in such a critical Situation as the last was, is scarcely in the power of Words to describe, and such as no Man who has experienced it once will ever undergo again.

If Congress should differ from me in Sentiment upon this point, I have only to beg, that they will do me the justice to believe, that I have nothing more in view than what to me appears necessary, to advance the publick Weal, although in the first Instance it will be attended with a capitol expence—And, that I have the honour to be with all due deference & respect theirs, and Your Most & Obedient & faithful Hble Servt

"A STRIKING PROOF OF YOUR GREAT POETICAL TALENTS"

To Phillis Wheatley

Mrs Phillis,   Cambridge February 28th 1776.
    Your favour of the 26th of October did not reach my hands 'till the middle of December. Time enough, you will say, to have given an answer ere this. Granted. But a variety of important occurrences, continually interposing to distract the mind and withdraw the attention, I hope will apologize for the delay, and plead my excuse for the seeming, but not real, neglect.

I thank you most sincerely for your polite notice of me, in the elegant Lines you enclosed; and however undeserving I may be of such encomium and panegyrick, the style and manner exhibit a striking proof of your great poetical Talents. In honour of which, and as a tribute justly due to you, I would have published the Poem, had I not been apprehensive, that, while I only meant to give the World this new instance of your genius, I might have incurred the imputation of Vanity. This, and nothing else, determined me not to give it place in the public Prints.

If you should ever come to Cambridge, or near Head Quarters, I shall be happy to see a person so favoured by the Muses, and to whom nature has been so liberal and beneficent in her dispensations. I am, with great Respect, Your obedt humble servant,

THE BRITISH EVACUATE BOSTON

To John Hancock

Sir   Head Quarters Cambridge 19 March 1776
    It is with the greatest pleasure I inform you that on Sunday last, the 17th Instant, about 9 O'Clock in the forenoon, The Ministerial Army evacuated the Town of Boston, and that the Forces of the United Colonies are now in actual possession

thereof. I beg leave to congratulate you Sir, & the honorable Congress—on this happy Event, and particularly as it was effected without endangering the lives & property of the remaining unhappy Inhabitants.

I have great reason to imagine their flight was precipitated by the appearance of a Work which I had Order'd to be thrown up last Saturday Night, on an Eminence at Dorchester which lay nearest to Boston Neck, call'd Newks Hill. The Town, although it has suffer'd greatly is not in so bad a state as I expected to find it, and I have a particular pleasure in being able to inform you Sir, that your house has receiv'd no damage worth mentioning. Your furniture is in tolerable Order and the family pictures are all left entire and untouch'd. Capt. Cazneau takes Charge of the whole until he shall receive further Orders from you.

As soon as the Ministerial Troops had quitted the Town, I order'd a thousand Men (who had had the Small Pox) under Command of General Putnam to take possession of the Heighths, which I shall endeavour to fortify in such a manner as to prevent their return should they attempt it, but as they are still in the Harbour I thought it not prudent to march off with the Main Body of the Army until I should be fully satisfied they had quitted the Coast—I have therefore only detach'd five Regiments, beside the Rifle Battalion, to New York, and shall keep the remainder here till all Suspicion of their return ceases.

The Situation in which I found their Works evidently discovered that their retreat was made with the greatest precipitation—They have left their Barracks & other Works of Wood at Bunkers Hill &c. all standing, & have destroy'd but a small part of their Lines. They have also left a number of fine pieces of Cannon, which they first spik'd up, also a very large Iron Mortar, and (as I am inform'd) they have thrown another over the end of your Wharf—I have employ'd proper Persons to drill the Cannon & doubt not shall save the most of them. I am not yet able to procure an exact list of all the Stores they have left, as soon as it can be done I shall take care to transmit it to you. From an Estimate of what the Quarter Master Gen'ral has already discover'd the Amount will be 25 or 30,000£.

Part of the Powder mention'd in yours of the 6th Instt, has already arriv'd—The remainder I have order'd to be stop'd on the Road as we shall have no occasion for it here. The Letter to General Thomas I immediately sent to him, he desir'd leave for three or four days to settle some of his private Affairs after which he will set out for his Command in Canada—I am happy that my Conduct in intercepting Lord Drummond's Letter is approv'd of by Congress. I have the honor to be, with sincere respect Sir Your most obedt Servt.

"NO MAN PERHAPS SINCE THE FIRST INSTITUTION OF ARMYS EVER COMMANDED ONE UNDER MORE DIFFICULT CIRCUMSTANCE THAN I"

To John Augustine Washington

Dear Brother,   Cambridge 31st March 1776.
    Your Letter of the 24th Ulto was duely forwarded to this Camp by Colo. Lee. and gave me the pleasure of hearing that you, my Sister and family were well. after your Post is established to Fredericksburg the Intercourse by Letter may become regular and certain (& when ever time, little of which God knows I have for friendly corrispondances, will permit, I shall be happy in writing to you)—I cannot call to mind the date of my last to you, but this I recollect, that I have wrote more Letters to than I have received from you.
    The Want of Arms, Powder &ca, is not peculiar to Virginia—this Country of which doubtless, you have heard such large and flattering Accounts, is more difficient of each than you can conceive, I have been here Months together with what will scarce be believed—not 30 rounds of Musket Cartridges a Man. have been obliged to submit to all the Insults of the Enemy's Cannon for want of Powder, keeping what little we had for Pistol distance. Another thing has been done, which added to the above, will put it in the power of this Army to say what perhaps none other with justice ever could. We have maintain'd our Ground against the Enemy under the above want of Powder—and, we have disbanded one Army & recruited another, within Musket Shot of two and Twenty Regimts, the Flower of the British Army when our strength have been little

if any, superior to theirs. and, at last have beat them, in a shameful & precipitate manner out of a place the strongest by Nature on this Continent—strengthen'd and fortified in the best manner, and at an enormous Expence.

As some Acct of the late Manouvres of both Armies, may not be unacceptable, I shall, hurried as I always am, devote a little time to it.

Having received a small supply of Powder then—very inadequate to our wants—I resolved to take possession of Dorchester Point, laying East of Boston; looking directly into it; and commanding (absolutely) the Enemys Lines on the Neck (Boston)—To effect this, which I knew would force the Enemy to an Ingagement, or subject them to be enphiladed by our Cannon, it was necessary in the first Instance to possess two heights (those mentioned in Genl Burgoynes Letter to Lord Stanley in his Acct of the Battle of Bunkers hill) which had the entire command of it—The grd at this time being froze upwards of two feet deep, & as impenetrable as a Rock, nothing could be attempted with Earth; we were oblig'd therefore to provide an amazing quantity of Chandeliers and Fascines for the Work, and on the Night of the 4th, after a previous severe Cannonade & Bombardment for three Nights together to divert the Enemy's attention from our real design, removed every material to the spot under Cover of Darkness, and took full possession of those heights without the loss of a Single Man.

Upon their discovery of the Works next Morning great preparations were made for attacking them, but not being ready before the Afternoon and the Weather getting very tempestuous, much blood was Saved, and a very important blow (to one side or the other) prevented—That this remarkable Interposition of Providence is for some wise purpose I have not a doubt; but as the principal design of the Manouvre was to draw the Enemy to an Ingagement under disadvantages—as a premeditated Plan was laid for this purpose, and seemed to be succeeding to my utmost wish and as no Men seem'd better disposed to make the Appeal than ours did upon that occasion, I can scarce forbear lamenting the disappointment, unless the dispute is drawing to an Accomodation, and the Sword going to be Sheathed.

But to return, the Enemy thinking (as we have since learnt)

that we had got too securely posted before the Second Morning to be much hurt by them, and apprehending great annoyance from our new Works resolved upon a retreat, and accordingly Imbark'd in as much hurry, precipitation and confusion as ever Troops did, the 17th, not taking time to fit their transports, but leaving Kings property in Boston to the amount, as is supposed, of thirty or £40,000 in Provisions, Stores, &ca—Many Pieces of Cannon, some Mortars, and a number of Shot, Shells &ca are also left—and Baggage Waggons, Artillery Carts &ca which they have been Eighteen Months preparing to take the Field with, were found destroyed —thrown into the Docks—and drifted upon every Shore—In short, Dunbars destruction of Stores after Genl Braddocks defeat, which made so much noise, affords but a faint Idea of what was to be met with here.

The Enemy lay from the 17th to the 27th In Nantasket & Kings Roads abt Nine Miles from Boston to take in Water (from the Islands thereabouts, surrounded by their Shipping) & to fit themselves for Sea—whither they are now bound, & where their Tents will be next pitched, I know not; but as New York and the Hudson's River are the most important objects they can have in view, as the latter secures the communication with Canada, at the same time it seperates the Northern and Southern Colonies Armies; and the former is thought to abound in disaffected Persons who only wait a favourable oppertunity, and support, to declare themselves openly, it became equally important for us to prevent their gaining Possession of these advantages, & therefore, so soon as they Imbarked I detach'd a Brigade of Six Regimts to that Government. so soon as they Sailed, another Brigade compos'd of the same number, and to morrow another of Five will March—In a day or two more I shall follow myself & be in New York ready to receive all but the first.

The Enemy left all their Works standing in Boston, & on Bunkers hill, and formidable they are—the Town has shared a much better Fate than was expected—the damage done to the Houses being nothing equal to report—but the Inhabitants have sufferd a good deal by being plunder'd by the Soldiery at their departure. All those who took upon themselves the Style, & title of Government Men in Boston in short all those who have acted an unfriendly part in this great Contest have Shipped themselves off in the same hurry, but under still greater disadvantages than the Kings Troops have done; being obliged to Man their own Vessels (for Seamen could not be had for the Transports for the Kings use) and submit to every hardship that can be conciv'd—One or two have done, what a great many ought to have done long ago—committed Suicide—By all Accts there never existed a more miserable set of Beings than these wretched Creatures now are—taught to believe that the Power of Great Britain was superior to all opposition, and that foreign Aid (if not) was at hand, they were even higher, & more insulting in their opposition than the Regulars—when the Order Issued therefore for Imbarking the Troops in Boston, no Electric Shock—no sudden Clap of thunder—in a word the last Trump—could not have Struck them with greater Consternation. they were at their Wits end, and conscious of their black ingratitude chose to commit themselves in the manner I have above describ'd to the Mercy of the Waves at a tempestuous Season rather than meet their offended Countrymen. but with this declaration the choice was made that if they thought the most abject Submission would procure them Peace they never would have stir'd.

I believe I may, with great truth affirm, that no Man perhaps since the first Institution of Armys ever commanded one under more difficult Circumstances than I have done—to enumerate the particulars would fill a volume—many of my difficulties and distresses were of so peculiar a cast that in order to conceal them from the Enemy, I was obliged to conceal them from my friends, indeed from my own Army thereby subjecting my Conduct to interpretations unfavourable to my Character—especially by those at a distance, who could not, in the smallest degree, be acquainted with the Springs that govern'd it—I am happy however to find, and to hear from different Quarters, that my reputation stands fair—that my Conduct hitherto has given universal Satisfaction—the Addresses which I have received, and which I suppose will be published, from the general Court of this Colony (the same as our Genl Assembly) and from the Selectmen of Boston upon the evacuation of the Town & my approaching departure from the Colony, exhibits a pleasing testimony of their approbation of my conduct, and of their personal regard, which I have found in various other Instances; and wch, in retirement, will afford many comfortable reflections.

The share you have taken in these Publick disputes is commendable and praiseworthy—it is a duty we owe our Country—a Claim posterity has on us—It is not sufficient for a Man to be a passive friend & well wisher to the Cause. This, and every other Cause, of such a Nature, must inevitably perish under such an opposition. every person should be active in some department or other, without paying too much attention to private Interest, It is a great stake we are playing for, and sure we are of winning if the Cards are well managed—Inactivity in some—disaffection in others—and timidity in many, may hurt the Cause; nothing else can, for Unanimity will carry us through triumphantly in spite of every exertion of Great Britain, if link'd together in one indissoluble Band—this they now know, & are practising every strategem which Human Invention can devise, to divide us, & unite their own People—upon this principle it is, the restraining Bill is past, and Commissioners are coming over. The device to be sure is shallow—the covering thin—But they will hold out to their own People that the Acts (complaind of) are repealed, and Commissioners sent to each Colony to treat with us, neither of which will we attend to &ca—this upon weak Minds among us will have its effect—they wish for reconciliation—or in other Words they wish for Peace without attending to the Conditions.

General Lee, I expect, is with you before this—He is the first Officer in Military knowledge and experience we have in the whole Army—He is zealously attachd to the Cause—honest, and well meaning, but rather fickle & violent I fear in his temper however as he possesses an uncommon share of good Sense and Spirit I congratulate my Countrymen upon his appointment to that Department. The appointment of Lewis I think was also judicious, for notwithstanding the odium thrown upon his Conduct at the Kanhawa I always look'd upon him as a Man of Spirit and a good Officer—his experience is equal to any one we have. Colo. Mercer would have supplied the place well but I question (as a Scotchman) whether it would have gone glibly down. Bullet is no favourite of mine, & therefore I shall say nothing more of him, than that his own opinion of himself always kept pace with what others pleas'd to think of him—if any thing, rather run a head of it.

As I am now nearly at the end of my Eighth page, I think it time to conclude, especially as I set out with prefacing, the little time I had for friendly Corrispondances—I shall only add therefore my Affectionate regards to my Sister and the Children, & Compliments to any enquiring friends and that I am with every Sentiment of true Affection yr Loving Brother & faithful friend.

ANNOUNCING THE DECLARATION
OF INDEPENDENCE

General Orders

Head Quarters, New York, July 9th 1776.
Parole Manchester.   Countersign Norfolk.

John Evans of Capt: Ledyards Company Col. McDougall's Regiment—Hopkins Rice of Capt: Pierce's Company Col. Ritzema's Regiment having been tried by a General Court Martial whereof Col. Read was President and found guilty of "Desertion," were sentenced to receive each Thirty-nine Lashes. The General approves the Sentences and orders them to be executed at the usual time & place.

Passes to go from the City are hereafter to be granted by John Berrien, Henry Wilmot and John Ray Junr a Committee of the City appointed for that purpose—Officers of the Guards at the Ferries and Wharves, to be careful in making this regulation known to the sentries, who are to see that the passes are signed by one of the above persons, and to be careful no Soldier goes over the Ferry without a pass from a General officer.

The North River Guard to be removed to the Market House near the Ferry-Stairs, as soon as it is fitted up.

The Honorable Continental Congress having been pleased to allow a Chaplain to each Regiment, with the pay of Thirty-three Dollars and one third   month—The Colonels or commanding officers of each regiment are directed to procure Chaplains accordingly; persons of good Characters and exemplary lives—To see that all inferior officers and soldiers pay them a suitable respect and attend carefully upon religious exercises: The blessing and protection of Heaven are at all times necessary but especially so in times of public distress and danger—The General hopes and trusts, that every officer, and man, will endeavour so to live, and act, as becomes a Christian Soldier defending the dearest Rights and Liberties of his country.

The Honorable the Continental Congress, impelled by the dictates of duty, policy and necessity, having been pleased to dissolve the Connection which subsisted between this Country, and Great Britain, and to declare the United Colonies of North America, free and independent STATES: The several brigades are to be drawn up this evening on their respective Parades, at six OClock, when the declaration of Congress, shewing the grounds & reasons of this measure, is to be read with an audible voice.

The General hopes this important Event will serve as a fresh incentive to every officer, and soldier, to act with Fidelity and Courage, as knowing that now the peace and safety of his Country depends (under God) solely on the success of our arms: And that he is now in the service of a State, possessed of sufficient power to reward his merit, and advance him to the highest Honors of a free Country.

The Brigade Majors are to receive, at the Adjutant Generals Office, several of the Declarations to be delivered to the Brigadiers General, and the Colonels of regiments.

The Brigade Majors are to be execused from farther attendance at Head Quarters, except to receive the Orders of the day, that their time and attention may be withdrawn as little as possible, from the duties of their respective brigades.

DEFEAT ON LONG ISLAND

To John Hancock

Sir   New York Head Qrs Septr 8th 1776
Since I had the honour of addressing you on the 6th Instt I have called a Council of the General Officers in order to take a

full & comprehensive view of our situation & thereupon form such a plan of future defence as may be immediately pursued & subject to no other alteration than a change of Operations on the Enemy's side may occasion. Before the Landing of the Enemy on Long Island, the point of Attack could not be known or any satisfactory Judgemt formed of their Intentions—It might be on Long Island—on Bergen, or directly on the City, this made It necessary to be prepared for each and has occasiond an expence of labour which now seems useless & is regretted by those who form a Judgement from after knowledge: But I trust men of discernment will think differently, and see that by such works & preparations we have not only delayed the Operations of the Campaign till It is too late to effect any capital Incursion into the Country, but have drawn the Enemy's forces to one point and obliged them to decline their plan, so as to enable us to form our defence on some certainty. It is now extremely obvious from all Intelligence—from their movements, & every other circumstance that having landed their whole Army on Long Island, (except about 4,000 on Staten Island) they mean to inclose us on the Island of New York by taking post in our Rear, while the Shipping effectually secure the Front; and thus either by cutting off our Communication with the Country oblige us to fight them on their own Terms or Surrender at discretion, or by a Brilliant stroke endeavour to cut this Army in peices & secure the collection of Arms & Stores which they will know we shall not be able soon to replace. Having therefore their System unfolded to us, It became an important consideration how It could be most successfully opposed—On every side there is a choice of difficulties, & every measure on our part, (however painfull the reflection is from experience) to be formed with some apprehension that all our Troops will not do their duty. In deliberating on this great Question, it was impossible to forget that History—our own experience—the advice of our ablest Friends in Europe—The fears of the Enemy, and even the Declarations of Congress demonstrate that on our side the War should be defensive, It has been even called a War of posts, that we should on all occasions avoid a general Action or put anything to the risque unless compelled by a necessity into which we ought never to be drawn. The Arguments on which such a System was founded were deemed unanswerable & experience has given her sanction —With these views & being fully persuaded that It would be presumption to draw out our young Troops into open Ground against their superiors both in number and discipline, I have never spared the Spade & Pickax: I confess I have not found that readiness to defend even strong posts at all hazards which is necessary to derive the greatest benefit from them. The honour of making a brave defence does not seem to be a sufficient stimulus when the success is very doubtfull and the falling into the Enemy's hands probable: But I doubt not this will be gradually attained. We are now in a strong post but not an Impregnable one, nay acknowledged by every man of Judgement to be untenable unless the Enemy will make the Attack upon Lines when they can avoid It and their Movements Indicate that they mean to do so—To draw the whole Army together in order to arrange the defence proportionate to the extent of Lines & works would leave the Country open for an approach and put the fate of this Army and Its stores on the Hazard of making a successfull defence in the City or the issue of an Engagement out of It—On the other hand to abandon a City which has been by some deemed defensible and on whose Works much Labor has been bestowed has a tendency to dispirit the Troops and enfeeble our Cause: It has also been considered as the Key to the Northern Country, But as to that I am fully of opinion that the establishing of Strong posts at Mount Washington on the upper part of this Island and on the Jersey side opposite to It with the assistance of the Obstructions already made, & which may be improved in the Water, that not only the Navigation of Hudsons River but an easier & better communication may be more effectually secured between the Northern & Southern States. This I beleive every one acquainted with the situation of the Country will readily agree to, and will appear evident to those who have an Opportunity of recurring to good Maps. These and the many other consequences which will be involved in the determination of our next measure have given our minds full employ & led every One to form a Judgement as the various Objects presented themselves to his view. The post at Kingsbridge is naturally strong & is pretty well fortified, the Heights about It are commanding and might soon be made more so. These are Important

Objects, and I have attended to them accordingly—I have also removed from the City All the Stores & Ammunition except what was absolutely necessary for Its defence and made every Other disposition that did not essentially interfere with that Object, carefully keeping in view untill It should be absolutely determined on full consideration, how far the City was to be defended at all events. In resolving points of such Importance many circumstances peculiar to our own Army also occur, being only provided for a Summers Campaign, their Cloaths, Shoes and Blankets will soon be unfit for the change of weather which we every day feel—At present we have not Tents for more than 2/3d, many of them old & worn out, but if we had a plentiful supply the season will not admit of continuing in them long—The Case of our Sick is also worthy of much consideration—their number by the returns forms at least 1/4 of the Army. policy and Humanity require they should be made as comfortable as possible—With these and many other circumstances before them, the whole Council of Genl Officers met yesterday in order to adopt some Genl line of conduct to be pursued at this Important crisis. I intended to have procured their separate Opinions on each point, but time would not admit, I was therefore Obliged to collect their sense more generally than I could have wished. All agreed the Town would not be tenable If the Enemy resolved to bombard & cannonade It—But the difficulty attending a removal operated so strongly, that a course was taken between abandoning It totally & concentring our whole strength for Its defence—Nor were some a little Influenced in their opinion to whom the determn of Congress was known, against an evacuation totally, as they were led to suspect Congress wished It to be maintained at every hazard—It was concluded to Arrange the Army under Three Divisions, 5000 to remain for the defence of the City, 9000 to Kingsbridge & Its dependancies as well to possess & secure those posts as to be ready to attack the Enemy who are moving Eastward on Long Island, If they should attempt to land on this side—The remainder to occupy the intermediate space & support either—That the Sick should be immediately removed to Orange Town, and Barracks prepared at Kingsbridge with all expedition to cover the Troops.

There were some Genl Officers in whose Judgemt and opinion

much confidence is to be reposed, that were for a total and immediate removal from the City, urging the great danger of One part of the Army being cut off before the other can support It, the Extremities being at least Sixteen miles apart—that our Army when collected is inferior to the Enemy's—that they can move with their whole force to any point of attack & consequently must succeed by weight of Numbers if they have only a part to oppose them—That by removing from hence we deprive the Enemy of the Advantage of their Ships which will make at least one half of the force to attack the Town—That we should keep the Enemy at Bay—put nothing to the hazard but at all events keep the Army together which may be recruited another Year, that the unspent Stores will also be preserved & in this case the heavy Artillery can also be secured—But they were overruled by a Majority who thought for the present a part of our force might be kept here and attempt to maintain the City a while longer.

I am sensible a retreating Army is encircled with difficulties, that the declining an Engagemt subjects a General to reproach and that the Common cause may be affected by the discouragement It may throw over the minds of many. Nor am I insensible of the contrary Effects if a brilliant stroke could be made with any probability of Success, especially after our Loss upon Long Island—But when the Fate of America may be at Stake on the Issue, when the wisdom of Cooler moments & experienced men have decided that we should protract the War, if possible, I cannot think it safe or wise to adopt a different System when the Season for Action draws so near a Close —That the Enemy mean to winter in New York there can be no doubt—that with such an Armament they can drive us out is equally clear. The Congress having resolved that It should not be destroyed nothing seems to remain but to determine the time of their taking possession—It is our Interest & wish to prolong It as much as possible provided the delay does not affect our future measures.

The Militia of Connecticut is reduced from 8000 to less than 2,000 and in a few days will be merely nominal—The arrival of some Maryland troops &c. from the flying Camp has in a great degree supplied the loss of men, but the Ammunition they have carried away will be a loss sensibly felt—the impulse for

going Home was so irresistable it answered no purpose to oppose It—tho I would not discharge, I have been obliged to
acquiesce & It affords one more melancholy proof how delu-
sive such dependencies are.

Inclosed I have the honor to transmit a Genl Return, the
first I have been able to procure for some time—Also a report
of Captn Newell from Our Works at Horn's Hook or Hell
Gate—their situation is extremely low and the Sound so very
narrow that the Enemy have 'em much within their Command.
I have the Honor to be with great respect Sir Yr Most Obed.
Servt

P.S. The Inclosed Informatn this minute came to Hand, I am
in hopes we shall henceforth get regular Intelligence of the
Enemies Movements.

"THIS IS A MOST UNFORTUNATE AFFAIR"

To John Augustine Washington

Dear Brother,   White plains Novr 6th 1776.
I have had the pleasure to receive your Letter of the 6th Ulto.
We have, I think, by one Manouvre and another, and with a
parcel of—but it is best to say nothing more about them—
Mixed, & ungovernable Troops, spun the Campaign out to
this time without coming to any decisive Action, or without
letting Genl How obtain any advantage which, in my opinion,
can contribute much to the completion of the business he is
come upon, or to the Honour and glory of the British Arms,
and those of their Auxilaries—Our numbers from the Beginning have been disjointed and confused, and much less than
were apprehended. had we ever hazarded a general Action with
them therefore, unless it had been in our Works at New York,
or Harlem heights, we undoubtedly should have risked a good
cause upon a very unfavourable Issue.

Whilst we lay at the upper end of York Island (or the heights
of Harlem) How suddenly Landed from the best Accts we cd
get, about 16,000 Men above us, on a place called Frogs point

on the East River, or Sound, this obliged Us, as his design was evidently to surround us, & cut of our Communication with the Country, thereby stopping all Supplies of Provisions (of which we were very scant) to remove our Camp and out Flank him, which we have done, & by degrees got Strongly posted on advantageous Grounds at this place.

It is not in my power to furnish you with so extensive a Draft as you require, as I have none but printed Maps of the Country you want to see deleniated, & have no person about me that has time enough to Copy one, but a rough sketch of the Country in wch we have been Manouvreing, & which I had taken off to carry in my pocket, I enclose you, as it will afford some Idea of the parts adjacent to New York.

Novr 19th at Hackensac: I began this Letter at the White plains as you will see by the first part of it; but by the time I had got thus far the Enemy advanced a Second time (for they had done it once before, & after engaging some Troops which I had posted on a Hill, & driving them from it with the loss of abt 300 killed & wounded to them, & little more than half the number to us) as if they meant a genel Attack but finding us ready to receive them, & upon such ground as they could not approach without loss, they filed of & retreated towards New York.

As it was conceived that this Manouvre was done with a design to attack Fort Washington (near Harlem heights) or to throw a body of Troops into the Jerseys, or what might be still worse, aim a stroke at Philadelphia, I hastend over on this side with abt 5000 Men by a round about March (wch we were obliged to take on Acct of the shipping opposing the passage at all the lower Ferries) of near 65 Miles, but did not get hear time enough to take Measures to save Fort Washington tho I got here myself a day or two before it surrendered, which happened on the 16th Instt after making a defence of about 4 or 5 hours only.

We have no particular Acct of the loss on either side, or of the Circumstances attending this matter, the whole Garrison after being drove from the out lines & retiring within the Fort surrendered themselves Prisoners of War, and giving me no Acct of the terms. By a Letter wch I have just receivd from Genl Greene at Fort Lee (wch is opposite to Fort Washington) I am informd that "one of the Train of Artillery came across the River last Night on a Raft—by his Acct the Enemy have suffered greatly on the North side of Fort Washington—Colo. Rawlings's Regiment (late Hugh Stephenson's) was posted there, and behaved with great Spirit—Colo. Magaw could not get the Men to Man the Lines, otherwise he would not have given up the Fort."

This is a most unfortunate affair and has given me great Mortification as we have lost not only two thousand Men that were there, but a good deal of Artillery, & some of the best Arms we had. And what adds to my Mortification is, that this Post after the last Ships went by it, was held contrary to my Wishes & opinion; as I conceived it to be a dangerous one: but being determind on by a full Council of General Officers, & receiving a resolution of Congress strongly expressive of their desires, that the Channel of the River (which we had been labouring to stop a long while at this place) might be obstructed, if possible; & knowing that this could not be done unless there were Batteries to protect the Obstruction I did not care to give an absolute Order for withdrawing the Garrison till I could get round & see the Situation of things & then it became too late as the Fort was Invested. I had given it, upon the passing of the last Ships, as my opinion to Genl Greene under whose care it was, that it would be best to evacuate the place—but—as the order was discretionary, & his opinion differed from mine, it unhappyly was delayd too long, to my great grief, as I think Genl Howe considering his Army & ours, would have had but a poor tale to have told without it & would have found it difficult, unless some Southern Expedition may prove successful, to have reconciled the People of England to the Conquest of a few pitiful Islands, none of wch were defensable considering the great number of their ships & the power they have by Sea to Surround & render them unapproachable.

Your Letter of the 30th of Octr was delivered to me a few days ago by Colo. Woodford—It is a matter of great grief and surprize to me, to find the different States so slow, and inattentive to that essential business of levying their quota's of Men— In ten days from this date, there will not be above 2000 Men, if that, on this Side Hudson's River (of the fixed & establish'd Regiments) to oppose Howes whole Army, and very little more on the other to secure the Eastern Colonies and the Important Passes leading through the Highlands to Albany & the Country about the Lakes. In short it is impossible for me in the compass of a Letter to give you any Idea of our Situation —of my difficulties—& the constant perplexities & mortifications I constantly meet with, derived from the unhappy policy of short enlistments, & delaying them too long. Last fall or Winter; before the Army which was then to be raised, was set about, I represented in clear & explicit terms the evils wch would arise from short Inlistments—the expence that must attend the raising of an Army every year—the futility of such an Army when raised; and, in a word, if I had spoke with a prophetick spirit, could not have foretold the evils with more accuracy than I did—all the year since I have been pressing them to delay no time in engaging Men upon such terms as would Insure success, telling them that the longer it was delayed the more difficult it would grow; but the measure was not set about till it was too late to be effected, & then in such a manner as to bid adieu to every hope of getting an Army from which any Services are to be expected. the different States without regard to the merits or qualifications of an Officer, quarrelling about the appointments; & nominating such as are not fit to be Shoe Blacks from the local attachments of this or that Member of Assembly.

I am wearied almost to death with the retrograde Motions of things, and Solemnly protest that a pecuniary rewd of 20,000 £s a year would not induce me to undergo what I do; and after all perhaps, to loose my Character as it is impossible, under such a variety of distressing Circumstances to conduct Matters agreeable to public expectation or even of those who employ me—as they will not make proper allowances for the difficulties their own errors have occasioned.

I am glad to find by your last Letter that your family are tolerably well recoverd from the Indispositions they labourd under. God grant you all health & happiness—nothing in this world would contribute so much to mine as to be once more fixed among you in the peaceable enjoymt of my own vine, & fig Tree. Adieu my dear Sir—remember me Affectionately to my Sister & the Family, & give my Compliments to those who enquire after Yr Sincerely Affectionate Brother

"A DESTRUCTIVE, EXPENSIVE, DISORDERLY MOB"

To John Hancock

Sir   Trenton Decr 5th 1776

As nothing but necessity obliged me to retire before the
Enemy, & leave so much of the Jerseys unprotected, I conceive
it my duty, and it corresponds with my Inclination to make
head against them so soon as there shall be the least probability
of doing it with propriety. That the Country might in some
measure be covered, I left two Brigades consisting of the Five
Virginia Regiments and that of Delaware, containing in the
whole about 1200 Men fit for duty, under the command of
Lord Stirling & Genl Stephen at Princeton, till the Baggage &
Stores could cross the Delaware, or the Troops under their
respective commands should be forced from thence. I shall now,
having removed the greatest part of the above Articles, face
about with such Troops as are here fit for service, and march
back to Princeton and there govern myself by circumstances
and the movements of Genl Lee. At any event the Enemy's
progress may be retarded by this means, if they intend to come
on, & the Peoples fears in some measure quieted, if they do
not. Sorry I am to observe however, that the frequent calls
upon the Militia of this State—the want of exertion in the
Principal Gentlemen of the Country—or a fatal supineness and
insensibility of danger, till it is too late to prevent an evil, that
was not only foreseen, but foretold, have been the causes of
our late disgraces. If the Militia of this State had stepped forth
in Season, and timely notice they had, we might have prevented
the Enemy's crossing the Heckenseck, although without some
previous notice of the time & place it was impossible to have
done this at the North River. We might with equal probability
of success, have made a stand at Brunswic on the Rariton; but
as both these Rivers were fordable in a variety of Places, (knee
deep only) it required many men to defend the passes & these
we had not. At Heckenseck our force was insufficient, because
a part was at Elizabeth Town, Amboy & Brunswick, guarding a
Coast which I thought most exposed to danger—and at Brunswic, because I was disappointed in my expectation of Militia,

and because on the day of the Enemy's approach, and probably the occasion of it, the term of the Jersey & Maryland Brigades service expired, neither of which would consent to stay an hour longer.

These among Ten thousand other Instances might be adduced to shew the disadvantages of Short inlistments & the little dependance upon Militia in times of real danger; But as yesterday cannot be recalled, I will not dwell upon a Subject which no doubt has given much uneasiness to Congress, as well as extreme pain and anxiety to myself. My first wish is, That Congress may be convinced of the impropriety of relying upon the Militia, and of the necessity of raising a larger standing Army than what they have voted. The saving in the article of Stores, Provisions and in a thousand other things, by having nothing to do with Militia unless in cases of extraordinary exigency, & such as could not be expected in the common course of events, would amply support a large Army, which well officered would be daily improving, instead of continuing a destructive, expensive, disorderly Mob.

I am clear in Opinion, that if 40,000 Men had been kept in constant pay since the first commencement of Hostilities, and the Militia had been excused doing duty during that period, the Continent would have saved Money. When I reflect on the losses we have sustained for want of good Troops, the certainty of this is placed beyond a doubt in my mind. In such case the Militia, who have been harrassed & tired by repeated calls upon them, and farming & manufactures in a manner suspended, would upon any pressing emergency have run with alacrity to Arms, Whereas the cry now is, they may be as well ruined in one way as another, & with difficulty are obtained. I mention these things to shew, that in my Opinion, if any dependance is placed in the Militia another year, Congress will be deceived. When danger is a little removed from them, they will not turn out at all—When it comes Home to 'em, the well affected instead of flying to Arms to defend themselves, are busily employed in removing their Families & Effects, whilst the disaffected are concerting measures to make their submission & spread terror & dismay all around to induce others to follow the example. daily experience & abundant proofs warrant this information.

I shall this day reinforce Lord Stirling with about 1200 Men which will make his Numbers about 2400—to morrow I mean to repair to Princeton myself & shall order the Pensylvania Troops (who are not yet arrived, except part of the German Batallion & a Company of Light Infantry), to the same place.

By my last advices the Enemy are still at Brunswic, and the Account adds that Genl Howe was expected at Elizabeth Town with a reinforcement to erect the King's Standard and demand a submission of this State. I can only give this as a report brought from the Enemys Camp by some of the Country people. I have the Honor to be with great respect Sir Yr Most Obedt Servt

"THE SUCCESS OF AN ENTERPRIZE"

To John Hancock

Sir   Head Quarters Newtown 27th Decemr 1776.

I have the pleasure of congratulating you upon the Success of an Enterprize, which I had formed against a Detachment of the Enemy lying in Trenton, and which was executed yesterday Morning.

The Evening of the 25th I ordered the Troops intended for this Service to parade back of McKonkey's Ferry, that they might begin to pass as soon as it grew dark, imagining we should be able to throw them all over, with the necessary Artillery, by 12 OClock, and that we might easily arrive at Trenton by five in the Morning, the distance being about nine Miles. But the quantity of Ice, made that Night, impeded the passage of Boats so much, that it was three OClock before the Artillery could all be got over, and near four, before the Troops took up their line of march.

This made me despair of surprizing the Town, as I well knew we could not reach it before the day was fairly broke, but as I was certain there was no making a Retreat without being discovered, and harassed on repassing the River, I determined to push on at all Events. I formed my Detatchment into two divisions one to march by the lower or River road, the other, by the upper or Pennington Road. As the Divisions had nearly the same distance to march, I ordered each of them, immediately upon forcing the out Guards, to push directly into the Town, that they might charge the Enemy before they had time to form. The upper division arrived at the Enemys advanced post, exactly at eight OClock, and in three Minutes after, I found from the fire on the lower Road that, that Division had also got up. The Out Guards made but small Opposition, tho', for their Numbers, they behaved very well, keeping up a constant retreating fire from behind Houses.

We presently saw their main Body formed, but from their Motions, they seem'd undetermined how to act.

Being hard pressed by our Troops, who had already got possession of part of their Artillery, they attempted to file off by a road on their right leading to Princetown, but perceiving their Intention, I threw a Body of Troops in their Way which immediately checked them. Finding from our disposition, that they were surrounded, and that they must inevitably be cut to peices if they made any further Resistance, they agreed to lay down their Arms. The Number, that submitted in this manner, was 23 Officers and 886 Men. Colo. Rall the commanding Officer and seven others were found wounded in the Town. I dont exactly know how many they had killed, but I fancy not above twenty or thirty, as they never made any regular Stand. Our Loss is very trifling indeed, only two Officers and one or two privates wounded.

I find, that the Detatchment of the Enemy consisted of the three Hessian Regiments of Lanspatch, Kniphausen and Rohl amounting to about 1500 Men, and a Troop of British Light Horse; but immediately, upon the beginning of the Attack, all those, who were not killed or taken, pushed directly down the Road towards Bordentown. These would likewise have fallen into our hands, could my plan have been compleatly carried into Execution. Genl Ewing was to have crossed before day at Trenton Ferry, and taken possession of the Bridge leading out of Town, but the Quantity of Ice was so great, that tho' he did every thing in his power to effect it, he could not get over. This difficulty also hindered Genl Cadwallader from crossing, with the Pennsylvania Militia, from Bristol, he got part of his Foot over, but finding it impossible to embark his Artillery, he was obliged to desist. I am fully confident, that could the Troops, under Generals Ewing and Cadwallader, have passed the River, I should have been able, with their Assistance, to have driven the Enemy from all their posts below Trenton. But the Numbers I had with me, being inferior to theirs below me, and a strong Battalion of Light Infantry being at Princetown above me, I thought it most prudent to return the same Evening, with the prisoners and the Artillery we had taken. We found no Stores of any Consequence in the Town.

In justice to the Officers and Men, I must add, that their Behaviour upon this Occasion, reflects the highest honor upon them. The difficulty of passing the River in a very severe Night, and their March thro' a violent Storm of Snow and Hail, did not in the least abate their Ardour. But when they came to the Charge, each seemed to vie with the other in pressing forward, and were I to give a preferance to any particular Corps, I should do great injustice to the others.

Colo. Baylor, my first Aid de Camp, will have the honor of delivering this to you, and from him you may be made acquainted with many other particulars; his spirited Behaviour upon every Occasion, requires me to recommend him to your particular Notice. I have the Honor to be with great Respect Sir Your most obt Servt

Inclosed you have a particular List of the Prisoners, Artillery and other Stores.

SUBORDINATING MILITARY
TO CIVILIAN AUTHORITY

To the Executive Committee of the Continental Congress

Gentlemen   Head Quarters Trenton 1st Jany 1777.
I have the honor and pleasure of acknowledging your favors of the 28th and 31st Decr and Mr Morris's of the 30th and 31st. The Messenger delivered me the two parcels of hard Money,

which I suppose will turn out right, not having had time to count it. The Sum that is lodged at Ticonderoga shall be ordered down, provided the Commander in the Northern Department, finds no better use for it there, than I can make of it here.

The Accounts you give me, in yours of the 28th Ulto of the good Effects that are likely to flow from our Success at Trenton, add not a little to the Satisfaction I have felt on that occasion. You are pleased to pay me many personal compliments, as if the merit of that Affair was due solely to me; but I assure you, the other General Officers, who assisted me in the plan and execution, have full as good right to your Encomiums as myself.

We are devising such Measures, as I hope, if they succeed, will add as much or more to the distress of the Enemy, than their defeat at Trenton, and I promise myself the greatest Advantages, from having engaged, a number of the Eastern Troops, to stay six Weeks beyond their Term of Inlistment, upon giving a Bounty of Ten Dollars. This I know is a most extravagant price, when compared to the time of Service, but the Example was set by the State of pennsylvania with respect to their Militia, and I thought it no time to stand upon Trifles when a Body of firm Troops, inured to danger, were absolutely necessary to lead on the more raw and undisciplined.

I shall know this day, how many of Colonel Glovers Regiment are willing to continue in the land Service, I dont expect many will be prevailed upon to stay, and I will endeavour to procure the rest for the purpose of fitting out the Frigates, upon the best terms I can.

The future and proper disposition of the Hessian Prisoners, struck me in the same light, in which you view it, for which Reason, I advised the Council of Safety to separate them from their Officers, and canton them in the German Counties. If proper pains are taken to convince them, how preferable the Situation of their Countrymen, the Inhabitants of those Counties, is to theirs, I think they may be sent back in the Spring, so fraught with a love of Liberty, and property too, that they may create a disgust to the Service among the remainder of the foreign Troops and widen that Breach which is already opened between them and the British.

Yours of the 31st last Month, incloses me sundry Resolves of Congress, by which I find, they have done me the honor to intrust me with powers, in my military Capacity, of the highest Nature and almost unlimited in extent. Instead of thinking myself free'd from all civil Obligations, by this mark of their Confidence, I shall constantly bear in Mind, that as the Sword was the last Resort for the preservation of our Liberties, so it ought to be the first thing laid aside, when those Liberties are firmly established.

I shall instantly set about making the most necessary Reforms in the Army, but it will not be in my power to make so great a progress, as if I had a little leisure time upon my Hands.

Mr Morris has my sincere thanks for the Advice and Assistance he promises to give Mr Commissary Wharton, and I beg he would remind him that all his Exertions will be necessary to support an Army in this exhausted Country. I am Gentlemen with the most perfect Respect and Esteem Yr most obt Servt

P.S. My best thanks to Mr Morris for procuring the Qr Cask Wine, which is not yet got to hand.

VICTORY AT PRINCETON

To John Hancock

Sir   Pluckamin January 5th 1777

I have the honor to inform you, that since the date of my last from Trenton, I have removed with the Army under my command to this place. The difficulty of crossing the Delaware on account of the ice made our passage over it tedious, and gave the Enemy an opportunity of drawing in their several cantonments and assembling their whole Force at Princeton. Their large Picquets advanced towards Trenton, their great preparations & some intelligence I had received, added to their knowledge, that the first of January brought on a dissolution of the best part of our Army, gave me the strongest reasons to conclude, that an attack upon us was meditating.

Our situation was most critical and our force small. to remove immediately was again destroying every dawn of hope which had begun to revive in the breasts of the Jersey Militia, and to bring those Troops which had first crossed the Delaware, and were laying at Croswix's under Genl Cadwalader & those under Genl Mifflin at Bordenton (amounting in the whole to about 3600) to Trenton, was to bring them to an exposed place; One or the other however was unavoidable, the latter was preferred & they were ordered to join us at Trenton, which they did by a Night march on the 1st Instt.

On the 2d according to my expectation the Enemy began to advance upon us, and after some skirmishing the Head of their Column reached Trenton about 4 OClock, whilst their rear was as far back as Maidenhead. They attempted to pass Sanpink Creek, which runs through Trenton at different places, but finding the Fords guarded, halted & kindled their Fires—We were drawn up on the other side of the Creek. In this situation we remained till dark, cannonading the Enemy & receiving the fire of their Field peices which did us but little damage.

Having by this time discovered that the Enemy were greatly superior in number and that their design was to surround us, I ordered all our Baggage to be removed silently to Burlington soon after dark, and at twelve OClock after renewing our fires & leaving Guards at the Bridge in Trenton and other passes on the same stream above, marched by a roundabout Road to Princeton, where I knew they could not have much force left and might have Stores. One thing I was certain of, that it would avoid the appearance of a retreat, (which was of course or to run the hazard of the whole Army being cut off) whilst we might by a fortunate stroke withdraw Genl Howe from Trenton and give some reputation to our Arms. happily we succeeded. We found Princeton about Sunrise with only three Regiments and three Troops of light Horse in it, two of which were on their march to Trenton—These three Regiments, especially the Two first, made a gallant resistance and in killed wounded and Prisoners must have lost 500 Men, upwards of One hundred of them were left dead in the Feild, and with what I have with me & what were taken in the pursuit & carried across the Delaware, there are near 300 prisoners 14 of which are Officers—all British.

This peice of good fortune is counterballanced by the loss of the brave and worthy Genl Mercer, Cols. Hazlet and Potter, Captn Neal of the Artillery, Captn Fleming who commanded the first Virginia Regiment and four or five other valuable Officers who with about twenty five or thirty privates were slain in the feild—Our whole loss cannot be ascertained, as many who were in pursuit of the Enemy, who were chaced three or four Miles, are not yet come in.

The rear of the Enemy's Army laying at Maidenhead (not more than five or Six miles from Princeton) was up with us before our pursuit was over, but as I had the precaution to destroy the Bridge over Stoney Brooke (about half a mile from the Feild of action) they were so long retarded there as to give us time to move off in good order for this place. We took Two Brass Feild peices but for want of Horses could not bring them away. We also took some Blankets—Shoes—and a few other trifling Articles—burnt the Hay & destroyed such other things as the shortness of the time would admit of.

My Original plan when I set out from Trenton was to have pushed on to Brunswic, but the harrassed State of our own Troops (many of them having had no rest for two nights & a day) and the danger of loosing the advantage we had gained by aiming at too much induced me by the advice of my Officers to relinquish the attempt, but in my Judgement Six or Eight hundred fresh Troops upon a forced march would have destroyed all their Stores and Magazines—taken as we have since learnt their Military Chest containing 70,000£ and put an end to the War. The Enemy from the best intelligence I have been able to get were so much alarmed at the apprehension of this, that they marched immediately to Brunswick without halting except at the Bridges, (for I also took up those on Millstone on the different routs to Brunswick) and got there before day.

From the best information I have received, Genl Howe has left no men either at Trenton or Princeton. The truth of this I am endeavouring to ascertain that I may regulate my movements accordingly—The Militia are taking spirit and I am told, are coming in fast from this State, but I fear those from Philadelphia will scarcely submit to the hardships of a winter Campaign much longer, especially as they very unluckily sent their Blankets with their Baggage to Burlington—I must do them justice however to add, that they have undergone more fatigue and hardship than I expected Militia (especially Citizens) would have done at this inclement Season. I am just moving to Morris town where I shall endeavour to put them under the best cover I can. hitherto we have been without any and many of our poor Soldiers quite bear foot & ill clad in other respects. I have the Honor to be with great respect Sir Yr Most Obedt

"FORTHWITH TO WITHDRAW
THEMSELVES AND FAMILIES"

Proclamation Concerning Loyalists

WHEREAS several persons, inhabitants of the United States of America, influenced by inimical motives, intimidated by the threats of the enemy, or deluded by a Proclamation issued the 30th of November last, by Lord and General Howe, stiled the King's Commissioners for granting pardons, &c. (now at open war and invading these states) have been so lost to the interest and welfare of their country, as to repair to the enemy, sign a declaration of fidelity, and, in some instances, have been compelled to take oaths of allegiance, and to engage not to take up arms, or encourage others so to do, against the King of Great-Britain. And whereas it has become necessary to distinguish between the friends of America and those of Great-Britain, inhabitants of these States, and that every man who receives a protection from and is a subject of any State (not being conscientiously scrupulous against bearing arms) should stand ready to defend the same against every hostile invasion, I do therefore, in behalf of the United States, by virtue of the powers committed to me by Congress, hereby strictly command and require every person, having subscribed such declaration, taken such oaths, and accepted protection and certificates from Lord or General Howe, or any person acting under their authority, forthwith to repair to Head-Quarters, or to the quarters of the nearest general officer of the Continental Army or Militia (until farther provision can be made by the civil authority) and there deliver up such protections, certificates, and passports, and take the oath of allegiance to the United States of America. Nevertheless, hereby granting full liberty to all such as prefer the interest and protection of Great-Britain to the freedom and happiness of their country, forthwith to withdraw themselves and families within the enemy's lines. And I do hereby declare that all and every person, who may neglect or refuse to comply with this order, within thirty days from the date hereof, will be deemed adherents to the King of Great-Britain, and treated as common enemies of the American States.

Given at Head-Quarters, Morris-Town, January 25, 1777.

"YOUR OWN FEELINGS MUST BE YOUR GUIDE"

To Benedict Arnold

Dear Sir   Head Quarters Morris Town 2d Apl 1777
I was this day favd with yours of the 26th last Month and a few days ago with that of the 11th.

It is needless for me to say much upon a subject, which must undoubtedly give you a good deal of uneasiness. I confess I was surprized when I did not see your Name in the list of Major Generals, and was so fully of opinion that there was some mistake in the matter, that I (as you may recollect) desired you not to take any hasty Step, before the intention of Congress was fully known. The point does not now admit of a doubt, and is of so delicate a nature, that I will not even undertake to advise, your own feelings must be your Guide—As no particular Charge is alledged agt you, I do not see upon what Ground you can demand a Court of Enquiry. Besides, Public Bodies are not amenable for their Actions. They place and displace at pleasure, and all the satisfaction that an individual can obtain when he is overlooked is, if innocent, a consciousness that he has not deserved such treatment for his honest exertions. Your determination, not to quit your present command, while any danger to the public might ensue from your leaving it, deserves my thanks, and justly entitles you to the thanks of your Country.

Genl Green who has lately been at Philada took occasion to

inquire upon what principle the Congress proceeded in their late promotion of General Officers—He was informed that the Members from each State seemed to insist upon having a proportion of General Officers adequate to the number of Men which they furnish, and that as Connecticut had already two Majors General it was their full share. I confess this is a strange mode of reasoning, but it may serve to shew you, that the promotion which was due to your seniority was not overlooked for want of Merit in you. I am Dear Sir Yr most obt Servt.

THE BATTLE OF BRANDYWINE CREEK

To John Hancock

Sir,   Chester Septr 11. 1777. 12 o'Clock at Night.
    I am sorry to inform you that in this days engagement we have been obliged to leave the enemy masters of the field. Unfortunately the intelligence received of the enemy's advancing up the Brandywine, & crossing at a ford about six miles above us, was uncertain & contradictory, notwithstanding all my pains to get the best. This prevented my making a disposition adequate to the force with which the enemy attacked us on our right; in consequence of which the troops first engaged were obliged to retire before they could be reinforced. In the midst of the attack on the right, that body of the enemy which remained on the other side of Chad's ford, crossed it, & attacked the division there under the command of General Wayne & the light troops under General Maxwell; who after a severe conflict also retired. The militia under the command of General Armstrong, being posted at a ford about two miles below Chad's, had no opportunity of engaging. But though we fought under many disadvantages, and were from the causes above mentioned, obliged to retire; yet our loss of men is not, I am persuaded, very considerable; I believe much less than the enemys. We have also lost seven or eight pieces of cannon, according to the best information I can at present obtain. The baggage having been previously moved off is all secure; saving

the mens' blankets, which being at their backs, many of them doubtless are lost.

I have directed all the troops to assemble behind Chester, where they are now arranging for this night. Notwithstanding the misfortune of the day, I am happy to find the troops in good spirits; and I hope another time we shall compensate for the losses now sustained.

The Marquis La Fayette was wounded in the leg, & General Woodford in the hand. Divers other officers were wounded, & some slain; but the numbers of either cannot now be ascertained. I have the honor to be, Sir, your obedient h'ble servant

P.S. It has not been in my power to send you earlier intelligence; the present being the first leisure moment I have had since the action.

"AS UNFORTUNATE A MEASURE, AS EVER WAS ADOPTED"

To Richard Henry Lee

Dear Sir   Matuchen Hills Phila. County 16th October 1777
Your favour of the 5th Inst. as also that of the 11th by Baron Kalb, are both to hand—It is not in my power at present to answer your quere respecting the appointment of this Gentleman; but Sir, if there is any truth in the report which has been handed to me, viz.—that congress has appointed Brigadier conway to be Major General in this Army, it will be as unfortunate a measure, as ever was adopted—I may add (& I think with truth) that it will give a fatal blow to the existance of this army—upon so interesting a subject I must speak plain—the duty I owe my country—the ardent desire I have to promote its true interests—and justice to Individuals require this of me.

General Conways' merit then, as an officer, and his importance in this Army, exists more in his own imagination than in reallity; for it is a maxim with him to leave no service of his own untold nor to want any thing which is to be obtained by importunity; but, as I do not want to detract from any merit he possesses, and only wish to have the matter taken up, on its true ground (after allowing him every thing that his warmest friends can contend for) I would only ask why the youngest Brigadier in the service (for I believe he is so) should be put over the heads of the oldest, & thereby take Rank, and command Gentlemen who yesterday only, were his Seniors—Gentn who I will be bold to say (in behalf of some of them at least) of sound judgment & unquestionable Bravery. If there was a degree of conspicuous merit in Genl Conway unpossessed by any of his Seniors the confusion which might be occasioned by it would stand Warranted upon the principles of Sound policy, for I do readily agree that this is no time for trifling; but at the same time, that I cannot Subscribe to the fact, this truth, I am very well assured of (tho I have not directly nor indirectly exchanged a word with any one of the Brigrs on the subject nor am I certain that any one of them have heard of the appointment) that they will not Serve under him; I leave you to guess therefore, at the situation this Army would be in at So important a crisis, if such an event should take place.

These Gentn have feelings as officers; & tho they do not dispute the authority of Congress to make appointments, they will judge of the propriety of acting under them—In a word the service is so dificult, & every necessary so expensive, that almost all your officers are tired out; do not therefor afford them good pretexts for retiring—no day passes over my head without applications for leave to resign—Within the last Six days, I am certain twenty commissions have been tendered to me. I must therefore conjure you to conjure Congress to consider this matter well, & not by a real act of injustice, compel some good officers to leave your service, & thereby incur a train of evels unforeseen and irremidiable.

To sum up the whole, I have been a Slave to the service: I have undergone more than most men are aware of, to harmonize so many discordant parts but it will be impossible for me to be of any further survice if such insuperable difficulties are thrown in my way—You may believe me my dear Sir, that I have no earthly view, but the public good in what I have said— I have no prejudice against Genl Conway, nor desire to serve any other Brigadier, further than I think the cause will be benefitted by it—to bring which to a speedy & happy isue is the most fervent wish of my Soul.

With respect to the wants of the Militia (as mentd in your favor of the 5th) in the articles of cloathing, you must be well convinced that it is not in my power to supply them in the smallest degree, when near one half of our Men are rendered unfit for service for want of these things—I can add no more at present than that I am Dear Sir Your Most Obed. Hbe Servt

THE BATTLE OF GERMANTOWN

To John Augustine Washington

Dear Brother   Phila. County Octr 18th 1777.

Your kind and Affectionate Letters of the 21st of Septr & 2d Instt came Safe to hand. when my last to you was dated I know not, for truely I can say, that my whole time is so much engross'd that I have scarce a moment (but sleeping ones) for relaxation, or to endulge myself in writing to a friend.

The anxiety you have been under, on Acct of this Army, I can easily conceive; would to God there had been less Cause for it. or, that our Situation at present, was such, as to promise much from it. The Enemy crossed the Schuylkill—which, by the by, above the Falls (& the Falls you know is only five Miles from the City) is as easily crossed in any place as Potomack Run, Aquia, or any other broad & shallow Water—rather by stratagem; tho I do not know that it was in our power to prevent it, as their Manœuvres made it necessary for us to attend to our Stores which lay at Reading, towards which they seemd bending their course, & the loss of which must have proved our Ruin—After they had crossed, we took the first favourable oppertunity of attacking them—this was attempted by a Nights March of fourteen Miles to surprize them (which we effectually did) so far as reaching their Guards before they had notice of our coming, and but for a thick Fog rendered so infinitely dark at times, as not to distinguish friend from Foe at the distance of 30 Yards, we should, I believe, have made a decisive & glorious day of it. But Providence—or some unaccountable something, designd it otherwise; for after we had driven the Enemy a Mile or two, after they were in the utmost confusion, and flying before us in most places, after we were upon the point (as it appeard to every body) of grasping a compleat Victory, our own Troops took fright & fled with precipitation and disorder. how to acct for this I know not, unless, as I before observd, the Fog represented their own Friends to them for a Reinforcement of the Enemy as we attacked in different Quarters at the sametime, & were about closing the Wings of our Army when this happened. one thing indeed contributed not a little to our Misfortune, and that was want of Ammunition on the right wing, which began the Ingagement, and in the course of two hours and 40 Minutes which it lasted, had (many of them) expended the 40 Rounds which they took into the Field.

After the Ingagement we removd to a place about 20 Miles from the Enemy, to collect our Force together—to take care of our Wounded—get furnished with necessaries again—& be in a better posture, either for Offensive, or defensive operations. we are now advancing towards the Enemy again, being at this time within 12 Miles.

Our loss in the late Action was, in killed, wounded, and Missing, about 1000, but of the missing, many, I dare say took advantage of the times, and deserted. Genl Nash of No. Carolina was Wounded and died two or three days after. many valuable Officers of ours was also wounded and some killed. The Enemys loss is variously reported. none make it less than 1500 (killed & Wounded) & many estimate it much larger—Genl Agnew of theirs was certainly killed & many Officers wounded among whom some of distinction—this we certainly know that the Hospital at Philadelphia & several large Meeting Houses are filled with their wounded besides private Houses with the Horses. In a word it was a bloody day—would to Heaven I could add, that it had been a more fortunate one for us.

Our distress on Acct of Cloathing is great, & in a little time must be very Sensibly felt, unless some expedient can be hit upon to obtain them. We have since the Battle got in abt 1200 Militia from Virginia—about the same number have gone off from this State and Jersey but others are promised in lieu of them—with truth however it may be said, that this State acts most infamously, the People of it I mean as we derive little or no assistance from them—In short they are, in a manner, totally, disaffected, or in a kind of Lethargy.

The Enemy are making vigorous efforts to remove the obstructions in the Delaware, & to possess themselves of the Works which have been constructed for the Defence of them—I am doing all I can in my present situation to save them: God only, knows which will succeed.

I very sincerely congratulate you on the change in your Family. tell the young couple, after wishing them joy of their union, that it is my sincere hope that it will be as happy, and lasting as their present joys are boundless. the Inclosed Letter of thanks to my Sister for her elegant present you will please to deliver and with sincere Affection for you all I am Dr Brother Yrs

P.S. I had scarce finish'd this Letter when by express from the State of New York, I received the Important and glorious News which follows. I most devoutly congratulate you, my Country, and every well wisher to the Cause on this Signal Stroke of Providence. Yrs as before.

SUFFERING AT VALLEY FORGE

To Henry Laurens

Sir   Valley Forge Decemb. 23d 1777.

Full as I was in my representation of matters in the Commissary's department yesterday, fresh and more powerful reasons oblige me to add, that I am now convinced beyond a doubt, that unless some great and capital change suddenly takes place in that line this Army must inevitably be reduced to one or other of these three things. Starve—dissolve—or disperse, in order to obtain subsistence in the best manner they can. rest assured, Sir, this is not an exaggerated picture, and that I have abundant reason to support what I say.

Yesterday afternoon receiving information that the Enemy, in force, had left the City, and were advancing towards Derby, with apparent design to forage and draw subsistence from that part of the Country, I ordered the Troops to be in readiness, that I might give every Opposition in my power; when behold! to my great mortification, I was not only informed, but convinced, that the Men were unable to stir on account of provision, and that a dangerous mutiny, begun the night before and which with difficulty was suppressed by the spirited exertions of some Officers, was still much to be apprehended for want of this Article.

This brought forth the only Commissary in the purchasing line in this Camp, and with him this melancholy and alarming truth, That he had not a single hoof of any kind to slaughter, and not more than 25 Barrells of Flour! From hence form an opinion of our situation, when I add, that he could not tell when to expect any.

All I could do under these circumstances was, to send out a few light parties to watch and harrass the Enemy, whilst other parties were instantly detached different ways to collect, if possible, as much provision as would satisfy the present pressing wants of the Soldiery—But will this answer? No Sir: three or four days bad weather would prove our destruction. What then is to become of the Army this Winter? and if we are as often without Provisions now, as with them, what is to become of us in the Spring, when our force will be collected, with the aid perhaps of Militia, to take advantage of an early campaign before the Enemy can be reinforced? These are considerations of great magnitude—meriting the closest attention, and will, when my own reputation is so intimately connected and to be affected by the event, justify my saying that the present Commissaries are by no means equal to the execution of the Office, or that the disaffection of the people is past beleif. The misfortune however does in my opinion proceed from both causes, and though I have been tender heretofore of giving any opinion or lodging complaints, as the change in that department took place contrary to my Judgement, and the consequences thereof were predicted; yet finding that the inactivity of the Army, whether for want of provisions, Cloaths, or other essentials is charged to my account, not only by the common vulgar, but those in power, it is time to speak plain in exculpation of myself. With truth then I can declare, that no Man in my opinion ever had his measures more impeded than I have, by every department. Since the month of July we have had no assistance from the Quarter Master General, and to want of assistance from this department, the Commissary General charges great part of his deficiency—to this I am to add, that notwithstanding it is a standing order and often repeated, that the Troops shall always have two days provisions by them, that they might be ready at any sudden call, yet no opportunity has scarcely ever offered of taking advantage of the Enemy, that has not been either totally obstructed, or greatly impeded on this account: and this the great & crying evil is not all. Soap—Vinegar and other articles allowed by Congress we see none of, nor have we seen them, I believe, since the battle of Brandywine. The first indeed we have now little occasion for, few men having more than one shirt—many only the moiety of one, and some none at all. In addition to which, as a proof of the little benefit received from a Cloathier General, and at the same time, as a farther proof of the inability of an Army under the circumstances of this, to perform the common duties of Soldiers, besides a number of Men confined to Hospitals for want of Shoes, & others in Farmers Houses on the same account, we have by a Field return this day made, no less than 2898 Men now in Camp unfit for duty, because they are barefoot and otherwise naked; and by the same return it appears, that our strength in continental Troops, including the Eastern Brigades which have joined since the surrender of Genl Burgoyne, exclusive of the Maryland Troops sent to Wilmington, amount to no more than 8200—in Camp fit for duty. Notwithstanding which, and that since the 4th Instant our numbers fit for duty from the hardships and exposures they have undergone, particularly on account of Blankets (numbers having been obliged and still are, to set up all night by fires, instead of taking comfortable rest in a natural and common way) have decreased near 2000 Men, we find Gentlemen without knowing whether the Army was really going into Winter Quarters or not (for I am sure no Resolution of mine would warrant the Remonstrance) reprobating the measure as much, as if they thought the Soldiery were made of Stocks or Stones, and equally insensible of Frost and Snow; and moreover, as if they conceived it easily practicable for an inferior Army, under the disadvantages I have described ours to be, which is by no means exaggerated, to confine a Superior one, in all respects well appointed and provided for a Winters Campaign, within the City of Philadelphia, and to cover from depredation and waste the States of pensylvania, Jersey, &ca. But what makes this matter still more extraordinary in my eye is, that these very Gentlemen, who were well apprized of the nakedness of the Troops from occular demonstration, who thought their own Soldiers worse clad than others and advised me near a month ago, to postpone the execution of a plan I was about to adopt in consequence of a Resolve of Congress for seizing Cloaths, under strong assurances, that an ample supply would be collected in ten days agreable to a decree of the State (not one article of which, by the bye, is yet come to hand) should think a Winters Campaign, and the covering these States from the invasion of an Enemy so easy and practicable a business. I can assure those Gentlemen, that it is a much easier and less distressing thing, to draw Remonstrances in a comfortable room by a good fire side, than to occupy a cold, bleak hill, and sleep under frost & snow without Cloaths or Blankets: However, although they seem to have little feeling for the naked and distressed Soldier, I feel superabundantly for them, and from my soul pity those miseries, which it is neither in my power to releive or prevent. It is for these reasons therefore, I have dwelt upon the subject, and it adds not a little to my other difficulties and distress, to find that much more is expected of me, than is possible to be performed; and, that upon the ground of safety and policy, I am obliged to conceal the true state of the Army from public view, and thereby expose myself to detraction & calumny.

The Honble Committee of Congress went from Camp fully possessed of my Sentiments respecting the Establishment of this Army—the necessity of Auditors of Accounts—Appointment of Officers—New Arrangements &c. I have no need therefore to be prolix on these Subjects, but shall refer to them, after adding a word or two to shew, First, the necessity of some better provision for binding the Officers by the tye of Interest to the service (as no day, nor scarcely an hour passes without an Offer of a resigned Commission) Otherwise, I much doubt the practicability of holding the Army together much longer. In this, I shall probably be thought more sincere, when I freely declare, that I do not myself expect to derive the smallest benefit from any establishment that Congress may adopt, Otherwise than as a Member of the Community at large in the good which I am persuaded will result from the measure, by making better Officers and better Troops; And Secondly, to point out the necessity of making the appointments, arrangements, &ca without loss of time. We have not more than three months to prepare a great deal of business in—if we let these slip or waste, we shall be labouring under the same difficulties all next Campaign, as we have done this, to rectify mistakes, and bring things to order for Military arrangements and movements, in consequence like the Mechanism of a Clock, will be imperfect, and disordered, by the want of a part. In a very sensible degree, have I experienced this in the course of the last Summer—Several Brigades having no Brigadiers appointed to them till late & some not at all. by which means it follows, that an additional weight is thrown upon the Shoulders of the Commander in Cheif to withdraw his attention from the great line of his duty. The Gentlemen of the Committee, when they were at Camp, talked of an expedient for adjusting these matters, which I highly approved and wish to see adopted; namely that two or three Members of the Board of War—or a Committee of Congress should repair immediately to Camp where the best aid can be had, and with the Commanding Officer, or a Committee of his appointment prepare and digest the most perfect plan, that can be divised for correcting all abuses—making New arrangements—considering what is to be done with the weak & debilitated Regiments (If the States to which they belong will not draft men to fill them, for as to enlisting Soldiers it seems to me to be totally out of the question) together with many other things that would occur in the course of such a conference: and after digesting matters in the best manner they can, to submit the whole to the ultimate determination of Congress. If this measure is approved of, I would earnestly advise the immediate execution of it. And that the Commissary General of purchases, whom I rarely see, may be directed to form Magazines without a moments delay in the Neighbourhood of this Camp in order to secure provision for us in case of bad weather. The Quarter Master General ought also to be busy in his department—In short, there is as much to be done in preparing for a Campaign, as in the active part of it. In fine every thing depends upon the preparation that is made in the Several departments in the course of this Winter and the success or misfortunes of next Campaign will more than probably originate with our activity or Supineness this Winter. I have the Honor to be Sir Your Most Obedt Servant

"THE MAN I DEEM MY ENEMY"

To Henry Laurens

Sir   Valley Forge January 2d 1778

I take the liberty of transmitting to you the Inclosed Copies of a Letter from me to Genl Conway since his return from York to Camp, and of Two Letters from him to me, which you will be pleased to lay before Congress. I shall not in this Letter animadvert upon them, but after making a single observation submit the whole to Congress.

If General Conway means by cool receptions mentioned in the last paragraph of his Letter of the 31st Ulto, that I did not receive him in the language of a warm and cordial Friend, I readily confess the charge. I did not, nor shall I ever, till I am capable of the arts of dissimulation. These I despise, and my feelings will not permit me to make professions of friendship to the man I deem my Enemy, and whose system of conduct forbids it. At the same time, Truth authorises me to say, that he was received & treated with proper respect to his Official character, and that he has had no cause to justifye the assertion, that he could not expect any support for fulfilling the duties of his Appointment. I have the Honor to be with great respect Sir Your Most Obedt Servt

P.S. The Inclosed Extract from the proceedings of a Council of Genl Officers will shew, the Office of Inspector Genl was a matter not of such modern date as Genl Conway mentions it to be, and that it was one of the Regulations in view for the reform of the Army. The Foreign Officers who had Commissions & no Commands and who were of ability, were intended to be recommended to execute it—particularly the Baron D'Arendt with whom the Idea originated, and whose capacity seemed to be well admitted.

EXPOSING "THE CONWAY CABAL"

To Horatio Gates

Sir,   Valley forge Jany 4th 1778

Your Letter of the 8th Ulto came to my hands a few days ago; and, to my great surprize informed me, that a copy of it had been sent to Congress—for what reason, I find myself unable to acct; but, as some end doubtless was intended to be answered by it, I am laid under the disagreeable necessity of returning my answer through the same channel, lest any member of that honble body, should harbour an unfavourable suspicion of my having practiced some indirect means, to come at the contents of the confidential Letters between you & General Conway.

I am to inform you then, that Colo. Wilkenson, in his way to Congress in the Month of October last, fell in with Lord Stirling at Reading; and, not in confidence that I ever understood, inform'd his Aid de Camp Majr McWilliams that Genl Conway had written thus to you "Heaven has been determined to save your Country; or a weak General and bad Counsellors would have ruined it"—Lord Stirling, from motives of friendship, transmitted the acct with this remark—"The inclosed was communicated by Colo. Wilkenson to Majr McWilliams, such wicked duplicity of conduct I shall always think it my duty to detect."

In consequence of this information, and without having any thing more in view than merely to shew that Gentn that I was not unapprized of his intrieguing disposition, I wrote him a Letter in these words. "Sir—A Letter which I received last night contained the following paragraph.

"In a Letter from Genl Conway to Genl Gates he says 'Heaven has been determined to save your Country; or a weak Genl and bad Counsellors would have ruined it—I am Sir & ca."

Neither this Letter, nor the information which occasioned it, was ever, directly, or indirectly, communicated by me to a single Officer in this army (out of my own family) excepting the Marquis de la Fayette, who having been spoken to on the subject by Genl Conway, applied for, and saw, under injunctions of secrecy, the Letter which contained Wilkensons information—so desirous was I, of concealing every matter that could, in its consequences, give the smallest Interruption to the tranquility of this army, or, afford a gleam of hope to the enemy by dissensions therein.

Thus Sir, with an openness and candour which I hope will ever characterize and mark my conduct, have I complied with your request. the only concern I feel upon the occasion (finding how matters stand) is, that in doing this, I have necessarily been obliged to name a Gentn whom I am perswaded (although I never exchanged a word with him upon the subject) thought he was rather doing an act of Justice, than committing an act of infidility; and sure I am, that, till Lord Stirlings Letter came to my hands, I never knew that Genl Conway (who I viewed in the light of a stranger to you) was a corrispondant of yours, much less did I suspect that I was the subject of your confidential Letters—pardon me then for adding, that so far from conceiving, that the safety of the States can be affected, or in the smallest degree injured, by a discovery of this kind; or, that I should be called upon in such solemn terms to point out the author, that I considered the information as coming from yourself; and given with a friendly view to forewarn, and consequently forearm me, against a secret enemy; or, in other words, a dangerous incendiary; in which character, sooner or later, this Country will know Genl Conway. But—in this, as in other matters of late, I have found myself mistaken. I am Sir yr Most Obedt Servt

"I MEAN NOT TO SHRINK IN THE CAUSE"

To William Gordon

Dear Sir, Valley-forge Feby 15th 1778.
Since my last to you abt the end of Jany I have been favour'd
with your Letter of the 12th of that Month, which did not
reach my hands till within these few days. The question there
put, was, in some degree, solved in my last—But to be more
explicit, I can assure you that no person ever heard me drop an
expression that had a tendency to resignation. the same principles that led me to embark in the opposition to the arbitrary
claims of Great Britn operate with additional force at this day;
nor is it my desire to withdraw my Services while they are
considered of importance in the present contest—but to report
a design of this kind is among the Arts wch those who are endeavouring to effect a change, are practicing, to bring it to
pass. I have said, & I still do say, that there is not an Officer in
the Service of the United States that would return to the
sweets of domestic life with more heart-felt joy than I should;
but I would have this declaration, accompanied by these Sentiments, that while the public are satisfied with my endeavours I
mean not to shrink in the cause—but, the moment her voice,
not that of faction, calls upon me to resign, I shall do it with as
much pleasure as ever the weary traveller retired to rest. This
my dear Doctor you are at liberty to assert, but in doing it, I
would have nothing formal—all things will come right again
& soon recover their proper tone as the design is not only seen
thro but reprobated. With sincere esteem and regard I am Dr
Sir Yr Most Obedt & Affecte Servt

P.S. Mrs Washington who is now with me joins in best respects
to Mrs Gordon with Yrs.

"SUCH LOW, & DIRTY TRICKS"

To Bryan Fairfax

Dear Sir,   Head Qrs Valley-forge Mar. 1st 1778.
  Your favor of the 8th of Decr came safe to my hands—after considerable delay in its passage.
  The Sentiments you have expressed of me in this Letter are highly flattering—meriting my warmest acknowledgements, as I have too good an opinion of your sincerity and candour, to believe that you are capable of unmeaning professions—& speaking a language foreign from your heart—The friendship I ever professed, & felt for you, met with no diminution from the difference in our political sentiments—I knew the rectitude of my own intentions & believing in the sincerity of yours, lamented, though I did not condemn, your renunciation of the creed I had adopted—nor do I think any person, or power ought to do it whilst your conduct is not opposed to the general Interest of the People, & the measures they are pursuing—The latter, that is our actions, depending on ourselves may be controuled, while the powers of thinking originating from higher causes, cannot always be moulded to our wishes.
  The determinations of Providence are always wise—often inscrutable—and, thô its decrees appear to bear hard upon us at times, is, nevertheless meant for gracious purposes—In this light I cannot help viewing your late disappointment; for if you had been permitted to have gone to England, unrestrained even by the rigid Oaths which are administred upon those occasions, your feelings as a husband, parent, &ca must have been considerably wounded in the prospect of a long—perhaps lasting seperation from your nearest relatives—what then must they have been if the obligation of an Oath had left you without a Will?
  Your hope of being instrumental in restoring peace, would prove as unsubstantial as mist before a Noon day Sun; and would as soon dispel; for believe me Sir, G. Britain understood herself perfectly well in this dispute, but did not comprehend America—She meant as Lord Cambden in his late speech in Parliament clearly, & explicitly declares, to drive America into

rebellion, that her own purposes might be more fully answered by it; but take this along with it, that this plan originating in a firm belief founded on mis-information, that no effectual opposition would, or could be made, they little dreamt of what has happened, and are disappointed in their views.

Does not every act of Administration from the Tea act to the present Sessions of Parliament declare this in plain & self-evident characters? Had the Commissioners any powers to treat with America? If they meant peace, would Lord Howe have been detained in England five Months after passing the Act? Would the powers of these Commissioners have been confined to mere acts of grace upon condition of absolute submission? No—surely No! they meant to drive us into what they termed rebellion, that they might be furnished with a pretext to disarm, and then strip us of the rights & previledges of Englishmen—If they were actuated by principles of Justice, why did they refuse, indignantly to accede to the terms which were humbly supplicated before hostilities commenced, and this Country deluged in blood, & now make their principal officers, and even the Commissioners themselves, say that these terms are just & reasonable; nay, that more will be granted than we have yet asked, if we will relinquish our claim to Independancy—what name does such conduct as this deserve? and what punishment is there in store for the Men who have distressed Millions—Involved thousands in ruin—and plunged numberless families in inextricable woe! Could that which is just & reasonable now have been unjust four years ago? If not, upon what principles I repeat, does Administration act? they must either be wantonly wicked & cruel or (which is only another mode of expressing the same thing) under false colours are now endeavouring to deceive the great body of the People by industriously propagating an Idea, that G. Britain is willing to offer any, & that we will accept of no terms; thereby hoping to poison, & disaffect the minds of those who wish for Peace, & create feuds and dissentions in consequence—In a word, having less dependance now on their Arms than their Arts, they are practicing such low, & dirty tricks, that Men of Sentiment and honor must blush for their fall. among other manœuvres in this way, they are forging Letters and publishing them as intercepted ones of mine, to prove that I am an enemy to the

present measures of this Continent; having been deceived, &
led on by Congress in hopes that at length, they would recede
from their claims & withdraw their opposition to G. Britain.

I am sorry to hear of the indisposition of Miss Fairfax—I
shd have been pleased, could I have congratulated you on a
Marriage wch I heard was in agitation between her & a Relation of mine Mr Whiting—My best respects to Mrs Fairfax &
yr family & believe me to be Dr Sr Yr Most Obed. & Affe.

NEWS OF THE FRENCH ALLIANCE

To John Augustine Washington

Dear Brother,   Valley-forge May 1778.
Your letter of the 27th of Mar. from Bushfield came safe to
hand, & gave me the pleasure of hearing, or rather inferring
(for you are not explicit) that my Sister and the rest of your
family were well. I thank you for your intelligence respecting
the pamphlet of forged Letters which Colo. Lee has, & said to
be written by me; not one sentence of which you may rely on
it, did I ever write; although so many little family circumstances
are interspersed through the whole performance to give it the
air of authenticity—The Arts of the enemy, and the low dirty
tricks which they are daily practising is an evincing proof that
they are lost to all sense of virtue & honor, and that they will
stick at nothing however incompatible with truth and manli-
ness to carry their points. They have lately forged, & industriously circulated, a resolve for Congress, purporting (after
reciting with great propriety, & plausibility, the inconveniencies of short enlistments) that all Soldiers who have been
drafted for periods short of the war, shall nevertheless continue
in Service during it; and by their emissaries have endeavoured,
& effected the injury of the Service by this means—alarming
the fears of the Soldiery & Country.

I am mistaken if we are not verging fast to one of the most
important periods that ever America saw—doubtless before
this reaches you, you will have seen the Draughts of two Bills

intended to be enacted into Laws, & Lord North's Speech upon the occasion; these our accts from Phila. say, will be immediately followed by the Commissioners; and Lord Amherst, Adml Keppel, & General Murray are said to be the Commissioners—These Gentlemen I presume, are to move in a civil and Military Line, as Genl Howe is certainly recalled, & report adds—Lord Howe also—Be this as it may, it will require all the skill—the wisdom—& policy—of the first abilities of these States, to manage the helm, and steer with judgment to the haven of our wishes through so many shelves and Rocks, as will be thrown in our way. This, more than ever, is the time for Congress to be replete with the first characters in every State, instead of having a thin Assembly, & many States totally unrepresented, as is the case at present. I have often regretted the pernicious (& what appears to me, fatal) policy of having our ablest men engaged in the formation of the more local Governments, and filling Offices in their respective States, leaving the great national concern, on wch the superstructure of all, and every of them does absolutely depend, and without which none can exist, to be managed by Men of more contracted abilities—indeed those at a distance from the Seat of War live in such perfect tranquility that they conceive the dispute to be at an end in a manner, and those near hand it, are so disaffected that they only serve as embarrassments—between the two, therefore, time slips away without the necessary means for opening the Campaign in time, or with propriety.

Your accts of the high prices of fresh Provisions in Philadelphia are true, but it affects the Inhabitants more than the Soldiery, who have plenty of Salt Meat, Pease &ca.

Since I began this Letter, authentic accts have come to my hands of France having declared the United States free and Independant, and guaranteeing to them all the Territory formerly ceeded by them to Great Britain. My acct (from the Gentleman who was going on to Congress with the Treaty) adds, that France have done this in the most generous manner, and to our utmost wish. This is great, 'tis glorious News and must put the Independency of America out of all manner of dispute. and accts for the gentle gales which have succeeded rude Boreas, of late. A publication of this important intelligence will no doubt be directed by Congress, & diffused through the Continent as Speedily as possible, I shall add nothing further therefore on the Subject.

It would have been a happy circumstance if the several States had been industrious in pushing their recruits into the field, early—but I see little prospect of it at present, if ever. My love and best wishes, in which Mrs Washington joins me attend my Sister & the rest of your family & with great truth I subscribe myself Yr Most Affecte Brothr

THE BATTLE OF MONMOUTH COURTHOUSE

To Henry Laurens

Sir   English Town 1st July 1778

I embrace this first moment of leisure, to give Congress a more full and particular account of the movements of the Army under my command, since its passing the Delaware, than the situation of our Affairs would heretofore permit.

I had the honor to advise them, that on the appearances of the enemy's intention to march thro' Jersey becoming serious, I had detached General Maxwells Brigade, in conjunction with the Militia of that State, to interrupt and impede their progress, by every obstruction in their power; so as to give time to the Army under my command to come up with them, and take advantage of any favorable circumstances that might present themselves. The Army having proceeded to Coryell's ferry and crossed the Delaware at that place, I immediately detached Colo. Morgan with a select Corps of 600 Men to reinforce General Maxwell, and marched with the main Body towards princetown.

The slow advance of the Enemy had greatly the air of design, and led me, with others, to suspect that General Clinton desirous of a general Action was endeavouring to draw us down into the lower Country, in order by a rapid movement to gain our Right, and take possession of the strong Grounds above us. This consideration, and to give the troops time to repose and refresh themselves from the fatigues they had experienced from rainy and excessive hot Weather, determined me to halt at Hopewell Township, about five Miles from princetown, where we remained till the Morning of the 25th On the preceding day I made a second detatchment of 1500 chosen troops under Brigadier Genl Scott, to reinforce those already in the vicinity of the Enemy, the more effectually to annoy and delay their march. The next day the Army moved to Kingston, and having received intelligence that the Enemy were prosecuting their Rout towards Monmouth Court House, I dispatched a thousand select men under Brigadier General Wayne, and sent the Marquis de la Fayette to take the command of the whole advanced Corps, including Maxwells Brigade and Morgans light Infantry; with orders to take the first fair opportunity of attacking the Enemy's Rear. In the evening of the same day, the whole Army marched from Kingston where our Baggage was left, with intention to preserve a proper distance for supporting the advanced Corps, and arrived at Cranberry early the next morning. The intense heat of the Weather, and a heavy storm unluckily coming on made it impossible to resume our march that day without great inconvenience and injury to the troops. Our advanced Corps being differently circumstanced, moved from the position it had held the night before, and took post in the evening on the Monmouth Road, about five Miles from the Enemy's Rear, in expectation of attacking them next morning on their march. The main Body having remained at Cranberry, the advanced Corps was found to be too remote, and too far upon the Right to be supported either in case of an attack upon, or from the Enemy, which induced me to send orders to the Marquis to file off by his left towards English Town, which he accordingly executed early in the Morning of the 27th.

The Enemy in marching from Allen Town had changed their disposition and placed their best troops in the Rear, consisting of all the Grenadiers, Light Infantry, and Chasseurs of the line. This alteration made it necessary to increase the number of our advanced Corps; in consequence of which I detatched Major General Lee with two Brigades to join the Marquis at English Town, on whom of course the command of the whole devolved, amounting to about five thousand Men. The main Body marched the same day and encamped within three Miles of that place. Morgans Corps was left hovering on the Enemy's right flank, and the Jersey Militia, amounting at this time to about 7 or 800 Men under General Dickinson on their left.

The Enemy were now encamped in a strong position, with their right extending about a Mile and an half beyond the Court House, in the parting of the Roads leading to Shrewsbury and Middletown, and their left along the Road from Allen Town to Monmouth, about three miles on this side the Court House. Their Right flank lay on the skirt of a small wood, while their left was secured by a very thick one, a Morass running towards their Rear, and their whole front covered by a wood, and for a considerable extent towards the left with a Morass. In this situation they halted till the morning of the 28th.

Matters being thus situated, and having had the best information, that if the Enemy were once arrived at the Heights of Middletown, ten or twelve Miles from where they were, it would be impossible to attempt any thing against them with a prospect of success I determined to attack their Rear the moment they should get in motion from their present Ground. I communicated my intention to General Lee, and ordered him to make his disposition for the attack, and to keep his Troops constantly lying upon their Arms, to be in readiness at the shortest notice. This was done with respect to the Troops under my immediate command.

About five in the Morning General Dickinson sent an Express, informing, that the Front of the Enemy had began their march. I instantly put the Army in motion, and sent orders by one of my Aids to General Lee to move on and attack them, unless there should be very powerful Reasons to the contrary; acquainting him at the same time, that I was marching to support him, and for doing it with the greater expedition and convenience, should make the Men disencumber themselves of their packs and Blankets.

After marching about five Miles, to my great surprize and mortification, I met the whole advanced Corps retreating, and, as I was told, by General Lee's orders without having made any opposition, except one fire given by a party under the command of Colo. Butler, on their being charged by the Enemy's Cavalry, who were repulsed. I proceeded immediately to the

Rear of the Corps, which I found closely pressed by the Enemy, and gave directions for forming part of the retreating troops, who by the brave and spirited conduct of the Officers, aided by some pieces of well served Artillery, checked the Enemy's advance, and gave time to make a disposition of the left Wing and second line of the Army upon an eminence, and in a wood a little in the Rear, covered by a morass in front. On this were placed some Batteries of Cannon by Lord Stirling, who commanded the left Wing, which played upon the Enemy with great effect, and seconded by parties of Infantry detatched to oppose them, effectually put a stop to their advance.

General Lee being detatched with the advanced Corps, the command of the Right Wing, for the occasion, was given to General Greene. For the expedition of the march, and to counteract any attempt to turn our Right, I had ordered him to file off by the new Church two Miles from English Town, and fall into the Monmouth Road, a small distance in the Rear of the Court House, while the rest of the Column moved directly on towards the Court House. On intelligence of the Retreat, he marched up and took a very advantagious position on the Right.

The Enemy, by this time, finding themselves warmly opposed in front made an attempt to turn our left Flank; but they were bravely repulsed and driven back by detatched parties of Infantry. They also made a movement to our Right, with as little success, General Greene having advanced a Body of Troops with Artillery to a commanding peice of Ground, which not only disappointed their design of turning our Right, but severely enfiladed those in front of the left Wing. In addition to this, General Wayne advanced with a Body of Troops and kept up so severe and well directed a fire that the Enemy were soon compelled to retire behind the defile, where the first stand in the beginning of the Action had been made.

In this situation, the Enemy had both their Flanks secured by thick Woods and Morasses, while their front could only be approached thro' a narrow pass. I resolved nevertheless to attack them, and for that purpose ordered General Poor with his own and the Carolina Brigade, to move round upon their Right, and General Woodford upon their left, and the Artillery to gall them in front: But the impediments in their way prevented their getting within reach before it was dark. They remained upon the Ground, they had been directed to occupy, during the Night, with intention to begin the attack early the next morning, and the Army continued lying upon their Arms in the Feild of Action, to be in readiness to support them. In the mean time the Enemy were employed in removing their wounded, and about 12 OClock at Night marched away in such silence, that tho' General Poor lay extremely near them, they effected their Retreat without his Knowledge. They carried off all their wounded except four Officers and about Forty privates whose wounds were too dangerous to permit their removal.

The extreme heat of the Weather—the fatigue of the Men from their march thro' a deep sandy Country almost entirely destitute of Water, and the distance the Enemy had gained by marching in the Night, made a pursuit impracticable and fruitless. It would have answered no valuable purpose, and would have been fatal to numbers of our Men, several of whom died the preceding day with Heat.

Were I to conclude my account of this days transactions without expressing my obligations to the Officers of the Army in general, I should do injustice to their merit, and violence to my own feelings. They seemed to vie with each other in manifesting their Zeal and Bravery. The Catalouge of those who distinguished themselves is too long to admit of particularizing individuals: I cannot however forbear mentioning Brigadier General Wayne whose good conduct and bravery thro' the whole action deserves particular commendation.

The Behaviour of the troops in general, after they recovered from the first surprize occasioned by the Retreat of the advanced Corps, was such as could not be surpassed.

All the Artillery both Officers and Men that were engaged, distinguished themselves in a remarkable manner.

Inclosed Congress will be pleased to receive a Return of our killed, wounded and missing. Among the first were Lieut. Colo. Bunner of Penna and Major Dickinson of Virginia both Officers of distinguished merit and much to be regretted. The Enemy's slain left on the Feild and buried by us, according to the Return of the persons assigned to that duty were four Officers and Two hundred and forty five privates. In the former number was the Honble Colo. Monckton. Exclusive of these they buried some themselves, as there were several new Graves near the feild of Battle. How many Men they may have had wounded cannot be determined; but from the usual proportion the number must have been considerable. There were a few prisoners taken.

The peculiar Situation of General Lee at this time, requires that I should say nothing of his Conduct. He is now in arrest. The Charges against him, with such Sentence as the Court Martial may decree in his Case, shall be transmitted for the approbation or disapprobation of Congress as soon as it shall have passed.

Being fully convinced by the Gentlemen of this Country that the Enemy cannot be hurt or injured in their embarkation at Sandy Hook the place to which they are going, and unwilling to get too far removed from the North River, I put the Troops in motion early this morning and shall proceed that way, leaving the Jersey Brigade, Morgans Corps and other light parties (the Militia being all dismissed) to hover about them—countenance desertion and to prevent their depredations as far as possible. After they embark, the former will take post in the Neighbourhood of Elizabeth Town—The latter rejoin the Corps from which they were detatched. I have the Honor to be with the greatest Respect Sir Yr most obt Servt

"THE HAND OF PROVIDENCE HAS BEEN SO
CONSPICUOUS IN ALL THIS"

To Thomas Nelson, Jr.

My dear Sir,   Camp at the White-plains Augt 20th 1778
In what terms can I sufficiently thank you for your polite attention to me, and agreeable present? and, which is still more to the purpose, with what propriety can I deprive you of a valuable, and favourite Horse? You have pressed me once, nay twice, to accept him as a gift; as a proof of my sincere attachment to, and friendship for you, I obey, with this assurance,

that from none but a Gentn for whom I have the highest regard, would I do this, notwithstanding the distressed situation
I have been in for want of one.

I am heartily disappointed at a late resolution of Congress
for the discontinuance of your Corps, because I pleased my self
with the prospect of seeing you, and many other Gentn of my
acquaintance from Virginia, in Camp—As you had got to
Philadelphia, I do not think the saving, or difference of expence
(taking up the matter even upon that ground, which under
present circumstances I think a very erroneous one) was by
any means an object suited to the occasion.

The arrival of the French Fleet upon the Coast of America is
a great, & striking event; but the operations of it have been
injured by a number of unforeseen & unfavourable cercum-
stances—which, tho they ought not to detract from the merit,
and good intention of our great Ally, has nevertheless lessened
the importance of their Services in a great degree—The length
of the passage in the first instance was a capitol misfortune, for
had even one of common length taken place, Lord Howe with
the British Ships of War and all the Transports in the River
Delaware must, inevitably, have fallen; and Sir Harry must
have had better luck than is commonly dispensed to Men of
his profession, under such circumstances, if he and his Troops
had not shared (at least) the fate of Burgoyne—The long passage of Count D'Estaign was succeeded by an unfavourable
discovery at the hook, which hurt us in two respects; first in a
defeat of the enterprize upon New York—the Shipping—&
Troops at that place; and next, in the delay that was used in
ascertaining the depth of Water over the Bar; which was essential to their entrance into the Harbour of New York—And
lastly after the enterprize upon Rhode Island had been planned,
and was in the moment of execution, that Lord Howe with the
British Ships should interpose, merely to create a diversion,
and draw the French fleet from the Island was again unlucky,
as the Count had not return'd on the 17th to the Island tho
drawn off from it the 10th; by which means the Land operations were retarded, and the whole subject to a miscarriage in
case of the arrival of Byrons Squadron.

I do not know what to make of the enemy at New York;
whether their stay at that place is the result of choice, or the

effect of necessity, proceeding from an inferiority in their Fleet
—want of Provisions—or other causes, I know not, but certain
it is that if it is not an act of necessity it is profoundly misterious unless they look for considerable reinforcements and are
waiting the arrival of them to commence their operations. time
will shew.

It is not a little pleasing, nor less wonderful to contemplate,
that after two years Manœuvering and undergoing the strang-
est vicissitudes that perhaps ever attended any one contest
since the creation both Armies are brought back to the very
point they set out from and, that that, which was the offending
party in the beginning is now reduced to the use of the spade
and pick axe for defence. The hand of Providence has been so
conspicuous in all this, that he must be worse than an infidel
that lacks faith, and more than wicked, that has not gratitude
enough to acknowledge his obligations—but—it will be time
enough for me to turn preacher, when my present appointment ceases; and therefore, I shall add no more on the Doctrine
of Providence; but make a tender of my best respects to your
good Lady—the Secretary & other friends and assure you that
with the most perfect regard I am Dr Sir Yr Most Affecte &
Obliged Hble Ser.

P.S. Since writing the foregoing, I have been favoured with
your Letter of the 25th Ulto from Baltimore, and 9th Instt
from Philadelphia—The method you propose to take with the
Public Horses in your volunteer Corps will be very proper &
agreeable to me.

"WHOSE FINANCES (THEIRS OR OURS)
IS MOST LIKELY TO FAIL"

To Gouverneur Morris

Dear Sir,   Fish-kill, Octr 4th 1778.
    My public Letters to the Presidt of Congress will inform you
of the Wind that wafted me to this place—nothing more
therefore need to be said on that head.

Your Letter of the 8th Ulto contains three questions & answers—to wit—Can the Enemy prosecute the War? Do they mean to stay on the Continent? And is it our interest to put impediments in the way of their departure? To the first you answer in the negative—To the second you are decided in opinion that they do not—and to the third say clearly No.

Much my good Sir, may be said in favor of these answers; and *some* things against the first & second—By way therefore of dissertation on the first, I will also beg leave to put a question, and give it an answer—Can *we* carry on the War much longer? certainly No; unless some measures can be devised, and speedily executed, to restore the credit of our Currency—restrain Extortion—and punish Forestallers.

Without these can be effected, what funds can stand the present Expences of the Army? And what Officer can bear the weight of prices, that every necessary article is now got to? A Rat, in the shape of a Horse, is not to be bought at this time for less than £200—A Saddle under Thirty or forty—Boots twenty—and Shoes and other articles in like proportion! How is it possible therefore for Officers to stand this, without an Increase of pay? And how is it possible to advance their pay, when Flour is selling (at different places) from five to fifteen pounds pr Ct—Hay from ten to thirty pounds pr Tunn—and Beef & other essentials in this proportion.

The true point of light then, in which to place, & consider this matter, is not simply whether G. Britain can carry on the War, but whose Finances (theirs or ours) is most likely to fail: which leads me to doubt, *very much*, the infallibility of the answer given to your second question, respecting the Enemy's leaving the Continent; for I believe, that they will not do it while even *hope*, & the chapter of *accidents* can give them a *chance* of bringing us to terms short of *Independance*—But this *you* perhaps will say, they are now bereft of *I* shall acknowledge that many things favour the idea; but add, that, upon a comparitive view of circumstances there is abundant matter to puzzle, & confound the judgment—To your third answer, I subscribe with my hand and heart. The opening is now fair, and God grant they may embrace the oppertunity of bidding an eternal adieu to our—once quit of them—happy Land. If the Spaniards would but join their Fleets to those of France, &

commence hostilities, my doubts would all subside—without it, I fear the British Navy has it too much in its power to counteract the schemes of France.

The high prices of every necessary—The little—indeed no benefit, which Officers have derived from the intended bounty of Congress in the Article of Cloathing. The change in the establishment, by which so many of them are discontinued—The unfortunate delay of this business, which kept them too long in suspence, and set a number of evil spirits to work—The unsettled Rank—and contradictory modes of adjusting it—with other causes which might be enumerated, have conspired to Sour the temper of the Army exceedingly; and has, I am told, been productive of a memorial, or representation of some kind, to Congress; which neither directly nor indirectly did I know, or ever hear was in agitation, till some days after it was dispatched—owing, as I apprehend, to the secrecy with which it was conducted, to keep it from my knowledged; as I had, in a similar instance last spring, discountenanced, & stifled a child of the same illigitimacy, in its birth—If you have any news worth communicating, do not put it under a bushel, but give it to Dr Sir Yrs sincerely

AGAINST FRENCH INTERVENTION IN CANADA

To Henry Laurens

Dear Sir   Fredericksburg in N. Yk Novr 14th 1778.

This will be accompanied by an Official Letter on the subject of the proposed Expedition against Canada—You will perceive I have only considered it in a Military light—indeed I was not authorized to consider it in any other, and I am not without apprehensions, that I may be thought in what I have done, to have exceeded the limits intended by Congress—But my sollicitude for the public welfare which I think deeply interested in this affair, will I hope justify me in the eyes of all those who view things through that just medium.

I do not know Sir what may be your Sentiments in the present case—but whatever they are, I am sure I can confide in your honor & friendship, and shall not hesitate to unbosom myself to you on a point of the most delicate and important nature. The question of the Canadian expedition in the form it now stands appears to me one of the most interesting that has hitherto agitated our national deliberations. I have one objection to it untouched in my public letter, which is in my estimation insurmountable—and alarms all my feelings for the true and permanent interests of my Country. This is the introduction of a large body of French Troops into Canada, and putting them in possession of the Capitol of that Province—attached to them by all the ties of blood, habits, manners, religion & former Connixion of Government. I fear this would be too great a temptation to be resisted by any power actuated by the common maxims of national policy.

Let us realize for a moment the striking advantages France would derive from the possession of Canada, the acquisition of an extensive territory abounding in supplies for the use of her Islands—the opening a vast source of the most beneficial commerce with the Indian Nations which she might then monopolise—she having ports of her own on the Continent independant on the precarious good will of an Ally—the engrossing the whole trade of Newfoundland whenever she pleased (the finest nursery of Seamen in the world)—the security afforded to her Islands—and finally of awing & controuling these States, the natural and most formidable rival of every Maratime power in Europe. Canada would be a solid acquisition to France on all these accts and because of the Numerous inhabitants, subjects to her by inclination, who would aid in preserving it under her power against the attempt of every other.

France acknowledged for some time past the most powerful Monarchy in Europe by land able now to dispute the empire of the Sea with Britain, and if joined with Spain, I may say certainly superior, in possession of Canada on our left, and the extensive territory anciently comprehended within its limits— while the other branch of the House of Bourbon possesses New Orleans—the Key of the Mississippi—on our right— seconded by the numerous tribes of Indians on our rear from one extremity to the other, a people so generally friendly to her, and whom she knows so well to conciliate—would it is much to be apprehended, have it in her power to give law to these States.

Let us suppose that, when the five thousand French Troops, (and under the idea of that number twice as many may be sent) were entered the City of Quebec, they should declare an intention to hold Canada as a pledge & security for the debt due to France from the United States—or under other specious pretences hold the place till they can find a bond for contention—and, in the Mean while, should excite the Canadians to engage in supporting their pretences & claims, what should we be able to say with only four or five thousand Men to carry on the dispute? It may be supposed that France would not choose to renounce our friendship by a step of this kind, as the consequence would probably be a reunion with England on some terms or other, and the loss of what she had acquired in so violent and unjustifiable a manner, with all the advantages of an alliance with us. This, in my opinion, is too slender a security against the Measure, to be relied on. The truth of the position will entirely depend on Naval Events—If France and Spain should unite, and obtain a decided superiority by Sea—a reunion with England would avail very little, and might be set at defiance—France with a numerous Army at command, might throw in what number of land forces she thought proper to support her pretensions, and England without Men, without Money, and inferior on her favourite element could give no effectual aid to oppose them, Resentment, reproaches, and submission seem to be all that would be left us. Men are very apt to run into extremes, hatred to England may carry some into an excess of confidence in France, especially, when motives of gratitude are thrown into the scale—Men of this description would be unwilling to suppose France capable of acting so ungenerous a part. I am heartily disposed to entertain the most favourable sentiments of our New Ally, and to cherish them in others, to a reasonable degree, but it is a maxim founded on the universal experience of Mankind, that no Nation is to be trusted farther than it is bound by its interest, And no prudent Statesman or politician will venture to depart from it. In our circumstances, we ought to be particularly cautious for we have not yet attained sufficient vigor and maturity to recover from the shock of any false step, into which we may unwarily fall.

If France should even engage in the scheme in the first instance with the purest intentions, there is the greatest danger that in the progress of the business, invited to it by circumstances perhaps urged on by the solicitations & wishes of the Canadians, she would alter her views. As the Marquis cloathed his proposition when he spoke of it to me, it would seem to originate wholly with himself, but it is far from impossible that it had its birth in the Cabinet of France, & was put into this artful dress, to give it the readier currency. I fancy, I read in the countenances of some people on this occasion, more than the disinterested zeal of Allies—I hope I am mistaken and my fears of mischief, make me refine too much and awaken jealousies that have no sufficient foundation.

But upon the whole, Sir, to waive every other consideration, I do not like to add to the number of National obligations—I would wish as much as possible, to avoid giving a foreign power new claims of merit for services performed to the United States, and would ask No assistance that is not indispensible. I am with the truest attachment, & most perfect Confidence, Dr Sir Yr Most Obed. & Obliged

"WHETHER MY PROPERTY IS IN NEGROES, OR LOAN OFFICE CERTIFICATES"

To Lund Washington

Middle Brook, February 24, 1779.

Dear Lund: I wrote to you by the last post, but in so hasty a manner as not to be so full and clear as the importance of the subject might require. In truth, I find myself at a loss to do it to my own satisfaction in this hour of more leisure and thought, because it is a matter of much importance and requires a good deal of judgment and foresight to time things in such a way as to answer the purposes I have in view.

The advantages resulting from the sale of my negroes, I have very little doubt of; because, as I observed in my last, if we should ultimately prove unsuccessful (of which I am under no apprehension unless it falls on us as a punishment for our want of public, and indeed private virtue) it would be a matter of very little consequence to me, whether my property is in Negroes, or loan office Certificates, as I shall neither ask for, nor expect any favor from his most gracious Majesty, nor any person acting under his authority; the only points therefore for me to consider, are, first, whether it would be most to my interest, in case of a fortunate determination of the present contest, to have negroes, and the Crops they will make; or the sum they will now fetch and the interest of the money. And, secondly, the critical moment to make this sale.

With respect to the first point (if a negro man will sell at, or near one thousand pounds, and woman and children in proportion) I have not the smallest doubt on which side the balance, placed in the scale of interest, will preponderate: My scruples arise from a reluctance in offering these people at public vendue, and on account of the uncertainty of timeing the sale well. In the first case, if these poor wretches are to be held in a state of slavery, I do not see that a change of masters will render it more irksome, provided husband and wife, and Parents and children are not separated from each other, which is not my intentions to do. And with respect to the second, the judgment founded in a knowledge of circumstances, is the only criterion for determining when the tide of depreciation is at an end; for like the flux and reflux of the water, it will no sooner have got to its full ebb or flow, but an immediate turn takes place, and every thing runs in a contrary direction. To hit this critical moment then, is the point; and a point of so much nicety, that the longer I reflect upon the subject, the more embarrassed I am in my opinion; for if a sale takes place while the money is in a depreciating state, that is, before it has arrived at the lowest ebb of depreciation; I shall lose the difference, and if it is delayed, 'till some great and important event shall give a decisive turn in favor of our affairs, it may be too late. Notwithstanding, upon a full consideration of the whole matter; if you have done nothing in consequence of my last letter, I wou'd have you wait 'till you hear further from me on this subject. I will, in the meanwhile, revolve the matter in my mind more fully, and may possibly be better able to draw some more precise conclusions than at present, while you may be employed in endeavouring to ascertain the highest prices Negroes sell at, in different parts of the Country, where, and in what manner it would be best to sell them, when such a measure is adopted, (which I think will very likely happen in the course of a few months.)

Inclosed is my Bond for conveyance of the Land purchased of the Ashfords &c. It is as well drawn as I can do it, and I believe it to be effectual.

February 26, 1779.

Your Letter of the 17th. inst: is just come to hand, your apprehensions on account of my health are groundless; the irregularity of the Post, and stoppage of your letters, or miscarriages of them, were the principal causes of my long silence. My last letter to you was full on the subject of corn; I shall not touch upon it therefore in this. I then desired, and again repeat my wish, that you would sell every thing about the house and plantations, that is not essentially necessary. Mr. Custis wrote to me for an Anchor, to be sold or lent, the former I prefer, as I wish to get quit of all those kind of things; the money arising from all which, the sale of Flour &c, I would have put in the continental loan office. I am glad to hear your success in Lambs is so great. Mrs. Washington joins in remembrance to yourself and Milly, with Dr. Lund, Your affecte. Servant.

"THE POLICY OF OUR ARMING SLAVES"

To Henry Laurens

Middle brook, March 20, 1779.

Dear Sir: I have to thank you, and I do it very sincerely, for your obliging favors of the 2d. and 16th Inst.; and for their several inclosures, containing articles of intelligence. I congratulate you most cordially on Campbells precipitate retreat from Fort Augusta. What was this owing to? it seems to have been a surprize even upon Williamson. but I rejoice much more on acct. of his disappointed application to the Creek Indians; this I think, is to be considered as a very important event, and may it not be the conjectural cause of his (Campbells) hasty return; this latter circumstance cannot but be a fresh proof to the disaffected (in that Country) that they are leaning upon a broken reed; severe examples should, in my judgment, be made of those who were forgiven former offences and again in Arms against us.

The policy of our arming Slaves is, in my opinion, a moot point, unless the enemy set the example; for should we begin to form Battalions of them, I have not the smallest doubt (if the War is to be prosecuted) of their following us in it, and justifying the measure upon our own ground; the upshot then must be, who can arm fastest, and where are our Arms? besides, I am not clear that a discrimination will not render Slavery more irksome to those who remain in it; most of the good and evil things of this life are judged of by comparison; and I fear a comparison in this case will be productive of much discontent in those who are held in servitude; but as this is a subject that has never employed much of my thoughts, these are no more than the first crude Ideas that have struck me upon the occasion.

I had not the smallest intimation of Monsr. Gerards passing through Jersey till I was favoured with your Letter, and am now ignorant of the cause, otherwise than by conjecture. The inclosed I return, as Mr. Laurens left this some days ago for Philadelphia, on his way to the Southward.

Mrs. Washington joins me in respectful compliments to you, and with every sentiment of regard and attachment. I am etc.

"I AM A WARRIOR. MY WORDS ARE FEW AND PLAIN"

Speech to the Delaware Chiefs

Head Quarters, Middle Brook, May 12, 1779.

Brothers: I am happy to see you here. I am glad the long Journey you have made, has done you no harm; and that you are in good health: I am glad also you left All our friends of the Delaware Nation well.

Brothers: I have read your paper. The things you have said are weighty things, and I have considered them well. The Delaware Nation have shown their good will to the United States. They have done wisely and I hope they will never repent. I rejoice in the new assurances you give of their friendship. The things you now offer to do to brighten the chain, prove your sincerity. I am sure Congress will run to meet you, and will do every thing in their power to make the friendship between the people of these States, and their Brethren of the Delaware nation, last forever.

Brothers: I am a Warrior. My words are few and plain; but I will make good what I say. 'Tis my business to destroy all the Enemies of these States and to protect their friends. You have seen how we have withstood the English for four years; and how their great Armies have dwindled away and come to very little; and how what remains of them in this part of our great Country, are glad to stay upon Two or three little Islands, where the Waters and their Ships hinder us from going to destroy them. The English, Brothers, are a boasting people. They talk of doing a great deal; but they do very little. They fly away on their Ships from one part of our Country to an other; but as soon as our Warriors get together they leave it and go to some other part. They took Boston and Philadelphia, two of our greatest Towns; but when they saw our Warriors in a great body ready to fall upon them, they were forced to leave them.

Brothers: We have till lately fought the English all alone. Now the Great King of France is become our Good Brother and Ally. He has taken up the Hatchet with us, and we have sworn never to bury it, till we have punished the English and made them sorry for All the wicked things they had in their Hearts to do against these States. And there are other Great Kings and Nations on the other side of the big Waters, who love us and wish us well, and will not suffer the English to hurt us.

Brothers: Listen well to what I tell you and let it sink deep into your Hearts. We love our friends, and will be faithful to them, as long as they will be faithful to us. We are sure our Good brothers the Delawares will always be so. But we have sworn to take vengeance on our Enemies, and on false friends. The other day, a handful of our young men destroyed the settlement of the Onondagas. They burnt down all their Houses, destroyed their grain and Horses and Cattle, took their Arms away, killed several of their Warriors and brought off many prisoners and obliged the rest to fly into the woods. This is but the beginning of the troubles which those Nations, who have taken up the Hatchet against us, will feel.

Brothers: I am sorry to hear that you have suffered for want of necessaries, or that any of our people have not dealt justly by you. But as you are going to Congress, which is the great Council of the Nation and hold all things in their hands, I shall say nothing about the supplies you ask. I hope you will receive satisfaction from them. I assure you, I will do every thing in my power to prevent your receiving any further injuries, and will give the strictest orders for this purpose. I will severely punish any that shall break them.

Brothers: I am glad you have brought three of the Children of your principal Chiefs to be educated with us. I am sure Congress will open the Arms of love to them, and will look upon them as their own Children, and will have them educated accordingly. This is a great mark of your confidence and of your desire to preserve the friendship between the Two Nations to the end of time, and to become One people with your Brethren of the United States. My ears hear with pleasure the other matters you mention. Congress will be glad to hear them too. You do well to wish to learn our arts and ways of life, and above all, the religion of Jesus Christ. These will make you a greater and happier people than you are. Congress will do every thing they can to assist you in this wise intention; and to tie the knot of friendship and union so fast, that nothing shall ever be able to loose it.

Brothers: There are some matters about which I do not open my Lips, because they belong to Congress, and not to us warriors; you are going to them, they will tell you all you wish to know.

Brothers: When you have seen all you want to see, I will then wish you a good Journey to Philadelphia. I hope you may find there every thing your hearts can wish, that when you return home you may be able to tell your Nation good things of us. And I pray God he may make your Nation wise and Strong, that they may always see their own true interest and have courage to walk in the right path; and that they never may be deceived by lies to do any thing against the people of these States, who are their Brothers and ought always to be one people with them.

To Marquis de Lafayette

West-point, September 30, 1779.

My dear Marqs: A few days ago I wrote you a letter in much haste. the cause a sudden notification of Monsr. Gerards having changed the place of his embarkation from Boston (as was expected) to Philadelphia, and the hurry Monsir. de la Colombe was in to reach the latter before the Minister should have left it. Since that, I have been honourd with the company of the Chevr. de la Luzerne, and by him was favourd with your obliging letter of the 12th. of June which filled me with equal pleasure and surprise; the latter at hearing that you had not received one of the many letters I had written to you, since you left the American Shore. I cannot at this time charge my memory with the precise dates of these letters but the first, which ought and I expected would have reached you at Boston and I much wished it to do so because it contained a Letter from me to Doctr Franklin expressive of the Sentiments I entertained of your Services and merit was put into the hands of a Captn. McQueen of Charles Town, who was to Sail from Phila. soon after. In March I wrote you once or twice, and in June or the first of July following, (when it was reported that Monsr. Gerard was about to leave us I took the liberty of committing to his care another of my lettrs. to you,) which sevl. efforts though they may have been unsuccessful will exhibit no bad specimen of my having kept you constantly in remembrance and a desire of giving you proofs of it.

It gave me infinite pleasure to hear from yourself of the favourable reception you met with from your Sovereign, and of the joy which your safe arrival in France had diffused among your friends. I had no doubt but that this wou'd be the case; to hear it from yourself adds pleasure to the acct. and here My dear friend let me congratulate you on your new, honourable and pleasing appointment in the Army commanded by the Count de Vaux which I shall accompy. with an assurance that none can do it with more warmth of Affection, or sincere joy than myself. Your forward zeal in the cause of liberty; Your singular attachment to this infant World; Your ardent and per-severing efforts, not only in America but since your return to France to serve the United States; Your polite attention to Americans, and your strict and uniform friendship for *me*, has ripened the first impressions of esteem and attachment which I imbibed for you into such perfect love and gratitude that nei-ther time nor absence can impair which will warrant my assur-ing you, that whether in the character of an Officer at the head of a Corps of gallant French (if circumstances should require this) whether as a Major Genl. commanding a division of the American Army; Or whether, after our Swords and Spears have given place to the plough share and pruning hook, I see you as a private Gentleman, a friend and Companion, I shall welcome you in all the warmth of friendship to Columbia's shore; and in the latter case, to my rural Cottage, where homely fare and a cordial reception shall be substituted for delicacies and costly living. this from past experience I know *you* can submit to; and if the lovely partner of your happiness will consent to partici-pate with *us* in such rural entertainment and amusemts. I can undertake in behalf of Mrs. Washington that she will do every thing in her power to make Virginia agreeable to the Marchio-ness. My inclination and endeavours to do this cannot be doubted when I assure you that I love everybody that is dear to you. consequently participate in the pleasure you feel in the prospt. of again becoming a parent and do most Sincerely con-gratulate you and your Lady on this fresh pledge she is about to give you of her love.

I thank you for the trouble you have taken, and your polite attention in favouring me with a Copy of your letter to Con-gress; and feel as I am perswaded they must do, the force of such ardent zeal as you there express for the interest of this Country. The propriety of the hint you have given them must carry conviction and I trust will have a salutary effect; tho' there is not, I believe, the same occasion for the admonition now, there was some months ago; many late changes have taken place in that honourable body which has removed in a very great degree, if not wholly, the discordant spirit which it is said prevailed in the Winter, and I hope measures will also be taken to remove those unhappy and improper differences which have extended themselves elsewhere to the prejudice of our affairs in Europe.

You enquire after Monsr. de la Colombe, and Colo. Neville; the first (who has been with Baron de Kalb) left this a few days ago, as I have already observed, for Phila., in expectation of a passage with Monsr. Gerard. Colo. Neville called upon me about a Month since and was to have dined with us the next day but did not come, since which I have not seen him, nor do I know at this time where he is; he had then but just returned from his own home; and it was the first time I had seen him since he parted with you at Boston. It is probable he may be with the Virginia Troops which lye at the mouth of Smiths clove abt. 30 Miles from hence.

I have had great pleasure in the visit which the Chevalier de la Luzerne and Monsr. Marbois did me the honor to make at this Camp; for both of whom I have imbibed the most favourable impressions, and thank you for the honourable mention you made of me to them. The Chevr. till he had announced himself at Congress, did not choose to be received in his public character. If he had, except paying him Military honors, It was not my intention to depart from that plain and simple manner of living which accords with the real Interest and policy of Men struggling under every difficulty for the attainment of the most inestimable blessing of life, *Liberty*; the Chevalier was polite enough to approve my principle, and condescended to appear pleased with our Spartan living. In a word he made us all exceeding happy by his affability and good humour, while he remained in Camp.

You are pleased my dear Marquis to express an earnest desire of seeing me in France (after the establishment of our Independancy) and do me the honour to add, that you are not singular in your request. let me entreat you to be perswaded, that to meet you anywhere after the final accomplishment of so glorious an event would contribute to my happiness; and that, to visit a country to whose generous aid we stand so much indebted, would be an additional pleasure; but remember my good friend, that I am unacquainted with your language. that I am too far advanced in years to acquire a knowledge of it. and that to converse through the medium of an interpreter upon common occasions, especially with the *Ladies* must appr. so extremely aukward, insipid, and uncouth, that I can scarce bear it in idea. I will therefore hold myself disengaged for the *present* and when I see you in Virginia, we will talk of this matter and fix our plans.

The declaration of Spain in favour of France has given universal joy to every Whig, while the poor Tory droops like a withering flower under a declining Sun.

We are anxiously expecting to hear of great and important events on your side the Atlantic. At prest. the immagination is left in the wide field of conjecture. Our eyes one moment are turned to an Invasion of England. then of Ireland. Minorca, Gibralter, &ca. In a word we hope every thing, but know not what to expect or where to fix.

The glorious successes of Count DEstaing in the West Indies at the sametime that it adds dominion to France and fresh lustre to her Arms is a source of *new* and unexpected misfortune to our *tender* and *generous parent* and must serve to convince her of the folly of quitting the substance in pursuit of a shadow; and as there is no experience equal to that which is bought I trust she will have a superabundance of this kind of knowledge and be convinced as I hope all the World, and every tyrant in it will that the best and only safe road to honour, glory, and true dignity, is *justice*.

We have such repeated advices of Count D'Estaings being in these Seas that (though I have no official information of the event) I cannot help giving entire credit to the report and looking for his arrival every moment and am preparing accordingly. The enemy at New York also expect it, and to guard agt. the consequences as much as it is in their power to do, are repairing and strengthening all the old fortifications and adding New ones in the vicinity of the City; their fear however does not retard an embarkation which was making (and generally believed) to be for the West Indies or Charles Town. It still goes forward, and by my intelligence will consist of a pretty large detachment. About 14 days ago one british Regiment (the 44th. compleated) and 3 Hessian Regiments were embarked and are gone, as is supposed, to Hallifax. Under convoy of Admiral Arbuthnot about the 20th. of last month the Enemy recd. a reinforcement consisting of two new raised Scotch Regts. some drafts and a few Recruits amounting altogether to about 3000 Men and a few days ago Sir Andw. Hammond arrived with (as it is said) abt. 2000 more; many of these new Troops died on their passage and since landing, the rest are very sickly as indeed their whole Army is while ours keeps remarkably healthy.

The Operations of the enemy this campaign have been confined to the establishment of works of defence. taking a post at Kings ferry, and burning the defenceless towns of New haven, Fairfield, Norwalk, &ca. on the sound within reach of their Shipping where little else was, or could be opposed to them than the cries of distressed Women and helpless children; but these were offered in vain; since these notable exploits they have never stepped out of their Works or beyond their lines. How a conduct of this kind is to effect the conquest of America the wisdom of a North, a Germaine, or Sandwich best can tell. it is too deep and refined for the comprehension of common understandings and general run of politicians.

Colo. Fleury who I expect will have the honour of presenting this letter to you, and who acted an important and honourable part in the event, will give you the particulars of the assault and reduction of Stony point the capture of the G. consg. of 600 men with their Colours, Arms, Baggage, Stores, 15 pieces of valuable ordnance, &ca. He led one of the columns; struck the colours of the garrison with his own hands; and in all respects behaved with that intrepidity and intelligence which marks his conduct upon all occasions.

Since that event we surprized and took Paulus hook a very strong fortified post of the enemys, opposite to the city of New York and within reach of the batteries of that place. The garrison consisting of about 160 Men with the colors were brought off, but none of the stores could be removed on acct. of its insular situation and the difficulty of removing them; the first of these enterprizes was made under the command of General Wayne; the other was conducted by Majr. Lee of the light Horse both of whom have acquired much honor by their gallant behaviour in the respective attacks.

By my last advices from Genl. Sullivan of the 9th. Instt. I am led to conclude that ere this he has completed the entire destruction of the whole Country of the Six nations, excepting so much of it as is inhabited by the Oneidas who have always lived in amity with us; and a few towns belonging to the Cayugas and Onondago's who were disposed to be friendly. At the time these advices came away he had penetrated to the heart of their settlements after having defeated in a general engagement the united force of Indians, Tories, and regulars from Niagara. Burnt between 15 and 20 Towns, destroyed their Crops and every thing that was to be found. He was then advancing to the exterior Towns with a view to complete the desolation of the whole Country, and Remove the cruel inhabitants of it to a greater distance, who were then fleeing in the utmost confusion, consternation and distress towards Niagara, distant 100 Miles through an uninhabited wilderness; experiencing a little of that distress, but nothing of those cruelties which they have exercised on our unhappy frontier Settlers, who (Men, Women and Children) have been deliberately murdered, in a manner shocking to humanity.

But to conclude, you requested from me a long letter, I have given you one; but methinks my dear Marquis, I hear you say, there is reason in all things; that this is too long. I am clearly in sentiment with you, and will have mercy on you in my next. But at present must pray your patience a while longer, till I can make a tender of my most respectful compliments to the Marchioness. Tell her (if you have not made a mistake, and offered your *own love* instead of *hers* to me) that I have a heart susceptable of the tenderest passion, and that it is already so strongly impressed with the most favourable ideas of her, that she must be cautious of putting loves torch to it; as you must be in fanning the flame. But here again methinks I hear you say, I am not apprehensive of danger. My wife is young, you are growing old and the atlantic is between you. All this is true, but know my good friend that no distance can keep *anxious* lovers long asunder, and that the Wonders of former ages may be revived in this. But alas! will you not remark that amidst all the wonders recorded in holy writ no instance can be produced where a young Woman from *real inclination* has prefered an old man.

This is so much against me that I shall not be able *I fear* to contest the prize with you, yet, under the encouragement you have given me I shall enter the list for so inestimable a Jewell.

I will now reverse the scene, and inform you, that Mrs. Washington (who set out for Virginia when we took the field in June) often has in, her letters to me, enquired if I had heard from you, and will be much pleased at hearing that you are well, and happy. In her name (as she is not here) I thank you for your polite attention to her; and shall speak her sense of the honor confered on her by the Marchioness.

When I look back to the length of this letter I am so much astonished and frightened at it myself, that I have not the courage to give it a careful reading for the purpose of correction. You must therefore receive it with all its imperfections, accompanied with this assurance that though there may be many incorrections in the letter, there is not a single defect in the friendship of my dear Marquis Yr., etc.

"FROM MY SOUL I ABHOR THEM!"

To Robert Howe

West-point, November 20, 1779.

Dear Sir: Herewith you will receive Mr. Pulteney's lucubrations, and my thanks for the perusal of them. He has made I perceive, the dependance of America essential to the existance of Great Britain as a powerful Nation. This I shall not deny; because I am in sentiment with him in thinking her fallen state in consequence of the seperation too obvious to be disputed. It was of magnitude sufficient to have made a wise and just people look before they leaped. But I am glad to find that he has placed the supplies necessary to support that dependance upon three things which I am perswaded will never again exist in his nation; namely Public virtue, public œconomy, and public union in her grand Council.

Stock Jobbing, speculation dissipation luxury and venality with all their concomitants are too deeply rooted to yield to virtue and the public good. *We* that are not yet hackneyed in vice, but infants as it were in the arts of corruption, and the knowledge of taking advantage of public necessity (tho' I am much mistaken if we shall not soon become very great adepts at them), find it almost, if not quite impossible to preserve virtue enough to keep the body politic and corporate in tolerable tune. It is scarcely to be expected therefore that a people who have reduced these things to a system and have actually interwoven them into their constitution should at once become immaculate.

I do not know which rises highest, my indignation or contempt for the Sentiments which pervade the Ministerial writings of this day; these hireling scribblers labour to describe and prove the ingratitude of America in not breaking faith with France, and returning to her Allegiance to the Crown of Great Britain after its having offered such advantageous terms of accommodation. Such Sentiments as these are insulting to common sense and affrontive to every principle of sound policy and common honesty. Why has She offered these terms? because after a bloody contest, carried on with unrelenting and savage fury on her part the issue (which was somewhat doubtful while we stood alone) is now become certain by the aid we derive from our Alliance; notwithstanding the manifest advantages of which, and the blood and treasure which has been spent to resist a tyranny which was unremitted as long as there remained a hope of subjugation we are told with an effrontery altogether unparrallelled that every cause of complaint is now done away by the generous offers of a tender parent; that it is ungrateful in us not to accept the proffered terms; and impolitic not to abandon a power (dangerous I confess to her but) which held out a Saving hand to us in the hour of our distress. What epithet does such Sentiments merit? How much shd. a people possessed of them be despised? From my Soul I abhor them! A Manly struggle, had it been conducted upon liberal ground; an honest confession that they were unequal to conquest, and wished for our friendship, would have had its proper weight; but their cruelties, exercised upon those who have fallen within their power; the wanton depredations committed by themselves and their faithful Allies the Indians; their low and dirty practices of Counterfeiting our money, forging letters, and condescending to adopt such arts as the meanest villain in private life would blush at being charged with has made me their fixed enemy.

I have received your letter by Colo. Moylan of yesterdays date. The Instructions given to —— are full and compleat. I have no thought of withdrawing the effective horse till the other Troops go into quarters. I am, etc.

"YOU ARE TO PROCEED TO WEST POINT AND TAKE THE COMMAND"

To Benedict Arnold

Head Quarters at Peekskill, August 3, 1780.

Sir: You are to proceed to West point and take the command of that post and its dependencies, in which are included all from Fishkill to Kings Ferry. The Corps of Infantry and Cavalry advanced towards the Enemy's lines on the East side of the River will also be under your orders and will take directions from you, and you will endeavour to obtain every intelligence of the Enemy's Motions. The Garrison of West point is to consist of the Militia of New Hampshire and Massachusetts, for which reason, as soon as the number from those States amounts to twelve hundd the New York Militia under the command of Colo. Malcom are to join the Main Army on the West side of the River, and when the number from Massachusetts-bay alone shall amount to fifteen hundred Rank and file, the Militia of New Hampshire will also march to the Main Army. Colo. James Livingstons Regiment is, till further orders, to garrison the Redoubts at Stoney and Verplanks points.

Claverac upon the North River is appointed for the place of rendezvous of the Militia of New Hampshire and Massachusetts, from whence you will have them brought down as fast as they arrive. A supply of provision will be necessary at that place, which you will order from time to time as there may be occasion.

You will endeavour to have the Works at West point carried on as expeditiously as possible by the Garrison, under the direction and superintendance of the Engineers. The Stores carefully preserved, and the provision safely deposited and often inspected, particularly the salted Meat. A certain quantity of provision has been constantly kept in each Work, to be ready against a sudden attack. Where there are Bomb proofs, they serve for Magazines; but in the smaller Works where there are none, you will have places erected sufficiently tight to preserve the provision from damage and pillage.

You will, as soon as possible, obtain and transmit an accurate Return of the Militia which have come in, and inform me regularly of their increase.

Should any Levies, from the State of New York or those to the Eastward of it, intended for the Continental Army arrive at West point, you will immediately forward them to the Lines to which they respectively belong.

The difficulties we shall certainly experience on the score of provisions render the utmost œconomy highly necessary. You will therefore attend frequently to the daily Issues, and by comparing them with your Returns, will be able to check any impositions.

DISCOVERING ARNOLD'S TREACHERY

To Samuel Huntington

Robinson's House in the Highlands,
September 26, 1780.

Sir: I have the honor to inform Congress that I arrived here yesterday about 12 o'clock on my return from Hartford. Some hours previous to my arrival Major General Arnold went from his quarters which were at this place; and as it was supposed over the river to the garrison at West-point, whether I proceeded myself in order to visit the post. I found General Arnold had not been there during the day, and on my return to his quarters, he was still absent. In the mean time a packet had arrived from Lt. Colonel Jamison announcing the capture of a John Anderson who was endeavouring to go to New-York, with the several interesting and important papers mentioned below, all in the hand writing of General Arnold. This was also accompanied with a letter from the prisoner avowing himself to be Major John André Adjt: General of the British army, relating the manner of his capture, and endeavouring to shew that he did not come under the description of a spy. From these several circumstances, and information that the General seemed to be thrown into some degree of agitation on receiving a letter a little time before he went from his quarters, I was led to conclude immediately that he had heard of Major André's captivity, and that he would if possible escape to the enemy, and accordingly took such measures as appeared the most probable to apprehend him. But he had embarked in a barge, and proceeded down the river under a flag to the vulture ship of war, which lay at some miles below Stony and Verplank's points. He wrote me after he got on board a letter, of which the inclosed is a copy. Major André is not arrived yet, but I hope he is secure and that he will be here to-day. I have been and am taking proper precautions, which I trust will prove effectual, to prevent the important consequences which this conduct on the part of General Arnold was intended to produce. I do not know the party that took Major André; but it is said, it consisted only of a few militia, who acted in such a manner upon the occasion as does them the highest honor and proves them to be men of great virtue. They were offered, I am informed, a large sum of money for his release, and as many goods as they would demand, but without any effect. Their conduct gives them a just claim to the thanks of their country, and I also hope they will be otherwise rewarded. As soon as I know their names I shall take pleasure in transmitting them to Congress. I have taken such measures with respect to the Gentlemen of General Arnolds family as prudence dictated; but from every thing that has hitherto come to my knowledge, I have the greatest reason to believe they are perfectly innocent. I early secured, Joshua Smith, the person mentioned in the close of General Arnolds letter, and find him to have had a considerable share in this business. I have the honor etc.

"LEARN THE DESIGNS OF THE ENEMY"

Instructions to Spies Going into New York

Get into the City.

There, in the best manner possible, learn the designs of the Enemy.

Whether they mean to evacuate New York wholly in part, or continue the Army there. A discovery of this kind will be best made by attending a little to the conduct of Delancy, Bayard, Matthews &ca., as they, more than probably, will be preparing for a Removal if the City is to be left, wholly, or in any considerable degree.

Or Secondly, whether they have any views of Operating against this Army, which will be best known by their preparations of Waggons, Horses &ca., these will want Shoeing, repairing, &ca. Collecting together.

Enquire whether the Transports are Wooding and Watering. Whether the Stores are removing from the City into them, and whether any Regimental Baggage is Imbarked. Enquire also, how the Enemy are off for Provisions; whether the Cork Fleet is arrived and the number of Provision Ships it consists of.

Enquire also if Admiral Byrons Fleet is arrived. Where Lord Howe and the New York Fleet is; whether within Sandy hook, or gone out to Sea, and for what purpose.

Whether any Troops have been Imbarked lately and for what place. Whether any have arrived from England lately, or are expected.

Whether the Merchants who came from Europe and those who have been attached to Government are packing up or selling off their goods. Attend particularly to Coffin and Anderson who keep a large dry good Store and supply their Officers and Army.

c. September 1780

"I SEE NOTHING BEFORE US
BUT ACCUMULATING DISTRESS"

To John Cadwalader

Head Qrs., Tappan, October 5, 1780.

Dear Sir: I have to acknowledge and thank you for your obliging and friendly letter of the 20th Ulto. It came to this place in my absence from the Army and during my necessary detention at West point on a very interesting but disgraceful incident in our Military occurrences.

Altho I have but little leizure for the gratification of private corrispondencies, I beg you to be assured, that from a warmth of friendship, any letters of yours will be gratefully accepted. and it is with much pleasure I receive fresh assurances of your regard and attachment to me.

We are now drawing an inactive Campaign to a close. The beginning of which appeared pregnant with events, of a favourable complexn, I hoped, but hoped in vain, that a prospect was displaying which wd. enable me to fix a period to my military pursuits, and restore me to domestic life. The favourable disposition of Spain; the promised succour from France; the combined force in the West Indies; The declaration of Russia (acceded to by other powers of Europe, humiliating to the Naval pride and power of Great Britain); the Superiority of France and Spain by Sea in Europe; The Irish claims and English disturbances, formed in the agregate, an opinion in my breast (which is not very susceptable of peaceful dreams) that the hour of deliverance was not far distant; for that however unwilling Great B: might be to yield the point, it would not be in her power to continue the contest. but alas! these prospects, flattering as they were, have prov'd delusory, and I see nothing before us but accumulating distress. We have been half of our time without provision and are like to continue so. We have no Magazines, nor money to form them, and in a little time we shall have no Men, if we had money to pay them. We have lived upon expedients till we can live no longer. In a word, the history of the War is a history of false hopes and temporary devices, instead of system and œconomy. It is in vain however to look back, nor is it our business to do so. Our case is not desperate, if virtue exists in the people and there is wisdom among our rulers; but to suppose that this great revolution can be accomplished by a temporary army; that this Army will be subsisted by State supplies, and that taxation alone is adequate to our wants, is, in my Opinion absurd and as unreasonable as to expect an Inversion in the order of nature to accommodate itself to our views. If it was necessary, it could easily be proved to any person of a moderate share of understanding, that an annual Army, or any Army raised on the spur of the occasion, besides being unqualified for the end designed, is, in various ways which could be enumerated, ten times more expensive than a permanent body of Men, under good organization and military discipline, which never was, nor never will be the case of New Troops. A thousand arguments, resulting from experience and the nature of things, might also be adduced to prove, that the Army, if it is to depend upon State supplies, must disband or starve; and that taxation alone (especially at this late hour) cannot furnish the mean to carry on the War. Is it not time then to retract from error, and benefit by experience? or do we want further proof of the ruinous system we have pertinaciously adhered to?

You seem to regret not having accepted the appointment of Congress to a command in the American Army. It is a circumstance that ever was, most sincerely, regretted by me, and it is the more to be lamented as we find an Officer high in rank, and Military reputation capable of turning apostate, and attempting to sell his Country. Men of independent spirit and firmness of mind, must step forth to rescue our affairs from the embarrassments they have fallen into, or they will suffer in the general Wreck. I do not mean to apply this more to the Military than civil line. We want the best, and ablest men in both.

To tell you, if any event shd. ever bring you to the army, and you have no *commd*. in it equal to your merit; nor *place* more agreeable to your wishes than being a member of my family, that I should be happy in seeing you there, would only be announcing a truth which has often been repeated and wch. I hope you are convinced of.

My best respects attend Mrs. Cadwalader, and compliments of congratulation to both of you on the increase of your family. With sentiments of the most sincere regard etc.

"ARNOLDS VILLAINOUS PERFIDY"

To John Laurens

Hd. Qrs., Passaic Falls, October 13, 1780.
My dear Laurens: Your friendly and Affectione. letter of the 4th. came to my hands on the 10th. and would have been acknowledged yesterday by the Baron de Steuben but for some important business I was preparing for Congress.

In no instance since the commencement of the War has the interposition of Providence appeared more conspicuous than in the rescue of the Post and Garrison of West point from Arnolds villainous perfidy. How far he meant to involve me in the catastrophe of this place does not appear by any indubitable evidence, and I am rather inclined to think he did not wish to hazard the more important object of his treachery by attempting to combine two events the lesser of which might have marred the greater. A combination of extraordinary circumstances. An unaccountable deprivation of presence of Mind in a man of the first abilities, and the virtuous conduct of three Militia men, threw the Adjutant General of the British forces in America (with full proofs of Arnolds treachery) into our hands; and but for the egregious folly, or the bewildered conception of Lieutt. Colo. Jameson who seemed lost in astonishment and not to have known what he was doing I should as certainly have got Arnold. André has met his fate, and with that fortitude which was to be expected from an accomplished man, and gallant Officer. But I am mistaken if at *this time,* Arnold is undergoing the torments of a mental Hell. He wants feeling! From some traits of his character which have lately come to my knowledge, he seems to have been so hackneyed in villainy, and so lost to all sense of honor and shame that while his faculties will enable him to continue his sordid pursuits there will be no time for remorse.

Believe me sincere when I assure you, that my warmest wishes accompany Captn. Wallops endeavours and your expectations of exchange; and that nothing but the principle of Justice and policy wch. I have religiously adhered to of exchanging Officers in the order of their Captivity (where rank would apply) has prevented my every exertion to obtain your release and restoration to a family where you will be receiv'd with open arms by every individual of it; but from none with more cordiality and true affection than Your Sincere friend etc.

P. S. The Baron not setting out as I expected becomes the bearer of this letter.

MUTINY IN THE PENNSYLVANIA LINE

Circular to
New England State Governments

Head Quarters, New Windsor, January 5, 1781.
Sir: It is with extreme anxiety, and pain of mind, I find myself constrained to inform Your Excellency that the event I have long apprehended would be the consequence of the complicated distresses of the Army, has at length taken place. On the night of the 1st instant a mutiny was excited by the Non Commissioned Officers and Privates of the Pennsylvania Line, which soon became so universal as to defy all opposition; in attempting to quell this tumult, in the first instance, some Officers were killed, others wounded, and the lives of several common Soldiers lost. Deaf to the arguments, entreaties, and utmost efforts of *all their Officers* to stop them, the Men moved off from Morris Town, the place of their Cantonment, with their Arms, and six pieces of Artillery: and from Accounts just received by Genl. Wayne's Aid De Camp, they were still in a body, on their March to Philadelphia, to demand a redress of their grievances. At what point this defection will stop, or how extensive it may prove God only knows; at present the Troops at the important Posts in this vicinity remain quiet, not being acquainted with this unhappy and alarming affair; but how

long they will continue so cannot be ascertained, as they labor under some of the pressing hardships, with the Troops who have revolted.

The aggravated calamities and distresses that have resulted, from the total want of pay for nearly twelve Months, for want of cloathing, at a severe season, and not unfrequently the want of provisions; are beyond description. The circumstances will now point out much more forcibly what ought to be done, than any thing that can possibly be said by me, on the subject.

It is not within the sphere of my duty to make requisitions, without the Authority of Congress, from individual States: but at such a crisis, and circumstanced as we are, my own heart will acquit me; and Congress, and the States (eastward of this) whom for the sake of dispatch, I address, I am persuaded will excuse me, when once for all I give it decidedly as my opinion, that it is in vain to think an Army can be kept together much longer, under such a variety of sufferings as ours has experienced: and that unless some immediate and spirited measures are adopted to furnish at least three Months pay to the Troops, in Money that will be of some value to them; And at the same time ways and means are devised to cloath and feed them better (more regularly I mean) than they have been, the worst that can befall us may be expected.

I have transmitted Congress a Copy of this Letter, and have in the most pressing manner requested them to adopt the measure which I have above recommended, or something similar to it, and as I will not doubt of their compliance, I have thought proper to give you this previous notice, that you may be prepared to answer the requisition.

As I have used every endeavour in my power to avert the evil that has come upon us, so will I continue to exert every means I am possessed of to prevent an extension of the Mischief, but I can neither foretell, or be answerable for the issue.

That you may have every information that an officer of rank and abilities can give of the true situation of our affairs, and the condition and temper of the Troops I have prevailed upon Brigadier Genl Knox to be the bearer of this Letter, to him I beg leave to refer your Excellency for many Matters which would be too tedious for a Letter. I have the honor etc.

"UNCONDITIONAL SUBMISSION"

To Robert Howe

West Point, January 22, 1781.

Sir: You are to take the command of the detachment, which has been ordered to march from this post against the mutineers of the Jersey line. You will rendezvous the whole of your command at Ringwood or Pompton as you find best from circumstances. The object of your detachment is to compel the mutineers to unconditional submission, and I am to desire you will grant no terms while they are with arms in their hands in a state of resistance. The manner of executing this I leave to your discretion according to circumstances. If you succeed in compelling the revolted troops to a surrender you will instantly execute a few of the most active and most incendiary leaders.

You will endeavour to collect such of the Jersey troops to your standard as have not followed the pernicious example of their associates, and you will also try to avail yourself of the services of the Militia, representing to them how dangerous to civil liberty the precedent is of armed soldiers dictating terms to their country.

You will open a correspondence with Colonels Dayton and Shreve of the Jersey line and Col Freelinghuosen of the Militia or any others.

"IT IS OUR DUTY TO BEAR PRESENT
EVILS WITH FORTITUDE"

General Orders

Head Quarters, New Windsor,
Tuesday, January 30, 1781.

Parole ——. Countersigns ——.

The General returns his thanks to Major General Howe for the judicious measures he pursued and to the officers and men under his command for the good conduct and alacrity with which they executed his orders for suppressing the late Mutiny in a part of the New Jersey line. It gave him inexpressible pain to have been obliged to employ their arms upon such an occasion and convinced that they themselves felt all the Reluctance which former Affection to fellow Soldiers could inspire. He considers the patience with which they endured the fatigues of the march through rough and mountainous roads rendered almost impassable by the depth of the Snow and the cheerfulness with which they performed every other part of their duty as the strongest proof of their Fidelity, attachment to the service, sense of subordination and abhorrence of the principles which actuated the Mutineers in so daring and atrocious a departure from what they owed to their Country, to their Officers to their Oaths and to themselves.

The General is deeply sensible of the sufferings of the army. He leaves no expedient unessayed to relieve them, and he is persuaded Congress and the several States are doing every thing in their power for the same purpose. But while we look to the public for the fullfilment of its engagements we should do it with proper allowance for the embarrassments of public affairs. We began a Contest for Liberty and Independence ill provided with the means for war, relying on our own Patriotism to supply the deficiency. We expected to encounter many wants and distresses and We should neither shrink from them when they happen nor fly in the face of Law and Government to procure redress. There is no doubt the public will in the event do ample justice to men fighting and suffering in its defence. But it is our duty to bear present Evils with Fortitude looking forward to the period when our Country will have it more in its power to reward our services.

History is full of Examples of armies suffering with patience extremities of distress which exceed those we have suffered, and this in the cause of ambition and conquest not in that of the rights of humanity of their country, of their families of themselves; shall we who aspire to the distinction of a patriot army, who are contending for every thing precious in society against every thing hateful and degrading in slavery, shall We who call ourselves citizens discover less Constancy and Military virtue than the mercenary instruments of ambition? Those who in the

present instance have stained the honor of the American soldiery and sullied the reputation of patient Virtue for which they
have been so long eminent can only atone for their pusillani-
mous defection by a life devoted to a Zealous and examplary
discharge of their duty. Persuaded that the greater part were
influenced by the pernicious advice of a few who probably have
been paid by the enemy to betray their Associates; The General
is happy in the lenity shewn in the execution of only two of the
most guilty after compelling the whole to an unconditional
surrender, and he flatters himself no similar instance will hereafter disgrace our military History. It can only bring ruin on
those who are mad enough to make the attempt; for lenity on
any future occasion would be criminal and inadmissible.

The General at the same time presents his thanks to Major
General Parsons for the prudent and Military dispositions he
made and to Lieutenant Colonel Hull and the officers and
Men under his command for the good conduct address and
Courage with which they executed the enterprize against a
Corps of the enemy in West Chester, having destroyed their
Barracks and a large quantity of Forage, burnt a bridge across
Haerlem, under the protection of one of their redoubts,
brought off fifty two prisoners and a number of Horses and
Cattle with inconsiderable Loss except in the death of Ensign
Thompson of the 6th. Massachusett's regiment an active and
enterprizing officer.

The General also thanks Colonel Hazen and his party for
their Conduct and bravery in covering Lieutenant Colonel
Hull's retreat and repelling the Enemy and Colonels Scammell
and Sherman and in general all the Officers and men of General
Parsons's command for their good Conduct in supporting the
advanced Corps.

"IT WOULD HAVE BEEN A LESS PAINFUL CIRCUMSTANCE TO ME, TO HAVE HEARD . . . THEY HAD BURNT MY HOUSE"

To Lund Washington

New Windsor, April 30, 1781.

Dear Lund: Your letter of the 18th. came to me by the last Post. I am very sorry to hear of your loss; I am a little sorry to hear of my own; but that which gives me most concern, is, that you should go on board the enemys Vessels, and furnish them with refreshments. It would have been a less painful circumstance to me, to have heard, that in consequence of your non-compliance with their request, they had burnt my House, and laid the Plantation in ruins. You ought to have considered yourself as my representative, and should have reflected on the bad example of communicating with the enemy, and making a voluntary offer of refreshments to them with a view to prevent a conflagration.

It was not in your power, I acknowledge, to prevent them from sending a flag on shore, and you did right to meet it; but you should, in the same instant that the business of it was unfolded, have declared, explicitly, that it was improper for you to yield to the request; after which, if they had proceeded to help themselves, *by force*, you could but have submitted (and being unprovided for defence) this was to be prefered to a feeble opposition which only serves as a pretext to burn and destroy.

I am thoroughly perswaded that you acted from your best judgment; and believe, that your desire to preserve my property, and rescue the buildings from impending danger, were your governing motives. But to go on board their Vessels; carry them refreshments; commune with a parcel of plundering Scoundrels, and request a favor by asking the surrender of my Negroes, was exceedingly ill-judged, and 'tis to be feared, will be unhappy in its consequences, as it will be a precedent for others, and may become a subject of animadversion.

I have no doubt of the enemys intention to prosecute the plundering plan they have begun. And, unless a stop can be put to it by the arrival of a superior naval force, I have as little doubt of its ending in the loss of all my Negroes, and in the destruction of my Houses; but I am prepared for the event, under the prospect of which, if you could deposit, in safety, at some convenient distance from the Water, the most valuable and least bulky articles, it might be consistent with policy and prudence, and a mean of preserving them for use hereafter. such, and so many things as are necessary for common, and present use must be retained and run their chance through the firy trial of this summer.

Mrs. Washington joins me in best and affectionate regard for you, Mrs. Washington and Milly Posey; and does most sincerely regret your loss. I do not know what Negros they may have left you; and as I have observed before, I do not know what number they will have left me by the time they have done; but this I am sure of, that you shall never want assistance, while it is in my power to afford it. I am etc.

A DECISIVE VICTORY IN VIRGINIA

Journal of the Yorktown Campaign

*   *   *   *

14th. Received dispatches from the Count de Barras announcing the intended departure of the Count de Grasse from Cape Francois with between 25 & 29 Sail of the line & 3200 land Troops on the 3d. Instant for Chesapeake bay and the anxiety of the latter to have every thing in the most perfect readiness to commence our operations in the moment of his arrival as he should be under a necessity from particular engagements with the Spaniards to be in the West Indies by the Middle of October—At the same time intimating his (Barras's) Intentions of enterprizing something against Newfoundland, & against which both Genl. Rochambeau and myself remonstrated as impolitic & dangerous under the probability of Rodneys coming upon this Coast.

Matters having now come to a crisis and a decisive plan to be determined on—I was obliged, from the Shortness of Count de Grasses premised stay on this Coast—the apparent disinclination in their Naval Officers to force the harbour of New York and the feeble compliance of the States to my requisitions for Men, hitherto, & little prospect of greater exertion in future, to give up all idea of attacking New York; & instead thereof to remove the French Troops & a detachment from the American Army to the Head of Elk to be transported to Virginia for the purpose of cooperating with the force from the West Indies against the Troops in that State.

15. Dispatched a Courier to the Marquis de la Fayette with information of this matter—requesting him to be in perfect readiness to second my views & to prevent if possible the retreat of Cornwallis toward Carolina. He was also directed to Halt the Troops under the Command of General Wayne if they had not made any great progress in their March to join the Southern Army.

16th. Letters from the Marqs. de la Fayette & others, inform that Lord Cornwallis with the Troops from Hampton Road, had proceeded up York River & landed at York & Gloucester Towns where they were throwing up Works on the 6th. Inst.

19th. The want of Horses, or bad condition of them in the French army delayed the March till this day. The same causes, it is to be feared, will occasion a slow and disagreeable March to Elk if fresh horses cannot be procured & better management of them adopted.

The detachment from the American is composed of the light Infantry under Scammell—two light companies of York to be joined by the like Number from the Connecticut line—the remainder of the Jersey line—two Regiments of York—Hazens Regiment & the Regiment of Rhode Island—together with Lambs regiment of Artillery with Cannon and other Ordnance for the field & Siege.

Hazens regiment being thrown over at Dobbs's ferry was ordered with the Jersey Troops to March & take Post on the heights between Spring field & Chatham & Cover a french Battery at the latter place to veil our real movement & create apprehensions for Staten Island. The Quarter Master Genl. was dispatched to Kings ferry—the only secure passage—to prepare for the speedy transportation of the Troops across the River.

Passed Singsing with the American column. The French column marched by the way of Northcastle, Crompond & Pinesbridge being near ten miles further.

20th. The head of the Americans arrived at Kings ferry about ten O'clock & immediately began to cross.

21st. In the course of this day the whole of the American Troop, all their baggage, artillery & Stores, crossed the river. Nothing remained of ours but some Waggons in the Commissary's & Qr. Mr. Generals departmt., which were delayed, that no interruption might be given to the passage of the French Army.

During the passing of the French Army I mounted 30 flat Boats (able to carry about 40 Men each) upon carriages—as well with a design to deceive the enemy as to our real movement, as to be useful to me in Virginia when I get there.

Some of the french Artillery wch. preceeded their Infantry got to the ferry & crossed it also.

22d. 23d. 24th. & 25th. Employed in transporting the French Army, its baggage & Stores over the river.

The 25th. the American Troops marched in two Columns— Genl. Lincoln with the light Infantry & first York Regiment pursuing the rout by Peramus to Springfield—while Colo. Lamb with his Regiment of Artillery—the Parke—Stores and Baggage of the Army covered by the Rhode Island Regt. proceeded to Chatham by the way of Pompton & the two bridges.

The Legion of Lauzen & the Regiments of Bourbonne & Duponts with the heavy Parke of the French Army also Marched for percipony by Suffrans Pompton &   .

The 26th. the remainder of the French army, its baggage & Stores, moved from the ferry and arrived at Suffrans—the ground the others had left.

28th. The American columns and 1st. division of the French Army arrived at the places assigned them.

29th. The Second division of French joined the first. The whole halted—as well for the purpose of bringing up our rear—as because we had heard not of the arrival of Count de Grasse & was unwilling to discover our real object to the enemy.

30th. As our intentions could be concealed one March more (under the idea of Marching to Sandy hook to facilitate the entrance of the French fleet within the Bay), the whole Army was put in motion in three columns—the left consisted of the light Infantry, first York Regiment, and the Regiment of Rhode Island—the Middle column consisted of the Parke Stores & Baggage—Lambs Regt. of Artillery—Hazens & the Corps of Sappers & Miners—the right column consisted of the whole French army, Baggage Stores &ca. This last was to march by the rout of Morristown—Bullions Tavern—Somerset Ct House & Princeton. The middl. was to go by Bound brooke to Somerset &ca. and the left to proceed by the way of Brunswick to Trenton, to which place the whole were to March Transports being ordered to meet them there.
    I set out myself for Philadelphia to arrange matters there—provide Vessels & hasten the transportation of the Ordnance Stores, &ca.—directing before I set out, the secd. York Regiment (which had not all arrived from Albany before we left Kings ferry) to follow with the Boats—Intrenching Tools &ca. the French Rear to Trenton.

31st. Arrived at Philadelphia to dinner and immediately hastened up all the Vessels that could be procured—but finding them inadequate to the purpose of transporting both Troops & Stores, Count de Rochambeau & myself concluded it would be best to let the Troops March by land to the head of Elk, & gave directions accordingly to all but the 2d. York Regiment which was ordered (with its baggage) to come down in the Batteaux they had in charge to Christiana bridge.

5th. The rear of the French army having reached Philadelphia and the Americans having passed it—the Stores having got up

& every thing in a tolerable train here; I left this City for the head of Elk to hasten the Embarkation at that place and on my way—(at Chester)—received the agreeable news of the safe arrival of the Count de Grasse in the Bay of Chesapeake with 28 Sail of the line & four frigates—with 3000 land Troops which were to be immediately debarked at James town & form a junction with the American Army under the command of the Marqs. de la Fayette.

Finding upon my arrival at the head of Elk a great deficiency of Transports, I wrote many letters to Gentn. of Influence on the Eastern shore, beseeching them to exert themselves in drawing forth every kind of Vessel which would answer for this purpose and agreed with the Count de Rochambeau that about 1000 American Troops (including the Artillery Regiment) and the Grenadiers & Chasseurs of the Brigade of Bourbonne with the Infantry of Lauzen's legion should be the first to Embark and that the rest of the Troops should continue their march to Baltimore proceeding thence by Land, or Water according to circumstances. The Cavalry of Lauzen, with the Saddle horses & such teams of both armies as the Qr. Masters thereof might judge necessary to go round by Land to the place of operation.

Judging it highly expedient to be with the army in Virginia as soon as possible, to make the necessary arrangements for the Siege, & to get the Materials prepared for it, I determined to set out for the Camp of the Marqs. de la Fayette without loss of time and accordingly in Company with the Count de Rochambeau who requested to attend me, and the Chevr. de Chastellux set out on the

8th. and reached Baltimore where I recd. and answered an address of the Citizens.

9th. I reached my own Seat at Mount Vernon (distant 120 Miles from the Hd. of Elk) where I staid till the 12th. and in three days afterwards that is on the 14th. reached Williamsburg. The necessity of seeing, & agreeing upon a proper plan of cooperation with the Count de Grasse induced me to make him a visit at Cape Henry where he lay with his fleet after a partial engagement with the British Squadron off the Capes under the Command of Admiral Graves whom he had driven back to Sandy hook.

17th. In company with the Count de Rochambeau—the Chevr. Chastellux—Genls. Knox & Duportail, I set out for the Interview with the Admiral & arrived on board the Ville de Paris (off Cape Henry) the next day by Noon and having settled most points with him to my satisfaction except not obtaining an assurance of sending Ships above York and one that he could not continue his fleet on this Station longer than the first of November I embarked on board the Queen Charlotte (the Vessell I went down in) but by hard blowing; & contrary Winds, did not reach Williamsburg again till the 22d.

22d. Upon my arrival in Camp I found that the 3d. Maryland Regiment had got in (under the Command of Colo. Adam) and that all except a few missing Vessels with the Troops from the head of Elk were arrived, & landing at the upper point of the College Creek—where Genl. Choisy with 600 Fr. Troops who had from R. Isld. had arrived in the Squadron of Count de Barras

had done before them during my absence.

25th. Admiral de Barras having Joined the Count de Grasse with the Squadron and Transports from Rhode Island, & the latter with some Frigates being sent to Baltimore for the remr. of the French army arrived this day at the usual port of debarkation above the College Creek and began to land the Troops from them.

28th. Having debarked all the Troops and their Baggage— Marched and Encamped them in Front of the City and having with some difficulty obtained horses & Waggons sufficient to move our field Artillery—Intrenching Tools & such other articles as were indispensably necessary—we commenced our March for the Investiture of the Enemy at York.

The American Continental, and French Troops formed one column on the left—the first in advance—the Militia composed the right column & marched by the way of Harwoods Mill.

Half a mile beyond the halfway Ho the French & Americans seperated. The former continued on the direct road to York, by the Brick House. The latter filed of to the right for Murfords bridge, where a junction with the Militia was to be made. About Noon the head of each column arrived at its ground, & some of the enemys Picquets were driven in on the left by a Corps of French Troops, advanced for the purpose, which afforded an oppertunity of reconnoitering them on their right. The enemy's Horse on the right were also obliged to retire from the ground they had Encamped on, & from whence they were employed in reconnoitering the right column.

The line being formed, all the Troops—Officers & Men— lay upon their arms during the Night.

29th. Moved the American Troops more to the right, and Encamped on the East side of Bever dam Creek, with a Morass in front, about Cannon shot from the enemys lines. Spent this day in reconnoitering the enemys position, & determining upon a plan of attack & approach which must be done without the assistance of Shipping above the Town as the Admiral (notwithstanding my earnest sollicitation) declined hazarding any Vessells on that Station.

30th. The Enemy abandoned all their exterior works, & the position they had taken without the Town; & retired within their Interior works of defence in the course of last Night— immediately upon which we possessed them, & made those on our left (with a little alteration) very serviceable to us. We also began two inclosed Works on the right of Pidgeon Hill— between that & the ravine above Mores Mill.

From this time till the 6th. of October nothing occurred of Importance—much deligence was used in debarking, & transporting the Stores—Cannon &ca. from Trebells Landing (distant 6 Miles) on James Riv., to Camp; which for want of Teams went on heavily and in preparing Fascines, Gabions, &ca. for the Siege—as also in reconnoitering the Enemys defences, & their situation as perfectly as possible, to form our parallels & mode of attack.

The Teams which were sent round from the head of Elk, having arrived about this time, we were enabled to bring forward our heavy Artillery & Stores with more convenience and dispatch and every thing being prepared for opening Trenches 1500 Fatiegue men & 2800 to cover them, were ordered for this Service.

6th. Before Morning the Trenches were in such forwardness as to cover the Men from the enemys fire. The work was executed with so much secresy & dispatch that the enemy were, I believe, totally ignorant of our labor till the light of the Morning discovered it to them. Our loss on this occasion was extremely inconsiderable, not more than one Officer (french) & about 20 Men killed & Wounded—the Officer & 15 of which were on our left from the Corps of the Marqs. de St. Simond, who was betrayed by a deserter from the Huzzars that went in & gave notice of his approaching his parrallel.

7th. & 8th. Was employed in compleating our Parallel—finishing the redoubts in them and establishing Batteries.

9th. About 3 o'clock P.M. the French opened a battery on our extreme left, of 4 Sixteen pounders, and Six Morters & Hawitzers and at 5 oclock an American battery of Six 18s & 24s; four Morters & 2 Hawitzers, began to play from the extremity of our right—both with good effect as they compelled the Enemy to withdraw from their ambrazures the Pieces which had previously kept up a constant firing.

10th. The French opened two batteries on the left of our front parallel—one of 6 twenty four pounders, & 2 Sixteens with 6 Morters & Hawitzers—the other of 4 Sixteen pounders and the Americans two Batteries between those last mentioned & the one on our extreme right the left of which containing 4 Eighteen pounders—the other two Mortars.

The whole of the batteries kept an incessant fire—the Cannon at the Ambrazures of the enemy, with a view to destroy them—the Shells into the Enemy's Works, where by the information of deserters they did much execution.

The French battery on the left, by red hot shot, set fire to (in the course of the Night) the Charon frigate & 3 large Transports which were entirely consumed.

11th. The French opened two other batteries on the left of the parallel, each consisting of 3 Twenty four pounders. These were also employed in demolishing the Ambrazures of the enemys Works & advancd Redoubts.

Two Gentlemen—a Major Granchien & Captn. D'Avilion being sent by Admiral de Grasse to reconnoiter the Enemys Water defences, & state of the River at and near York, seemed favourably disposed to adopt the measure which had been strongly urged of bringing Ships above the Town & made representations accordingly to the Count de Grasse.

12th. Began our second parallel within abt. 300 yards (& in some places less) of the enemys lines and got it so well advanced in the course of the Night as to cover the Men before morning. This business was conducted with the same secresy as the former & undertaken so much sooner than the enemy expected (we should commence a second parallel) that they did not by their conduct, & mode of firing, appear to have had any suspicion of our Working parties till day light discovered them to their Picquets; nor did they much annoy the Trenches in the course of this day (the Parallel being opened last Night from the ravene in front, and on the right flank of the Enemy till it came near to the intersection of the line of fire from the American 4 Gun Battery to the enemy's advanced redoubts on their left. The french Batteries fired over the second parallel.

13th. The fire of the enemy this Night became brisk—both from their Cannon and royals and more injurious to us than it had been; several Men being killed, and many wounded in the Trenches, but the works were not in the smallest degree retarded by it. Our Batteries were begun in the course of the Night and a good deal advanced.

14th. The day was spent in compleating our parallel, and maturing the Batteries of the second parallel. The old batteries were principally directed against the abattis & salient angles of the enemys advanced redoubts on their extreme right & left to prepare them for the intended assault for which the necessary dispositions were made for attacking the two on the left and,

At half after Six in the Evening both were carried—that on their left (on the Bank of the river) by the Americans and the other by the French Troops. The Baron Viominel commanded the left attack & the Marqs. de la fayette the right on which the light Infantry were employed.

In the left redoubt (assaulted by the Americans) there were abt. 45 men under the command of a Major Campbell; of which the Major a Captn. & Ensign, with 17 Men were made Prisoners—But few were killed on the part of the Enemy & the remainder of the Garrison escaped. The right Redoubt attacked by the French, consisted of abt. 120 Men, commanded by a Lieutenant Colo.—of these 18 were killed, & 42 taken Prisoners—among the Prisoners were a Captain and two Lieutenants. The bravery exhibited by the attacking Troops was emulous and praiseworthy—few cases have exhibited stronger proofs of Intripidity coolness and firmness than were shown upon this occasion. The following is our loss in these attacks and since the Investiture of York.

American

Periods	Killed								Wounded								Total
	Colo.	Lt. Colo.	Maj.	Captn.	C. Lieu	Lieut.	Sergt.	R & F	Colo.	Lt. Colo.	Majr.	Captn.	C. Lt.	Lieut.	Sergt.	R & F	
From the Investe. to openg. 1st. parall.	1						1	4								8	14
To the opening of the 2d. parl.								2								6	8
To the Storm on the 14th.			1					6			1					14	22
At the Storm								8	2	1	2	1	1	1		28	44
Total	1		1				1	20	2	1	3	1	1	1		56	88

The loss of the French from the Investiture to the Assault of the Redoubts Inclusive, is as follow—viz.—

```
Officers—killed  . . . . . . . . . . .    2
            Wounded  . . . . . . . . . .    7  . . .
                                                        9
Soldiers . . . Killed . . . . . . . . . .   50
            Wounded . . . . . . . .   127
                                                      177
            Total . . . . . . . . . . . . . . .   186
```

15th. Busily employed in getting the Batteries of the Second parallel compleated, and fixing on New ones contiguous to the Redoubts which were taken last Night. Placed two Hawitzers in each of the Captured Redoubts wch. were opened upon the enemy about 5 oclock in the Afternoon.

16th. About four O'clock this Morning the enemy made a Sortee upon our Second parallel and spiked four French pieces of Artillery & two of ours—but the guards of the Trenches advancing quickly upon them they retreated precipitately. The Sally being made upon that part of the parallel which was guarded by the French Troops they lost an officer & 12 Men killed and 1 Officer taken prisoner. The American loss was one Sergeant of Artillery (in the American battery) Wounded. The Enemy, it is said, left 10 dead and lost 3 Prisoners.

About 4 Oclock this afternoon the French opened two Batteries of 2. 24s. & four 16s. each. 3 pieces from the American grand battery were also opened—the others not being ready.

17th. The French opened another Battery of four 24s. & two 16s. and a Morter Battery of 10 Morters and two Hawitzers. The American grand Battery consisting of 12 twenty fours and Eighteen prs.—4 Morters and two Hawitzers.

About ten Oclock the Enemy beat a parley and Lord Cornwallis proposed a cessation of Hostilities for 24 hours, that Commissioners might meet at the house of a Mr. Moore (in the rear of our first parallel) to settle terms for the surrender of the Posts of York and Gloucester. To this he was answered, that a desire to spare the further effusion of Blood would readily incline me to treat of the surrender of the above Posts but previous to the meeting of Commissioners I wished to have his proposals in writing and for this purpose would grant a cessation of hostilities two hours—Within which time he sent out A letter with such proposals (tho' some of them were inadmissable) as led me to believe that there would be no great difficulty in fixing the terms. Accordingly hostilities were suspended for the Night & I proposed my own terms to which if he agreed Commissioners were to meet to digest them into form.

18th. The Commissioners met accordingly; but the business was so procrastinated by those on their side (a Colo. Dundas & a Majr. Ross) that Colo. Laurens & the Viscount De Noailles who were appointed on our part could do no more than make the rough draft of the Articles which were to be submitted for Lord Cornwallis's consideration.

19th. In the Morning early I had them copied and sent word to Lord Cornwallis that I expected to have them signed at 11 Oclock and that the Garrison would March out at two O'clock—both of which were accordingly done. Two redoubts on the Enemys left being possessed (the one by a detachment of French Grenadiers, & the other by American Infantry) with orders to prevent all intercourse between the army & Country and the Town—while Officers in the several departments were employed in taking acct. of the public Stores &ca.

RESISTING A CROWN

To Lewis Nicola

Newburgh, May 22, 1782.
Sir: With a mixture of great surprise and astonishment I have read with attention the Sentiments you have submitted to my perusal. Be assured Sir, no occurrence in the course of the War, has given me more painful sensations than your information of there being such ideas existing in the Army as you have expressed, and I must view with abhorrence, and reprehend with

severety. For the present, the communicatn. of them will rest in my own bosom, unless some further agitation of the matter, shall make a disclosure necessary.

I am much at a loss to conceive what part of my conduct could have given encouragement to an address which to me seems big with the greatest mischiefs that can befall my Country. If I am not deceived in the knowledge of myself, you could not have found a person to whom your schemes are more disagreeable; at the same time in justice to my own feelings I must add, that no Man possesses a more sincere wish to see ample justice done to the Army than I do, and as far as my powers and influence, in a constitutional way extend, they shall be employed to the utmost of my abilities to effect it, should there be any occasion. Let me conjure you then, if you have any regard for your Country, concern for yourself or posterity, or respect for me, to banish these thoughts from your Mind, and never communicate, as from yourself, or any one else, a sentiment of the like Nature. With esteem I am.

"IT IS HIGH TIME FOR A PEACE"

To Benjamin Lincoln

Head Quarters, October 2, 1782.

My dear Sir: Painful as the task is to describe the dark side of our affairs, it some times becomes a matter of indispensable necessity. Without disguize or palliation, I will inform you candidly of the discontents which, at this moment, prevail universally throughout the Army.

The Complaint of Evils which they suppose almost remediless are, the total want of Money, or the means of existing from One day to another, the heavy debts they have already incurred, the loss of Credit, the distress of their Families (i e such as are Maried) at home, and the prospect of Poverty and Misery before them. It is vain Sir, to suppose that Military Men will acquiesce *contently* with bare rations, when those in the Civil walk of life (unacquainted with half the hardships they endure) are regularly paid the emoluments of Office; while the human Mind is influencd by the same passions, and have the same inclinations to endulge it cannt. be. A Military Man has the same turn to sociability as a person in Civil life; he conceives himself equally called upon to live up to his rank; and his pride is hurt when circumstans. restrain him. Only conceive then, the mortification they (even the Genl. Officers) must suffer when they cannot invite a French Officer, a visiting friend, or travelling acquaintance to a better repast than stinking Whiskey (and not always that) and a bit of Beef without Vegitables, will afford them.

The Officers also complain of other hardships which they think might and ought to be remedied without delay, viz, the stopping Promotions where there have been vacancy's open for a long time, the withholding Commissions from those who are justly entitled to them and have Warrants or Certificates of their Appointments from the Executive of their States, and particularly the leaving the compensation for their services, in a loose equivocal state, without ascertaining their claims upon the public, or making provision for the future payment of them.

While I premise, that tho' no one that I have seen or heard of, appears opposed to the principle of reducing the Army as circumstances may require; Yet I cannot help fearing the Result of the measure in contemplation, under present circumstances when I see such a Number of Men goaded by a thousand stings of reflexion on the past, and of anticipation on the future, about to be turned into the World, soured by penury and what they call the ingratitude of the Public, involved in debts, without one farthing of Money to carry them home, after having spent the flower of their days and many of them their patrimonies in establishing the freedom and Independence of their Country, and suffered every thing human Nature is capable of enduring on this side of death; I repeat it, these irritable circumstances, without one thing to sooth their feelings, or frighten the gloomy prospects, I cannot avoid apprehending that a train of Evils will follow, of a very serious and distressing Nature. On the other hand could the Officers be placed in as good a situation as when they came into service, the contention, I am persuaded, would be not who should continue in the field, but who should retire to private life.

I wish not to heighten the shades of the picture, so far as the real life would justify me in doing, or I would give Anecdotes of patriotism and distress which have scarcely ever been paralleled, never surpassed in the history of Mankind; but you may rely upon it, the patience and long sufferance of this Army are almost exhausted, and that there never was so great a spirit of Discontent as at this instant: While in the field, I think it may be kept from breaking out into Acts of Outrage, but when we retire into Winter Quarters (unless the Storm is previously dissipated) I cannot be at ease, respecting the consequences. It is high time for a Peace.

To you, my dear Sir, I need not be more particular in describing my Anxiety and the grounds of it. You are too well acquainted, from your own service, with the real sufferings of the Army to require a longer detail; I will therefore only add that exclusive of the common hardships of a Military life, Our Troops have been, and still are obliged to perform more services, foreign to their proper duty, without gratuity or reward, than the Soldiers of any other Army; for example, the immense labours expended in doing the duties of Artificers in erecting Fortifications and Military Works; the fatigue of building themselves Barracks or Huts annually; And of cutting and transporting Wood for the use of all our Posts and Garrisons, without any expence whatever to the Public.

Of this Letter, (which from the tenor of it must be considered in some degree of a private nature) you may make such use as you shall think proper. Since the principal objects of it were, by displaying the Merits, the hardships, the disposition and critical state of the Army, to give information that might eventually be useful, and to convince you with what entire confidence and esteem. I am etc.

"THE EXPECTATIONS OF AMERICA
WERE MUCH RAISED"

To Benjamin Franklin

Head Quarters, October 18, 1782.
Sir: I have been honored with two Favors of your Excellency; One presented by the Count de Segur, of the 2d. of

April, the other delivered by the Prince de Broglie, of the 8th. both which were rendered doubly agreeable, by the pleasure I had in receiving them from the Hands of two such amiable and accomplished Young Gentlemen.

Independent of my Esteem for your Excellency. Be assured Sir! that my respect and Regard for the french Nation at large, to whom this Country is under so great Obligations, as well as the very favorable Impressions I have conceived for their particular Characters, will secure my warmest attention to the persons of these distinguished young Noblemen.

I am much obliged by the political Information, which you have taken the trouble to convey to me; but feel myself much embarrassed in my Wish to make you a Return in kind. At the first of the Season, the Expectations of America were much raised, in Consequence of the Change of the British Ministry and the Measures of Parliament; but Events have shewn, that their Hopes have risen too high. The Death of the Marquis of Rockingham, the Advancement of the Earl of Shelburne, and the Delays of Negotiation, have given us very different Impressions from those we at first conceived. We now begin again to reflect upon the persevering Obstinacy of the King, the wickedness of his Ministry, and the haughty Pride of the Nation, which Ideas recall to our Minds very disagreeable prospects, and a probable Continuance of our present Trouble.

The military Operations of the Campaign, are drawing to a Close, without any very important Events, on this Side the Water, unless the Evacuation of Charlestown, which is generally expected, but not yet known to me, should take place and form a paragraph in the Page of this Years History.

The British Fleet from the West Indies, still continues in N York. I have not been able yet to decide on the Enemy's Intentions there. It is generally tho't that a detachment of their Troops will sail with them when the fleet returns to the West Indies, where it is conjectured their Efforts for the Winter, will be prosecuted with Vigor. I have the honr etc.

"POSTERITY WILL BESTOW ON THEIR LABORS
THE EPITHET AND MARKS OF FICTION"

To Nathanael Greene

Newburgh, February 6, 1783.

My dear Sir: I have the pleasure to inform you that your Packet for Govr. Greene which came inclosed to me (in your private Letter of the 12th. of December) was forwarded in an hour after it came to my hands by a Gentleman returning to Rhode Island (Welcome Arnold Esquire); there can be no doubt therefore of its having got safe to the Governor.

It is with a pleasure which friendship only is susceptible of, I congratulate you on the glorious end you have put to hostilities in the Southern States; the honor and advantage of it, I hope, and trust, you will live long to enjoy. when this hemisphere will be equally free is yet in the womb of time to discover; a little while, however 'tis presumed, will disclose the determinations of the British Senate with respect to Peace or War as it seems to be agreed on all hands, that the present Premeir (especially if he should find the opposition powerful) intends to submit the decision of these matters to Parliament. The Speech, the Addresses, and Debates for which we are looking in every direction, will give a data from which the bright rays of the one, or the gloomy prospect of the other, may be discovered.

If Historiographers should be hardy enough to fill the page of History with the advantages that have been gained with unequal numbers (on the part of America) in the course of this contest, and attempt to relate the distressing circumstances under which they have been obtained, it is more than probable that Posterity will bestow on their labors the epithet and marks of fiction; for it will not be believed that such a force as Great Britain has employed for eight years in this Country could be baffled in their plan of Subjugating it by numbers infinitely less, composed of Men oftentimes half starved; always in Rags, without pay, and experiencing, at times, every species of distress which human nature is capable of undergoing.

I intended to have wrote you a long letter on sundry matters but Majr. Burnett popped in unexpectedly, at a time when I was preparing for the Celebration of the day; and was just going to a review of the Troops, previous to the Fue de joy. As he is impatient, from an apprehension of the Sleighing failing. and as he can give you the occurrences of this quarter more in detail than I have time to do, I will refer you to him. I cannot omit informing you however, that I let no oppertunity slip to enquire after your Son George at Princeton, and that it is with pleasure I hear he enjoys good health, and is a fine promising boy.

Mrs. Washington joins me in most Affectionate regards, and best wishes for Mrs Greene and yourself. With great truth and sincerity and every sentiment of friendship. I am etc.

CHASTISING A NEGLIGENT MANAGER

To Lund Washington

Newburgh, February 12, 1783.

Dear Lund: Your letter of the 29th. of Jany. came by the last Post. You do not seem to have considered the force and tendency of the words of yr. letter when you talk of the probability *only* of sending me "the long promised account" "the irregularity of them"; not you add "for want of knowledge in keeping them but neglect; your aversion to writing" &ca. &ca. These are but other words for saying, "as I am not fond of writing, and it is *quite* immaterial whether you have any knowledge or information of your private concerns or whether the accts. are kept properly or not, I have delayed, and do not know how much longer I may continue to delay bringing you acquainted with these accts. irregular as they are."

Delicacy hitherto, and a hope that you long ago would have seen into the propriety of the measure, without a hint of it from me, has restrained me from telling you that annual Accts. of my Crops, together with the receipts and expenditure of my money, state of my stocks, &ca. ought to have been sent to me as regularly as the year came about. It is not to be supposed, that all the avocations of my public duties, great and laborious as they have been, could render me totally insensible to the *only means* by which myself and family; and the character I am to maintain in life hereafter, is to be supported, or that a precise acct. of these matters would not have been exceedingly satisfactory to me. Instead of this, except the Acct. rendered at Valley forge in the year 1778 I have received none since I left home; and not till after two or 3 applications in the course of last year could I get any acct. of the Crop of the preceeding one; and then only of the Corn by the Post on Sunday last.

I have often told you, and I repeat it with much truth; that the entire confidence which I placed in your integrity made me easy, and I was always happy at thinking that my Affairs were in your hands, which I could not have been, if they had been under the care of a common Manager; but this did not exempt me from the desires which all men have, of knowing the exact state of them. I have now to beg that you will not only send me the Account of your receipts, and expenditures of Specie; but of every kind of money subsequent to the Acct. exhibited at Valley Forge, which ended sometime in April 1778.

I want to know before I come home (as I shall come home with empty pockets whenever Peace shall take place) how Affairs stand with me, and what my dependence is.

I wish to know also, what I have to expect from the Wheat of 1781 and 82, as you say the two Crops are so blended that they cannot be rendered seperately? How are settlements to be made with and justice done to the several Parties Interested under these circumstances?

"THE PREDICAMENT IN WHICH I STAND AS
CITIZEN & SOLDIER"

To Alexander Hamilton

Newburgh 4th. Mar: 1783

Dear Sir,

I have received your favor of February   & thank you for the information & observations it has conveyed to me. I shall always think myself obliged by a free communication of sentiments,

& have often thought (but suppose I thought wrong as it did not accord with the practice of Congress) that the public interest might be benefitted, if the Commander in Chief of the Army was let more into the political & pecuniary state of our affairs than he is. Enterprises, & the adoption of Military & other arrangements that might be exceedingly proper in some circumstances, would be altogether improper in others. It follows then by fair deduction, that where there is a want of information there must be chance medley; & a man may be upon the brink of a precipice before he is aware of his danger—when a little foreknowledge might enable him to avoid it. But this by the by. The hint contained in your letter, and the knowledge I have derived from the public Gazettes respecting the nonpayment of Taxes contain all the information I have received of the danger that stares us in the face, on acct. of our funds, and so far was I from conceiving that our finances were in so deplorable a state, *at this time*, that I had imbibed ideas from some source or another, that with the prospect of a loan from Holland we should be able to rub along.

To you, who have seen the danger, to which the Army has been exposed, to a political dissolution for want of subsistence, & the unhappy spirit of licentiousness which it imbibed by becoming in one or two instances its own proveditors, no observations are necessary to evince the fatal tendency of such a measure; but I shall give it as my opinion, that it would at this day be productive of Civil commotions & end in blood. Unhappy situation this! God forbid we should be involved in it.

The predicament in which I stand as Citizen & Soldier, is as critical and delicate as can well be conceived. It has been the subject of many contemplative hours. The sufferings of a complaining army on one hand, and the inability of Congress and tardiness of the States on the other, are the forebodings of evil; & may be productive of events which are more to be depricated than prevented; but I am not without hope, if there is such a disposition shewn as prudence & policy dictates, to do justice, your apprehensions, in case of Peace, are greater than there is cause for. In this however I may be mistaken, if those ideas, which you have been informed are propagated in the Army, should be extensive; the source of which may be easily traced; as the old leven, *it is said*, for I have no proof of it, is again beginning to work, under the mask of the most perfect dissimulation & apparent cordiallity.

Be these things as they may, I shall pursue the same steady line of conduct which has governed me hitherto; fully convinced that the sensible, and discerning part of the army, cannot be unacquainted (although I never took pains to inform them) of the services I have rendered it, on more occasions than one. This, and pursuing the suggestions of your letter, which I am happy to find coincides with my own practice for several months past, & which was the means of directing the business of the Army into the Channel it now is, leaves me under no *great* apprehension of its exceeding the bounds of reason & moderation, nothwithstanding the prevailing sentiment in the Army is, that the prospect of compensation for past Services will terminate with the War.

The just claims of the Army ought, and it is to be hoped will, have their weight with every sensible Legislature in the Union, if Congress point to their demands; shew (if the case is so) the reasonableness of them, and the impracticability of complying with them without their aid. In any other point of view it would, in my opinion, be impolitic to introduce the Army on the Tapis; lest it should excite jealousy, and bring on its concomitants. The States cannot, surely, be so devoid of common sense, common honesty, & common policy as to refuse their aid on a full, clear, & candid representation of facts from Congress; more especially if these should be enforced by members of their own body; who might demonstrate what the inevitable consequences of failure must lead to.

In my opinion it is a matter worthy of consideration how far an Adjournment of Congress for a few months is advisable. The Delegates in that case, if they are in unison themselves respecting the great defects of their Constitution may represent them fully & boldly to their Constituents. To me, who know nothing of the business which is before Congress, nor of the arcanum, it appears that such a measure would tend to promote the public weal; for it is clearly my opinion, unless Congress have powers competent to all *general* purposes, that the distresses we have encountered, the expences we have incurred, and the blood we have spilt in the course of an Eight years war, will avail us nothing.

The contents of your letter is known only to myself and your prudence will direct what should be done with this. With great esteem and regard I am Dr Sir Yr. Most Obedt. Servt

"SUCH AN IRREGULAR INVITATION"

General Orders

Head Quarters, Newburgh, Tuesday, March 11, 1783.
Parole Quebec.   Countersigns Richmond, Sunbury.
For the day tomorrow Major Reading.
For duty the 5th. Massachusetts regiment.

The Commander in Chief having heard that a General meeting of the officers of the Army was proposed to be held this day at the Newbuilding in an anominous paper which was circulated yesterday by some unknown person conceives (altho he is fully persuaded that the good sense of the officers would induce them to pay very little attention to such an irregular invitation) his duty as well as the reputation and true interest of the Army requires his disapprobation of such disorderly proceedings, at the same time he requests the General and Field officers with one officer from each company and a proper representative of the staff of the Army will assemble at 12 o'clock on Saturday next at the Newbuilding to hear the report of the Committee of the Army to Congress.

After mature deliberation they will devise what further measures ought to be adopted as most rational and best calculated to attain the just and important object in view. The senior officer in Rank present will be pleased to preside and report the result of the Deliberations to the Commander in Chief.

Congress have been pleased to promote Captain Job Sumner of the 3d Massachusetts regiment to be a Major in the Army and to take rank from the 1st. of October 1782.

To Alexander Hamilton

Newburgh 12th. Mar. 1783.

Dear Sir,

When I wrote to you last we were in a state of tranquility, but after the arrival of a certain Gentleman, who shall be nameless at present, from Philadelphia, a storm very suddenly arose with unfavourable prognostics; which tho' diverted for a moment is not yet blown over, nor is it in my power to point to the issue.

The Papers which I send officially to Congress, will supercede the necessity of my remarking on the tendency of them. The notification and address, both appeared at the same instant, on the day preceding the intended meeting. The first of these I got hold of the same afternoon; the other, not till next morning.

There is something very misterious in this business. It appears, reports have been propagated in Philadelphia, that dangerous combinations were forming in the Army; and this at a time when there was not a syllable of the kind in agitation in Camp. It also appears, that upon the arrival in Camp of the Gentleman above alluded to such sentiments as these were immediately circulated: That it was universally expected the army would not disband untill they had obtained justice; That the public creditors looked up to them for Redress of their own grievances, wd afford them every aid, and even join them in the Field if necessary; That some members of Congress wished the measure might take effect, in order to compel the public, particularly the delinquent States, to do justice; with many other suggestions of a similar nature.

From this, and a variety of other considerations, it is firmly believed, by *some*, the scheme was not only planned but also digested and matured in Philadelphia; but in my opinion shall be suspended till I have a better ground to found one on. The matter was managed with great art; for as soon as the Minds of the Officers were thought to be prepared for the transaction, the anonymous invitations and address to the Officers were put in circulation, through every state line in the army. I was obliged therefore, in order to arrest on the spot, the foot that stood wavering on a tremendous precipice; to prevent the Officers from being taken by surprize while the passions were all inflamed, and to rescue them from plunging themselves into a gulph of Civil horror from which there might be no receding, to issue the order of the 11th. This was done upon the principle that it is easier to divert from a wrong, and point to a right path, than it is to recall the hasty and fatal steps which have been already taken.

It is commonly supposed if the Officers had met agreeably to the anonymous summons, with their feelings all alive, Resolutions might have been formed the consequences of which may be more easily conceived than described. Now they will have leizure to view the matter more calmly, and will act more seriously. It is to be hoped they will be induced to adopt more rational measures, and wait a while longer for a settlement of their accts., the postponing of which, appears to be the most plausible and almost the only article of which designing men can make an improper use, by insinuating (which they really do) that it is done with design that Peace may take place and prevent any adjustment of accts. which say they would inevitably be the case if the war was to cease tomorrow. Or supposing the best, you would have to dance attendance at public Offices at great distances perhaps, and equally great expences to obtain a settlement, which would be highly injurious, nay ruinous to you. This is their language.

Let me beseech you therefore, my good Sir, to urge this matter earnestly, and without further delay. The situation of these Gentlemen I do verily believe, is distressing beyond description. It is affirmed to me, that a large part of them have no better prospect before them than a Goal, if they are turned loose without liquidation of accts. and an assurance of that justice to which they are so worthily entitled. To prevail on the Delegates of those States through whose means these difficulties occur, it may, in my opinion, with propriety be suggested to them, if any disastrous consequences should follow, by reason of their delinquency, that they must be answerable to God & their Country for the ineffable horrors which may be occasioned thereby.

I am Dear Sir Yr. Most Obedt. Serv

P.S. I have received your letter of the 5th. & have put that matter in train which was mentioned in it.

I am this instant informed, that a second address to the Officers, distinguished No. 2, is thrown into circulation. The Contents, evidently prove that the Author is in, or near Camp; and that the following words, erazed in the second page of this Letter, ought not to have met with this treatment. viz: "By others, that it is the illegitimate offspring of a person in the army."

"BUT HERE, GENTLEMEN, I WILL DROP THE CURTAIN"

Speech to the Officers of the Army

Head Quarters, Newburgh, March 15, 1783.

Gentlemen: By an anonymous summons, an attempt has been made to convene you together; how inconsistent with the rules of propriety! how unmilitary! and how subversive of all order and discipline, let the good sense of the Army decide.

In the moment of this Summons, another anonymous production was sent into circulation, addressed more to the feelings and passions, than to the reason and judgment of the Army. The author of the piece, is entitled to much credit for the goodness of his Pen and I could wish he had as much credit for the rectitude of his Heart, for, as Men see thro' different Optics, and are induced by the reflecting faculties of the Mind, to use different means, to attain the same end, the Author of the Address, should have had more charity, than to mark for Suspicion, the Man who should recommend moderation and longer forbearance, or, in other words, who should not think as he thinks, and act as he advises. But he had another plan in view, in which candor and liberality of Sentiment; regard to justice, and love of Country, have no part; and he was right, to insinuate the darkest suspicion, to effect the blackest designs.

That the Address is drawn with great Art, and is designed to answer the most insidious purposes. That it is calculated to impress the Mind, with an idea of premeditated injustice in the Sovereign power of the United States, and rouse all those resentments which must unavoidably flow from such a belief. That the secret mover of this Scheme (whoever he may be) intended to take advantage of the passions, while they were warmed by the recollection of past distresses, without giving time for cool, deliberative thinking, and that composure of Mind which is so necessary to give dignity and stability to measures is rendered too obvious, by the mode of conducting the business, to need other proof than a reference to the proceeding.

Thus much, Gentlemen, I have thought it incumbent on me to observe to you, to shew upon what principles I opposed the irregular and hasty meeting which was proposed to have been held on Tuesday last: and not because I wanted a disposition to give you every oppertunity consistent with your own honor, and the dignity of the Army, to make known your grievances. If my conduct heretofore, has not evinced to you, that I have been a faithful friend to the Army, my declaration of it at this time wd. be equally unavailing and improper. But as I was among the first who embarked in the cause of our common Country. As I have never left your side one moment, but when called from you on public duty. As I have been the constant companion and witness of your Distresses, and not among the last to feel, and acknowledge your Merits. As I have ever considered my own Military reputation as inseperably connected with that of the Army. As my Heart has ever expanded with joy, when I have heard its praises, and my indignation has arisen, when the mouth of detraction has been opened against it, it can *scarcely be supposed*, at this late stage of the War, that I am indifferent to its interests. But, how are they to be promoted? The way is plain, says the anonymous Addresser. If War continues, remove into the unsettled Country; there establish yourselves, and leave an ungrateful Country to defend itself. But who are they to defend? Our Wives, our Children, our Farms, and other property which we leave behind us. or, in this state of hostile seperation, are we to take the two first (the latter cannot be removed), to perish in a Wilderness, with hunger, cold and nakedness? If Peace takes place, never sheath your Swords Says he untill you have obtained full and ample justice; this dreadful alternative, of either deserting our Country in the extremest hour of her distress, or turning our Arms against it, (which is the apparent object, unless Congress can be compelled into instant compliance) has something so shocking in it, that humanity revolts at the idea. My God! what can this writer have in view, by recommending such measures? Can he be a friend to the Army? Can he be a friend to this Country? Rather, is he not an insidious Foe? Some Emissary, perhaps, from New York, plotting the ruin of both, by sowing the seeds of discord and seperation between the Civil and Military powers of the Continent? And what a Compliment does he pay to our Understandings, when he recommends measures in either alternative, impracticable in their Nature?

But here, Gentlemen, I will drop the curtain, because it wd. be as imprudent in me to assign my reasons for this opinion, as it would be insulting to your conception, to suppose you stood in need of them. A moment's reflection will convince every dispassionate Mind of the physical impossibility of carrying either proposal into execution.

There might, Gentlemen, be an impropriety in my taking notice, in this Address to you, of an anonymous production, but the manner in which that performance has been introduced to the Army, the effect it was intended to have, together with some other circumstances, will amply justify my observations on the tendency of that Writing. With respect to the advice given by the Author, to suspect the Man, who shall recommend moderate measures and longer forbearance, I spurn it, as every Man, who regards that liberty, and reveres that justice for which we contend, undoubtedly must; for if Men are to be precluded from offering their Sentiments on a matter, which may involve the most serious and alarming consequences, that can invite the consideration of Mankind, reason is of no use to us; the freedom of Speech may be taken away, and, dumb and silent we may be led, like sheep, to the Slaughter.

I cannot, in justice to my own belief, and what I have great reason to conceive is the intention of Congress, conclude this

Address, without giving it as my decided opinion, that that Honble Body, entertain exalted sentiments of the Services of the Army; and, from a full conviction of its merits and sufferings, will do it compleat justice. That their endeavors, to discover and establish funds for this purpose, have been unwearied, and will not cease, till they have succeeded, I have not a doubt. But, like all other large Bodies, where there is a variety of different Interests to reconcile, their deliberations are slow. Why then should we distrust them? and, in consequence of that distrust, adopt measures, which may cast a shade over that glory which, has been so justly acquired; and tarnish the reputation of an Army which is celebrated thro' all Europe, for its fortitude and Patriotism? and for what is this done? to bring the object we seek nearer? No! most certainly, in my opinion, it will cast it at a greater distance.

For myself (and I take no merit in giving the assurance, being induced to it from principles of gratitude, veracity and justice), a grateful sence of the confidence you have ever placed in me, a recollection of the chearful assistance, and prompt obedience I have experienced from you, under every vicissitude of Fortune, and the sincere affection I feel for an Army, I have so long had the honor to Command, will oblige me to declare, in this public and solemn manner, that, in the attainment of compleat justice for all your toils and dangers, and in the gratification of every wish, so far as may be done consistently with the great duty I owe my Country, and those powers we are bound to respect, you may freely command my Services to the utmost of my abilities.

While I give you these assurances, and pledge myself in the most unequivocal manner, to exert whatever ability I am possessed of, in your favor, let me entreat you, Gentlemen, on your part, not to take any measures, which, viewed in the calm light of reason, will lessen the dignity, and sully the glory you have hitherto maintained; let me request you to rely on the plighted faith of your Country, and place a full confidence in the purity of the intentions of Congress; that, previous to your dissolution as an Army they will cause all your Accts. to be fairly liquidated, as directed in their resolutions, which were published to you two days ago, and that they will adopt the most effectual measures in their power, to render ample justice to you, for your faithful and meritorious Services. And let me conjure you, in the name of our common Country, as you value your own sacred honor, as you respect the rights of humanity, and as you regard the Military and National character of America, to express your utmost horror and detestation of the Man who wishes, under any specious pretences, to overturn the liberties of our Country, and who wickedly attempts to open the flood Gates of Civil discord, and deluge our rising Empire in Blood. By thus determining, and thus acting, you will pursue the plain and direct road to the attainment of your wishes. You will defeat the insidious designs of our Enemies, who are compelled to resort from open force to secret Artifice. You will give one more distinguished proof of unexampled patriotism and patient virtue, rising superior to the pressure of the most complicated sufferings; And you will, by the dignity of your Conduct, afford occasion for Posterity to say, when speaking of the glorious example you have exhibited to Mankind, "had this day been wanting, the World had never seen the last stage of perfection to which human nature is capable of attaining."

PEACE!

To Nathanael Greene

Head Quarters, March 31, 1783.

Dear Sir: I have the pleasure to inclose to you a letter from the Marquis de la fayette, which came under cover to me, by the Packet Triumph, dispatched by the Marquis and the Count de Estaing from Cadiz to Phila.

All the Accounts which this Vessel has bro't, of a Conclusion of a General Peace, you will receive before this can reach you.

You will give the highest Credit to my Sincerity, when I beg you to accept my warmest Congratulations on this glorious and happy Event, an Event which crowns all our Labors and will sweeten the Toils which we have experienced in the Course of Eight Years distressing War. The Army here, universally participate in the general Joy which this Event has diffused, and, from this Consideration, together with the late Resolutions of Congress, for the Commutation of the Half pay, and for a Liquidation of all their Accounts, their Minds are filled with the highest Satisfaction. I am sure you will join with me in this additional occasion of joy.

It remains only for the States to be Wise, and to establish their Independence on that Basis of inviolable efficacious Union, and firm Confederation, which may prevent their being made the Sport of European Policy; may Heaven give them Wisdom to adopt the Measures still necessary for this important Purpose. I have the honor etc.

"NO MAN PERHAPS HAS FELT THE
BAD EFFECTS OF IT MORE SENSIBLY"

To Alexander Hamilton

Dear Sir,   Newburgh 31st. March 1783
  I have duly received your favors of the 17th. & 24th. ulto. I rejoice most exceedingly that there is an end to our warfare, and that such a field is opening to our view as will, with wisdom to direct the cultivation of it, make us a great, a respectable, and happy People; but it must be improved by other means than State politics, and unreasonable jealousies & prejudices; or (it requires not the second sight to see that) we shall be instruments in the hands of our Enemies, & those European powers who may be jealous of our greatness in Union to dissolve the confederation; but to attain this, altho the way seems extremely plain, is not so easy.

My wish to see the Union of these States established upon liberal & permanent principles, & inclination to contribute my mite in pointing out the defects of the present Constitution, are equally great. All my private letters have teemed with these Sentiments, & whenever this topic has been the subject of conversation, I have endeavoured to diffuse & enforce them; but how far any further essay, by me, might be productive of the wished for end, or appear to arrogate more than belongs to me, depends so much upon popular opinion, & the temper

& disposition of People, that it is not easy to decide. I shall be obliged to you however for the thoughts which you have promised me on this subject, and as soon as you can make it convenient.

No man in the United States is, or can be more deeply impressed with the necessity of a reform in our present Confederation than myself. No man perhaps has felt the bad effects of it more sensibly; for to the defects thereof, & want of Powers in Congress may justly be ascribed the prolongation of the War, & consequently the Expences occasioned by it. More than half the perplexities I have experienced in the course of my command, and almost the whole of the difficulties & distress of the Army, have there origin here; but still, the prejudices of some, the designs of others, and the mere machinery of the majority, makes address & management necessary to give weight to opinions which are to Combat the doctrine of those different classes of men, in the field of Politics.

I would have been more full on this subject but the bearer (in the clothing department) is waiting. I wish you may understand what I have written.

I am Dr Sir Yr. Most Obedt Servt

Honble. Alexr Hamilton.

The inclosed extract of a Letter to Mr Livingston, I give you in confidence. I submit it to your consideration, fully persuaded that you do not want inclination to gratify the Marquis's wishes as far as is consistent with our National honor.

WASHINGTON'S LEGACY

Circular to State Governments

Head Quarters, Newburgh, June 8, 1783.
Sir: The great object for which I had the honor to hold an appointment in the Service of my Country, being accomplished, I am now preparing to resign it into the hands of Congress, and to return to that domestic retirement, which, it is well known, I left with the greatest reluctance, a Retirement,

for which I have never ceased to sigh through a long and painful absence, and in which (remote from the noise and trouble of the World) I meditate to pass the remainder of life in a state of undisturbed repose; But before I carry this resolution into effect, I think it a duty incumbent on me, to make this my last official communication, to congratulate you on the glorious events which Heaven has been pleased to produce in our favor, to offer my sentiments respecting some important subjects, which appear to me, to be intimately connected with the tranquility of the United States, to take my leave of your Excellency as a public Character, and to give my final blessing to that Country, in whose service I have spent the prime of my life, for whose sake I have consumed so many anxious days and watchfull nights, and whose happiness being extremely dear to me, will always constitute no inconsiderable part of my own.

Impressed with the liveliest sensibility on this pleasing occasion, I will claim the indulgence of dilating the more copiously on the subjects of our mutual felicitation. When we consider the magnitude of the prize we contended for, the doubtful nature of the contest, and the favorable manner in which it has terminated, we shall find the greatest possible reason for gratitude and rejoicing; this is a theme that will afford infinite delight to every benevolent and liberal mind, whether the event in contemplation, be considered as the source of present enjoyment or the parent of future happiness; and we shall have equal occasion to felicitate ourselves on the lot which Providence has assigned us, whether we view it in a natural, a political or moral point of light.

The Citizens of America, placed in the most enviable condition, as the sole Lords and Proprietors of a vast Tract of Continent, comprehending all the various soils and climates of the World, and abounding with all the necessaries and conveniencies of life, are now by the late satisfactory pacification, acknowledged to be possessed of absolute freedom and Independency; They are, from this period, to be considered as the Actors on a most conspicuous Theatre, which seems to be peculiarly designated by Providence for the display of human greatness and felicity; Here, they are not only surrounded with every thing which can contribute to the completion of private and domestic enjoyment, but Heaven has crowned all its other blessings, by giving a fairer oppertunity for political happiness, than any other Nation has ever been favored with. Nothing can illustrate these observations more forcibly, than a recollection of the happy conjuncture of times and circumstances, under which our Republic assumed its rank among the Nations; The foundation of our Empire was not laid in the gloomy age of Ignorance and Superstition, but at an Epocha when the rights of mankind were better understood and more clearly defined, than at any former period, the researches of the human mind, after social happiness, have been carried to a great extent, the Treasures of knowledge, acquired by the labours of Philosophers, Sages and Legislatures, through a long succession of years, are laid open for our use, and their collected wisdom may be happily applied in the Establishment of our forms of Government; the free cultivation of Letters, the unbounded extension of Commerce, the progressive refinement of Manners, the growing liberality of sentiment, and above all, the pure and benign light of Revelation, have had a meliorating influence on mankind and increased the blessings of Society. At this auspicious period, the United States came into existence as a Nation, and if their Citizens should not be completely free and happy, the fault will be intirely their own.

Such is our situation, and such are our prospects: but notwithstanding the cup of blessing is thus reached out to us, notwithstanding happiness is ours, if we have a disposition to seize the occasion and make it our own; yet, it appears to me there is an option still left to the United States of America, that it is in their choice, and depends upon their conduct, whether they will be respectable and prosperous, or contemptable and miserable as a Nation; This is the time of their political probation, this is the moment when the eyes of the whole World are turned upon them, this is the moment to establish or ruin their national Character forever, this is the favorable moment to give such a tone to our Federal Government, as will enable it to answer the ends of its institution, or this may be the ill-fated moment for relaxing the powers of the Union, annihilating the cement of the Confederation, and exposing us to become the sport of European politics, which may play one State against another to prevent their growing importance, and to serve their own interested purposes. For, according to the system of

Policy the States shall adopt at this moment, they will stand or fall, and by their confirmation or lapse, it is yet to be decided, whether the Revolution must ultimately be considered as a blessing or a curse: a blessing or a curse, not to the present age alone, for with our fate will the destiny of unborn Millions be involved.

With this conviction of the importance of the present Crisis, silence in me would be a crime; I will therefore speak to your Excellency, the language of freedom and of sincerity, without disguise; I am aware, however, that those who differ from me in political sentiment, may perhaps remark, I am stepping out of the proper line of my duty, and they may possibly ascribe to arrogance or ostentation, what I know is alone the result of the purest intention, but the rectitude of my own heart, which disdains such unworthy motives, the part I have hitherto acted in life, the determination I have formed, of not taking any share in public business hereafter, the ardent desire I feel, and shall continue to manifest, of quietly enjoying in private life, after all the toils of War, the benefits of a wise and liberal Government, will, I flatter myself, sooner or later convince my Countrymen, that I could have no sinister views in delivering with so little reserve, the opinions contained in this Address.

There are four things, which I humbly conceive, are essential to the well being, I may even venture to say, to the existence of the United States as an Independent Power:

1st. An indissoluble Union of the States under one Federal Head.

2dly. A Sacred regard to Public Justice.

3dly. The adoption of a proper Peace Establishment, and

4thly. The prevalence of that pacific and friendly Disposition, among the People of the United States, which will induce them to forget their local prejudices and policies, to make those mutual concessions which are requisite to the general prosperity, and in some instances, to sacrifice their individual advantages to the interest of the Community.

These are the Pillars on which the glorious Fabrick of our Independency and National Character must be supported; Liberty is the Basis, and whoever would dare to sap the foundation, or overturn the Structure, under whatever specious pretexts he may attempt it, will merit the bitterest execration, and the severest punishment which can be inflicted by his injured Country.

On the three first Articles I will make a few observations, leaving the last to the good sense and serious consideration of those immediately concerned.

Under the first head, altho' it may not be necessary or proper for me in this place to enter into a particular disquisition of the principles of the Union, and to take up the great question which has been frequently agitated, whether it be expedient and requisite for the States to delegate a larger proportion of Power to Congress, or not, Yet it will be a part of my duty, and that of every true Patriot, to assert without reserve, and to insist upon the following positions, That unless the States will suffer Congress to exercise those prerogatives, they are undoubtedly invested with by the Constitution, every thing must very rapidly tend to Anarchy and confusion, That it is indispensable to the happiness of the individual States, that there should be lodged somewhere, a Supreme Power to regulate and govern the general concerns of the Confederated Republic, without which the Union cannot be of long duration. That there must be a faithfull and pointed compliance on the part of every State, with the late proposals and demands of Congress, or the most fatal consequences will ensue, That whatever measures have a tendency to dissolve the Union, or contribute to violate or lessen the Sovereign Authority, ought to be considered as hostile to the Liberty and Independency of America, and the Authors of them treated accordingly, and lastly, that unless we can be enabled by the concurrence of the States, to participate of the fruits of the Revolution, and enjoy the essential benefits of Civil Society, under a form of Government so free and uncorrupted, so happily guarded against the danger of oppression, as has been devised and adopted by the Articles of Confederation, it will be a subject of regret, that so much blood and treasure have been lavished for no purpose, that so many sufferings have been encountered without a compensation, and that so many sacrifices have been made in vain. Many other considerations might here be adduced to prove, that without an entire conformity to the Spirit of the Union, we cannot exist as an Independent Power; it will be sufficient for my purpose to mention but one or two which seem to me of the greatest importance. It is only in our united Character as an Empire, that our Independence is acknowledged, that our power can be regarded, or our Credit supported among Foreign Nations. The Treaties of the European Powers with the United States of America, will have no validity on a dissolution of the Union. We shall be left nearly in a state of Nature, or we may find by our own unhappy experience, that there is a natural and necessary progression, from the extreme of anarchy to the extreme of Tyranny; and that arbitrary power is most easily established on the ruins of Liberty abused to licentiousness.

As to the second Article, which respects the performance of Public Justice, Congress have, in their late Address to the United States, almost exhausted the subject, they have explained their Ideas so fully, and have enforced the obligations the States are under, to render compleat justice to all the Public Creditors, with so much dignity and energy, that in my opinion, no real friend to the honor and Independency of America, can hesitate a single moment respecting the propriety of complying with the just and honorable measures proposed; if their Arguments do not produce conviction, I know of nothing that will have greater influence; especially when we recollect that the System referred to, being the result of the collected Wisdom of the Continent, must be esteemed, if not perfect, certainly the least objectionable of any that could be devised; and that if it shall not be carried into immediate execution, a National Bankruptcy, with all its deplorable consequences will take place, before any different Plan can possibly be proposed and adopted; So pressing are the present circumstances! and such is the alternative now offered to the States!

The ability of the Country to discharge the debts which have been incurred in its defence, is not to be doubted, an inclination, I flatter myself, will not be wanting, the path of our duty is plain before us, honesty will be found on every experiment, to be the best and only true policy, let us then as a Nation be just, let us fulfil the public Contracts, which Congress had undoubtedly a right to make for the purpose of carrying on the War, with the same good faith we suppose ourselves bound to perform our private engagements; in the mean time, let an attention to the chearfull performance of their proper business, as Individuals, and as members of Society, be earnestly inculcated on the Citizens of America, that will they strengthen the hands of Government, and be happy under its protection: every one will reap the fruit of his labours, every one will enjoy his own acquisitions without molestation and without danger.

In this state of absolute freedom and perfect security, who will grudge to yield a very little of his property to support the common interest of Society, and insure the protection of Government? Who does not remember, the frequent declarations, at the commencement of the War, that we should be compleatly satisfied, if at the expence of one half, we could defend the remainder of our possessions? Where is the Man to be found, who wishes to remain indebted, for the defence of his own person and property, to the exertions, the bravery, and the blood of others, without making one generous effort to repay the debt of honor and of gratitude? In what part of the Continent shall we find any Man, or body of Men, who would not blush to stand up and propose measures, purposely calculated to rob the Soldier of his Stipend, and the Public Creditor of his due? and were it possible that such a flagrant instance of Injustice could ever happen, would it not excite the general indignation, and tend to bring down, upon the Authors of such measures, the aggravated vengeance of Heaven? If after all, a spirit of disunion or a temper of obstinacy and perverseness, should manifest itself in any of the States, if such an ungracious disposition should attempt to frustrate all the happy effects that might be expected to flow from the Union, if there should be a refusal to comply with the requisitions for Funds to discharge the annual interest of the public debts, and if that refusal should revive again all those jealousies and produce all those evils, which are now happily removed, Congress, who have in all their Transaction shewn a great degree of magnanimity and justice, will stand justified in the sight of God and Man, and the State alone which puts itself in opposition to the aggregate Wisdom of the Continent, and follows such mistaken and pernicious Councils, will be responsible for all the consequences.

For my own part, conscious of having acted while a Servant of the Public, in the manner I conceived best suited to promote the real interests of my Country; having in consequence of my fixed belief in some measure pledged myself to the Army, that their Country would finally do them compleat and ample Justice; and not wishing to conceal any instance of my official conduct from the eyes of the World, I have thought proper to transmit to your Excellency the inclosed collection of Papers, relative to the half pay and commutation granted by Congress to the Officers of the Army; From these communications, my decided sentiment will be clearly comprehended, together with the conclusive reasons which induced me, at an early period, to recommend the adoption of the measure, in the most earnest and serious manner. As the proceedings of Congress, the Army, and myself are open to all, and contain in my opinion, sufficient information to remove the prejudices and errors which may have been entertained by any; I think it unnecessary to say any thing more, than just to observe, that the Resolutions of Congress, now alluded to, are undoubtedly as absolutely binding upon the United States, as the most solemn Acts of Confederation or Legislation. As to the Idea, which I am informed has in some instances prevailed, that the half pay and commutation are to be regarded merely in the odious light of a Pension, it ought to be exploded forever; that Provision, should be viewed as it really was, a reasonable compensation offered by Congress, at a time when they had nothing else to give, to the Officers of the Army, for services then to be performed. It was the only means to prevent a total dereliction of the Service, It was a part of their hire, I may be allowed to say, it was the price of their blood and of your Independency, it is therefore more than a common debt, it is a debt of honour, it can never be considered as a Pension or gratuity, nor be cancelled until it is fairly discharged.

With regard to a distinction between Officers and Soldiers, it is sufficient that the uniform experience of every Nation of the World, combined with our own, proves the utility and propriety of the discrimination. Rewards in proportion to the aids the public derives from them, are unquestionably due to all its Servants; In some Lines, the Soldiers have perhaps generally had as ample a compensation for their Services, by the large Bounties which have been paid to them, as their Officers will receive in the proposed Commutation, in others, if besides the donation of Lands, the payment of Arrearages of Cloathing and Wages (in which Articles all the component parts of the

Army must be put upon the same footing) we take into the estimate, the Bounties many of the Soldiers have received and the gratuity of one Year's full pay, which is promised to all, possibly their situation (every circumstance being duly considered) will not be deemed less eligible than that of the Officers. Should a farther reward, however, be judged equitable, I will venture to assert, no one will enjoy greater satisfaction than myself, on seeing an exemption from Taxes for a limited time, (which has been petitioned for in some instances) or any other adequate immunity or compensation, granted to the brave defenders of their Country's Cause; but neither the adoption or rejection of this proposition will in any manner affect, much less militate against, the Act of Congress, by which they have offered five years full pay, in lieu of the half pay for life, which had been before promised to the Officers of the Army.

Before I conclude the subject of public justice, I cannot omit to mention the obligations this Country is under, to that meritorious Class of veteran Non-commissioned Officers and Privates, who have been discharged for inability, in consequence of the Resolution of Congress of the 23d of April 1782, on an annual pension for life, their peculiar sufferings, their singular merits and claims to that provision need only be known, to interest all the feelings of humanity in their behalf: nothing but a punctual payment of their annual allowance can rescue them from the most complicated misery, and nothing could be a more melancholy and distressing sight, than to behold those who have shed their blood or lost their limbs in the service of their Country, without a shelter, without a friend, and without the means of obtaining any of the necessaries or comforts of Life; compelled to beg their daily bread from door to door! suffer me to recommend those of this discription, belonging to your State, to the warmest patronage of your Excellency and your Legislature.

It is necessary to say but a few words on the third topic which was proposed, and which regards particularly the defence of the Republic, As there can be little doubt but Congress will recommend a proper Peace Establishment for the United States, in which a due attention will be paid to the importance of placing the Militia of the Union upon a regular and respectable footing; If this should be the case, I would beg leave to urge the great advantage of it in the strongest terms. The Militia of this Country must be considered as the Palladium of our security, and the first effectual resort in case of hostility; It is essential therefore, that the same system should pervade the whole; that the formation and discipline of the Militia of the Continent should be absolutely uniform, and that the same species of Arms, Accoutrements and Military Apparatus, should be introduced in every part of the United States; No one, who has not learned it from experience, can conceive the difficulty, expence, and confusion which result from a contrary system, or the vague Arrangements which have hitherto prevailed.

If in treating of political points, a greater latitude than usual has been taken in the course of this Address, the importance of the Crisis, and the magnitude of the objects in discussion, must be my apology: It is, however, neither my wish or expectation, that the preceding observations should claim any regard, except so far as they shall appear to be dictated by a good intention, consonant to the immutable rules of Justice; calculated to produce a liberal system of policy, and founded on whatever experience may have been acquired by a long and close attention to public business. Here I might speak with the more confidence from my actual observations, and, if it would not swell this Letter (already too prolix) beyond the bounds I had prescribed myself: I could demonstrate to every mind open to conviction, that in less time and with much less expence than has been incurred, the War might have been brought to the same happy conclusion, if the resourses of the Continent could have been properly drawn forth, that the distresses and disappointments which have very often occurred, have in too many instances, resulted more from a want of energy, in the Continental Government, than a deficiency of means in the particular States. That the inefficiency of measures, arising from the want of an adequate authority in the Supreme Power, from a partial compliance with the Requisitions of Congress in some of the States, and from a failure of punctuality in others, while it tended to damp the zeal of those which were more willing to exert themselves; served also to accumulate the expences of the War, and to frustrate the best concerted Plans, and that the discouragement occasioned by the complicated difficulties and embarrassments, in which our affairs were, by this means involved, would have long ago produced the dissolution of any Army, less patient, less virtuous and less persevering, than that which I have had the honor to command. But while I mention these things, which are notorious facts, as the defects of our Federal Constitution, particularly in the prosecution of a War, I beg it may be understood, that as I have ever taken a pleasure in gratefully acknowledging the assistance and support I have derived from every Class of Citizens, so shall I always be happy to do justice to the unparalleled exertion of the individual States, on many interesting occasions.

I have thus freely disclosed what I wished to make known, before I surrendered up my Public trust to those who committed it to me, the task is now accomplished, I now bid adieu to your Excellency as the Chief Magistrate of your State, at the same time I bid a last farewell to the cares of Office, and all the imployments of public life.

It remains then to be my final and only request, that your Excellency will communicate these sentiments to your Legislature at their next meeting, and that they may be considered as the Legacy of One, who has ardently wished, on all occasions, to be useful to his Country, and who, even in the shade of Retirement, will not fail to implore the divine benediction upon it.

I now make it my earnest prayer, that God would have you, and the State over which you preside, in his holy protection, that he would incline the hearts of the Citizens to cultivate a spirit of subordination and obedience to Government, to entertain a brotherly affection and love for one another, for their fellow Citizens of the United States at large, and particularly for their brethren who have served in the Field, and finally, that he would most graciously be pleased to dispose us all, to do Justice, to love mercy, and to demean ourselves with that Charity, humility and pacific temper of mind, which were the Characteristicks of the Divine Author of our blessed Religion, and without an humble imitation of whose example in these things, we can never hope to be a happy Nation.

PEACE AND THE INDIANS

To James Duane

Rocky Hill, September 7, 1783.

Sir: I have carefully perused the Papers which you put into my hands relative to Indian Affairs.

My Sentiments with respect to the proper line of Conduct to be observed towards these people coincides precisely with those delivered by Genl. Schuyler, so far as he has gone in his Letter of the 29th. July to Congress (which, with the other Papers is herewith returned), and for the reasons he has there assigned; a repetition of them therefore by me would be unnecessary. But independant of the arguments made use of by him the following considerations have no small weight in my Mind.

To suffer a wide extended Country to be over run with Land Jobbers, Speculators, and Monopolisers or even with scatter'd settlers, is, in my opinion, inconsistent with that wisdom and policy which our true interest dictates, or that an enlightened People ought to adopt and, besides, is pregnant of disputes both with the Savages, and among ourselves, the evils of which are easier, to be conceived than described; and for what? but to aggrandize a few avaricious Men to the prejudice of many, and the embarrassment of Government. for the People engaged in these pursuits without contributing in the smallest degree to the support of Government, or considering themselves as amenable to its Laws, will involve it by their unrestrained conduct, in inextricable perplexities, and more than probable in a great deal of Bloodshed.

My ideas therefore of the line of Conduct proper to be observed not only towards the Indians, but for the government of the Citizens of America, in their Settlement of the Western Country (which is intimately connected therewith) are simply these.

First and as a preliminary, that all Prisoners of whatever age or Sex, among the Indians shall be delivered up.

That the Indians should be informed, that after a Contest of eight years for the Sovereignty of this Country G: Britain has ceded all the Lands of the United States within the limits dis-cribed by the ____ arte. of the Provisional Treaty.

That as they (the Indians) maugre all the advice and admo-nition which could be given them at the commencemt; and during the prosecution of the War could not be restrained from acts of Hostility, but were determined to join their Arms to those of G Britain and to share their fortune; so, conse-quently, with a less generous People than Americans they would be made to share the same fate; and be compelld to re-tire along with them beyond the Lakes. But as we prefer Peace to a state of Warfare, as we consider them as a deluded People; as we perswade ourselves that they are convinced, from experi-ence, of their error in taking up the Hatchet against us, and that their true Interest and safety must now depend upon *our* friendship. As the Country, is large enough to contain us all; and as we are disposed to be kind to them and to partake of their Trade, we will from these considerations and from mo-tives of Compn., draw a veil over what is past and establish a boundary line between them and us beyond which we will *en-deavor* to restrain our People from Hunting or Settling, and within which they shall not come, but for the purposes of Trading, Treating, or other business unexceptionable in its nature.

In establishing this line, in the first instance, care should be taken neither to yield nor to grasp at too much. But to en-deavor to impress the Indians with an idea of the generosity of our disposition to accommodate them, and with the necessity we are under, of providing for our Warriors, our Young People who are growing up, and strangers who are coming from other Countries to live among us. and if they should make a point of it, or appear dissatisfied at the line we may find it necessary to establish, compensation should be made them for their claims within it.

It is needless for me to express more explicitly because the tendency of my observns. evinces it is my opinion that if the Legislature of the State of New York should insist upon expel-ling the Six Nations from all the Country they Inhabited previ-ous to the War, within their Territory (as General Schuyler seems to be apprehensive of) that it will end in another Indian War. I have every reason to believe from my enquiries, and the information I have received, that they will not suffer their Country (if it was our policy to take it before we could settle it) to be wrested from them without another struggle. That they would compromise for a part of it I have very little doubt, and that it would be the cheapest way of coming at it, I have no doubt at all. The same observations, I am perswaded, will hold good with respect to Virginia, or any other state which has powerful Tribes of Indians on their Frontiers; and the reason of my mentioning New York is because General Schuyler has expressed his opinion of the temper of its Legislature; and because I have been more in the way of learning the Sentimts. of the Six Nations, than of any other Tribes of Indians on this Subject.

The limits being sufficiently extensive (in the New Ctry.) to comply with all the engagements of Government and to admit such emigrations as may be supposed to happen within a given time not only from the several States of the Union but from Foreign Countries, and moreover of such magnitude as to form a distinct and proper Government; a Proclamation in my opinion, should issue, making it Felony (if there is power for the purpose and if not imposing some very heavy restraint) for any person to Survey or Settle beyond the Line; and the Officers Commanding the Frontier Garrison should have pointed and peremptory orders to see that the Proclamation is carried into effect.

Measures of this sort would not only obtain Peace from the Indians, but would, in my opinion, be the surest means of preserving it. It would dispose of the Land to the best advantage; People the Country progressively, and check Land Jobbing and Monopolizing (which is now going forward with great avidity) while the door would be open, and the terms known for every one to obtain what is reasonable and proper for himself upon legal and constitutional ground.

Every advantage that could be expected or even wished for would result from such a mode of proceedure our Settlements would be compact, Government well established, and our Barrier formidable, not only for ourselves but against our Neighbours, and the Indians as has been observed in Genl Schuylers Letter will ever retreat as our Settlements advance upon them and they will be as ready to sell, as we are to buy; That it is the cheapest as well as the least distressing way of dealing with them, none who are acquainted with the Nature of Indian warfare, and has ever been at the trouble of estimating the expence of one, and comparing it with the cost of purchasing their Lands, will hesitate to acknowledge.

Unless some such measures as I have here taken the liberty of suggesting are speedily adopted one of two capital evils, in my opinion, will inevitably result, and is near at hand; either that the settling, or rather overspreading the Western Country will take place, by a parcel of Banditti, who will bid defiance to all Authority while they are skimming and disposing of the Cream of the Country at the expence of many suffering officers and Soldiers who have fought and bled to obtain it, and are now waiting the decision of Congress to point them to the promised reward of their past dangers and toils, or a renewal of Hostilities with the Indians, brought about more than probably, by this very means.

How far agents for Indian Affrs. are indispensably necessary I shall not take upon me to decide; but if any should be appointed, their powers in my opinion should be circumscribed, accurately defined, and themselves rigidly punished for every infraction of them. A recurrence to the conduct of these People under the British Administration of Indian Affairs will manifest the propriety of this caution, as it will there be found, that self Interest was the principle by which their Agents were actuated; and to promote this by accumulating Lands and passing large quantities of Goods thro their hands, the Indians were made to speak any language they pleased by their representation; were pacific or hostile as their purposes were most likely to be promoted by the one or the other. No purchase under any pretence whatever should be made by any other authority than that of the Sovereign power, or the Legislature of the State in which such Lands may happen to be. Nor should the Agents be permitted directly or indirectly to trade; but to have a fixed, and ample Salary allowed them as a full compensation for their trouble.

Whether in practice the measure may answer as well as it appears in theory to me, I will not undertake to say; but I think, if the Indian Trade was carried on, on Government Acct., and with no greater advance than what would be necessary to defray the expence and risk, and bring in a small profit, that it would supply the Indians upon much better terms than they usually are; engross their Trade, and fix them strongly in our Interest; and would be a much better mode of treating them than that of giving presents; where a few only are benefitted by them. I confess there is a difficulty in getting a Man, or set of Men, in whose Abilities and integrity there can be a perfect reliance; without which, the scheme is liable to such abuse as to defeat the salutary ends which are proposed from it. At any rate, no person should be suffered to Trade with the Indians without first obtaining a license, and giving security to conform to such rules and regulations as shall be prescribed; as was the case before the War.

In giving my Sentiments in the Month of May last (at the request of a Committee of Congress) on a Peace Establishmt. I took the liberty of suggesting the propriety, which in my opinion there appeared, of paying particular attention to the French and other Settlers at Detroit and other parts within the limits of the Western Country; the perusal of a late Pamphlet entitled "Observations on the Commerce of the American States with Europe and the West Indies" impresses the necessity of it more forcibly than ever on my Mind. The author of that Piece strongly recommends a liberal change in the Government of Canada, and tho' he is too sanguine in his expectations of the benefits arising from it, there can be no doubt of the good policy of the measure. It behooves us therefore to counteract them, by anticipation. These People have a disposition towards us susceptible of favorable Impressions; but as no Arts will be left unattempted by the British to withdraw them from our Interest, the prest. moment should be employed by us to fix them in it, or we may loose them forever; and with them, the advantages, or disadvantages consequent of the choice they may make. From the best information and Maps of that Country, it would appear that from the Mouth of the Great Miami River wch. empties into the Ohio to its confluence with the Mad River, thence by a Line to the Miami Fort and Village on the other Miami River wch. empties into Lake Erie, and Thence by a Line to include the Settlement of Detroit would with Lake Erie to the No. ward Pensa. to the Eastwd. and the Ohio to the Soward form a Governmt. sufficiently extensive to fulfill all the public engagements, and to receive moreover a large population by Emigrants, and to confine The Settlement of the New States within these bounds would, in my opinion, be infinitely better even supposing no disputes were to happen with the Indians and that it was not necessary to guard against those other evils which have been enumerated than to suffer the same number of People to roam over a Country of at least 500,000 Square Miles contributing nothing to the support, but much perhaps to the Embarrassment of the Federal Government.

Was it not for the purpose of comprehending the Settlement of Detroit within the Jurisdn. of the New Governmt a more compact and better shaped district for a State would be for the line to proceed from the Miami Fort and Village along the River of that name to Lake Erie. leaving In that case the Settlement of Detroit, and all the Territory No. of the Rivers Miami and St. Josephs between the Lakes Erie, St. Clair, Huron, and Michigan to form, hereafter, another State equally large compact and water bounded.

At first view, it may seem a little extraneous, when I am called upon to give an opinion upon the terms of a Peace proper to be made with the Indians, that I should go into the formation of New States; but the Settlemt. of the Western Country and making a Peace with the Indians are so analogous that there can be no definition of the one without involving considerations of the other. for I repeat it, again, and I am clear in my opinion, that policy and œconomy point very strongly to the expediency of being upon good terms with the Indians, and the propriety of purchasing their Lands in preference to attempting to drive them by force of arms out of their Country; which as we have already experienced is like driving the Wild Beasts of the Forest which will return us soon as the pursuit is at an end and fall perhaps on those that are left there; when the gradual extension of our Settlements will as certainly cause the Savage as the Wolf to retire; both being beasts of prey tho' they differ in shape. In a word there is nothing to be obtained by an Indian War but the Soil they live on and this can be had by purchase at less expence, and without that bloodshed, and those distresses which helpless Women and Children are made partakers of in all kinds of disputes with them.

If there is any thing in these thoughts (which I have fully and freely communicated) worthy attention I shall be happy and am Sir Yr. etc.

P. S. A formal Address, and memorial from the Oneida Indians when I was on the Mohawk River, setting forth their Grievances and distresses and praying relief, induced me to order a pound of Powder and 3 lbs. of Lead to be issued to each Man, from the Military Magazines in the care of Colo. Willet; this, I presume, was unknown to Genl. Schuyler at the time he recommended the like measure in his Letter to Congress.

"ONE PATRIOTIC BAND OF BROTHERS"

Farewell Address to the Armies of the United States

Rock Hill, near Princeton, November 2, 1783.
The United States in Congress assembled after giving the most honorable testimony to the merits of the fœderal Armies, and presenting them with the thanks of their Country for their long, eminent, and faithful services, having thought proper by their proclamation bearing date the 18th. day of October last. to discharge such part of the Troops as were engaged for the war, and to permit the Officers on furlough to retire from service from and after to-morrow; which proclamation having been communicated in the publick papers for the information and government of all concerned; it only remains for the Comdr in Chief to address himself once more, and that for the last time, to the Armies of the U States (however widely dispersed the individuals who compose them may be) and to bid them an affectionate, a long farewell.

But before the Comdr in Chief takes his final leave of those he holds most dear, he wishes to indulge himself a few moments in calling to mind a slight review of the past. He will then take the liberty of exploring, with his military friends, their future prospects, of advising the general line of conduct, which in his opinion, ought to be pursued, and he will conclude the Address by expressing the obligations he feels himself under for the spirited and able assistance he has experienced from them in the performance of an arduous Office.

A contemplation of the compleat attainment (at a period earlier than could have been expected) of the object for which we contended against so formidable a power cannot but inspire us with astonishment and gratitude. The disadvantageous circumstances on our part, under which the war was undertaken, can never be forgotten. The singular interpositions of Providence in our feeble condition were such, as could scarcely escape the attention of the most unobserving; while the unparalleled perseverance of the Armies of the U States, through almost every possible suffering and discouragement for the space of eight long years, was little short of a standing miracle.

It is not the meaning nor within the compass of this address to detail the hardships peculiarly incident to our service, or to describe the distresses, which in several instances have resulted from the extremes of hunger and nakedness, combined with the rigours of an inclement season; nor is it necessary to dwell on the dark side of our past affairs. Every American Officer and Soldier must now console himself for any unpleasant circumstances which may have occurred by a recollection of the uncommon scenes in which he has been called to Act no inglorious part, and the astonishing events of which he has been a witness, events which have seldom if ever before taken place on the stage of human action, nor can they probably ever happen again. For who has before seen a disciplined Army form'd at once from such raw materials? Who, that was not a witness, could imagine that the most violent local prejudices would cease so soon, and that Men who came from the different parts of the Continent, strongly disposed, by the habits of education, to despise and quarrel with each other, would instantly become but one patriotic band of Brothers, or who, that was not on the spot, can trace the steps by which such a wonderful revolution has been effected, and such a glorious period put to all our warlike toils?

It is universally acknowledged, that the enlarged prospects of happiness, opened by the confirmation of our independence and sovereignty, almost exceeds the power of description. And shall not the brave men, who have contributed so essentially to these inestimable acquisitions, retiring victorious from the field of War to the field of agriculture, participate in all the blessings which have been obtained; in such a republic, who will exclude them from the rights of Citizens and the fruits of their labour. In such a Country, so happily circumstanced, the pursuits of Commerce and the cultivation of the soil will unfold to industry the certain road to competence. To those hardy Soldiers, who are actuated by the spirit of adventure the Fisheries will afford ample and profitable employment, and the extensive and fertile regions of the West will yield a most happy asylum to those, who, fond of domestic enjoyments are seeking for personal independence. Nor is it possible to conceive, that any one of the U States will prefer a national bankruptcy and a dissolution of the union, to a compliance with the requisitions of Congress and the payment of its just debts; so that the Officers and Soldiers may expect considerable assistance in recommencing their civil occupations from the sums due to them from the public, which must and will most inevitably be paid.

In order to effect this desirable purpose and to remove the prejudices which may have taken possession of the minds of any of the good people of the States, it is earnestly recommended to all the Troops that with strong attachments to the Union, they should carry with them into civil society the most conciliating dispositions; and that they should prove themselves not less virtuous and useful as Citizens, than they have been persevering and victorious as Soldiers. What tho, there should be some envious individuals who are unwilling to pay the debt the public has contracted, or to yield the tribute due to merit; yet, let such unworthy treatment produce no invective or any instance of intemperate conduct; let it be remembered that the unbiassed voice of the few Citizens of the United States has promised the just reward, and given the merited applause; let it be known and remembered, that the reputation of the fœderal Armies is established beyond the reach of malevolence; and let a conscientiousness of their achievements and fame still unite the men, who composed them to honourable actions; under the persuasion that the private virtues of œconomy, prudence, and industry, will not be less amiable in civil life, than the more splendid qualities of valour, perseverance, and enterprise were in the Field. Every one may rest assured that much, very much of the future happiness of the Officers and Men will depend upon the wise and manly conduct which shall be adopted by them when they are mingled with the great body of the community. And, altho the General has so frequently given it as his opinion, in the most public and explicit manner, that, unless the principles of the federal government were properly supported and the powers of the union increased, the honour, dignity, and justice of the nation would be lost forever. Yet he cannot help repeating, on this occasion, so interesting a sentiment, and leaving it as his last injunction to every Officer and every Soldier, who may view the subject in the same serious point of light, to add his best endeavours to those of his worthy fellow Citizens towards effecting these great and valuable purposes on which our very existence as a nation so materially depends.

The Commander in chief conceives little is now wanting to enable the Soldiers to change the military character into that of the Citizen, but that steady and decent tenor of behaviour which has generally distinguished, not only the Army under his immediate command, but the different detachments and seperate Armies through the course of the war. From their good sense and prudence he anticipates the happiest consequences; and while he congratulates them on the glorious occasion, which renders their services in the field no longer necessary, he wishes to express the strong obligations he feels himself under for the assistance he has received from every Class, and in every instance. He presents his thanks in the most serious and affectionate manner to the General Officers, as well for their counsel on many interesting occasions, as for their Order in promoting the success of the plans he had adopted. To the Commandants of Regiments and Corps, and to the other Officers for their great zeal and attention, in carrying his orders promptly into execution. To the Staff, for their alacrity and exactness in performing the Duties of their several Departments. And to the Non Commissioned Officers and private Soldiers, for their extraordinary patience in suffering, as well as their invincible fortitude in Action. To the various branches of the Army the General takes this last and solemn opportunity of professing his inviolable attachment and friendship. He wishes more than bare professions were in his power, that he were really able to be useful to them all in future life. He flatters himself however, they will do him the justice to believe, that whatever could with propriety be attempted by him has been done, and being now to conclude these his last public Orders, to take his ultimate leave in a short time of the military character, and to bid a final adieu to the Armies he has so long had the honor to Command, he can only again offer in their behalf his recommendations to their grateful country, and his prayers to the God of Armies. May ample justice be done them here, and may the choicest of heaven's favours, both here and hereafter, attend those who, under the devine auspices, have secured innumerable blessings for others; with these wishes, and this benediction, the Commander in Chief is about to retire from Service. The Curtain of seperation will soon be drawn, and the military scene to him will be closed for ever.

"I RETIRE FROM THE GREAT THEATRE OF ACTION"

Address to Congress on Resigning Commission

Mr. President: The great events on which my resignation depended having at length taken place; I have now the honor of offering my sincere Congratulations to Congress and of presenting myself before them to surrender into their hands the trust committed to me, and to claim the indulgence of retiring from the Service of my Country.

Happy in the confirmation of our Independence and Sovereignty, and pleased with the oppertunity afforded the United States of becoming a respectable Nation, I resign with satisfaction the Appointment I accepted with diffidence. A diffidence in my abilities to accomplish so arduous a task, which however was superseded by a confidence in the rectitude of our Cause, the support of the Supreme Power of the Union, and the patronage of Heaven.

The Successful termination of the War has verified the most sanguine expectations, and my gratitude for the interposition of Providence, and the assistance I have received from my Countrymen, encreases with every review of the momentous Contest.

While I repeat my obligations to the Army in general, I should do injustice to my own feelings not to acknowledge in this place the peculiar Services and distinguished merits of the Gentlemen who have been attached to my person during the War. It was impossible the choice of confidential Officers to compose my family should have been more fortunate. Permit me Sir, to recommend in particular those, who have continued in Service to the present moment, as worthy of the favorable notice and patronage of Congress.

I consider it an indispensable duty to close this last solemn act of my Official life, by commending the Interests of our dearest Country to the protection of Almighty God, and those who have the superintendence of them, to his holy keeping.

Having now finished the work assigned me, I retire from the great theatre of Action; and bidding an Affectionate farewell to this August body under whose orders I have so long acted, I here offer my Commission, and take my leave of all the employments of public life.

Annapolis, December 23, 1783

"WE SHALL WANTON AND RUN RIOT"

To Benjamin Harrison

My Dear Sir,   Mount Vernon 18th Jany 1784

I have just had the pleasure to receive your letter of the 8th—for the friendly & affectionate terms in which you have welcomed my return to this Country & to private life; & for the favourable light in which you are pleased to consider, & express your sense of my past services, you have my warmest & most grateful acknowledgments.

That the prospect before us is, as you justly observe, fair, none can deny; but what use we shall make of it, is exceedingly problematical; not but that I believe, all things will come right at last; but like a young heir, come a little prematurely to a large inheritance, we shall wanton and run riot until we have brought our reputation to the brink of ruin, & then like him shall have to labor with the current of opinion when *compelled* perhaps, to do what prudence & common policy pointed out as plain as any problem in Euclid, in the first instance.

The disinclination of the individual States to yield competent powers to Congress for the Fœderal Government—their unreasonable jealousy of that body & of one another—& the disposition which seems to pervade each, of being all-wise & all-powerful within itself, will, if there is not a change in the system, be our downfal as a Nation. This is as clear to me as the A, B.C.; & I think we have opposed Great Britain, & have arrived at the present state of peace & independency, to very little purpose, if we cannot conquer our own prejudices. The powers of Europe begin to see this, & our newly acquired friends the British, are already & professedly acting upon this ground; & wisely too, if we are determined to persevere in our folly. They know that individual opposition to their measures is futile, & *boast* that we are not sufficiently united as a Nation to give a general one! Is not the indignity alone, of this declaration, while we are in the very act of peace-making & conciliation, sufficient to stimulate us to vest more extensive & adequate powers in the sovereign of these United States? For my own part, altho' I am returned to, & am now mingled with the class of private citizens, & like them must suffer all the evils of a Tyranny, or of too great an extension of fœderal powers; I have no fears arising from this source; in my mind, but I have many, & powerful ones indeed which predict the worst consequences from a half starved, limping Government, that appears to be always moving upon crutches, & tottering at every step. Men, chosen as the Delegates in Congress are, cannot officially be dangerous—they depend upon the breath—nay, they are so much the creatures of the people, under the present Constitution, that they can have no views (which could possibly be carried into execution), nor any interests, distinct from those of their constituents. My political creed therefore is, to be wise in the choice of Delegates—support them like Gentlemen while they are our representatives—give them competent powers for all fœderal purposes—support them in the due exercise thereof —& lastly, to compel them to close attendance in Congress during their delegation. These things under the present mode for, & termination of elections, aided by annual instead of constant Sessions, would, or I am exceedingly mistaken, make us one of the most wealthy, happy, respectable & powerful Nations, that ever inhabited the terrestrial Globe—without them, we shall in my opinion soon be every thing which is the direct reverse of them.

I shall look for you, in the first part of next month, with such other friends as may incline to accompany you, with great pleasure, being with best respects to Mrs Harrison, in which Mrs Washington joins me, Dear Sir, Your Most Obedt & affecte hble servant

"THE DERANGED SITUATION OF MY PRIVATE CONCERNS"

To Marquis de Lafayette

Mount Vernon 1st Feby 1784

At length my Dear Marquis I am become a private citizen on the banks of the Potomac, & under the shadow of my own Vine & my own Fig tree, free from the bustle of a camp & the busy scenes of public life, I am solacing myself with those tranquil enjoyments, of which the Soldier who is ever in pursuit of fame—the Statesman whose watchful days & sleepless Nights are spent in devising schemes to promote the welfare of his own—perhaps the ruin of other countries, as if this Globe was insufficient for us all—& the Courtier who is always watching the countenance of his Prince, in hopes of catching a gracious smile, can have very little conception. I am not only retired from all public employments, but I am retireing within myself; & shall be able to view the solitary walk, & tread the paths of private life with heartfelt satisfaction—Envious of none, I am determined to be pleased with all. & this my dear friend, being the order for my march, I will move gently down the stream of life, until I sleep with my Fathers.

Except an introductory letter or two, & one countermanding my request respecting Plate, I have not written to you since the middle of Octobr by Genl Duportail. To inform you at this late hour, that the City of New York was evacuated by the British forces on the 25th of Novembr—that the American Troops took possession of it the same day, & delivered it over to the civil authority of the State—that good order, contrary to the expectation & predictions of Gl Carleton, his Officers & all the loyalists, was immediately established—and that the harbour of New York was finally cleared of the British flag about the 5th or 6th of Decemr, would be an insult to your intelligence. And to tell you that I remained eight days in New York after we took possession of the City—that I was very much hurried during that time, which was the reason I did not write to you from thence—that taking Phila. in my way, I was obliged to remain there a week—that at Annapolis, where Congress were then, and are now sitting, I did, on the 23d of December present them my Commission, & made them my last bow—& on the Eve of Christmas entered these doors an older man by near nine years, than when I left them, is very uninteresting to any but myself. Since that period we have been fast locked up in frost & snow, & excluded in a manner from all kinds of intercourse, the winter having been, & still continues to be, extremely severe.

I have now to acknowledge, and thank you for your favors of the 22d of July & 8th of September, both of which, altho' the first is of old date, have come to hand since my letter to you of October. The accounts contained therein of the political & commercial state of affairs as they respect America, are interesting, & I wish I could add that they were altogether satisfactory; & the Agency, you have had in both, particularly with regard to the Free ports in France, is a fresh evidence of your unwearied endeavours to serve this Country; but there is no part of your Letters to Congress My Dear Marquis, which bespeaks the excellence of your heart more plainly than that, which contains those noble & generous sentiments on the justice which is due to the faithful friends & Servants of the public; but I must do Congress the justice to declare, that as a body, I believe there is every disposition in them, not only to acknowledge the merits, but to reward the services of the army:

there is a contractedness, I am sorry to add, in some of the States, from whence all our difficulties on this head, proceed; but it is to be hoped, the good sense & perserverance of the rest, will ultimately prevail, as the spirit of meanness is beginning to subside.

From a letter which I have just received from the Governor of this State I expect him here in a few days, when I shall not be unmindful of what you have written about the bust, & will endeavour to have matters respecting it, placed on their proper basis. I thank you most sincerely My Dear Marqs for your kind invitation to your house, if I should come to Paris. At present I see but little prospect of such a voyage, the deranged situation of my private concerns, occasioned by an absence of almost nine years, and an entire disregard of all private business during that period, will not only suspend, but may put it forever out of my power to gratify this wish. This not being the case with you, come with Madame la Fayette & view me in my domestic walks—I have often told you, & I repeat it again, that no man could receive you in them with more friendship & affection than I should do; in which I am sure Mrs Washington would cordially join me. We unite in respectful compliments to your Lady, & best wishes for your little flock. With every sentiment of esteem, Admiration & Love, I am, My Dr Marqs Your Most Affecte friend

"THEY MAY BE MAHOMETANS, JEWS,
OR CHRISTIANS OF ANY SECT—OR
THEY MAY BE ATHIESTS"

To Tench Tilghman

Dear Sir,   Mount Vernon Mar. 24th 1784

I am informed that a Ship with Palatines is gone up to Baltimore, among whom are a number of Tradesmen. I am a good deal in want of a House Joiner & Bricklayer, (who really understand their profession) & you would do me a favor by purchasing one of each, for me. I would not confine you to Palatines. If they are good workmen, they may be of Assia, Africa, or

Europe. They may be Mahometans, Jews, or Christian of any Sect—or they may be Athiests—I would however prefer middle aged, to young men. and those who have good countenances & good characters on ship board, to others who have neither of these to recommend them—altho, after all, the proof of the pudding must be in the eating. I do not limit you to a price, but will pay the purchase money on demand—This request will be in force 'till complied with, or countermanded, because you may not succeed at this moment, and have favourable ones here after to do it in. My best respects, in which Mrs Washington joins, are presented to Mrs Tilghman & Mrs Carroll—and I am Dr Sir Yr Affecte Hble Servt

"PEOPLE HAVE GOT IMPATIENT"

To Richard Henry Lee

Dear Sir,   Mount Vernon 14th Decr 84
    The letter which you did me the honor to write to me on the 20th of last Month, only came to my hands by the Post preceeding the date of this.
    For the copy of the treaty held with the Six Nations at Fort Stanwix, you will please to accept my thanks. These people have given, I think, all that the United States could reasonably have asked of them; more perhaps than the State of New York conceive ought to have been required from them, by any other, than their own Legislature. I wish they were better satisfied. Individual States opposing the measures of the United States—encroaching upon the territory of one another—and setting up old and obsolete claims, is verifying the predictions of our enemies; and, in reallity, is truly unfortunate. If the Western tribes are as well disposed to treat with us as the Northern Indians have been, & will cede a competent district of Country North West of the Ohio, to answer our present purposes, it would be a circumstance as unexpected, as pleasing to me; for it was apprehended, if they agreed to the latter at all, it would be reluctantly. but the example of the Six Nations who (if they have not relinquished their claim) have pretensions to a large part of

those Lands, may have a powerful influence on the Western gentry, & smooth the way for the Commissioners, who have proceeded to Fort Pitt.

It gave me pleasure to find by the last Gazettes, that a sufficient number of States had Assembled to form a Congress, and that you had been placed in the Chair of it—On this event, permit me to offer my Compliments of congratulation. To whatever causes the delay of this meeting may have been ascribed, it most certainly has an unfavorable aspect—contributes to lessen—(already too low)—the dignity and importance of the fœderal government. and is hurtful to our National character, in the eyes of Europe.

It is said (how founded I know not) that our Assembly have repealed their former act respecting British debts. If this be true, & the State of New York have not acted repugnant to the terms of the treaty, the British government can no longer hold the western posts under that cover; but I shall be mistaken if they do not intrench themselves behind some other expedient, to effect it; or, will appoint a time for surrendering them, of which we cannot avail ourselves—the probable consequence whereof will be, the destruction of the Works.

The Assemblies of Virginia and Maryland have now under consideration the extension of the inland navigation of the rivers Potomack & James; and opening a communication between them, and the Western Waters. They seem fully impressed with the political, as well as the commercial advantages which would result from the accomplishment of these great objects; & I hope will embrace the present moment to put them in a train for execution—Would it not at the same time, be worthy the wisdom, & attention of Congress to have the Western Waters well explored; the Navigation of them fully ascertained; accurately laid down; and a complete & perfect Map made of the Country; at least as far Westerly—as the Miamies, running into the Ohio & Lake Erie; and to see how the Waters of these communicates with the river St Joseph, which emptys into the Lake Michigan, & with the Wabash? for I cannot forbear observing that the Miami village in Hutchins Map, if it and the Waters are laid down with accuracy points to a very important Post for the Union—The expence attending such an undertaking could not be great—the advantages would be unbounded—for sure

I am Nature has made such a display of her bounties in those regions that the more the Country is explored the more it will rise in estimation—consequently greater will the revenue be, to the Union.

Would there be any impropriety do you think Sir, in reserving for special Sale, all Mines, Minerals & Salt Springs in the general grants of land, from the United States? The public, instead of the few knowing ones might, in that case, receive the benefits which would proceed from the Sale of them; without infringing any rule of justice that occurs to me, or their own laws—but on the contrary, inflict just punishment upon those who, in defiance of the latter, have dared to create enemies to disturb the public tranquility, by roaming over the Country marking & Surveying the valuable spots in it, to the great disquiet of the Western tribes of Indians, who have viewed these proceedings with jealous indignation.

To hit upon a happy medium price for the Western Lands, for the prevention of Monopoly on one hand—and not discouraging useful Settlers on the other, will, no doubt, require consideration; but ought not in my opinion to employ too much time before the terms are announced. The Spirit of emigration is great—People have got impatient—and tho' you cannot stop the road, it is yet in your power to mark the way; a little while, & you will not be able to do either—It is easier to prevent, than to remedy an evil.

I shall be very happy in the continuation of your corrispondence—& with sentiments of great esteem & respect I have the honor to be Dr Sir Yr Most Obedt Hble Servt

A BIT OF RIBALDRY

To William Gordon

Dear sir,   Mount Vernon 20th Decr 1784.
I am indebted to you for several letters; & am as much so for the Fish you kindly intended, as if it had actually arrived, & I was in the act of paying my respects to it at table—the chance, however, of doing this would be greater, was it at Boston, than in

York-town in this State, where, I am informed it was landed at the time the Marqs de la Fayette did; who proceeded from thence to richmond, where I met him, & conducted him to Annapolis on his way to New York; the place of his intended embarkation for France, about the middle of this month.

I am glad to hear that my old acquaintance Colo. Ward is yet under the influence of vigorous passions—I will not ascribe the intrepidity of his late enterprize to a mere *flash* of desires, because, in his military career he would have learnt how to distinguish between false alarms & a serious movement. Charity therefore induces me to suppose that like a prudent general, he had reviewed his *strength*, his arms, & ammunition before he got involved in an action—But if these have been neglected, & he has been precipitated into the measure, let me advise him to make the *first* onset upon his fair del Tobosa, with vigor, that the impression may be deep, if it cannot be lasting, or frequently renewed.

We are all well at this time except Miss Custis, who still feels the effect, & sometimes the return of her fever—Mrs Lund Washington has added a daughter to her family—She, child and husband are well, & become house keepers at the distance of about four miles from this place.

We have a dearth of News, but the fine weather keeps us busy, & we have leisure for cogitation. All join in best wishes for you. Doctr & Mrs Stuart are of those who do it. I am Dr sir yrs &c.

"ALL THIS NAVIGATION BUSINESS"

To Benjamin Harrison

My Dr Sir,   Mount Vernon 22d Jan. 1785.
It is not easy for me to decide by which my mind was most affected upon the receipt of your letter of the 6th inst.—surprize or gratitude: both were greater than I have words to express. The attention & good wishes which the Assembly have evidenced by their act for vesting in me 150 shares in the navigation of each of the rivers Potomac & James, is more than mere

compliment—there is an unequivocal & substantial meaning annexed—But believe me sir, notwithstanding these, no circumstance has happened to me since I left the walks of public life, which has so much embarrassed me. On the one hand, I consider this act, as I have already observed, as a noble and unequivocal proof of the good opinion, the affection, & disposition of my Country to serve me; & I should be hurt, if by declining the acceptance of it, my refusal should be construed into disrespect, or the smallest slight put upon the generous intention of the Country: or, that an ostentatious display of disinterestedness or public virtue, was the source of the refusal.

On the other hand, it is really my wish to have my mind, & the actions which are the result of contemplation, as free & independent as the air, that I may be more at liberty (in things which my opportunities & experience have brought me to the knowledge of) to express my sentiments, & if necessary, to suggest what may occur to me, under the fullest conviction, that altho' my judgment may be arraigned, there will be no suspicion that sinister motives had the smallest influence in the suggestion. Not content then with the bare consciousness of my having, in all this navigation business, acted upon the clearest conviction of the political importance of the measure; I would wish that every individual who may hear that it was a favorite plan of mine, may know also that I had no other motive for promoting it than the advantage I conceived it would be productive of to the Union, & to this State in particular, by cementing the Eastern and Western Territory together, at the same time that it will give vigor & encrease to our Commerce, & be a convenience to our Citizens.

How would this matter be viewed then by the eye of the world; and what would be the opinion of it, when it comes to be related that G: W——n exerted himself to effect this work—and G.W. has received 20,000 Dollars, and £5,000 Sterling of the public money as an interest therein? Would not this in the estimation of it (if I am entitled to any merit for the part I have acted; & without it there is no foundation for the act) deprive me of the principal thing which is laudable in my conduct? Would it not, in some respects, be considered in the same light as a pension? And would not the apprehension of this make me more reluctantly offer my sentiments in future? In a word, under what ever pretence, & however customary these gratuitous gifts are made in other Countries, should I not thence forward be considered as a dependant? one moments thought of which would give me more pain, than I should receive pleasure from the product of all the tolls, was every farthing of them vested in me: altho' I consider it as one of the most certain & increasing Estates in the Country.

I have written to you with an openess becoming our friendship—I could have said more on the subject; but I have already said enough to let you into the State of my mind. I wish to know whether the ideas I entertain occurred to, & were expressed by any member in or out of the House. Upon the whole, you may be assured my Dr Sir, that my mind is not a little agitated—I want the best information & advice to settle it. I have no inclination (as I have already observed) to avail myself of the generosity of the Country: nor do I want to appear ostentatiously disinterested, (for more than probable my refusal would be ascribed to this motive) or that the Country should harbour an idea that I am disposed to set little value on her favours—the manner of granting which is as flattering as the grant is important. My present difficulties however shall be no impediment to the progress of the undertaking. I will receive the full & frank opinions of my friends with thankfulness. I shall have time enough between this & the sitting of the next Assembly to consider the tendency of the act—& in this, as in all other matters, will endeavor to decide for the best.

My respectful compliments & best wishes, in which Mrs Washington & Fanny Bassett (who is much recovered) join, are offered to Mrs Harrison & the rest of your family. It would give us great pleasure to hear that Mrs Harrison had her health restored to her. With every sentiment of esteem, regard & friendship, I am My Dr Sir &c. &c.

"I AM CONSCIOUS OF A
DEFECTIVE EDUCATION"

To David Humphreys

My dear Humphreys   Mount Vernon July 25th 1785.

Since my last to you I have received your letters of the 15th of Jany and (I believe) that of the 11th of Novr; & thank you for them both—It always gives me pleasure to hear from you; and I should think, if amusements would spare you, business could not so much absorb your time as to prevent your writing to me more frequently; especially as there is a regular & safe conveyance once a month, by the Packett.

As the complexion of European politics seem now (from the letters I have received from the Marquisses de la Fayette & Chastellux—the Chevr de la Luzerne, &ca) to have a tendency to Peace, I will say nothing of War, nor make any animadversions upon the contending Powers—otherwise I might possibly have added, that the retreat from it seemed impossible, after the explicit declarations of the Parties.

My first wish is, to see this plague to Mankind banished from the Earth; & the Sons & daughters of this World employed in more pleasing & innocent amusements than in preparing implements, & exercising them for the destruction of the human race. Rather than quarrel abt territory, let the poor, the needy, & oppressed of the Earth; and those who want Land, resort to the fertile plains of our Western Country, to the second Land of promise, & there dwell in peace, fulfilling the first & great Commandment.

In a former letter I informed you, My dear Humphreys, that if I had talents for it, I have not leizure to devote my time & thoughts to commentaries. I am conscious of a defective education, & want of capacity to fit me for such an undertaking. What with Company, letters, & other Matters, many of them extraneous, I have not yet been able to arrange my own private concerns so as to rescue them from that disordered state into which they have been thrown, by the War; and to do which, is become indispensibly necessary for my support, whilst I remain on this stage of human action.

The sentiment of your last letter on this subject gave me great pleasure. I should indeed be pleased to see you undertake this business. Your abilities as a writer—Your discernment respecting the principles which lead to the decision by Arms—Your personal knowledge of many facts as they occurred, in the progress of the War—Your disposition to justice, candour & impartiallity, and your diligence in investigating truth, combining, fits you, in the vigor of life, for this task. and I should with great pleasure not only give you the perusal of all my Papers, but any oral information of circumstances which cannot be obtained from the latter, that my memory will furnish. And I can with great truth add, that my House would not only be at your Service during the period of your preparing this work, but (and without an unmeaning compliment I say it) I shoud be exceedingly happy if you would make it your home. You might have an Apartment to yourself in which you could command your own time. You would be considered, & treated as one of the family. And would meet with that cordial reception & entertainment, which are characteristic of the sincerest friendship.

To reverberate European News would be idle; and we have little of a domestic kind worthy of attention. We have held treaties indeed with the Indians, but they were so unseasonably delayed that these people from our last accts from the Westward are in a discontented mood—supposed by many to be instigated thereto by our late enemy—now, to be sure, good & fast friends; who, from anything I can learn, under the indefinite expression of the treaty, hold, & seem resolved to retain, possession of our Western Posts. Congress have also—after long & tedeous deliberation—passed an Ordinance for laying of the Western territory into States, & for disposing of the Land; but in a manner, and on terms, which few people (in the Southern States) conceive can be accomplished. Both sides are sure, & the event is appealed to—time must decide. It is to be regretted however, that local politics, & self interested views, obtrude themselves into every measure of public utility. But on such characters, be the obloquy—My attention is more immediately engaged in a project which I think is big with great political, as well as Commercial consequences to these States, especially the middle ones. It is, by removing the obstructions—and extending the inland Navigations of our Rivers, to bring the States on the Atlantic in close connection with those forming to the Westward, by a short & easy Land transportation. Without this is effected, I can readily conceive that the Western Settlers will have different views—seperate interests—and other connections.

I may be singular in my ideas, but they are these, that to open the front door to, & make easy the way for those Settlers to the Westward (which ought to progress regularly & compactly) before we make any stir about the Navigation of the Mississipi, and before our settlements are far advanced towards that River would be our true line of policy. It can I think be demonstrated, that the produce of the Western territory (if the Navigations which are now in hand succeed, and of which I have no doubt) as low down the Ohio as the Great Kanhawa (I believe to the Falls) and between the parts above, & the Lakes, may be brought to the highest shipping Port either on this, or James River, at a less expence, with more ease (including the return) and in a much shorter time than it can be carried to New Orleans, if the Spaniards, instead of restrictions were to throw open their ports, & envite our trade—But if the commerce of that Country shd embrace this channel, and connections be formed, experience has taught us (and there is a very recent one in proof, with Great Britain) how next to impracticable it is to divert it—and if that shd be the case, the Atlantic States (especially as those to the Westward will, in a great degree, fill with foreigners) except to excite—perhaps with too much cause—our fears that the Country of California, which is still more to the Westward, & belonging to another Power. Mrs Washington presents her compliments to you, and with every wish for your happiness I am—My dear Humphreys Yr sincere friend and Affectionate Hble Servt

"ACTS OF TYRANNY & OPPRESSION"

To Robert Morris

Dr Sir,   Mt Vernon 12th April 1786
   I give you the trouble of this letter at the instance of Mr Dalby of Alexandria; who is called to Philadelphia to attend what he conceives to be a vexatious law-suit respecting a slave of his, which a Society of Quakers in the City (formed for such purposes) have attempted to liberate. The merits of this case will no doubt appear upon trial; but from Mr Dalby's state of the matter, it should seem that this Society is not only acting repugnant to justice so far as its conduct concerns strangers, but, in my opinion extremely impolitickly with respect to the State—the City in particular; & without being able (but by Acts of tyranny & oppression) to accomplish their own ends. He says the conduct of this society is not sanctioned by Law: had the case been otherwise, whatever my opinion of the Law might have been, my respect for the policy of the State would on this occasion have appeared in my silence; because against the penalties of promulgated Laws one may guard; but there is no avoiding the snares of individuals, or of private societies—and if the practice of this Society of which Mr Dalby speaks, is not discountenanced, none of those whose *misfortune* it is to have slaves as attendants will visit the City if they can possibly avoid it; because by so doing they hazard their property—or they must be at the expence (& this will not always succeed) of providing servants of another description for the trip.
   I hope it will not be conceived from these observations, that it is my wish to hold the unhappy people who are the subject of this letter, in slavery. I can only say that there is not a man living who wishes more sincerely than I do, to see a plan adopted for the abolition of it—but there is only one proper and effectual mode by which it can be accomplished, & that is by Legislative authority: and this, as far as my suffrage will go, shall never be wanting.
   But when slaves who are happy & content to remain with their present masters, are tampered with & seduced to leave them; when masters are taken at unawares by these practices;

when a conduct of this sort begets discontent on one side and resentment on the other, & when it happens to fall on a man whose purse will not measure with that of the Society, & he looses his property for want of means to defend it—it is oppression in the latter case, & not humanity in any; because it introduces more evils than it can cure.

I will make no apology for writing to you on this subject; for if Mr Dalby has not misconceived the matter, an evil exists which requires a remedy; if he has, my intentions have been good though I may have been too precipitate in this address. Mrs Washington joins me in every good & kind wish for Mrs Morris & your family, and I am &c.

"SOMETHING MUST BE DONE,
OR THE FABRICK MUST FALL"

To John Jay

Dear Sir,   Mount Vernon 18th May 1786.

In due course of Post, I have been honoured with your favours of the 2d & 16th of March; since which I have been a good deal engaged, and pretty much from home.

For the inclosure which accompanied the first, I thank you. Mr Littlepage seems to have forgot what had been his situation—What was due to you—and indeed what was necessary for his own character. And his Guardian I think, seems to have forgot every thing.

I coincide perfectly in sentiment with you, my dear Sir, that there are errors in our National Government which call for correction; loudly I will add; but I shall find my self happily mistaken if the remedies are at hand. We are certainly in a delicate situation, but my fear is that the people are not yet sufficiently misled to retract from error! To be plainer, I think there is more wickedness than ignorance, mixed with our councils. Under this impression, I scarcely know what opinion to entertain of a general Convention. That it is necessary to revise, and amend the articles of Confederation, I entertain *no* doubt; but what may be the consequences of such an attempt *is* doubtful.

Yet, something must be done, or the fabrick must fall. It certainly is tottering! Ignorance & design, are difficult to combat. Out of these proceed illiberality, *improper* jealousies, and a train of evils which oftentimes, in republican governments, must be sorely felt before they can be removed. The former, that is ignorance, being a fit soil for the latter to work in, tools are employed which a generous mind would disdain to use; and which nothing but time, and their own puerile or wicked productions, can show the inefficacy and dangerous tendency of. I think often of our situation, and view it with concern. From the high ground on which we stood—from the plain path which invited our footsteps, to be so fallen!—so lost! is really mortifying. But virtue, I fear, has, in a great degree, taken its departure from our Land, and the want of disposition to do justice is the sourse of the national embarrassments; for under whatever guise or colourings are given to them, this, I apprehend, is the origin of the evils we now feel, & probably shall labour for sometime yet. With respectful Complimts to Mrs Jay—and sentiments of sincere friendship—I am—Dear Sir Yr most Obedt Hble Servt

P.S. Will you do me the favor to forward the enclosed, with any dispatches of your own, for England?

"MAY OUR COUNTRY NEVER WANT PROPS TO
SUPPORT THE GLORIOUS FABRICK!"

To Thomas Jefferson

Dear Sir,   Mount Vernon Augt 1st 1786.
The letters you did me the favor to write to me on the 4th & 7th of Jany have been duly received.

In answer to your obliging enquiries respecting the dress, attitude &ca which I would wish to have given to the Statue in question—I have only to observe that not having a sufficient knowledge in the art of sculpture to oppose my judgment to the taste of Connoisseiurs, I do not desire to dictate in the matter —on the contrary I shall be perfectly satisfied with whatever may be judged decent and proper. I should even scarcely have ventured to suggest that perhaps a servile adherence to the garb of antiquity might not be altogether so expedient as some little deviation in favor of the modern custom, if I had not learnt from Colo. Humphreys that this was a circumstance hinted in conversation by Mr West to Houdon. This taste, which has been introduced in painting by West, I understand is received with applause & prevails extensively.

I have taken some pains to enquire into the facts respecting the medals of the Cincinnati, which Majr L'Enfant purchased in France. It seems that when he went to Europe in 1783 he had money put into his hands to purchase a certain number, and that conceiving it to be consonant with the intentions of the Society, he purchased to a still greater amount—insomuch that a Committee of the Genl Meeting, upon examining his Acct reported a balle due to him of Six hundred & thirty dollars, wch report was accepted. This money is still due, and is all that is due from the Society of the Cincinnati as a Society. General Knox has offered to pay the amount to Majr L'Enfant, but as it has become a matter of some public discussion, the latter wished it might remain until the next Genl Meeting, which will be in May next. In the meantime Genl Knox (who is Secretary Genl) has, or will write fully on the Subject to the Marquis de la Fayette, from whom he has had a letter respecting the business.

We have no news of importance And if we had, I should hardly be in the way of learning it; as I divide my time between the superintendence of opening the navigations of our rivers & attention to my private concerns. Indeed I am too much secluded from the world to know with certainty, what sensation the refusal of the British to deliver up the Western posts, has made on the public mind. I fear the edge of its sensibility is somewhat blunted. Fœderal measures are not yet universally adopted. New York, wch was as well disposed a State as any in the Union is said to have become in a degree antifœderal. Some other States are, in my opinion, falling into very foolish & wicked plans of emitting paper money. I cannot however give up my hopes & expectations that we shall 'ere long adopt a more liberal system of policy. What circumstances will lead, or what misfortunes will compel us to it, is more than can be told without the spirit of prophecy.

In the meantime the people are industrious, œconomy begins to prevail, and our internal governments are, in general, tolerably well administered.

You will probably have heard of the death of Genl Greene before this reaches you, in which case you will, in common with your Countrymen, have regretted the loss of so great and so honest a man. Genl McDougall, who was a brave Soldier & a disinterested patriot, is also dead—he belonged to the Legislature of his State, the last act of his life, was (after being carried on purpose to the Senate) to give his voice against the emission of a paper currency. Colo. Tilghman, who was formerly of my family, died lately & left as fair a reputation as ever belonged to a human character. Thus some of the pillars of the revolution fall. Others are mouldering by insensible degrees. May our Country never want props to support the glorious fabrick! With sentiments of the highest esteem & regard, I have the honor to be Dear Sir Yr Most Obedt & very Hble Servt

"OUR AFFAIRS ARE RAPIDLY
DRAWING TO A CRISIS"

To John Jay

Dear Sir   Mount Vernon 15th Augt 1786

I have to thank you very sincerely for your interesting letter of the 27th of June, as well as for the other communications you had the goodness to make at the same time.

I am sorry to be assured, of what indeed I had little doubt before, that we have been guilty of violating the treaty in some instances. What a misfortune it is the British should have so well grounded a pretext for their palpable infractions?—and what a disgraceful part, out of the choice of difficulties before us, are we to act?

Your sentiments, that our affairs are drawing rapidly to a crisis, accord with my own. What the event will be is also beyond the reach of my foresight. We have errors to correct. We have probably had too good an opinion of human nature in forming our confederation. Experience has taught us, that men will not adopt & carry into execution, measures the best calculated for their own good without the intervention of a coercive power. I do not conceive we can exist long as a nation, without having lodged somewhere a power which will pervade the whole Union in as energetic a manner, as the authority of the different state governments extends over the several States. To be fearful of vesting Congress, constituted as that body is, with ample authorities for national purposes, appears to me the very climax of popular absurdity and madness. Could Congress exert them for the detriment of the public without injuring themselves in an equal or greater proportion? Are not their interests inseperably connected with those of their constituents? By the rotation of appointment must they not mingle frequently with the mass of citizens? Is it not rather to be apprehended, if they were possessed of the powers before described, that the individual members would be induced to use them, on many occasions, very timidly & inefficatiously for fear of loosing their popularity & future election? We must take human nature as we find it. Perfection falls not to the share of mortals. Many are of opinion that Congress have too frequently made use of the suppliant humble tone of requisition, in applications to the States, when they had a right to assume their imperial dignity and command obedience. Be that as it may, requisitions are a perfect nihility, where thirteen sovereign, independent, disunited States are in the habit of discussing & refusing compliance with them at their option. Requisitions are actually little better than a jest and a bye word through out the Land. If you tell the Legislatures they have violated the treaty of peace and invaded the prerogatives of the confederacy they will laugh in your face. What then is to be done? Things cannot go on in the same train forever. It is much to be feared, as you observe, that the better kind of people being disgusted with the circumstances will have their minds prepared for any revolution whatever. We are apt to run from one extreme into another. To anticipate & prevent disasterous contingencies would be the part of wisdom & patriotism.

What astonishing changes a few years are capable of producing! I am told that even respectable characters speak of a monarchical form of government without horror. From thinking proceeds speaking, thence to acting is often but a single step. But how irrevocable & tremendous! What a triumph for the advocates of despotism to find that we are incapable of governing ourselves, and that systems founded on the basis of equal liberty are merely ideal & falacious! Would to God that wise measures may be taken in time to avert the consequences we have but too much reason to apprehend.

Retired as I am from the world, I frankly acknowledge I cannot feel myself an unconcerned spectator. Yet having happily assisted in bringing the ship into port & having been fairly discharged; it is not my business to embark again on a sea of troubles. Nor could it be expected that my sentiments and opinions would have much weight on the minds of my Countrymen—they have been neglected, tho' given as a last legacy in the most solemn manner. I had then perhaps some claims to public attention. I consider myself as having none at present. With sentiments of sincere esteem & friendship I am, my dear Sir, Yr most Obedt & Affecte Hble Servant

"THE SPRING OF REANIMATION"

To James Madison

My Dr Sir,   Mount Vernon 18th Novr 1786.

Not having sent to the Post Office with my usual regularity, your favor of the 8th did not reach me in time for an earlier acknowledgment than of this date.

It gives me the most sensible pleasure to hear that the Acts of the present Session, are marked with wisdom, justice & liberality. They are the palladium of good policy, & the only paths that lead to national happiness. Would to God every State would let these be the leading features of their constituent characters: those threatening clouds which seem ready to burst on the Confederacy, would soon dispel. The unanimity with which the Bill was received, for appointing Commissioners agreeably to the recommendation of the Convention at Annapolis;

and the uninterrupted progress it has met with since, are indications of a favourable issue. It is a measure of equal necessity & magnitude; & may be the spring of reanimation.

Altho' I have bid a public adieu to the public walks of life, & had resolved never more to tread that theatre; yet, if upon an occasion so interesting to the well-being of the Confederacy it should have been the wish of the Assembly that I should have been an associate in the business of revising the fœderal System; I should, from a sense of the obligation I am under for repeated proofs of confidence in me, more than from any opinion I should have entertained of my usefulness, have obeyed its call; but it is now out of my power to do this with any degree of consistency—the cause I will mention.

I presume you heard Sir, that I was first appointed & have since been rechosen President of the Society of the Cincinnati; & you may have understood also that the triennial Genl Meeting of this body is to be held in Philada the first monday in May next. Some particular reasons combining with the peculiar situation of my private concerns; the necessity of paying attention to them; a wish for retirement & relaxation from public cares, and rheumatic pains which I begin to feel very sensibly, induced me on the 31st ulto to address a circular letter to each State society informing them of my intention not to be at the next Meeting, & of my desire not to be rechosen President. The Vice President is also informed of this, that the business of the Society may not be impeded by my absence. Under these circumstances it will readily be perceived that I could not appear at the same time & place on any other occasion, with out giving offence to a very respectable & deserving part of the Community—the late officers of the American Army.

I feel as you do for our acquaintance Colo. Lee; better never have delegated, than left him out; unless some glaring impropriety of conduct has been ascribed to him. I hear with pleasure that you are in the new choice. With sentiments of the highest esteem & affectn I am &c.

"NOW WE ARE UNSHEATHING
THE SWORD TO OVERTURN THEM!"

To David Humphreys

My dear Humphreys   Mount Vernon Decr 26th 1786
I am much indebted to you for your several favors of the 1st
9th & 16th of November. The last came first. Mr Morse keeping in Mind the old proverb, was determined not to make more
haste than good speed in prosecuting his journey to Georgia—
so I got the two first but lately.

For your publication respecting the confinement of Captn
Asgill, I am exceedingly obliged to you. The manner of making it was as good as could be devised; and the matter, will
prove the injustice, as well as illiberality of the reports which
have been circulated on that occasion, and which are fathered
on that Officer, as the author.

It is with the deepest, and most heart felt concern, I perceive
by some late paragraphs extracted from the Boston Gazettes,
that the Insurgents of Massachusetts—far from being satisfied
with the redress offered by their General Court—are still acting in open violation of Law & Government; & have obliged
the Chief Magistrate in a decided tone, to call upon the militia
of the State to support the Constitution. What, gracious God,
is man! that there should be such inconsistency & perfidious-
ness in his conduct? It is but the other day we were shedding
our blood to obtain the Constitutions under which we now
live—Constitutions of our own choice and framing—and now
we are unsheathing the Sword to overturn them! The thing is
so unaccountable, that I hardly know how to realize it, or to
persuade my self that I am not under the vision of a dream.

My mind previous to the receipt of your letter of the first
Ulto had often been agitated by thoughts similar to those you
have expressed, respecting an old frd of yours; but heaven forbid that a crisis should arrive when he shall be driven to the
necessity of making choice of either of the alternatives there-
mentioned. Let me entreat you, my dear Sir, to keep me advised of the situation of Affairs in your quarter. I can depend
upon your Accts. Newspaper paragraphs unsupported by other

testimony, are often contradictory & bewildering. At one time these insurgents are represented as a mere Mob—At other times as systematic in all their proceedings. If the first, I would fain hope that like other Mobs, it will, however formidable, be of short duration. If the latter, there surely are men of consequence and abilities behind the Curtain, who move the puppits. The designs of whom may be deep & dangerous. They may be instigated by British Councils—actuated by ambitious motives—or being influenced by dishonest principles, had rather see the Country plunged in civil discord than do what Justice would dictate to an honest mind.

Private and Confidential

I had hardly dispatched my circular letters to the several State Societies of the Cincinnati, when I received Letters from some of the principal members of our Assembly, expressing a wish that they might be permitted to name me as one of the Deputies to the Convention proposed to be held at Philadelphia, the first of May next. I immediately wrote to my particular friend Madison (& similarly to the rest) the answer contained in the extract No. 1—In reply I got No. 2—This obliged me to be *more* explicit & confidential with him, on points which a recurrence to the conversations we have had on this Subject will bring to your mind without my hazarding the recital of them in a letter—Since this interchange, I have received from the Governor the letter No. 4 to whom I returned the answer No. 5. If this business should be further prest (which I hope it will not, as I have no inclination to go) what had I best do? *You*, as an *indifferent person*—& one who is much better acquainted with the Sentiments, & views of the Cincinnati than I am (for in this State, where the recommendations of the General meeting have been acceded to, hardly any thing is said about it) as also with the temper of the people, and the state of Politics at large, can determine upon fuller evidence, & better ground than myself—especially as you will know in what light the States to the Eastward consider *the Convention* & the measures they are pursuing to contravene, or give efficacy to it. On the last occasion, only five States were represented—none East of New York. Why the New England Governments did not appear I am yet to learn; for of all others the distractions &

turbulent temper of their people would, I should have thought, have afforded the strongest evidence of the *necessity* of competent powers somewhere. That the fœderal Government is nearly, if not quite at a stand none will deny: The question then is, can it be propt—or shall it be anihilated? If the former, the proposed Convention is an object of the first magnitude, and should be supported by all the friends of the present Constitution. In the other case, if on a full and dispassionate revision thereof, the continuances shall be adjudged impracticable, or unwise, would it not be better for such a meeting to suggest some other to avoid, if possible, civil discord, or other impending evils. Candour however obliges me to confess that as we could not remain quiet more than three or four years (in time of peace) under the constitutions of our own choice, which it was believed, in many instances, were formed with deliberation & wisdom, I see little prospect either of our agreeing upon any other, or that we should remain long satisfied under it if we could—Yet I would wish to see *any thing* and every thing essayed to prevent the effusion of blood, and to avert the humiliating, & contemptible figure we are about to make, in the Annals of Mankind.

If this second attempt to convene the States for the purposes proposed in the report of the partial representation at Annapolis in September last, should also prove abortive it may be considered as an unequivocal proof that the States are not likely to agree in any general measure which is to pervade the Union, & consequently, that there is an end put to Fœderal Government. The States therefore who make this last dying essay to avoid the misfortune of a dissolution would be mortified at the issue: and their deputies would return home chagreened at their ill success & disappointment. This would be a disagreeable predicament for any of them to be in, but more particularly so for a person in my situation. If no further application is made to me, of course I do not attend. If there is, I am under no obligation to do it; but as I have had so many proofs of your friendship—know your abilities to judge—and your opportunities of learning the politicks of the day, on the points I have enumerated, you would oblige me by a *full* & *confidential* communication of your sentiments thereon.

Peace & tranquility prevail in this State. The Assembly by a very great Majority, and in very emphatical terms have rejected an application for paper money; and spurned the idea of fixing the value of Military certificates by a scale of depreciation. In some other respects too, the proceedings of the present Session have been marked with Justice, and a strong desire of supporting the fœderal system.

Although I lament the effect, I am pleased at the cause which has deprived us of your aid in the Attack of Christmas Pyes. We had one yesterday on which all the company (and pretty numerous it was) were hardly able to make an impression. Mrs Washington, George & his wife (Mr Lear I had occasion to send into the Western Country) join in affectionate regard for you—& with sentiments of the warmest friendship I am— sincerely Yours

A DUTIFUL, AND EXASPERATED, SON

To Mary Ball Washington

Hond Madam,   Mount Vernon February 15 1787

In consequence of your communication to George Washington, of your want of money, I take the (first safe) conveyance by Mr John Dandridge to send you 15 Guineas which believe me is all I have and which indeed ought to have been paid many days ago to another agreeable to my own assurances. I have now demands upon me for more than 500£ three hundred and forty odd of which is due for the tax of 1786; and I know not where, or when I shall receive one shilling with which to pay it. In the last two years I made no Crops. In the first I was obliged to buy Corn and this year have none to sell, and my wheat is so bad I cannot neither eat it myself nor sell it to others, and Tobaca I make none. Those who owe me money cannot or will not pay it without Suits and to sue is like doing nothing, whilst my expences, not from any extravagance, or an inclination on my part to live splendidly but for the absolute support of my family and the visitors who are constantly here are exceedingly high; higher indeed than I can support, without selling part of my estate which I am disposed to do rather than run in debt or continue to be so but this I cannot do, without taking much less than the lands I have offered for sale are worth. This is really and truely my situation—I do not however offer it as any excuse for not paying you what may really be due—for let this be little or much I am willing; however unable to pay to the utmost farthing; but it is really hard upon me when you have taken every thing you wanted from the Plantation by which money could be raised—When I have not received one farthing, directly nor indirectly from the place for more than twelve years if ever—and when, in that time I have paid, as appears by Mr Lund Washingtons account against me (during my absence) Two hundred and Sixty odd pounds, and by my own account Fifty odd pounds out of my own Pocket to you. besides (if I am rightly informed) every thing that has been raised by the Crops on the Plantation. who to blame, or whether any body is to blame for these things I know not, but these are facts. and as the purposes for which I took the Estate are not answered nor likely to be so but dissatisfaction on all sides have taken place, I do not mean to have any thing more to say to your Plantation or Negros since the first of January except the fellow who is here, and who will not, as he has formed connections in this neighbourhood leave it as experience has proved him I will hire. of this my intention I informed my brother John some time ago, whoes death I sincerely lament on many Accounts and on this painful event condole with you most sincerely. I do not mean by this declaration to with hold any aid or support I can give from you; for whilst I have a shilling left you shall have part, if it is wanted, whatever my own distresses may be. what I shall then give I shall have creadit for. now I have not for tho' I have received nothing from your Quarter, and am told that every farthing goes to you, and have moreover paid between 3 & 4 hundred pounds besides out of my own pocket I am viewed as a delinquent. & considered perhaps by the world as unjust and undutiful Son. My advice to you therefore, is, to do one of two things with the Plantation—either let your grandson Bushrod Washington, to whom the land is given by his Father have the whole interest there, that is lands and negros, at a reasonable rent—or, next year (for I presume it is too late this, as the overseer may be engaged) to let him have the land at a certain yearly rent during your life; and hire out the negros—this would ease you of all care and trouble—make your income certain—and your support ample. Further, my sincere, and pressing advice to you is, to break up housekeeping, hire out all the rest of your servants except a man and a maid and live with one of your Children. This would relieve you entirely from the cares of this world, and leave your mind at ease to reflect, undisturbedly on that which aught to come. On this subject I have been full with my Brother John and it was determined he should endeavor to get you to live with him—He alas is no more & three only of us remain—My House is at your service, & would press you most sincerely & most devoutly to accept it, but I am sure and candour requires me to say it will never answer your purposes, in any shape whatsoever —for in truth it may be compared to a well resorted tavern, as scarcely any strangers who are going from north to south, or from south to north do not spend a day or two at it—This would, were you to be an inhabitant of it, oblige you to do one of 3 things, 1st to be always dressing to appear in company, 2d to come into in a dishabille or 3d to be as it were a prisoner in your own chamber The first yould not like, indeed for a person at your time of life it would be too fateiguing. The 2d I should not like because those who resort here are as I observed before strangers and people of the first distinction. and the 3d, more than probably, would not be pleasing to either of us— nor indeed could you be retired in any room in my house; for what with the sitting up of Company; the noise and bustle of servants—and many other things you would not be able to enjoy that calmness and serenity of mind, which in my opinion you ought now to prefer to every other consideration in life. If you incline to follow this advice the House and lotts on which you now live you may rent, and enjoy the benefit of the money arising there from as long as you live—this with the rent of the land at the little falls & the hire of your negros would bring you in an income which would be much more than sufficient to answer all your wants and make ample amends to the child you live with; for myself I should desire nothing, if it did not, I would, most chearfully contribute more. a man, a maid, The Phæten and two horses, are all you would want—to lay in a sufficiency for the support of these would not require 1/4 of your income, the rest would purchase every necessary you could possibly want, and place it in your power to be serviceable to those wth whom you may live, which no doubt, would be agreeable to all parties.

There are such powerful reasons in my mind for giving this advice, that I cannot help urging it with a degree of earnestness which is uncommon for me to do. It is I am convinced, the only means by which you can be happy. the cares of a family without any body to assist you—The charge of an estate the proft of which depend upon wind weather—a good Overseer— an honest man—and a thousand other circumstance, cannot be right, or proper at your advanced age & for me, who am absolutely prevented from attending to my own plantations which are almost within call of me to attempt the care of yours would be folly in the extreme; but the mode I have pointed out, you may reduce your income to a certainty, be eased of all trouble—and, if you are so disposed, may be perfectly happy— for happiness depends more upon the internal frame of a persons own mind—than on the externals in the world. of the last if you will pursue the plan here recommended I am sure you can want nothing that is essential—the other depends wholy upon your self, for the riches of the Indies cannot purchase it.

Mrs Washington, George & Fanny Join me in every good wish for you and I am honored Madam, Yr most dutiful & affe. Son

"IT WILL, I FEAR, HAVE A TENDENCY
TO SWEEP ME BACK INTO THE
TIDE OF PUBLIC AFFAIRS"

To Edmund Randolph

Dear Sir,   Mount Vernon 28th Mar. 1787
Your favor of the 11th did not come to my hand till the 24th; and since then, till now, I have been too much indisposed to acknowledge the receipt of it. To what cause to ascribe the

detention of the letter I know not, as I never omit sending once, and oftener twice a week to the Post Office—In Alexandria.

It was the decided intention of the letter I had the honor of writing to your Excellency the 21st of December last, to inform you, that it would not be convenient for me to attend the Convention proposed to be holden in Philadelphia in May next; and I had entertained hopes that another had been, or soon would be, appointed in my place; inasmuch as it is not only inconvenient for me to leave home, but because there will be, I apprehend, too much cause to charge my conduct with inconsistency, in again appearing on a public theatre after a public declaration to the contrary; and because it will, I fear, have a tendency to sweep me back into the tide of public affairs, when retirement and ease is so essentially necessary for, and is so much desired by me.

However, as my friends, with a degree of sollicitude which is unusual, seem to wish my attendance on this occasion, I have come to a resolution to go if my health will permit, provided, from the lapse of time between the date of your Excellencys letter and this reply, the Executive may not—the reverse of which wd be highly pleasing to me—have turned its thoughts to some other character—for independantly of all other considerations, I have, of late, been so much afflicted with a rheumatic complaint in my shoulder that at times I am hardly able to raise my hand to my head, or turn myself in bed. This, consequently, might prevent my attendance, and eventually a representation of the State; which wd afflict me more sensibly than the disorder which occasioned it.

If after the expression of these sentiments, the Executive should consider me as one of the Delegates, I would thank your Excellency for the earliest advice of it; because if I am able, and should go to Philadelpa, I shall have some previous arrangements to make, and would set of for that place the first, or second day of May, that I may be there in time to account, personally, for my conduct to the General Meeting of the Cincinnati which is to convene on the first Monday of that month—My feelings would be much hurt if that body should otherwise, ascribe my attendance on the one, and not on the other occasion, to a disrespectful inattention to the Society; when the fact is, that I shall ever retain the most lively and affectionate regard for the members of which it is composed, on acct of their attachment to, and uniform support of me, upon many trying occasions; as well as on acct of their public virtues, patriotism, and sufferings.

I hope your Excellency will be found among the *attending* delegates. I should be glad to be informed who the others are —and cannot conclude without once more, and in emphatical terms, praying that if there is not a *decided* representation in *prospect*, without me, that another, for the reason I have assigned, may be chosen in my room without ceremony and without delay; for it would be unfortunate indeed if the State which was the mover of this Convention, should be unrepresented in it. With great respect I have the honor to be Yr Excellys Most Obedt Ser.

"I *ALMOST* DISPAIR OF SEEING
A FAVOURABLE ISSUE"

To Alexander Hamilton

Dear Sir,   Philadelphia 10th July 1787.

I thank you for your Communication of the 3d. When I refer you to the State of the Councils which prevailed at the period you left this City—and add, that they are now, if possible, in a worse train than ever; you will find but little ground on which the hope of a good establishment, can be formed. In a word, I *almost* dispair of seeing a favourable issue to the proceedings of the Convention, and do therefore repent having had any agency in the business.

The Men who oppose a strong & energetic government are, in my opinion, narrow minded politicians, or are under the influence of local views. The apprehension expressed by them that the people will not accede to the form proposed is the ostensible, not the real cause of the opposition—but admitting that the present sentiment is as they prognosticate, the question ought nevertheless to be, is it or is it not the best form? If the former, recommend it, and it will assuredly obtain mauger opposition.

I am sorry you went away—I wish you were back. The crisis is equally important and alarming, and no opposition under such circumstances should discourage exertions till the signature is fixed. I will not, at this time trouble you with more than my best wishes and sincere regards. I am Dear Sir Yr obedt Servt

"THE BUSINESS BEING THUS CLOSED"

Diary Entry

Monday 17th. Met in Convention when the Constitution received the Unanimous assent of 11 States and Colo. Hamilton's from New York (the only delegate from thence in Convention) and was subscribed to by every Member present except Govr. Randolph and Colo. Mason from Virginia & Mr. Gerry from Massachusetts. The business being thus closed, the Members adjourned to the City Tavern, dined together and took a cordial leave of each other—after which I returned to my lodgings —did some business with, and received the papers from the secretary of the Convention, and retired to meditate on the momentous wk. which had been executed, after not less than five, for a large part of the time Six, and sometimes 7 hours sitting every day, sundays & the ten days adjournment to give a Comee. opportunity & time to arrange the business for more than four Months.

September 17, 1787

"THE CONSTITUTION IS NOW BEFORE
THE JUDGMENT SEAT"

To Henry Knox

My dear Sir,   Mount Vernon October 15th 1787
    Your favor of the 3d instt came duly to hand.
    The fourth day after leaving Phila. I arrived at home, and found Mrs Washington and the family tolerably well, but the

fruits of the Earth almost entirely destroyed by one of the severest droughts (in this neighbourhood) that ever was experienced. The Crops generally, below the Mountains are injured; but not to the degree that mine, & some of my Neighbours, are here.

The Constitution is now before the judgment seat. It has, as was expected, its adversaries, and its supporters; which will preponderate is yet to be decided. The former, it is probable, will be most active because the Major part of them it is to be feared, will be governed by sinester and self important considerations on which no arguments will work conviction—the opposition from another class of them (if they are men of reflection, information and candour) may perhaps subside in the solution of the following plain, but important questions. 1. Is the Constitution which is submitted by the Convention preferable to the government (if it can be called one) under which we now live? 2. Is it probable that more confidence will, at this time, be placed in another Convention (should the experiment be tried) than was given to the last? and is it likely that there would be a better agreement in it? Is there not a Constitutional door open for alterations and amendments, & is it not probable that real defects will be as readily discovered after, as before, trial? and will not posterity be as ready to apply the remedy as ourselves, if there is occasion for it, when the mode is provided? To think otherwise will, in my judgment, be ascribing more of the amor patria—more wisdom—and more foresight to ourselves, than I conceive we are entitled to.

It is highly probable that the refusal of our Govr and Colo. Mason to subscribe to the proceedings of the Convention will have a bad effect in this State; for as you well observe, they *must* not only assign reasons for the justification of their conduct, but it is highly probable these reasons will appear in terrific array, with a view to alarm the people—Some things are already addressed to their fears and will have their effect. As far however as the sense of *this* part of the Country has been taken it is strongly in favor of the proposed Constitution. further I cannot speak with precision—If a powerful opposition is given to it the weight thereof will, I apprehend, come from the Southward of James River, & from the Western Counties.

Mrs Washington & the family join me in every good wish

for you and Mrs Knox—and with great and sincere regard I am, My dear Sir Yr Affecte

"I DO NOT CONCEIVE THAT WE ARE MORE INSPIRED . . . THAN THOSE WHO WILL COME AFTER US"

To Bushrod Washington

Dear Bushrod,   Mount Vernon Novr 9th 1787.

In due course of Post, I received your letters of the 19th & 26th Ult.; and since, the one which you committed to the care of Mr Powell. I thank you for the communications therein, & for a continuation, in matters of importance, I shall be obliged to you.

That the Assembly would afford the people an opportunity of deciding on the proposed Constitution I had hardly a doubt; the only question with me was, whether it would go forth under favourable auspices, or be branded with the mark of disapprobation. The opponents, I expected, (for it has ever been, that the adversaries to a measure are more active than its friends) would endeavour to give it an unfavourable complexion, with a view to biass the public mind. This, evidently, is the case with the writers in opposition; for their objections are better calculated to alarm the fears, than to convince the judgment of their readers. They build them upon principles which do not exist in the Constitution—which the known & litteral sense of it, does not support them in; and this too, after being flatly told that they are treading on untenable ground and after an appeal has been made to the letter, & spirit thereof, for proof: and then, as if the doctrine was uncontrovertable, draw such consequences as are necessary to rouse the apprehensions of the ignorant, & unthinking. It is not the interest of the major part of these characters to be convinced; nor will their local views yield to arguments which do not accord with their present, or future prospects; and yet, a candid solution of a single question, to which the understanding of almost every man is competent, must decide the point in dispute—namely—is it best for the States to unite, or not to unite?

If there are men who prefer the latter, then, unquestionably, the Constitution which is offered, must, in their estimation, be inadmissible from the first Word to the last signature, inclusively. But those who may think differently, and yet object to parts of it, would do well to consider, that it does not lye with *one* State, nor with a *minority* of the States, to superstruct a Constitution for the *whole*. The seperate interests, as far as it is practicable, must be consolidated—and local views as far as the general good will admit, must be attended to. Hence it is that *every* state has some objection to the *proposed* form; and that these objections are directed to different points. That which is most pleasing to one, is obnoxious to another, and vice versa. If then the Union of the whole is a desirable object, the parts which compose it, must yield a little in order to accomplish it; for without the latter, the former is unattainable. For I again repeat it, that not a single state nor a minority of the States, can force a Constitution on the majority. But admitting they had (from their importance) the power to do it, will it not be granted that the attempt would be followed by civil commotions of a very serious nature? But to sum up the whole, let the opponants of the proposed Constitution, *in this State*, be asked —it is a question they ought certainly to have asked themselves; What line of conduct they would advise it to adopt, if nine other States should accede to it, of which I think there is little doubt? Would they recommend that it should stand on its own basis—seperate & distinct from the rest? Or would they connect it with Rhode Island, or even say two others, checkerwise, & remain with them as outcasts from the Society, to shift for themselves? or will they advise a return to our former dependence on Great Britain for their protection & support? or lastly would they prefer the mortification of comg in, when they will have no credit there from? I am sorry to add in this place that Virginians entertain *too* high an opinion of the importance of their own Country. In extent of territory—In number of Inhabitants (*of all descriptions*) & In wealth I will readily grant that it certainly stands first in the Union; but in point of *strength*, it is, comparitively, weak. To this point, my opportunities authorise me to speak, decidedly; and sure I am, in every point of view, in which the subject can be placed, it is not (considering also the Geographical situation of the State) more the interest of any one of them to confederate, than it is the one in which we live.

The warmest friends to and the best supporters of the Constitution, do not contend that it is free from imperfections; but these were not to be avoided, and they are convinced if evils are likely to flow from them, that the remedy must come thereafter; because, in the *present moment* it is not to be obtained. And as there is a Constitutional door open for it, I think the people (for it is with them to judge) can, as they will have the aid of experience on their side, decide with as much propriety on the alterations and amendments wch shall be found necessary, as ourselves; for I do not conceive that we are more inspired—have more wisdom—or possess more virtue than those who will come after us. The power under the Constitution will always be with the people. It is entrusted for certain defined purposes and for a certain limited period to representatives of their own chusing; and whenever it is exercised contrary to their interests, or not according to their wishes, their Servants can, and undoubtedly will be, recalled. There will not be wanting those who will bring forward complaints of mal-administration whensoever they occur. To say that the Constitution *may be strained*, and an *improper* interpretation given to some of the clauses or articles of it, will apply to any that can be framed—in a word renders any one nugatory—for not one, more than another, can be binding, if the spirit and letter of the expression is disregarded. It is agreed on all hands that no government can be well administred without powers; and yet, the instant these are delegated, altho those who are entrusted with the Administration are taken from the people—return shortly to them again—and must feel the bad effect of oppressive measures—the persons holding them, as if their natures were immediately metamorphosed, are denominated tyrants and no disposition is allowed them, but to do wrong. Of these things in a government so constituted and guarded as the proposed one is, I can have no idea; and do firmly believe that whilst many ostensible reasons are held out against the adoption of it the true ones are yet behind the Curtain; not being of a nature to appear in open day. I believe further, supposing these objections to be founded in purity it-self that as great evils result from too much jealousy, as from the want of it. And I adduce several of the Constitutions of these States, as proof thereof. No man is a warmer advocate for *proper* restraints, and *wholesome* checks in every department of government than I am; but neither my reasoning, nor my ex-perience, has yet been able to discover the propriety of pre-venting men from doing good, because there is a possibility of their doing evil.

If Mr Ronald can place the finances of this Country upon so respectable a footing as he has intimated, he will deserve its warmest, and most grateful thanks. In the attempt, my best wishes—which is all I have to offer—will accompany him.

I hope there remains virtue enough in the Assembly of this State, to preserve inviolate public treaties, and private con-tracts. If these are infringed, farewell to respectability, and safety in the Government.

I never possessed a doubt, but if any had ever existed in my breast, re-iterated proofs would have convinced me of the im-policy, of all commutable taxes. If wisdom is not to be acquired from experience, where is it to be found? But why ask the question? Is it not believed by every one that *these* are time-serving jobs by which a few are enriched, at the public expence! but whether the plan originates for this purpose, or is the child of ignorance, oppression is the result.

You have, I find, broke the ice (as the saying is). one piece of advice only I will give you on the occasion (if you mean to be a respectable member, and to entitle yourself to the Ear of the House)—and that is—except in local matters which respect your Constituants and to which you are obliged, by duty, to speak, rise but seldom—let this be on important matters—and then make yourself thoroughly acquainted with the subject. Never be agitated by *more than* a decent *warmth*, & offer your sentiments with modest diffidence—opinions thus given, are listened to with more attention than when delivered in a dicta-torial stile. The latter, if attended to at all, altho they may *force* conviction, is sure to convey disgust also.

Your aunt, and the family here join me in every good wish for you. and I am with sentiments of great regd and Affecte.— Yours.

P.S. The letter you sent by Mr Powell for Nancy was forwarded next day to Doctr Brown, for the best conveyance that should offer from alexandria.

"THE PRESIDENCY . . . HAS NO ENTICING CHARMS"

To Marquis de Lafayette

Mount Vernon April 28th 1788

I have now before me, my dear Marqs your favor of the 3d of August in the last year; together with those of the 1st of January, the 2d of January and the 4th of February in the present—Though the first is of so antient a date, they all came to hand lately, and nearly at the same moment. The frequency of your kind remembrance of me, and the endearing expressions of attachment, are by so much the more satisfactory, as I recognise them to be a counterpart of my own feelings for you. In truth, you know I speak the language of sincerity and not of flattery, when I tell you, that your letters are ever most wellcome and dear to me.

This I lay out to be a letter of Politics. We are looking anxiously a cross the atlantic for news and you are looking anxiously back again for the same purpose. It is an interesting subject, to contemplate how far the war, kindled in the north of Europe, may extend its conflagrations, and what may be the result before its extinction. The Turke appears to have lost his old and acquired a new connection. Whether England has not, in the hour of her pride, overacted her part and pushed matters too far for her own interest, time will discover: but, in my opinion (though from my distance and want of minute information I should form it with diffidence) the affairs of that nation cannot long go on in the same prosperous train: in spite of expedients and in spite of resources, the Paper bubble will one day burst. And it will whelm many in the ruins. I hope the affairs of France are gradually sliding into a better state. Good effects may, and I trust will ensue, without any public convulsion. France, were her resources properly managed and her administrations wisely conducted, is (as you justly observe) much more potent in the scale of empire, than her rivals at present seem inclined to believe.

I notice with pleasure the additional immunities and facilities in trade, which France has granted by the late Royal Arret to the United States. I flatter myself it will have the desired effect, in some measure, of augmenting the commercial intercourse. From the productions and wants of the two countries, their trade with each other is certainly capable of great amelioration, to be actuated by a spirit of unwise policy. For so surely as ever we shall have an efficient government established; so surely will that government impose retaliating restrictions, to a certain degree, upon the trade of Britain, at present, or under our existing form of Confederations, it would be idle to think of making comercial regulations on our part. One State passes a prohibitory law respecting some article—another State opens wide the avenue for its admission. One Assembly makes a system —another Assembly unmakes it. Virginia, in the very last session of her Legislature, was about to have passed some of the most extravigant and preposterous Edicts on the subject of trade, that ever Stained the leaves of a Legislative Code. It is in vain to hope for a remedy of these and innumerable other evils, untill a general Government shall be adopted.

The Convention of Six States only have as yet accepted the new Constitution. No one has rejected it. It is believed that the Convention of Maryland, which is now in session; and that of South Carolina, which is to assemble on the 12th of May, will certainly adopt it. It is, also, since the elections of Members for the Convention have taken place in this State, more general believed that it will be adopted here than it was before those elections were made. There will, however, be powerful and elequent speeches on both sides of the question in the Virginia Convention. but as Pendelton, Wythe, Blair, Madison, Jones, Nicholas, Innis and many other of our first characters will be advocates for its adoption, you may suppose the weight of abilities will rest on that side. Henry and Masson are its great adversaries—The Governor, if he opposes it at all will do it feebly.

On the general Merits of this proposed Constitution, I wrote

to you, some time ago my sentiments pretty freely. That letter
had not been received by you, when you addressed to me the
last of yours which has come to my hands. I had never supposed that perfection could be the result of accomodation and
mutual concession. The opinion of Mr Jefferson & yourself is
certainly a wise one, that the Constitution ought by all means
to be accepted by nine States before any attempt should be
made to procure amendments. For, if that acceptance shall not
previously take place, men's minds will be so much agitated
and soured, that the danger will be greater than ever of our
becoming a disunited People. Whereas, on the other hand,
with prudence in temper and a spirit of moderation, every essential alteration, may in the process of time, be expected.

You will doubtless, have seen, that it was owing to this con-
ciliatory and patriotic principle that the Convention of Massachusetts adopted the Constitution in toto; but recommended
a number of specific alterations and quieting explanations, as
an early, serious and unremitting subject of attention. Now,
although it is not to be expected that every individual, in Society, will or can ever be brought to agree upon what is, exactly,
the best form of govenment; yet, there are many things in the
Constitution which only need to be explained, in order to
prove equally satisfactory to all parties. For example: there was
not a member of the convention, I believe, who had the least
objection to what is contended for by the Advocates for a *Bill
of Rights* and *Tryal by Jury*. The first, where the people evidently retained every thing which they did not in express terms
give up, was considered nugatory as you will find to have been
more fully explained by Mr Wilson and others: And as to the
second, it was only the difficulty of establishing a mode which
should not interfere with the fixed modes of any of the States,
that induced the Convention to leave it, as a matter of future
adjustment.

There are other points on which opinions would be more
likely to vary. As for instance, on the ineligibility of the same
person for President, after he should have served a certain
course of years. Guarded so effectually as the proposed Constitution is, in respect to the prevention of bribery and undue
influence in the choice of President: I confess, I differ widely
myself from Mr Jefferson and you, as to the necessity or expe-

diency of rotation in that appointment. The matter was fairly discussed in the Convention, & to my full convictions; though I cannot have time or room to sum up the arguments in this letter. There cannot, in my Judgment, be the least danger that the President will by any practicable intrigue ever be able to continue himself one moment in office, much less perpetuate himself in it—but in the last stage of corrupted morals and political depravity: and even then there is as much danger that any other species of domination would prevail. Though, when a people shall have become incapable of governing themselves and fit for a master, it is of little consequence from what quarter he comes.

Under an extended view of this part of the subject, I can see no propriety in precluding ourselves from the services of any man, who on some great emergency, shall be deemed, universally, most capable of serving the Public. In answer to the observations you make on the probability of my election to the Presidency (knowing me as you do) I need only say, that it has no enticing charms, and no fascinating allurements for me. However, it might not be decent for me to say I would refuse to accept or even to speak much about an appointment, which may never take place: for in so doing, one might possibly incur the application of the moral resulting from that Fable, in which the Fox is represented as inveighing against the sourness of the grapes, because he could not reach them. All that it will be necessary to add, my dear Marquis, in order to shew my decided predelection, is, that, (at my time of life and under my circumstances) the encreasing infirmities of nature and the growing love of retirement do not permit me to entertain a wish, beyond that of living and dying an honest man on my own farm. Let those follow the pursuits of ambition and fame, who have a keener relish for them, or who may have more years, in store, for the enjoyment!

Mrs Washington, while she requests that her best Compliments may be presented to you, Joins with me in soliciting that the same friendly and affectionate memorial of our constant remembrance and good wishes may be made acceptable to Madam de la Fayette and the little ones—I am &c.

P.S. May 1st.

Since writing the foregoing letter, I have received Authentic Accounts that the Convention of Maryland have ratified the new Constitution by a Majority of 63 to 11.

"I LIKE NOT MUCH THE SITUATION OF AFFAIRS IN FRANCE"

To Marquis de Lafayette

Mount Vernon June 18th 1788

I cannot account for your not having received some of my letters, my dear Marquis, before you wrote yours of the 18th of March; as I have been writing to you, at short intervals, constantly since last autumn. To demonstrate the satisfaction I enjoy on the receipt of your favours; I always answer them almost as soon as they arrive—Although, on account of my retirement from the busy scenes of life and the want of diversity in the tenour of our affairs, I can promise to give you little novelty or entertainment in proportion to what I expect in return. Were you to acknowledge the receipt of my letters, and give the dates of them when you write to me, I should be able to ascertain which of them had reached you—and which of them had miscarried. I am left in doubt whether the Indian Vocabularies &c. &c. have got to you or not.

There seems to be a great deal of bloody work cut out for this summer in the North of Europe. If war, want and plague are to desolate those huge armies that are assembled, who that has the feelings of a man can refrain from shedding a tear over the miserable victims of Regal Ambition? It is really a strange thing that there should not be room enough in the world for men to live, without cutting one anothers throats. As France, Spain and England have hardly recovered from the wounds of the late war, I would fain hope they will hardly be dragged into this. However, if the war should be protracted (and not end in a campain as you intimate it possibly may) there seems to be a probability of other powers being engaged on one side or the other. by the British papers (which are our principal source of intellegence, though not always to be relied upon, as you know) it appears that the Spaniards are fitting out a considerable fleet and that the English Ministry have prohibited the subjects of their Kingdom from furnishing transports for the Empress of Russia. France must be too intent on its own domestic affairs to wish to interfere; and all have not heard that the King of Prussia, since his exploits in Holland, has taken it into his head to meddle with other people's business. I cannot say that I am sorry to hear that the Algerines and other piratical powers are about to assist the Porte, because I think Russia will not forget and that she will take some leisure moment, Just to keep her fleets in exercise, for exterminating those nests of Miscreants.

I like not much the situation of affairs in France. The bold demands of the Parliaments and the decisive tone of the King, shew that but little more irritation would be necessary to blow up the spark of discontent into a flame that might not easily be quenched. If I were to advise, I would say that great moderation should be used on both sides. Let it not, my dear Marquis, be considered as a derogation from the good opinion that I entertain of your prudence, when I caution you, as an individual desirous, of signalising yourself in the cause of your country and freedom, against running into extremes and prejudicing your cause. The King, though I think from every thing I have been able to learn, he is really a good-hearted, tho' a warm-spirited man, if thwarted injudiciously in the execution of pre-rogatives that belonged to the Crown, and in plans which he conceives calculated to promote the national good, may dis-close qualities he has been little thought to possess. On the other hand, such a spirit seems to be awakened in the Kingdom, as, if managed with extreem prudence, may produce a gradual and tacit Revolution much in favour of the subjects, by abol-ishing Lettres de Cachet and defining more accurately the powers of government. It is a wonder to me, there should be found a single monarch, who does not realize that his own glory and felicity must depend on the prosperity and happiness of his People. How easy is it for a sovereign to do that which shall not only immortalize his, name, but attract the blessings of Millions.

In a letter I wrote you a few days ago by Mr Barlow (but which might not possibly have reached New York untill after his departure) I mentioned the accession of Maryland to the proposed government and give you the state of politics, to that period. Since which the Convention of South Carolina has ratified the Constitution by a great majority: that of this State has been setting almost three weeks and so nicely does it appear to be ballanced, that each side asserts that it has a preponderancy of votes in its favour. It is probable, therefore, the majority will be small, let it fall on which ever part it may; I am inclined to believe it will be in favour of the adoption. The Convention of New York and New Hampshire assemble both this week—a large proportion of members, with the Governor at their head, in the former are said to be opposed to the government in contemplation: New Hampshire it is thought will adopt it without much hesitation or delay. It is a little strange that the men of large property in the South, should be more afraid that the Constitution will produce an Aristocracy or a Monarchy, then the genuine democratical people of the East. Such are our actual prospects. The accession of one State more will complete the number, which by the Constitutional provision, will be sufficient in the first instance to carry the Government into effect.

And then, I expect, that many blessings will be attributed to our new government, which are now taking their rise from that industry and frugality into the practice of which the people have been forced from necessity. I really believe that there never was so much labour and economy to be found before in the country as at the present moment. If they persist in the habits they are acquiring, the good effects will soon be distinguishable. When the people shall find themselves secure under an energetic government, when foreign Nations shall be disposed to give us equal advantages in commerce from dread of retaliation, when the burdens of the war shall be in a manner done away by the sale of western lands, when the seeds of happiness which are sown here shall begen to expand themselves, and when every one (under his own vine and fig-tree) shall begin to taste the fruits of freedom—then all these blessings (for all these blessings will come) will be referred to the fostering influence of the new government. Whereas many causes will have conspired to produce them. you see I am not less enthusiastic than ever I have been, if a belief that peculiar scenes of felicity are reserved for this country, is to be denominated enthusiasm. Indeed, I do not believe that Providence has done so much for nothing. It has always been my creed that we should not be left as an awful monument to prove, "that Mankind, under the most favourable circumstances for civil liberty and happiness, are unequal to the task of Governing themselves, and therefore made for a Master."

We have had a backward spring and summer, with more rainy and cloudy weather than almost ever has been known: still the appearance of crops in some parts of the country is favorable— as we may generally expect will be the case, from the difference of soil and variety of climate in so extensive a region—insomuch that, I hope, some day or another we shall become a storehouse and granary For the world. In addition to our former channels of trade, salted provisions, butter, cheese &c. are exported, with propht from the eastern States to the East Indies. In consequence of a Contract, large quantities of flour are lately sent from Baltimore for supplying the garrison of Gibralter. With sentiments of the tenderest affection—I am &c. &c.

RECOMMENDED READING

To Richard Henderson

Sir,   Mount Vernon June 19th 1788
   Your favour of the 5th instant was lodged at my house, while I was absent on a visit to my Mother. I am now taking the earliest opportunity of noticing its contents and those of its Enclosure. Willing as I am to give satisfaction so far as I am able, to every reasonable enquire (and this is certainly not only so, but may be highly important and interesting) I must however, rather deal in general than particular observations: as I think you will be able, from the length of your residence in the country and the extensiveness of your acquaintance with its affairs, to make the necessary applications and add the proper details. Nor would I choose that my interference in the business should be transmitted, lest, in a malicious world, it might

be represented that I was officiously using the arts of seduction to depopulate other countries, for the sake of peopling our own.

In the first place it is a point conceded, that America, under an efficient government, will be the most favorable Country of any in the world for persons of industry and frugality, possessed of a moderate capital, to inhabit. It is also believed that it will not be less advantageous to the happiness of the lowest class of people because of the equal distribution of property the great plenty of unocupied lands, and the facility of procuring the means of subsistance. The scheme of purchasing a good tract of freehold estate and bringing out a number of able-boded men, indented for a certain time appears to be indisputably a rationale one. All the interior arrangements of transferring the property and commencing the establishment you are as well acquainted with, as I can possibly be. It might be considered as a point of more difficulty, to decide upon the place which should be most proper for a settlement. Although, I believe, that Emigrants from other countries to this, who shall be well-disposed and conduct themselves properly, would be treated with equal friendship and kindness in all parts of it; yet in the old settled States, land is so much occupied and the value so much enhanced by the contiguous cultivation, that the price would in general be an objection. The land in western country, or that on the Ohio, like all others, has its *advantages and disadvantages*. The neighbourhood of the Savages and the difficulty of transportation were the great objections. The danger of the first will soon cease by the strong establishments now taking place—the inconveniencies of the second will be, in a great degree, remidied by opening the internal Navigation. No Colony in America was ever settled under such favorable auspicies as that which has just commenced at the Muskingum Information, property and strength will be its characteristics. I know many of the settlers personally & that there never were men better calculated to promote the wellfare of such a community.

If I was a young man, just preparing to begin the world or if advanced in life, and had a family to make a provision for, I know of no country, where I should rather fix my habitation than in some part of that region; for which the writer of the quæries seems to have a predilection. he might be informed that his name-sake and distant relation, Genl St Clair, is not only in high repute, but that he is Governor of all the Territory westward of the Ohio and that there is a Gentleman (to wit Mr Joel Barlow) come from New York by The last French Packet, who will be in London in the course of this year and who is authorised to dispose of a very large body of land in that Country. The author of the quæries may then be referred "to the Information for those who would wish to remove to America": published in Europe in the year 1784, by the great Philosopher Dr Franklin. Short as it is, it contains almost every thing that need to be known on the subject of migrating to this Country. you may find that excellent little Treatise, in "Carey's American Museum for September 1787." It is worthy of being republished in Scotland and every other part of Europe.

As to the European Publications respecting the United States, they are commonly very defective. The Abbe Raynale is quite erroneous. Guthrie, though somewhat better informed, is not absolutely correct. There is now "an American Geography preparing for the press by a Mr Morse of New Haven in Connecticut" which, from the pains the Author has taken in travelling through the States and acquiring information from the principal characters in each, will probably be much more exact and useful. of books at present existing, Mr Jefferson's "Notes on Virginia," will give the best idea of this part of the Continent to a Foreigner: and the "American Farmer's Letters" —written by Mr Crevecœur (commonly called Mr St John) the French Consul in New York (who actually resided 20 years as a farmer in that State) will afford a great deal of profitable and amusive Information, respecting *the private Life* of the Americans; as well as the progress of agriculture, manufactures and arts in their Country. Perhaps the picture he gives, though founded in fact, is in some instances embellished with rather too flattering circumstances—I am &ca

PRAISING THE FEDERALIST PAPERS

To Alexander Hamilton

Dear Sir,   Mount Vernon Augt 28th 1788.

I have had the pleasure to receive your letter dated the 13th —accompanied by one addressed to General Morgan. I will forward the letter to Generl Morgan by the first conveyance, and add my particular wishes that he would comply with the request contained in it. Although I can scarcely imagine how the Watch of a British Officer, killed within their lines, should have fallen into his hands (who was many miles from the scene of action) yet, if it so happened, I flatter myself there will be no reluctance or delay in restoring it to the family.

As the perusal of the political papers under the signature of Publius has afforded me great satisfaction, I shall certainly consider them as claiming a most distinguished place in my library. I have read every performance which has been printed on one side and the other of the great question lately agitated (so far as I have been able to obtain them) and, without an unmeaning compliment, I will say that I have seen no other so well calculated (in my judgment) to produce conviction on an unbiassed mind, as the *Production* of your *Triumvirate*. When the transient circumstances & fugitive performances which attended this *crisis* shall have disappeared, that work will merit the notice of Posterity; because in it are candidly discussed the principles of freedom & the topics of government, which will be always interesting to mankind so long as they shall be connected in Civil Society.

The circular Letter from your Convention, I presume, was the equivalent by wch you obtained an acquiescence in the proposed Constitution: Notwithstanding I am not very well satisfied with the tendency of it; yet the Fœderal affairs have proceeded, with few exceptions, in so good a train, that I hope the political Machine may be put in motion, without much effort or hazard of miscarrying.

On the delicate subject with which you conclude your letter, I can say nothing; because the event alluded to may never happen; and because, in case it should occur, it would be a point of prudence to defer forming one's ultimate and irrevocable decision, so long as new data might be afforded for one to act with the greater wisdom & propriety. I would not wish to conceal my prevailing sentiment from you. For you know me well enough, my good Sir, to be persuaded that I am not guilty of affection, when I tell you, it is my great and sole desire to live and die, in peace and retirement, on my own farm. Were it even indispensable, a different line of conduct should be adopted; while you and some others who are acquainted with my heart would acquit, the world and Posterity might probably accuse me of inconsistency and ambition. Still I hope I shall always possess firmness and virtue enough to maintain (what I consider the most enviable of all titles) the character of an honest man, as well as prove (what I desire to be considered in reality) that I am, with great sincerity & esteem, Dear Sir Your friend and Most obedient Hble Servt

AGONIZING OVER THE PRESIDENCY

To Alexander Hamilton

Dear Sir,   Mount Vernon October 3d 1788
In acknowledging the receipt of your canded and kind letter by the last Post; little more is incumbent upon me, than to thank you sincerely for the frankness with which you communicated your sentiments, and to assure you that the same manly tone of intercourse will always be more than barely wellcome, Indeed it will be highly acceptable to me. I am particularly glad, in the present instance; you have dealt thus freely and like a friend. Although I could not help observing from several publications and letters that my name had been sometimes spoken of and that it was possible the *Contingency* which is the subject of, your letter might happen; yet I thought it best to maintain a guarded silence and to lack the *counsel* of my best friends (which I certainly hold in the highest estimation) rather than to hazard an imputation unfriendly to the delicacy of my feelings. For, situated as I am, I could hardly bring the question into the slightest discussion, or ask an opinion even in the most

confidential manner; without betraying, in my Judgment, some impropriety of conduct, or without feeling an apprehension that a premature display of anxiety, might be construed into a vainglorious desire of pushing myself into notice as a Candidate. Now, if I am not grossly deceived in myself, I should unfeignedly rejoice, in case the Electors, by giving their votes in favor of some other person, would save me from the dreaded Dilemma of being forced to accept or refuse. If that may not be—I am, in the next place, earnestly desirous of searching out the truth, and of knowing whether there does not exist a probability that the government would be just as happily and effectually carried into execution, without my aid, as with it. I am *truly* solicitous to obtain all the previous information which the circumstances will afford, and to determine (when the determination can with propriety be no longer postponed) according to the principles of right reason, and the dictates of a clear conscience; without too great a referrence to the unforeseen consequences, which may affect my person or reputation. Untill that period, I may fairly hold myself open to conviction —though I allow your sentiments to have weight in them; and I shall not pass by your arguments without giving them as dispassionate a consideration, as I can possibly bestow upon them.

In taking a survey of the subject in whatever point of light I have been able to place it; I will not surpress the acknowledgment, my Dr Sir that I have always felt a kind of gloom upon my mind, as often as I have been taught to expect, I might, and perhaps must ere long be called to make a decision. You will, I am well assured, believe the assertion (though I have little expectation it would gain credit from those who are less acquainted with me) that if I should receive the appointment and if I should be prevailed upon to accept it; the acceptance would be attended with more diffidence and reluctance than ever I experienced before in my life. It would be, however, with a fixed and sole determination of lending whatever assistance might be in my power to promote the public, weal, in hopes that at a convenient and an early period, my services might be dispensed with, and that I might be permitted once more to retire—to pass an unclouded evening, after the stormy day of life, in the bosom of domestic tranquility. But why these anticipations? if the friends to the Constitution conceive that my administering the government will be a means of its acceleration and strength, is it not probable that the adversaries of it may entertain the same ideas? and of course make it an object of opposition? That many of this description will become Electors, I can have no Doubt of: any more than that their oppinion will extend to any character who (from whatever cause) would be likely to thwart their measures—It might be impolite in them to make this declaration *previous* to the Election, but I shall be out in my conjectures if they do not act conformably thereto—and from that the seeming moderation by which they appear to be actuated at present is neither more nor less than a finesse to lull and deceive. Their plan of opposition is systemised, and a regular intercourse, I have much reason to believe between the Leaders of it in the several States is formed to render it more effectual. With sentiments of sincere regard and esteem—I have, the honor to be &c.

"I THINK, I SEE A *PATH*, AS CLEAR AND AS
DIRECT AS A RAY OF LIGHT"

To Marquis de Lafayette

My dear Marqs   Mount Vernon Jany 29 1789
By the last Post, I was favored with the receipt of your letter, dated the 5th of September last. Notwithstanding the distance of its date, it was peculiarly welcome to me: for I had not, in the mean time received any satisfactory advices respecting yourself or your country. By that letter, my mind was placed much more at its ease, on both those subjects, than it had been for many months.

The last letter, which I had the pleasure of writing to you, was forwarded by Mr Gouverneur Morris. Since his departure from America, nothing very material has occurred. The minds of men, however, have not been in a stagnant State. But patriotism, instead of faction, has generally agitated them. It is not a matter of wonder, that, in proportion as we approached to the time fixed for the organization and operation of the new government, their anxiety should have been encreased, rather than diminished. The choice of Senators, Representatives and Electors, whh (excepting in that of the last description) took place at different times, in the different States, has afforded abundant topics for domestic News, since the beginning of Autumn. I need not enumerate the several particulars, as I imagine you see most of them detailed, in the American Gazettes. I will content myself with only saying, that the elections have been hitherto vastly more favorable than we could have expected, that federal sentiments seem to be growing with uncommon rapidity, and that this encreasing unanimity is not less indicative of the good disposition than the good sense of the Americans. Did it not savour so much of partiality for my Countrymen I might add, that I cannot help flattering myself the new Congress on account of the self-created respectability and various talents of its Members, will not be inferior to any Assembly in the world. From these and some other circumstances, I really entertain greater hopes, that America will not finally disappoint the expectations of her Friends, than I have at almost any former period. Still however, in such a fickle state of existence, I would not be too sanguine in indulging myself with the contemplation of scenes of uninterupted prosperity; lest some unforeseen mischance or perverseness should occasion the greater mortification, by blasting the enjoyment in the very bud.

I can say little or nothing new, in consequence of the repetition of your opinion, on the expediency there will be, for my accepting the office to which you refer. Your sentiments, indeed, coincide much more nearly with those of my other friends, than with my own feelings. In truth my difficulties encrease and magnify as I drew towards the period, when, according to the common belief, it will be necessary for me to give a definitive answer, in one way or another. Should the circumstances render it, in a manner inevitably necessary, to be in the affirmative: Be assured, my dear Sir, I shall assume the task with the most unfeigned reluctance, and with a real diffidence for which I shall probably receive no credit from the world. If I know my own heart, nothing short of a conviction of duty will induce me again to take an active part in public affairs—and, in that case, if I can form a plan for my own conduct, my endeavours shall be unremittingly exerted (even at the hazard of former fame or present popularity) to extricate my country from the embarrassments in which it is entangled, through want of credit; and to establish, a general system of policy, which, if pursued will insure permanent felicity to the Commonwealth. I think, I see a *path*, as clear and as direct as a ray of light, which leads to the attainment of that object. Nothing but harmony, honesty, industry and frugality are necessary to make us a great and happy people. Happily the present posture of affairs and the prevailing disposition of my countrymen promise to co-operate, in establishing those four great and essential pillars of public felicity.

What has been considered at the moment as a disadvantage, will probably turn out for our good. While our commerce has been considerably curtailed, for want of that extensive credit formerly given in Europe, and for fault of remittance; the use-full arts have been almost imperceptibly pushed to a consider-able degree of perfection. Though I would not force the introduction of manufactures, by extravagant encouragements, and to the prejudice of agriculture; yet, I conceive, much might be done in that way by woman, children & others; without taking one really necessary hand from tilling the earth. Certain it is, great savings are already made in many articles of apparel, furniture and consumption. Equally certain it is, that no dimi-nution in agriculture has taken place, at the time when greator and more substantial improvements in manufactures were making, than were ever before known in America. In Pennsyl-vania they have attended particularly to the fabrication of cot-ten cloths, hats, and all articles in leather. In Massachusetts they are establishing factories of Duck, Cordage, Glass and several other extensive and useful branches. The number of shoes made in one town and nails in another is incredible. In that State and Connecticut are also factories of superfine and other broad cloths. I have been writing to our friend Genl Knox this day, to procure me homespun broad cloth, of the Hartford fabric, to make a suit of cloaths for myself. I hope it will not be a great while, before it will be unfashionable for a gentleman to appear in any other dress. Indeed we have already been to long subject to British prejudices. I use no porter or cheese in my family, but such as is made in America—both those articles may now be purchased of an excellent quality.

While you are quarreling among yourselves in Europe—
while one King is running mad—and others acting as if they
were already so, by cutting the throats of the subjects of their
neighbours: I think you need not doubt, My Dear Marquis we
shall continue in tranquility here—And that population will be
progressive so long as there shall continue to be so many easy
means for obtaining a subsistence, and so ample a field for the
exertion of talents and industry.

All my family join in Compliments to Madam la Fayette and
yours. Adieu, my dear Marqs believe me, what I am—With &c.

"THE PLACE OF HIS EXECUTION"

To Henry Knox

My dear Sir,   Mount Vernon April 1st 1789
    The Mail of the 30th brought me your favor of the 23d—For
which, & the regular information you have had the goodness
to transmit of the state of things in New York, I feel myself
very much obliged, and thank you accordingly.

I feel for those Members of the new Congress, who, hitherto,
have given an unavailing attendance at the theatre of business.
For myself, the delay may be compared to a reprieve; for in confidence I can assure *you*—with the *world* it would obtain *little
credit*—that my movements to the chair of Government will
be accompanied with feelings not unlike those of a culprit who
is going to the place of his execution: so unwilling am I, in the
evening of a life nearly consumed in public cares, to quit a
peaceful abode for an Ocean of difficulties, without that com-
petency of political skill—abilities & inclination which is necessary to manage the helm. I am sensible, that I am embarking
the voice of my Countrymen and a good name of my own, on
this voyage, but what returns will be made for them—Heaven
alone can foretell. Integrity & firmness is all I can promise—
these, be the voyage long or short; never shall forsake me although I may be deserted by all men. For of the consolations
which are to be derived from these (under any circumstances)

the world cannot deprive me. With best wishes for Mrs Knox, & sincere friendship for yourself—I remain Your affectionate

"A MIND OPPRESSED"

Diary Entries

About ten o'clock I bade adieu to Mount Vernon, to private life, and to domestic felicity; and with a mind oppressed with more anxious and painful sensations than I have words to express, set out for New York in company with Mr. Thompson, and colonel Humphries, with the best dispositions to render service to my country in obedience to its call, but with less hope of answering its expectations.

The display of boats which attended and joined us on this occasion, some with vocal and some with instrumental music on board; the decorations of the ships, the roar of cannon, and the loud acclamations of the people which rent the skies, as I passed along the wharves, filled my mind with sensations as painful (considering the reverse of this scene, which may be the case after all my labors to do good) as they are pleasing.

April 16 and 23, 1789

"THE EXPERIMENT ENTRUSTED TO THE
HANDS OF THE AMERICAN PEOPLE"

First Inaugural Address

Fellow Citizens of the Senate and
of the House of Representatives
   Among the vicissitudes incident to life, no event could have filled me with greater anxieties than that of which the notification was transmitted by your order, and received on the fourteenth day of the present month. On the one hand, I was

summoned by my Country, whose voice I can never hear but with veneration and love, from a retreat which I had chosen with the fondest predilection, and, in my flattering hopes, with an immutable decision, as the asylum of my declining years: a retreat which was rendered every day more necessary as well as more dear to me, by the addition of habit to inclination, and of frequent interruptions in my health to the gradual waste committed on it by time. On the other hand, the magnitude and difficulty of the trust to which the voice of my Country called me, being sufficient to awaken in the wisest and most experienced of her citizens, a distrustful scrutiny into his qualifications, could not but overwhelm with despondence, one, who, inheriting inferior endowments from nature and unpractised in the duties of civil administration, ought to be peculiarly conscious of his own deficiencies. In this conflict of emotions, all I dare aver, is, that it has been my faithful study to collect my duty from a just appreciation of every circumstance, by which it might be affected. All I dare hope, is, that, if in executing this task I have been too much swayed by a grateful remembrance of former instances, or by an affectionate sensibility to this transcendent proof, of the confidence of my fellow-citizens; and have thence too little consulted my incapacity as well as disinclination for the weighty and untried cares before me; my *error* will be palliated by the motives which misled me, and its consequences be judged by my Country, with some share of the partiality in which they originated.

Such being the impressions under which I have, in obedience to the public summons, repaired to the present station; it would be peculiarly improper to omit in this first official Act, my fervent supplications to that Almighty Being who rules over the Universe, who presides in the Councils of Nations, and whose providential aids can supply every human defect, that his benediction may consecrate to the liberties and happiness of the People of the United States, a Government instituted by themselves for these essential purposes: and may enable every instrument employed in its administration, to execute with success, the functions allotted to his charge. In tendering this homage to the Great Author of every public and private good, I assure myself that it expresses your sentiments not less than my own; nor those of my fellow-citizens at large, less than either:

No People can be bound to acknowledge and adore the invisible hand, which conducts the Affairs of men more than the People of the United States. Every step, by which they have advanced to the character of an independent nation, seems to have been distinguished by some token of providential agency. And in the important revolution just accomplished in the system of their United Government, the tranquil deliberations, and voluntary consent of so many distinct communities, from which the event has resulted, cannot be compared with the means by which most Governments have been established, without some return of pious gratitude along with an humble anticipation of the future blessings which the past seem to presage. These reflections, arising out of the present crisis, have forced themselves too strongly on my mind to be suppressed. You will join me I trust in thinking, that there are none under the influence of which, the proceedings of a new and free Government can more auspiciously commence.

By the article establishing the Executive Department, it is made the duty of the President "to recommend to your consideration, such measures as he shall judge necessary and expedient." The circumstances under which I now meet you, will acquit me from entering into that subject, farther than to refer to the Great Constitutional Charter under which you are assembled; and which, in defining your powers, designates the objects to which your attention is to be given. It will be more consistent with those circumstances, and far more congenial with the feelings which actuate me, to substitute, in place of a recommendation of particular measures, the tribute that is due to the talents, the rectitude, and the patriotism which adorn the characters selected to devise and adopt them. In these honorable qualifications, I behold the surest pledges, that as on one side, no local prejudices, or attachments; no seperate views, nor party animosities, will misdirect the comprehensive and equal eye which ought to watch over this great Assemblage of communities and interests: so, on another, that the foundations of our national policy, will be laid in the pure and immutable principles of private morality; and the pre-eminence of free Government, be exemplified by all the attributes which can win the affections of its Citizens, and command the respect of the world. I dwell on this prospect with every satisfaction which an ardent love for my Country can inspire: since there is no truth more thoroughly established, than that there exists in the œconomy and course of nature, an indissoluble union between virtue and happiness, between duty and advantage, between the genuine maxims of an honest and magnanimous policy, and the solid rewards of public prosperity and felicity: Since we ought to be no less persuaded that the propitious smiles of Heaven, can never be expected on a nation that disregards the eternal rules of order and right, which Heaven itself has ordained: And since the preservation of the sacred fire of liberty, and the destiny of the Republican model of Government, are justly considered as *deeply*, perhaps as *finally* staked, on the experiment entrusted to the hands of the American people.

Besides the ordinary objects submitted to your care, it will remain with your judgment to decide, how far an exercise of the occasional power delegated by the Fifth article of the Constitution is rendered expedient at the present juncture by the nature of objections which have been urged against the System, or by the degree of inquietude which has given birth to them. Instead of undertaking particular recommendations on this subject, in which I could be guided by no lights derived from official opportunities, I shall again give way to my entire confidence in your discernment and pursuit of the public good: For I assure myself that whilst you carefully avoid every alteration which might endanger the benefits of an United and effective Government, or which ought to await the future lessons of experience; a reverence for the characteristic rights of freemen, and a regard for the public harmony, will sufficiently influence your deliberations on the question how far the former can be more impregnably fortified, or the latter be safely and advantageously promoted.

To the preceding observations I have one to add, which will be most properly addressed to the House of Representatives. It concerns myself; and will therefore be as brief as possible. When I was first honoured with a call into the service of my Country, then on the eve of an arduous struggle for its liberties, the light in which I contemplated my duty required that I should renounce every pecuniary compensation. From this resolution I have in no instance departed—And being still under the impressions which produced it, I must decline as inapplicable to myself, any share in the personal emoluments, which may be indispensably included in a permanent provision for the Executive Department; and must accordingly pray that the pecuniary estimates for the Station in which I am placed, may, during my continuance in it, be limited to such actual expenditures as the public good may be thought to require.

Having thus imparted to you my sentiments, as they have been awakened by the occasion which brings us together, I shall take my present leave; but not without resorting once more to the benign Parent of the human race, in humble supplication that since he has been pleased to favour the American people, with opportunities for deliberating in perfect tranquility, and dispositions for deciding with unparellelled unanimity on a form of Government, for the security of their Union, and the advancement of their happiness; so this divine blessing may be equally *conspicuous* in the enlarged views—the temperate consultations, and the wise measures on which the success of this Government must depend.

April 30, 1789

"THE FIRST OF EVERYTHING"

To James Madison

My dear Sir,   New York May 5th 1789.
    Notwithstanding the conviction I am under of the labour which is imposed upon you by Public Individuals as well as public bodies—yet, as you have begun, so I could wish you to finish, the good work in a short reply to the Address of the House of Representatives (which I now enclose) that there may be an accordance in this business.

Thursday 12 Oclock, I have appointed to receive the Address. The proper place is with the House to determine. As the first of everything, in *our situation* will serve to establish a Precedent, it is devoutly wished on my part, that these precedents may be fixed on true principles. With affectionate regard I am ever Yours

"GREAT AND DURABLE CONSEQUENCES"

To John Adams

The President of the United States wishes to avail himself of your sentiments on the following points.

1st Whether a line of conduct, equally distant from an association with all kinds of company on the one hand and from a total seclusion from Society on the other, ought to be adopted by him? and, in that case, how is it to be done?

2d What will be the least exceptionable method of bringing any system, which may be adopted on this subject, before the Public and into use?

3d Whether, after a little time, one day in every week will not be sufficient for receiving visits of Compliment?

4th Whether it would tend to prompt impertinent applications & involve disagreeable consequences to have it known, that the President will, every Morning at 8 Oclock, be at leisure to give Audiences to persons who may have business with him?

5th Whether, when it shall have been understood that the President is not to give general entertainment in the manner the Presidents of Congress have formerly done, it will be practicable to draw such a line of discrimination in regard to persons, as that Six, eight or ten official characters (including in the rotation the members of both Houses of Congress) may be invited informally or otherwise to dine with him on the days fixed for receiving Company, without exciting clamours in the rest of the Community?

6th Whether it would be satisfactory to the Public for the President to make about four great entertainmts in a year on such great occasions as—the Anniversary of the Declaration of Independence, the Alliance with France—the Peace with Great Britain—the Organization of the general government: and whether arrangements of these two last kinds could be in danger of diverting too much of the Presidents time from business, or of producing the evils which it was intended to avoid by his living more recluse than the Presidents of Congress have heretofore lived.

7th Whether there would be any impropriety in the Presidents making informal visits—that is to say, in his calling upon his Acquaintances or public Characters for the purposes of sociability or civility—and what (as to the form of doing it) might evince these visits to have been made in his private character, so as that they might not be construed into visits from the President of the United States? and in what light would his appearance *rarely* at *Tea* parties be considered?

8th Whether, during the recess of Congress, it would not be advantageous to the interests of the Union for the President to make the tour of the United States, in order to become better acquainted with their principal Characters & internal Circumstances, as well as to be more accessible to numbers of well-informed persons, who might give him useful informations and advices on political subjects?

9th If there is a probability that either of the arrangements may take place, which will eventually cause additional expenses, whether it would not be proper that these ideas should come into contemplation, at the time when Congress shall make a permanent provision for the support of the Executive.

Remarks

On the one side no augmentation can be effected in the pecuniary establishment which shall be made, in the first instance, for the support of the Executive—on the other, all monies destined to that purpose beyond the actual expenditures, will be left in the Treasury of the United States or sacredly applied to the promotion of some national objects.

Many things which appear of little importance in themselves and at the beginning, may have great and durable consequences from their having been established at the commencement of a new general Government. It will be much easier to commence the administration, upon a well adjusted system built on tenable grounds, than to correct errors or alter inconveniences after they shall have been confirmed by habit. The President in all matters of business & etiquette, can have no object but to demean himself in his public character, in such a manner as to maintain the dignity of Office, without subjecting himself to the imputation of superciliousness or unnecessary reserve. Under these impressions, he asks for your candid and undisguised opinions.

May 10, 1789

"THE MIND CAN HARDLY REALIZE THE FACT"

To Gouverneur Morris

Dear Sir,   New York, October 13th 1789.

In my first moments of leisure I acknowledge the receipt of your several favors of the 23 of February, 3 of March and 29 of April.

To thank you for the interesting communications contained in those letters, and for the pains you have taken to procure me a watch, is all, or nearly all I shall attempt in this letter—for I could only repeat things, were I to set about it, which I have reason to believe have been regularly communicated to you in detail, at the periods which gave birth to them.

It may not however be unpleasing to you to hear in one word that the national government is organized, and as far as my information goes, to the satisfaction of all parties—That opposition to it is either no more, or hides its head.

That it is hoped and expected it will take strong root, and that the non acceding States will very soon become members of the union—No doubt is entertained of North Carolina, nor would there be of Rhode Island had not the majority of that People bid adieu, long since to every principle of honor—common sense, and honesty. A material change however has taken place, it is said, at the late election of representatives, and confident assurances are given from that circumstance of better dispositions in their Legislature at its next session, now about to be held.

The revolution which has been effected in France is of so wonderful a nature that the mind can hardly realise the fact—If it ends as our last accounts to the first of August predict that nation will be the most powerful and happy in Europe; but I fear though it has gone triumphantly through the first paroxysm, it is not the last it has to encounter before matters are finally settled.

In a word the revolution is of too great magnitude to be effected in so short a space, and with the loss of so little blood—The mortification of the King, the intrigues of the Queen, and the discontents of the Princes, and the Noblesse will foment divisions, if possible, in the national assembly, and avail themselves of every faux pas in the formation of the constitution if they do not give a more open, active opposition.

To these the licentiousness of the People on one hand and sanguinary punishments on the other will alarm the best disposed friends to the measure, and contribute not a little to the overthrow of their object—Great temperance, firmness, and foresight are necessary in the movements of that Body. To forbear running from one extreme to another is no easy matter, and should this be the case, rocks and shelves not visible at present may wreck the vessel.

This letter is an evidence, though of a trifling sort, that in the commencement of any work one rarely sees the progress or end of it. I declared to you in the beginning that I had little to say. I have got beyond the second page, and find I have a good deal to add; but that no time or paper may be wasted in a useless preface I will come to the point.

Will you then, my good Sir, permit me to ask the favor of you to provide and send to me by the first Ship, bound to this place, or Philadelphia mirrors for a table, with neat and fashionable but not expensive ornaments for them—such as will do credit to your taste—The mirrors will of course be in pieces that they may be adapted to the company, (the size of it I mean) the aggregate length of them may be ten feet—the breadth two feet—The panes may be plated ware, or any thing else more fashionable but not more expensive. If I am defective recur to what you have seen on Mr Robert Morris's table for my ideas *generally*. Whether these things can be had on better terms and in a better style in Paris than in London I will not undertake to decide. I recollect however to have had plated ware from both places, and those from the latter came cheapest—but a single instance is no evidence of a general fact.

Of plated ware may be made I conceive handsome and useful Coolers for wine *at* and *after* dinner. Those I am in need of viz. *eight* double ones (for madeira and claret the wines usually drank at dinner) each of the apertures to be sufficient to contain a pint decanter, with an allowance in the depth of it for ice at bottom so as to raise the neck of the decanter above the cooler—between the apertures a handle is to be placed by which these double coolers may with convenience be removed from one part of the table to another. For the wine *after* dinner *four* quadruple coolers will be necessary each aperture of which to be of the size of a *quart* decanter or quart bottle for four sorts of wine—These decanters or bottles to have ice at bottom, and to be elevated thereby as above—a central handle here also will be wanting—Should my description be defective your imagination is fertile and on this I shall rely. One idea however I must impress you with and that is in whole or part to avoid extravagance. For extravagance would not comport with my own inclination, nor with the example which ought to be set— The reason why I prefer an aperture for *every* decanter or bottle to coolers that would contain two and four is that whether full or empty the bottles will always stand upright and never be at variance with each other.

The letter enclosed with your draught accompanying it will provide the means for payment—The clumsy manner in which Merchants (or rather their Tradesmen) execute commissions, where taste is required, for persons at a distance must be my apology, and the best that can be offered by Dear Sir Your most obedient and affecte humble Servant

Mrs Washington presents her compliments to you.
P.S. I was in the very act of sealing this letter when yours of the 31st of July from Dieppe was put into my hands—accept my sincere thanks for the important communications contained in it, and for the tables which accompanied. I shall add no more now, except that in the morning I commence a tour, though rather late in the season, through the States eastward of this. Adieu, yours

"TO BE PREPARED FOR WAR IS ONE OF
THE MOST EFFECTUAL MEANS
OF PRESERVING PEACE"

First Annual Message to Congress

United States January 8th 1790
Fellow Citizens of the Senate, and House of Representatives.

I embrace with great satisfaction the opportunity, which now presents itself, of congratulating you on the present favourable prospects of our public affairs. The recent accession of the important State of North Carolina to the Constitution of the United States (of which official information has been recieved) —the rising credit and respectability of our Country—the general and increasing good will towards the Government of the Union—and the concord, peace and plenty, with which we are blessed, are circumstances, auspicious, in an eminent degree to our national prosperity.

In resuming your consultations for the general good, you cannot but derive encouragement from the reflection, that the measures of the last Session have been as satisfactory to your Constituents, as the novelty and difficulty of the work allowed you to hope. Still further to realize their expectations, and to secure the blessings which a Gracious Providence has placed within our reach, will in the course of the present important Session, call for the cool and deliberate exertion of your patriotism, firmness and wisdom.

Among the many interesting objects, which will engage your attention, that of providing for the common defence will merit particular regard. To be prepared for war is one of the most effectual means of preserving peace.

A free people ought not only to be armed but disciplined; to which end a Uniform and well digested plan is requisite: And their safety and interest require that they should promote such manufactures, as tend to render them independent on others, for essential, particularly for military supplies.

The proper establishment of the Troops which may be deemed indispensible, will be entitled to mature consideration. In the arrangements which may be made respecting it, it will be of importance to conciliate the comfortable support of the Officers and Soldiers with a due regard to œconomy.

There was reason to hope, that the pacific measures adopted with regard to certain hostile tribes of Indians would have relieved the inhabitants of our Southern and Western frontiers from their depredations. But you will percieve, from the information contained in the papers, which I shall direct to be laid before you (comprehending a communication from the Commonwealth of Virginia) that we ought to be prepared to afford protection to those parts of the Union; and, if necessary, to punish aggressors.

The interests of the United States require, that our intercourse with other nations should be facilitated by such provisions as will enable me to fulfil my duty in that respect, in the manner, which circumstances may render most conducive to the public good: And to this end, that the compensations to be made to the persons, who may be employed, should, according to the nature of their appointments, be defined by law; and a competent fund designated for defraying the expenses incident to the conduct of foreign affairs.

Various considerations also render it expedient, that the terms on which foreigners may be admitted to the rights of Citizens, should be speedily ascertained by a uniform rule of naturalization.

Uniformity in the Currency, Weights and Measures of the United States is an object of great importance, and will, I am persuaded, be duly attended to.

The advancement of Agriculture, commerce and Manufactures, by all proper means, will not, I trust, need recommendation. But I cannot forbear intimating to you the expediency of giving effectual encouragement as well to the introduction of new and useful inventions from abroad, as to the exertions of skill and genius in producing them at home; and of facilitating the intercourse between the distant parts of our Country by a due attention to the Post-Office and Post Roads.

Nor am I less pursuaded, that you will agree with me in opinion, that there is nothing, which can better deserve your patronage, than the promotion of Science and Literature. Knowledge is in every Country the surest basis of public happiness. In one, in which the measures of Government recieve their impression so immediately from the sense of the Community as in our's, it is proportionably essential. To the security of a free Constitution it contributes in various ways: By convincing those, who are entrusted with the public administration, that every valuable end of Government is best answered by the enlightened confidence of the people: And by teaching the people themselves to know and to value their own rights; to discern and provide against invasions of them; to distinguish between oppression and the necessary exercise of lawful authority; between burthens proceeding from a disregard to their convenience and those resulting from the inevitable exigencies of Society; to discriminate the spirit of liberty from that of licentiousness, cherishing the first, avoiding the last, and uniting a speedy, but temperate vigilence against encroachments, with an inviolable respect to the laws.

Whether this desirable object will be best promoted by affording aids to Seminaries of Learning already established—by the institution of a national University—or by any other expedients, will be well worthy of a place in the deliberations of the Legislature.

Gentlemen of the House of Representatives.

I saw with peculiar pleasure, at the close of the last Session, the resolution entered into by you expressive of your opinion, that an adequate provision for the support of the public Credit is a matter of high importance to the national honor and prosperity. In this sentiment, I entirely concur. And to a perfect confidence in your best endeavours to divise such a provision, as will be truly consistent with the end, I add an equal reliance on the chearful co-operation of the other branch of the Legislature. It would be superfluous to specify inducements to a measure in which the character and permanent interests of the United States are so obviously and so deeply concerned; and which has recieved so explicit a sanction from your declaration.

Gentlemen of the Senate and House of Representatives.

I have directed the proper Officers to lay before you respectively such papers and estimates as regard the affairs particularly recommended to your consideration, and necessary to convey to you that information of the state of the Union, which it is my duty to afford.

The welfare of our Country is the great object to which our cares and efforts ought to be directed. And I shall derive great satisfaction from a co-operation with you, in the pleasing though arduous task of ensuring to our fellow Citizens the blessings, which they have a right to expect, from a free, efficient and equal Government.

WOOING A SECRETARY OF STATE

To Thomas Jefferson

Dear Sir   New York Jany 21st 1790

I had the pleasure to receive duly your letter dated the 15th of Decr last; but I thought proper to delay answering or mentioning the contents of it, until after the arrival of Mr Madison, who I understood had been with you. He arrived yesterday, and I now take the earliest opportunity of mentioning to you the result of my reflections; and the expediency of your deciding, at as early a period as may consist with your convenience, on the important subject before you.

Previous to any remarks on the nature of the Office to which you have been recently appointed, I will premise, that I feel such delicacy & embarrassment in consequence of the footing on which you have placed your final determination, as to make it necessary for me to recur to the first ground on which I rested the matter. In confidence, therefore, I will tell you plainly that I wish not to oppose your inclinations; and that, after you shall have been made a little farther acquainted with the light in which I view the Office of Secretary of State, it must be at your option to determine relative to your acceptance of it, or continuance in your Office abroad.

I consider the successful Administration of the general Government as an object of almost infinite consequence to the present and future happiness of the Citizens of the United States. I consider the Office of Secretary for the Department of State as *very* important on many accts: and I know of no person, who, in my judgment, could better execute the Duties of it than yourself. Its duties will probably be not quite so arduous & complicated in their execution, as you might have been led at the first moment to imagine. At least, it was the opinion of Congress, that, after the division of all the business of a domestic nature between the Department of the Treasury, War and State, that those wch would be comprehended in the latter might be performed by the same Person, who should have the charge of conducting the Department of foreign Affairs. The experiment was to be made; and if it shall be found that

the fact is different, I have little doubt that a farther arrangement or division of the business in the Office of the Department of State will be made, in such manner as to enable it to
be performed, under the superintendance of one man, with
facility to himself, as well as with advantage & satisfaction to
the Public. These observations, however, you will be pleased
to remark are merely matters of opinion. But, in order that you
may be the better prepared to make your ultimate decision on
good grounds, I think it necessary to add one fact, which is
this, so far as I have been able to obtain information from all
quarters, your late appointment has given very extensive and
very great satisfaction to the Public. My original opinion &
wish may be collected from my nomination.

As to what you mention in the latter part of your letter, I
can only observe, I do not know that any alteration is likely to
take place in the Commission from the United States to the
Court of France. The necessary arrangements with regard to
our intercourse with Foreign Nations have never yet been taken
up on a great scale by the Government: because the Department which comprehended affairs of that nature has never
been properly organised, so as to bring the business well and
systematically before the Executive. If you shd finally determine to take upon yourself the duties of the Department of
State, it would be highly requisite for you to come on immediately, as many things are required to be done while Congress is
in Session rather than at any other time; and as, in that case,
your presence might doubtless be much better dispensed with
after a little time than at the present moment. Or, in all events,
it will be essential that I should be informed of your conclusive
option, so that, if you return to France, another Person may
be, at as early a day as possible, nominated to fill the Department of State. With sentiments of the highest regard and esteem I am, Dear Sir Your Most Obedt Hble Servt

SECTIONALISM AND THE
NEW FEDERAL GOVERNMENT

To David Stuart

Dear Sir,   New York March 28th 1790.

Your letter of the 15th enclosing the Act of Assembly autho-
rising an agreement with Mr Alexander came to my hand in
the moment my last to you was dispatched.

I am sorry such jealousies as you relate should be gaining
ground, & poisoning the minds of the Southern people. But,
admit the fact which is alledged as the cause of them, and give
it full scope, does it amount to more than what was known to
every man of information before, at, and since the adoption of
the Constitution? Was it not always believed that there are
some points which peculiarly interest the Eastern States? And
did any one who reads human nature, & more especially the
character of the Eastern people, conceive that they would not
pursue them steadily by a combination of their force? Are there
not other points which equally concern the Southern States? If
these States are less tenacious of their interest, or, if whilst the
Eastern move in a solid phalanx to effect their purposes, the
Southern are always divided, which of the two is most to be
blamed? That there is diversity of interests in the Union none has
denied. That this is the case also in every State is equally certain
—and that it extends even to Counties, can be as readily
proved. Instance the Southern & Northern parts of Virginia—
the upper & lower parts of So. Carolina &ca—have not the
interests of these always been at varience? Witness the County
of Fairfax, has not the interests of the people thereof varied, or
the Inhabitants been taught to believe so? These are well known
truths, and yet it did not follow that seperation was to result
from the disagreement.

To constitute a dispute there must be two parties. To understand it well both the parties & all the circumstances must be
fully understood. And to accomodate differences good temper
& mutual forbearance is requisite. Common danger brought
the States into Confederacy, and on their Union our safety &
importance depend. A spirit of accomodation was the basis of

the present Constitution; can it be expected then that the Southern or the Eastern part of the Empire will succeed in all their Measures? certainly not. but I will readily grant that more points will be carried by the latter than the former, and for the reason which has been mentioned—namely—that in all great national questions they move in unison, whilst the others are divided; but I ask again which is most blameworthy, those who see & will steadily pursue their interests, or those who cannot see, or seeing, will not act wisely? and I will ask another question (of the highest magnitude in my mind) and that is, if the Eastern & Northern States are dangerous *in Union*, will they be less so *in seperation*? If self interest is their governing principle, will it forsake them, or be less restrained by such an event? I hardly think it would. Then, independent of other considerations what would Virginia (and such other States as might be inclined to join her) gain by a seperation? Would they not, most unquestionably, be the weaker party?

Men who go from hence without *feeling* themselves of so much consequence as they wished to be considered—disappointed expectants—and malignant designing characters that miss no opportunity to aim a blow at the Constitution, paint highly on one side without bringing into view the arguments which are offered on the other. It is to be lamented that the Editors of the several Gazettes of the Union do not more generally & more connectedly publish the debates in Congress on all great National questions that affect different interests instead of stuffing their papers with scurrility & malignant declamation, which few would read if they were apprised of the contents. That they might do this with very little trouble is certain. The principles upon which the difference in opinion arises, as well as the decision, would, in that case, come fully before the public, & afford the best data for its judgment.

Mr Madison, on the question of discrimination, was actuated, I am persuaded, by the purest motives; & most heartfelt conviction; but the Subject was delicate, & perhaps had better not have been stirred. The assumption of the State debts by the United States is another subject that has given birth to long and laboured debates without having yet taken a final form. The Memorial of the Quakers (& a very mal-apropos one it was) has at length been put to sleep, from which it is not [   ] it will awake before the year 1808. With much truth I am Sir Yr Affecte Hble Servt

"IT IS NOW NO MORE THAT TOLERATION IS SPOKEN OF"

To the Hebrew Congregation in Newport, Rhode Island

Gentlemen

While I receive, with much satisfaction, your Address replete with expressions of affection and esteem; I rejoice in the opportunity of assuring you, that I shall always retain a grateful remembrance of the cordial welcome I experienced in my visit to Newport, from all classes of Citizens.

The reflection on the days of difficulty and danger which are past is rendered the more sweet, from a consciousness that they are succeeded by days of uncommon prosperity and security. If we have wisdom to make the best use of the advantages with which we are now favored, we cannot fail, under the just administration of a good Government, to become a great and a happy people.

The Citizens of the United States of America have a right to applaud themselves for having given to mankind examples of an enlarged and liberal policy: a policy worthy of imitation. All possess alike liberty of conscience and immunities of citizenship. It is now no more that toleration is spoken of, as if it was by the indulgence of one class of people, that another enjoyed the exercise of their inherent natural rights. For happily the Government of the United States, which gives to bigotry no sanction, to persecution no assistance requires only that they who live under its protection should demean themselves as good citizens, in giving it on all occasions their effectual support.

It would be inconsistent with the frankness of my character not to avow that I am pleased with your favorable opinion of my Administration, and fervent wishes for my felicity. May the Children of the Stock of Abraham, who dwell in this land, continue to merit and enjoy the good will of the other Inhabitants; while every one shall sit in safety under his own vine and figtree, and there shall be none to make him afraid. May the father of all mercies scatter light and not darkness in our paths, and make us all in our several vocations useful here, and in his own due time and way everlastingly happy.

August 18, 1790

"THE PROGRESS OF PUBLIC CREDIT"

Second Annual Message to Congress

Fellow Citizens of the Senate, and House of Representatives.
United States Decr 8th 1790

In meeting you again I feel much satisfaction in being able to repeat my congratulations on the favorable prospects which continue to distinguish our public affairs. The abundant fruits of another year have blessed our Country with plenty, and with the means of a flourishing commerce. The progress of public credit is witnessed by a considerable rise of American Stock abroad as well as at home. And the revenues allotted for this and other national purposes, have been productive beyond the calculations by which they were regulated. This latter circumstance is the more pleasing as it is not only a proof of the fertility of our resources, but as it assures us of a further increase of the national respectability and credit; and let me add, as it bears an honorable testimony to the patriotism and integrity of the mercantile and marine part of our Citizens. The punctuality of the former in discharging their engagements has been exemplary.

In conforming to the powers vested in me by Acts of the last Session, a loan of three Millions of florins, towards which some provisional measures had previously taken place, has been compleated in Holland. As well the celerity with which it has been filled as the nature of the terms (considering the more than ordinary demand for borrowing created by the situation of Europe) give a reasonable hope that the further execution of those powers may proceed with advantage and success. The

Secretary of the Treasury has my direction to communicate such further particulars as may be requisite for more precise information.

Since your last Sessions I have received communications by which it appears that the District of Kentucky, at present a part of Virginia, has concurred in certain propositions contained in a law of that State; in consequence of which the District is to become a distinct member of the Union, in case the requisite sanction of Congress be added. For this sanction application is now made. I shall cause the Papers on this very important transaction to be laid before you. The liberality and harmony with which it has been conducted will be found to do great honor to both the parties; and the sentiments of warm attachment to the Union and its present Government expressed by our fellow Citizens of Kentucky cannot fail to add an affectionate concern for their particular welfare to the great national impressions under which you will decide on the case submitted to you.

It has been heretofore known to Congress that frequent incursions have been made on our frontier settlements by certain banditti of Indians from the North West side of the Ohio. These with some of the tribes dwelling on and near the Wabash have of late been particularly active in their depridations; and being emboldened by the impunity of their crimes, and aided by such parts of the Neighbouring tribes as could be seduced to join in their hostilities or afford them a retreat for their prisoners and plunder, they have, instead of listening to the humane invitations and overtures made on the part of the United States renewed their voilences with fresh alacrity and greater effect. The lives of a number of valuable Citizens have thus been sacrificed, and some of them under circumstances peculiarly shocking; whilst others have been carried into a deplorable captivity.

These aggravated provocations render'd it essential to the safety of the Western settlements that the aggressors should be made sensible that the Government of the Union is not less capable of punishing their crimes, than it is disposed to respect their rights and reward their attachments. As this object could not be effected by defensive measures it became necessary to put in force the Act which empowers the President to call out the Militia for the protection of the frontiers. And I have accordingly authorised an Expedition in which the regular troops in that quarter are combined with such draughts of Militia as were deemed sufficient. The event of the measure is yet unknown to me—The Secretary at War is directed to lay before you a statement of the information on which it is founded, as well as an estimate of the expence with which it will be attended.

The disturbed situation of Europe, and particularly the critical posture of the great maritime powers, whilst it ought to make us the more thankful for the general peace and security enjoyed by the United States reminds us at the sametime of the circumspection with which it becomes us to preserve these blessings. It requires also that we shou'd not overlook the tendency of a War and even of preparations for a War, among the nations most concerned in active commerce with this Country, to abridge the means and thereby at least enhance the price of transporting its valuable productions to their proper markets. I recommend to your serious reflections how far and in what mode, it may be expedient to guard against embarrassments fromt these contingencies, by such encouragements to our own navigation as will render our commerce and agriculture less dependent on foreign Bottoms, which may fail us in the very moments most interesting to both of these great objects. Our sheries and the transportation of our own produce offer us abundant means for guarding ourselves against this evil.

Your attention seems to be not less due to that particular branch of our trade which belongs to the Mediterranean. So many circumstances unite in rendering the present state of it distressful to us, that you will not think any deliberations misemployed which may lead to its relief and protection.

The laws you have already passed for the establishment of a Judiciary system have opened the doors of Justice to all descriptions of persons. You will consider, in your wisdom, whether improvements in that system may yet be made; and particularly whether an uniform process of Execution on sentences issuing from the federal Courts be not desireable through all the States.

The patronage of our commerce, of our Merchants and Seamen, has called for the appointment of Consuls in foreign Countries. It seems expedient to regulate by law the exercise of that jurisdiction and those functions which are permitted them, either by express Convention, or by a friendly indulgence in the places of their residence. The Consular Convention too with his Most Christian Majesty has stipulated in certain cases, the aid of the national authority to his Consuls established here. Some legislative provision is requisite to carry these stipulations into full effect.

The establishment of the Militia—of a Mint—of Standards of Weights and Measures—of the Post Office and Post Roads, are subjects which (I presume) you will resume of course, and which are abundantly urged by their own importance.

Gentlemen of the House of Representatives.

The sufficiency of the revenues you have established for the objects to which they are appropriated, leaves no doubt that the residuary provisions will be commensurate to the other objects for which the public faith stands now pledged. Allow me moreover to hope that it will be a favorite policy with you not merely to secure a payment of the interest of the debt funded, but as far and as fast as the growing resources of the Country will permit, to exonerate it of the principal itself. The appropriation you have made of the Western lands explain your dispositions on this subject: and I am persuaded the sooner that valuable fund can be made to contribute along with other means to the actual reduction of the public debt, the more salutary will the measure be to every public interest, as well as the more satisfactory to our Constituents.

Gentlemen of the Senate and House of Representatives.

In persuing the various and weighty business of the present Session I indulge the fullest persuasion that your consultations will be equally marked with wisdom, and animated by the love of your Country. In whatever belongs to my duty, you shall have all the co-operation which an undiminished zeal for its welfare can inspire. It will be happy for us both and our best reward, if by a successful administration of our respective trusts we can make the established Government more and more instrumental in promoting the good of our fellow Citizens, and more and more the object of their attachment and confidence.

"HERE THEN IS THE SECURITY FOR THE
REMAINDER OF YOUR LANDS"

To the Chiefs of the Seneca Nation

I, the President of the United States, by my own mouth, and by a written speech signed with my own hand, and sealed with the seal of the United States, speak to the Seneka Nation, and desire their Attention, and that they would keep this speech in remembrance of the friendship of the United States.

I have received your Speech with satisfaction, as a proof of your confidence in the justice of the United States—and I have attentively examined the several objects which you have laid before me, whether delivered by your Chiefs at Tioga point in the last month to Colonel Pickering, or laid before me in the present month by the Cornplanter and the other Seneka Chiefs now in Philadelphia.

In the first place I observe to you, and I request it may sink in your minds, that it is my desire, and the desire of the United States that all the miseries of the late war should be forgotten and buried forever. That in future, the United States and the six nations should be truly brothers, promoting each other's prosperity by acts of mutual justice & friendship.

I am not uninformed that the six nations have been led into some difficulties with respect to the sale of their lands since the peace. But I must inform you that these arose before the present government of the United States was established, when the separate States, and individuals under their authority, undertook to treat with the Indian tribes respecting the sale of their lands.

But the case is now entirely altered—the general government only has the power to treat with the Indian nations, and any treaty formed and held without its authority will not be binding.

Here then is the security for the remainder of your lands— No state nor person can purchase your lands, unless at some public treaty held under the Authority of the United States. The general Government will never consent to your being defrauded—But it will protect you in all your just rights.

Hear well, and let it be heard by every person in your nation, that the President of the United States declares, that the general government considers itself bound to protect you in all the lands secured to you by the treaty of Fort Stanwix, the 22d of October 1784, excepting such parts as you may since have fairly sold to persons properly authorized to purchase of you.

You complain of John Livingston and Oliver Phelps have obtained your lands, assisted by Mr Street of Niagara, and they have not complied with their agreement.

It appears, upon enquiry of the Governor of New York, that John Livingston was not legally authorized to treat with you, and that every thing he did with you has been declared null and void, so that you may rest easy on that account.

But it does not appear from any proofs yet in the possession of government, that Oliver Phelps has defrauded you.

If, however you should have any just cause of complaint against him, and can make satisfactory proof thereof, the federal Courts will be open to you for redress, as to all other persons.

But your great object seems to be the security of your remaining lands, and I have therefore upon this point, meant to be sufficiently strong and clear.

That in future you cannot be defrauded of your lands—That you possess the right to sell, and the right of refusing to sell your lands.

That, therefore, the sale of your lands in future, will depend entirely upon yourselves.

But that when you may find it for your interest to sell any parts of your lands, the United States must be present by their Agent, and will by your security that you shall not be defrauded in the Bargain you may make.

It will, however, be important, before you make any further sales of your land, that you should determine among yourselves, who are the persons among you that shall give sure conveyances thereof as shall be binding upon your nation, and forever preclude all disputes relative to the validity of the sale.

That besides the before mentioned security for your land, you will perceive by the law of Congress, for regulating trade and intercourse with the Indian-tribes, the fatherly care the United States intend to take of the Indians. For the particular meaning of this law, I refer you to the explanations given thereof by Colonel Pickering at Tioga, which with the law, are herewith delivered to you.

You have said in your Speech that the game is going away from you, and that you thought it the design of the great spirit, that you should till the ground. But before you speak upon this subject, you want to know whether the United States meant to leave you any land to till?

You know now that all the lands secured to you by the treaty of Fort Stanwix, expecting such parts as you may since have fairly sold are your's, and that only your own Acts can convey them away—speak therefore your wishes on the subject of tilling the ground. The United States will be happy to afford you every assistance in the only business which will add to your numbers and happiness.

The murders that have been committed upon some of your people, by the bad white men, I sincerely lament and reprobate—and I earnestly hope that the real murderers will be secured and punished as they deserve. This business has been sufficiently explained to you here by the Governor of Pennsylvania, and by Colonel Pickering on behalf of the United States, at Tioga.

The Senekas may be assured, that the rewards offered for apprehending the murderers, will be continued until they are secured for trial, and that when they shall be apprehended, that they will be tried and punished as if they had killed Whitemen.

Having answered the most material parts of your speech, I shall inform you, that some bad Indians, and the outcast of several tribes who reside at the Miamee Village, have long continued their murders and depredations upon the frontiers laying along the Ohio. That they have not only refused to listen to my voice inviting them to peace, but that upon receiving it, they renewed their incursions and murders with greater violence than ever. I have therefore been obliged to strike those bad people, in order to make them sensible of their madness. I sincerely hope they will harken to reason, and not require to be further chastised. The United States desire to be the friends of the Indians, upon terms of justice & humanity—But they will not suffer the depredations of the bad people to go unpunished.

My desire is that you would caution all the Senekas and six

nations to prevent their rash young men from joining the Miamee Indians. For the United States cannot distinguish the tribes to which bad Indians belong, and every tribe must take care of their own people.

The merits of the Cornplanter and his friendship for the United States are well known to me, and shall not be forgotten —And as a mark of the esteem of the United States, I have directed the Secretary of War to make him a present of Two hundred and fifty dollars, either in money or goods, as the Cornplanter shall like best—And he may depend upon the future care and kindness of the United States—And I have also directed the Secretary of War to make suitable presents to their other Chiefs present in Philadelphia—and also that some further tokens of friendship to be forwarded to the other Chiefs now in their nation.

Remember my words, Senekas, continue to be strong in your friendship for the United States, as the only rational ground of your future happiness—and you may rely upon their kindness and protection.

An Agent shall soon be appointed to reside in some place convenient to the Senekas and six nations—He will represent the United States—apply to him on all occasions.

If any man brings you evil reports of the intentions of the United States, mark that man as your enemy, for he will mean to deceive you, and lead you into trouble. The United States will be true & faithful to their engagements. Given under my hand, and the Seal of the United States at the City of Philadelphia, this twenty ninth day of December, in the year of our Lord One thousand seven hundred & ninety one, and in the fifteenth year of the sovereignty & Independence of the United States.

Philadelphia, December 29, 1790

"TO A PHILANTHROPIC MIND THE
HAPPINESS OF 24 MILLIONS OF PEOPLE
CANNOT BE INDIFFERENT"

To Marquis de Lafayette

Philadelphia, July 28. 1791.

I have, my dear Sir, to acknowledge the receipt of your favors of the 7 of March and 3 of May, and to thank you for the communications which they contain relative to your public affairs. I assure you I have often contemplated, with great anxiety, the danger to which you are personally exposed by your peculiar and delicate situation in the tumult of the times, and your letters are far from quieting that friendly concern. But to one, who engages in hazardous enterprises for the good of his country, and who is guided by pure and upright views, (as I am sure is the case with you) life is but a secondary consideration.

To a philanthropic mind the happiness of 24 millions of people cannot be indifferent—and by an American, whose country in the hour of distress received such liberal aid from the french, the disorders and incertitude of that Nation are to be peculiarly lamented—we must, however, place a confidence in that Providence who rules great events, trusting that out of confusion he will produce order, and notwithstanding the dark clouds which may threaten at present, that right will ultimately be established.

The tumultous populace of large cities are ever to be dreaded —Their indiscriminate violence prostrates for the time all public authority—and its consequences are sometimes extensive and terrible—In Paris we may suppose these tumults are peculiarly disastrous at this time, when the public mind is in a ferment, and when (as is always the case on such occasions) there are not wanting wicked and designing men, whose element is confusion, and who will not hesitate in destroying the public tranquillity to gain a favorite point—But until your Constitution is fixed—your government organised—and your representative Body renovated—much tranquillity cannot be expected—for, until these things are done, those who are unfriendly to the revolution, will not quit the hope of bringing matters back to their former state.

The decrees of the National Assembly respecting our tobacco and oil do not appear to be very pleasing to the people of this country; but I do not presume that any hasty measures will be adopted in consequence thereof; for we have never entertained a doubt of the friendly disposition of the french Nation towards us, and are therefore persuaded that if they have done any thing which seems to bear hard upon us, at a time when the Assembly must have been occupied in very important matters, and which perhaps could not allow time for a due consideration of the subject, they will, in the moment of calm deliberation, alter it, and do what is right.

I readily perceive, my dear Sir, the critical situation in which you stand—and never can you have greater occasion to shew your prudence, judgment, and magnanimity.

On the 6 of this month I returned from a tour through the southern States, which had employed me for more than three months—In the course of this journey I have been highly gratified in observing the flourishing state of the Country, and the good dispositions of the people—Industry and economy have become very fashionable in those parts, which were formerly noted for the opposite qualities, and the labours of man are assisted by the blessings of Providence—The attachment of all Classes of citizens to the general Government seems to be a pleasing presage of their future happiness and respectability.

The complete establishment of our public credit is a strong mark of the confidence of the people in the virtue of their Representatives, and the wisdom of their measures—and, while in Europe, wars or commotions seem to agitate almost every nation, peace and tranquillity prevail among us, except on some parts of our western frontiers where the Indians have been troublesome, to reclaim or chastise whom proper measures are now pursuing—This contrast between the situation of the people of the United States, and those of Europe is too striking to be passed over even by the most superficial observer, and may, I believe, be considered as one great cause of leading the people here to reflect more attentively on their own prosperous state, and to examine more minutely, and consequently approve more fully of the government under which they live, than they otherwise would have done. But we do not wish to be the only people who may taste the sweets of an equal and good government—we look with an anxious eye for the time when happiness and tranquillity shall prevail in your country— and when all Europe shall be freed from commotions, tumults, and alarms.

Your friends in this country often express their great attachment to you by their anxiety for your safety.

Knox, Jay, Hamilton, Jefferson remember you with affection—but none with more sincerity and true attachment than, My dear Sir, Your affectionate

SUPPORTING REPRESSION OF THE SLAVE
REVOLT IN SAINT-DOMINGUE

To Jean Baptiste Ternant

Sir,   Mount Vernon Sepr 24th 1791.
I have not delayed a momt since the receipt of your communications of the 22d instant, in dispatching orders to the Secretary of the Treasury to furnish the money, and to the Secretary of War to deliver the arms and ammunition, which you have applied to me for.

Sincerely regretting, as I do, the cause which has given rise to this application, I am happy in the opportunity of testifying how well disposed the United States are to render every aid in their power to our good friends and Allies the French to quell "the alarming insurrection of the Negros in Hispaniola" and of the ready disposition to effect it, of the Executive authority thereof.

FRANK ADVICE FROM THE PRESIDENT

To Gouverneur Morris

Private
My dear Sir,   Philadelphia Jany 28th 1792
Your favor of the 30th of September came duly to hand, and
I thank you for the important information contained in it.

The official communications from the Secretary of State,
accompanying this letter, will convey to you the evidence of
my *nomination*, and *appointment* of you to be Minister Plenipotentiary for the United States at the Court of France; and
my assurances that both were made with *all my heart*, will, I
am persuaded, satisfy you as to that fact. I wish I could add,
that the *advice* & *consent* flowed from a similar source. Candour forbids it—and friendship requires that I should assign
the causes, as far as they have come to my knowledge.

Whilst your abilities, knowledge in the affairs of this Country, & disposition to serve it were adduced, and asserted on
one hand, you were charged on the other hand, with levity,
and imprudence of conversation and conduct. It was urged,
that your habit of expression, indicated a hauteur disgusting
to those who happen to differ from you in sentiment; and
among a people who study civility and politeness more than
any other nation, it must be displeasing. That in France you
were considered as a favourer of Aristocracy, & unfriendly to
its Revolution—(I suppose they meant Constitution). That
under this impression you could not be an acceptable public
character—of consequence, would not be able, however willing, to promote the interests of this Country in an essential
degree. That in England you indiscretely communicated the
purport of your mission, in the first instance, to the Minister of
France, at that Court; who, availing himself in the same moment of the occasion, gave it the appearance of a movement
through his Court. This, and other circumstances of a cimilar
nature, joined to a closer intercourse with the opposition
members, occasioned distrust, & gave displeasure to the Ministry; which was the cause, it is said, of that reserve which you

experienced in negotiating the business which had been entrusted to you.

But not to go further into detail—I will place the ideas of
your political adversaries in the light which their arguments
have presented them to my view—viz.—That the promptitude
with wch your brilliant, & lively imagination is displayed, allows too little time for deliberation, and correction; and is the
primary cause of those sallies which too often offend, and of
that ridicule of characters which begets enmity not easy to be
forgotten, but which might easily be avoided if it was under
the control of more caution and prudence. In a word, that it is
indispensably necessary that more circumspection should be
observed by our Representatives abroad than they conceive
you are disposed to adopt.

In this statement you have the pros & the cons; by reciting
them, I give you a proof of my friendship, if I give none of my
policy or judgment. I do it on the presumption, that a mind
conscious of its own rectitude, fears not what is said of it; but
will bid defiance to and dispise shafts that are not barbed with
accusations against honor or integrity; and because I have the
fullest confidence (supposing the alligations to be founded in
whole or part) that you would find no difficulty, being apprised
of the exceptionable light in which they are received, and
considering yourself as the representative of this Country, to
effect a change; and thereby silence, in the most unequivocal
and satisfactory manner, your political opponents. Of my good
opinion, & of my friendship & regard, you may be assured—
and that I am always—Yr affecte

"WE ARE *ALL* THE CHILDREN OF
THE SAME COUNTRY"

To James Madison

My dear Sir,   Mount Vernon May 20th 1792.
As there is a possibility if not a probability, that I shall not
see you on your return home; or, if I should see you, that it

may be on the Road and under circumstances which will prevent my speaking to you on the subject we last conversed upon; I take the liberty of committing to paper the following thoughts, & requests.

I have not been unmindful of the sentiments expressed by you in the conversations just alluded to: on the contrary I have again, and again revolved them, with thoughtful anxiety; but without being able to dispose my mind to a longer continuation in the Office I have now the honor to hold. I therefore still look forward to the fulfilment of my fondest and most ardent wishes to spend the remainder of my days (which I can not expect will be many) in ease & tranquility.

Nothing short of conviction that my deriliction of the Chair of Government (if it should be the desire of the people to continue me in it) would involve the Country in serious disputes respecting the chief Magestrate, & the disagreeable consequences which might result therefrom in the floating, & divided opinions which seem to prevail at present, could, in any wise, induce me to relinquish the determination I have formed: and of this I do not see how any evidence can be obtained previous to the Election. My vanity, I am sure, is not of that cast as to allow me to view the subject in this light.

Under these impressions then, permit me to reiterate the request I made to you at our last meeting—namely—to think of the proper time, and the best mode of anouncing the intention; and that you would prepare the latter. In revolving this subject myself, my judgment has always been embarrassed. On the one hand, a previous declaration to retire, not only carries with it the appearance of vanity & self importance, but it may be construed into a Manœuvre to be invited to remain. And on the other hand, to say nothing, implys consent; or, at any rate, would leave the matter in doubt; and to decline afterwards might be deemed as bad, & uncandid.

I would fain carry my request to you farther than is asked above, although I am sensible that your compliance with it must add to your trouble; but as the recess may afford you leizure, and I flatter myself you have dispositions to oblige me, I will, without apology desire (if the measure in itself should strike you as proper, & likely to produce public good, or private honor) that you would turn your thoughts to a Valadictory address from me to the public; expressing in plain & modest terms—that having been honored with the Presidential Chair, and to the best of my abilities contributed to the Organization & Administration of the government—that having arrived at a period of life when the private Walks of it, in the shade of retirement, becomes necessary, and will be most pleasing to me; and the spirit of the government may render a rotation in the Elective Officers of it more congenial with their ideas of liberty & safety, that I take my leave of them as a public man; and in bidding them adieu (retaining no other concern than such as will arise from fervent wishes for the prosperity of my Country) I take the liberty at my departure from civil, as I formerly did at my military exit, to invoke a continuation of the blessings of Providence upon it—and upon all those who are the supporters of its interests, and the promoters of harmony, order & good government.

That to impress these things it might, among other things be observed, that we are *all* the Children of the same country—A Country great & rich in itself—capable, & promising to be, as prosperous & as happy as any the Annals of history have ever brought to our view—That our interest, however deversified in local & smaller matters, is the same in all the great & essential concerns of the Nation. That the extent of our Country—the diversity of our climate & soil—and the various productions of the States consequent of both, are such as to make one part not only convenient, but perhaps indispensably necessary to the other part; and may render the whole (at no distant period) one of the most independant in the world. That the established government being the work of our own hands, with the seeds of amendment engrafted in the Constitution, may by wisdom, good dispositions, and mutual allowances; aided by experience, bring it as near to perfection as any human institution ever aproximated; and therefore, the only strife among us ought to be, who should be foremost in facilitating & finally accomplishing such great & desirable objects; by giving every possible support, & cement to the Union. That however necessary it may be to keep a watchful eye over public servants, & public measures, yet there ought to be limits to it; for suspicions unfounded, and jealousies too lively, are irritating to honest feelings; and oftentimes are productive of more evil than good.

To enumerate the various subjects which might be introduced into such an Address would require thought; and to mention them to you would be unnecessary, as your own judgment will comprehend *all* that will be proper; whether to touch, specifically, any of the exceptionable parts of the Constitution may be doubted. All I shall add therefore at present, is, to beg the favor of you to consider—1st the propriety of such an Address. 2d if approved, the several matters which ought to be contained in it—and 3d the time it should appear: that is, whether at the declaration of my intention to withdraw from the service of the public—or to let it be the closing Act of my Administration—which, will end with the next Session of Congress (the probability being that that body will continue sitting until March,) when the House of Representatives will also dissolve.

'Though I do not wish to hurry you (the cases not pressing) in the execution of either of the publications beforementioned, yet I should be glad to hear from you generally on both—and to receive them in time, if you should not come to Philadelphia until the Session commences, in the form they are finally to take. I beg leave to draw your attention also to such things as you shall conceive fit subjects for Communication on that occasion; and, noting them as they occur, that you would be so good as to furnish me with them in time to be prepared, and engrafted with others for the opening of the Session. With very sincere and Affectionate regard I am—ever Yours

CALLING IN THE SECRETARY OF STATE

To Thomas Jefferson

Dear Sir   George Town July 17th 1792

I am extremely sorry to find by the enclosed letter that the affairs of France put on so disagreeable an aspect.

As I know it is your intention to proceed immediately on, I

will not ask you to call at Mt Vernon now but hope it is unnecessary to say that I shall be glad to see you on your way going or Returning. I am sincerely & Affecy Yrs

CHALLENGING THE SECRETARY OF THE TREASURY

To Alexander Hamilton

(Private & confidential)

My dear Sir,   Mount Vernon July 29th 1792

I have not yet received the new regulation of allowances to the Surveyors, or Collectors of the duties on Spirituous liquors; but this by the bye. My present purpose is to write you a letter on a more interesting and important subject. I shall do it in strict confidence, & with frankness & freedom.

On my way home, and since my arrival here, I have endeavoured to learn from sensible & moderate men—known friends to the Government—the sentiments which are entertained of public measures. These all agree that the Country is prosperous & happy; but they seem to be alarmed at that system of policy, and those interpretations of the Constitution which have taken place in Congress.

Others, less friendly perhaps to the Government, and more disposed to arraign the conduct of its Officers (among whom may be classed my neighbour & quandom friend Colo. M.) go further, & enumerate a variety of matters—wch as well as I can recollect, may be adduced under the following heads. Viz.

First—That the public debt is greater than we can possibly pay before other causes of adding new debt to it will occur; and that this has been artificially created by adding together the whole amount of the debtor & creditor sides of the accounts, instead of taking only their balances; which could have been paid off in a short time.

2d—That this accumulation of debt has taken forever out of our power those easy sources of Revenue, which, applied to the ordinary necessities and exigencies of Government, would have answered them habitually, and covered us from habitual murmerings against taxes & tax gatherers; reserving extraordinary calls, for extraordinary occasions, would animate the People to meet them.

3d—That the calls for money have been no greater than we must generally expect, for the same or equivalent exigencies; yet we are already obliged to strain the *impost* till it produces clamour, and will produce evasion, and war on our citizens to collect it, and even to resort to an *Excise* law, of odious character with the people; partial in its operation; unproductive unless enforced by arbitrary & vexatious means; and committing the authority of the Government in parts where resistance is most probable, & coercion least practicable.

4th—They cite propositions in Congress, and suspect other projects on foot, still to encrease the mass of the debt.

5th—They say that by borrowing at 2/3 of the interest, we might have paid off the principal in 2/3 of the time; but that from this we are precluded by its being made irredeemable but in small portions, & long terms.

6th—That this irredeemable quality was given it for the avowed purpose of inviting its transfer to foreign Countries.

7th—They predict that this transfer of the principal, when compleated, will occasion an exportation of 3 Millions of dollars annually for the interest; a drain of Coin, of which as there has been no example, no calculation can be made of its consequences.

8th—That the banishment of our Coin will be compleated by the creation of 10 millions of paper money, in the form of Bank-bills now issuing into circulation.

9th—They think the 10 or 12 pr Ct annual profit, paid to the lenders of this paper medium are taken out of the pockets of the people, who would have had without interest the coin it is banishing.

10th—That all the Capitol employed in paper speculation is barren & useless, producing, like that on a gaming table, no accession to itself, and is withdrawn from Commerce and Agriculture where it would have produced addition to the common mass.

11th—That it nourishes in our citizens vice & idleness instead of industry & morality.

12th—That it has furnished effectual means of corrupting

such a portion of the legislature, as turns the balance between the honest Voters which ever way it is directed.

13th—That this corrupt squadron, deciding the voice of the legislature, have manifested their dispositions to get rid of the limitations imposed by the Constitution on the general legislature; limitations, on the faith of which, the States acceded to that instrument.

14th—That the ultimate object of all this is to prepare the way for a change, from the present republican form of Government, to that of a monarchy; of which the British Constitution is to be the model.

15th—That this was contemplated in the Convention, they say is no secret, because its partisans have made none of it—to effect it then was impracticable; but they are still eager after their object, and are predisposing every thing for its ultimate attainment.

16th—So many of them have got into the legislature, that, aided by the corrupt squadron of paper dealers, who are at their devotion, they make a majority in both houses.

17th—The republican party who wish to preserve the Government in its present form, are fewer even when joined by the two, three, or half a dozen antifederalists, who, tho' they dare not avow it, are still opposed to any general Government: but being less so to a Republican than a Monarchical one, they naturally join those whom they think pursuing the lesser evil.

18th—Of all the mischiefs objected to the system of measures beforementioned, none they add is so afflicting, & fatal to every honest hope, as the corruption of the legislature. As it was the earliest of these measures it became the instrument for producing the rest, and will be the instrument for producing in future a King, Lords & Commons; or whatever else those who direct it may chuse. Withdrawn such a distance from the eye of their Constituents, and these so dispersed as to be inaccessible to public information, and particularly to that of the conduct of their own Representatives, they will form the worst Government upon earth, if the means of their corruption be not prevented.

19th—The only hope of safety they say, hangs now on the numerous Representation which is to come forward the ensuing year; but should the majority of the new members be still in the same principles with the present—shew so much deriliction to republican government, and such a disposition to encroach upon, or explain away the limited powers of the constitution in order to change it, it is not easy to conjecture what would be the result, nor what means would be resorted to for correction of the evil. True wisdom they acknowledge should direct temperate & peaceable measures; but add, the division of sentiment & interest happens unfortunately, to be so geographical, that no mortal can say that what is most wise & temperate, would prevail against what is more easy & obvious; they declare, they can contemplate no evil more incalculable than the breaking of the Union into two, or more parts; yet, when they view the mass which opposed the original coalescence, when they consider that it lay chiefly in the Southern quarter—that the legislature have availed themselves of no occasion of allaying it, but on the contrary whenever Northern & Southern prejudices have come into conflict, the latter have been sacraficed and the former soothed.

20th—That the owers of the debt are in the Southern and the holders of it in the Northern division.

21st—That the antifederal champions are now strengthened in argument by the fulfilment of their predictions, which has been brought about by the monarchical federalists themselves; who, having been for the new government merely as a stepping stone to monarchy, have themselves adopted the very construction, of which, when advocating its acceptance before the tribunal of the people, they declared it insuceptable; whilst the Republican federalists, who espoused the same government for its intrinsic merits, are disarmed of their weapons, that which they denied as prophecy being now become true history. Who, therefore, can be sure they ask, that these things may not proselyte the small number which was wanting to place the majority on the other side—and this they add is the event at which they tremble.

These, as well as my memory serves me, are the sentiments which, directly and indirectly, have been disclosed to me.

To obtain light, and to pursue truth, being my sole aim; and wishing to have before me *explanations* of as well as the *complaints* on measures in which the public interest, harmony and peace is so deeply concerned, and my public conduct so much involved; it is my request, and you would oblige me in furnishing me, with your ideas upon the discontents here enumerated —and for this purpose I have thrown them into heads or sections, and numbered them that those ideas may apply to the corrispondent numbers. Although I do not mean to hurry you in giving your thoughts on the occasion of this letter, yet, as soon as you can make it convenient to yourself it would—for more reasons than one—be agreeable, & very satisfactory to me.

The enclosure in your letter of the 16th was sent back the Post after I received it, with my approving Signature; and in a few days I will write to the purpose mentioned in your letter of the 22d both to the Secretary of War & yourself—At present all my business—public & private—is on my own shoulders, the two young Gentlemen who came home with me, being on visits to their friends—and my Nephew, the Major, too much indisposed to afford me any aid, in copying or in other matters. With affectionate regard I am always—Yours

"INTERNAL DISSENTIONS . . .
TEARING OUR VITALS"

To Thomas Jefferson

(Private)
My dear Sir,   Mount Vernon Augt 23d 1792.

Your letters of the 12th & 13th came duly to hand—as did that enclosing Mr Blodgets plan of a Capitol. The latter I forwarded to the Commissioners, and the enclosures of the two first are now returned to you.

I believe we are never to hear *from* Mr Carmichael; nor *of him* but through the medium of a third person. His——I realy do not know with what epithet to fill the blank, is, to me, amongst the most unaccountable of all the unaccountable things! I wish much to hear of the arrival of Mr Short at Madrid, and the result of their joint negotiations at that Court, as we have fresh, and much stronger Representations from Mr Seagrove of the extraordinary interference of the Spaniards in West Florida, to prevent running the boundary line which had been established by treaty between the United States & the Creeks—of their promising them support in case of their refusal —and of their endeavouring to disaffect the four Southern tribes of Indians towards this Country. In the execution of these projects Seagrove is convinced McGillivray & his partner Panton are embarked, & have become principal Agents and there are suspicions entertained, he adds, that the Capture of Bowles was a preconcerted measure between the said Bowles & the Spaniards—That the former is gone to Spain (& to Madrid I think) is certain. That McGillivray has removed from little Tellassee to a place he has within, or bordering on the Spanish line. That a Captn Oliver, (a Frenchman, but) an Officer in a Spanish Regiment at New Orleans has taken his place at Tellassee and is holding talks with the Chiefs of the several Towns in the Nation. And that every exertion is making by the Governor of West Florida to obtain a full & general meeting of the Southern Tribes at Pensicola, are facts that admit of *no doubt*. It is also affirmed that five Regiments of about 600 men each, and a large quantity of Ordnance & Stores arrived lately at New Orleans, and that the like number of Regiments (but this can only be from report) was expected at the same place from the Havanna. Recent accts from Arthur Campbell (I hope without *much* foundation) speak of very hostile dispositions in the lower Cherokees, and of great apprehension for the safety of Govr Blount & Genl Pickens who had set out for the proposed meeting with the Chicasaws & Choctaws at Nashville—& for the Goods which were going down the Tenessee by Water, for that Meeting.

Our accounts from the Western Indns are not more favourable than those just mentioned. No doubt remains of their having put to death Majr Trueman & Colo. Hardin; & the Harbingers of their mission. The report from their grand Council is, that War was, or soon would be, decided on; and that they will admit no Flags. The meeting was numerous & not yet dissolved that we have been informed of. What influence our Indn Agents may have at it, remains to be known. Hendricks left Buffaloe Creek between the 18th & 20th of June, accompanied by two or three of the Six Nations; some of the Chiefs of those Nations were to follow in a few days—only waiting, it was said, for the Caughnawaga Indians from Canada.

And Captn Brandt would not be long after them. If these attempts to disclose the just & pacific disposition of the United States to these people, should also fail, there remains no alternative but the Sword, to decide the difference; & recruiting goes on heavily.

If Spain is really intrieguing with the Southern Indians as represented by Mr Seagrove, I shall entertain strong suspicions that there is a very clear understanding in all this business between the Courts of London and Madrid; & that it is calculated to check, as far as they can, the rapid encrease, extension & consequence of this Country; for there cannot be a doubt of the wishes of the former (if we may judge from the conduct of its Officers) to impede any eclaircissment of ours with the Western Indians, and to embarrass our negotiations with them, any more than there is of their Traders & some others who are subject to their Government, aiding and abetting them in acts of hostilities.

How unfortunate, and how much is it to be regretted then, that whilst we are encompassed on all sides with avowed enemies & insidious friends, that internal dissentions should be harrowing & tearing our vitals. The last, to me, is the most serious—the most alarming—and the most afflicting of the two. And without more charity for the opinions & acts of one another in Governmental matters—or some more infalible criterion by which the truth of speculative opinions, before they have undergone the test of experience, are to be forejudged than has yet fallen to the lot of fallibility, I believe it will be difficult, if not impracticable, to manage the Reins of Government or to keep the parts of it together: for if, instead of laying our shoulders to the machine after measures are decided on, one pulls this way & another that, before the utility of the thing is fairly tried, it must, inevitably, be torn asunder—And, in my opinion the fairest prospect of happiness & prosperity that ever was presented to man, will be lost—perhaps for ever!

My earnest wish, and my fondest hope therefore is, that instead of wounding suspicions, & irritable charges, there may be liberal allowances—mutual forbearances—and temporising yieldings on *all sides*. Under the exercise of these, matters will go on smoothly, and, if possible, more prosperously. Without them every thing must rub—the Wheels of Government will clog—our enemies will triumph—& by threwing their weight into the disaffected Scale, may accomplish the ruin of the goodly fabric we have been erecting.

I do not mean to apply these observations, or this advice to any particular person, or character—I have given them in the same general terms to other Officers of the Government—because the disagreements which have arisen from difference of opinions—and the Attacks wch have been made upon almost all the measures of government, & most of its Executive Officers, have, for a long time past, filled me with painful sensations; and cannot fail I think, of producing unhappy consequences at home & abroad.

The nature of Mr Seagroves communications was such, and the evidence in support of them so strongly corroborative, that I gave it as my sentiment to Genl Knox that the Commissioners of Spain ought to have the matter brought before them again in the manner it was before, but in stronger (though not in committing) language; as the Government was embarrassed, and its Citizens in the Southern States made uneasy by such proceedings, however unauthorised they might be by their Court.

I pray you to note down, or rather to frame into paragraphs or sections such matters as may occur to you as fit & proper for general communication at the opening of the next Session of Congress—not only in the department of State, but on any other subject applicable to the occasion, that I may, in due time, have every thing before me. With sincere esteem & friendship I am, always, Your Affectionate

"OPINIONS . . . PUSHED WITH
TOO MUCH TENACITY"

To Alexander Hamilton

(Private)
My dear Sir,   Mount Vernon Augt 26th 1792
    Your letter of the 18th, enclosing answers to certain objections communicated to you in my letter of the 29th Ulto came

duly to hand; and although I have not, as yet, from a variety of causes, been able to give them the attentive reading I mean to bestow, I feel myself much obliged by the trouble you have taken to answer them; as I persuade myself, from the full manner in which you appear to have taken the matter up, that I shall receive both satisfaction and profit from the perusal.

Differences in political opinions are as unavoidable as, to a certain point, they may perhaps be necessary; but it is to be regretted, exceedingly, that subjects cannot be discussed with temper on the one hand, or decisions submitted to without having the motives which led to them, improperly implicated on the other: and this regret borders on chagrin when we find that Men of abilities—zealous patriots—having the same *general* objects in view, and the same upright intentions to prosecute them, will not exercise more charity in deciding on the opinions, & actions of one another. When matters get to such lengths, the natural inference is, that both sides have strained the Cords beyond their bearing—and that a middle course would be found the best, until experience shall have pointed out the right mode—or, which is not to be expected, because it is denied to mortals—there shall be some *infallible* rule by which we could *fore* judge events.

Having premised these things, I would fain hope that liberal allowances will be made for the political opinions of one another; and instead of those wounding suspicions, and irritating charges with which some of our Gazettes are so strongly impregnated, & cannot fail if persevered in, of pushing matters to extremity, & thereby tare the Machine asunder, that there might be mutual forbearances and temporising yieldings *on all sides.* Without these I do not see how the Reins of Government are to be managed, or how the Union of the States can be much longer preserved.

How unfortunate would it be, if a fabric so goodly—erected under so many Providential circumstances—and in its first stages, having acquired such respectibility, should, from diversity of Sentiments, or internal obstructions to some of the acts of Government (for I cannot prevail on myself to believe that these measures are, as yet, the deliberate Acts of a determined party) should be harrowing our vitals in such a manner as to have brought us to the verge of dissolution—Melancholy

thought! But one, at the sametime that it shows the consequences of diversified opinions, when pushed with too much
tenacity; exhibits evidence also of the necessity of accomodation; and of the propriety of adopting such healing measures as
will restore harmony to the discordant members of the Union,
& the governing powers of it.

I do not mean to apply this advice to measures which are
passed, or to any character in particular. I have given it in the
same *general* terms to other Officers of the Government. My
earnest wish is, that balsam may be poured into *all* the wounds
which have been given, to prevent them from gangrening; &
from those fatal consequences which the community may sustain if it is withheld. The friends of the Union must wish this—
those who are not, but wish to see it rended, will be disappointed
—and all things I hope will go well.

We have learnt through the medium of Mr Harrison to
Doctr Craik, that you have it in contemplation to take a trip
this way. I felt pleasure at hearing it, and hope it is unnecessary
to add that it would be considerably encreased by seeing you
under this roof, for you may be assured of the sincere and Affectionate regard of Yours

P.S. I pray you to note down whatever may occur to you, not
only in your own department but other matters also of general
import that may be fit subjects for the Speech at the opening
of the ensuing Session.

"IMPOSSIBLE . . . FOR ANY MAN
LIVING TO MANAGE THE HELM"

To Edmund Randolph

(Private)
My dear Sir,   Mount Vernon Augt 26th 1792
    The purpose of this letter is merely to acknowledge the re-
ceipt of your favors of the 5th & 13th instt, and to thank you
for the information contained in both without entering into
the details of either.

With respect, however, to the interesting subject treated on in that of the 5th, I can express but one sentiment at this time, and that is a wish—a devout one—that whatever my ultimate determination shall be, it may be for the best. The subject never recurs to my mind but with additional poignancy; and from the declining State in the health of my Nephew, to whom my concerns of a domestic & private nature are entrusted it comes with aggrivated force—But as the allwise disposer of events has hitherto watched over my steps, I trust that in the important one I may soon be called upon to take, he will mark the course so plainly, as that I cannot mistake the way. In full hope of this, I will take no measure, yet awhile, that will not leave me at liberty to decide from circumstances, & the best lights, I can obtain on the subject.

I should be happy in the mean time to see a cessation of the abuses of public Officers—and of those attacks upon almost every measure of government with which some of the Gazettes are so strongly impregnated; & which cannot fail, if persevered in with the malignancy they now team, of rending the Union asunder. The Seeds of discontent—distrust & irritations which are so plentifully sown—can scarcely fail to produce this effect and to Mar that prospect of happiness which perhaps never beamed with more effulgence upon any people under the Sun—and this too at a time when all Europe are gazing with admiration at the brightness of our prospects. and for what is all this? Among other things, to afford Nuts for our transatlantic—what shall I call them? Foes!

In a word if the Government and the Officers of it are to be the constant theme for News-paper abuse, and this too without condescending to investigate the motives or the facts, it will be impossible, I conceive, for any man living to manage the helm, or to keep the machine together—But I am running from my text, and therefore will only add assurances of the Affecte esteem & regard with which I am always—Yours.

"I HAVE PURSUED *ONE* UNIFORM COURSE"

To John Francis Mercer

Sir,   Mount Vernon Septr 26. 1792.

Your Letter of the 15th inst: was presented to me by Mr Corbin, on his return from Philada.

As my object in taking your Land near Monocasy (in payment of the Debt due from the Estate of your deceased Father to me) is to convert it into Cash as soon as possible *without loss*, I can have no other objection to an advantageous partition of the Tract than what might result from the uncertainty of the price that may be affixed to it, and the consequent possibility that the amount of a moiety may exceed the sum which is due to me by the last settlement of the Accots—thereby occasioning a payment of money, instead of receiving it. If these difficulties were removed, I have none other to your proposal of dividing the Tract into two equal parts, & fixing the property therein by lot. A mean of doing this, I will suggest. It is—if you have not heard the sentiments of the Gentlemen, or either of them, who were chosen to affix a *ready money* price on the Land (& I give you my honor I have not, and moreover that I have never exchanged a word on the subject with any one, except what I told you was Colo. Wm Deakins's opinion of it's worth)—I will allow you seven Dollars pr acre for a moiety; to be ascertained in the manner before mentioned. I name seven dollars for the following reasons—1st because I have been assured by the above Gentleman (who professes to be well acquainted with the Land) that, in his judgment, it would not sell for more than six Dollars Cash, or seven dollars on credit; & 2d because you have set it at Eight Dollars your self, without being able to obtain that price. Five hundred & fifty acres (if the tract contains 1100) would then be within the compass of my claim; & the surplus, if any, I would receive in young Cows, or full grown heifers from Marlborough at three pounds a head, if more agreeable to you than to pay the Cash—Your answer to this proposal, soon, would be convenient to me, as I shall be on my return to Philada in a short time.

I come now to another part of your Letter, and in touching

upon it, do not scruple to declare to you that I was not a little displeased to find by a letter from Captn Campbell, to a Gentleman in this neighbourhood, that my name had been freely used by you, or your friends, for electioneering purposes, when I had never associated your name & the Election together; and when there had been the most scrupulous & pointed caution observed on my part, not to express a sentiment respecting the fitness, or unfitness of any Candidate for representation, that could be construed, by the most violent torture of the words, into an interference in favor of one, or to the prejudice of another. Conceiving that the exercise of an influence (if I really possessed any) however remote, would be highly improper; as the people ought to be entirely at liberty to chuse whom they pleased to represent them in Congress. Having pursued this line of conduct *steadily*— my surprise, and consequent declaration can be a matter of no wonder. when I read the following words in the letter above alluded to—"I arrived yesterday from Philadelphia, since which I find Colo. Mercer has openly declared, that Mr Richd Sprigg junr informed him, that Bushrod Washington told him that the President in his presence declared, that he hoped Colo. Mercer would not be left out of the next representation in Congress; and added that he thought him the best representative that now goes, or ever did go to that Body from this State."

I instantly declared to the person who shewed me the letter, "that to the best of my recollection, I never had exchanged a word to, or before Bushrod Washington on the subject of your Election—much less to have given such a decided opinion. That such a measure would have been incompatible with the rule I had prescrib'd to myself, & which I had invariably observed— of not interfering directly or indirectly with the suffrages of the People, in the choice of their representatives: and added, that I wished B. Washington might be called upon to certify what, or whether any conversation had ever passed between us on this subject, as it was my desire that every thing should stand upon it's proper foundation." Other sentiments have been reported as mine, that are equally erroneous.

Whether you have, upon any occasion, expressed your self in disrespectful terms of me, I know not: it has never been the subject of my enquiry. If nothing impeaching my honor, or honesty, is said, I care little for the rest. I have pursued *one* uniform course for three score years, and am happy in *believing* that the world have thought it a right one—if its being so, I am so well satisfied myself, that I shall not depart from it by turning either to the right or to the left, until I arrive at the end of my Pilgrimage. I am, Sir, Your very hble Servt

"I HAVE A GREAT—A SINCERE ESTEEM &
REGARD FOR YOU BOTH"

To Thomas Jefferson

(Private)
My dear Sir   Phila. Octobr 18th 1792.

I did not require the evidence of the extracts which you enclosed me, to convince me of your attachment to the Constitution of the United States, or of your disposition to promote the general Welfare of this Country. But I regret—deeply regret —the difference in opinions which have arisen, and divided you and another principal Officer of the Government; and wish, devoutly, there could be an accomodation of them by mutual yieldings.

A Measure of this sort would produce harmony, and consequent good in our public Councils; the contrary will, inevitably, introduce confusion, & serious mischiefs—and for what?— because mankind cannot think alike, but would adopt different means to attain the same end. For I will frankly, & solemnly declare that, I believe the views of both of you are pure, and well meant; and that experience alone will decide with respect to the salubrity of the measures wch are the subjects of dispute.

Why then, when some of the best Citizens in the United States—Men of discernment—Uniform and tried Patriots, who have no sinister views to promote, but are chaste in their ways of thinking and acting are to be found, some on one side, and some on the other of the questions which have caused these agitations, shd either of you be so tenacious of your opinions as to make no allowances for those of the other?

I could, and indeed was about to add more on this interesting subject; but will forbear, at least for the present; after expressing a wish that the cup wch has been presented, may not be snatched from our lips by a discordance of *action* when I am persuaded there is no discordance in your *views*. I have a great—a sincere esteem & regard for you both, and ardently wish that some line could be marked out by which both of you could walk. I am always—Yr Affecte

"SUBJECT TO THE UPBRAIDINGS OF ALL"

Second Inaugural Address

FELLOW-CITIZENS:

I am again called upon, by the voice of my country, to execute the functions of its Chief Magistrate. When the occasion proper for it shall arrive, I shall endeavour to express the high sense I entertain of this distinguished honor, and of the confidence which has been reposed in me by the people of United America.

Previous to the execution of any official act of the PRESIDENT, the Constitution requires an oath of office. This oath I am now about to take, and in your presence; that if it shall be found, during my administration of the Government, I have in any instance, violated, willingly or knowingly, the injunction thereof, I may (besides incurring Constitutional punishment) be subject to the upbraidings of all who are now witnesses of the present solemn ceremony.

Philadelphia, March 4, 1793

THE NATIONAL INTEREST

To Gouverneur Morris

(Private)
My dear Sir,   Philadelphia March 25th 1793.
    It was not 'till the middle of February that I had the pleasure to receive your letter of the 23d of October.

If you, who are at the fountain head of those great and important transactions which have lately engrossed the attention of Europe & America, cannot pretend to say what will be their event—surely we, in this distant quarter, should be presumptious indeed, in venturing to predict it. And unwise should we be in the extreme to involve ourselves in the contests of European Nations, where our weight could be but Small—tho' the loss to ourselves would be certain. I can however with truth aver, that this Country is not guided by such narrow and mistaken policy as will lead it to wish the destruction of any Nation, under an idea that our importance will be encreased in proportion as that of others is lessened. We should rejoice to see every Nation enjoying all the advantages that nature & its circumstances wd admit, consistent with civil liberty and the rights of other nations. Upon this ground the prosperity of this Country wd unfold itself every day—and every day would it be growing in political importance.

Mr Jefferson will communicate to you such official information as we have to give, & will transmit the laws—public papers —&ca.

I have thought it best, my dear Sir, not to let slip this opportunity of acknowledging the receipt of your letter lest no other should occur to me very Soon—as I am called to Mount Vernon by the death of my Nephew, Major Washington, and am on the point of setting out for that place (to morrow)—I need not tell you that this is, of course, a very busy moment with me. It will therefore account for the conciseness of this letter—by which however you must not measure my Regard.

You see me again entering upon the arduous duties of an important Office. It is done so contrary to my intention, that it would Require more time than I have allowed myself, to assign the reasons; and therefore, I shall leave them to your own Suggestion—aided by the publications which you will find in the Gazettes. I am always Your sincere friend & Affecte Servant

AFFIRMING NEUTRALITY

To Thomas Jefferson

Dear Sir,   Mount Vernon April 12th 1793.

Your letter of the 7th instant was brought to me by the last Post. War having actually commenced between France and Great Britain, it behoves the Government of this Country to use every means in it's power to prevent the citizens thereof from embroiling us with either of those powers, by endeavouring to maintain a strict neutrality. I therefore require that you will give the subject mature consideration, that such measures as shall be deemed most likely to effect this desirable purpose may be adopted without delay; for I have understood that vessels are already designated as Privateers, & preparing accordingly.

Such other measures as may be necessary for us to pursue against events which it may not be in our Power to avoid or controul you will also think of, and lay them before me at my arrival in Philadelphia, for which place I shall set out Tomorrow; but will leave it to the advices which I may receive to night by the Post, to determine whether it is to be by the most direct Rout, or by the one I proposed to have come—that is, by Reading, the Canals between the Rivers of Pennsylvania, Harrisburgh, Carlisle &ca. With very great esteem & regard I am, Dear Sir, Your mo: humble Servant

"THE TROUBLE THEY GIVE IS
HARDLY TO BE DESCRIBED"

To Henry Lee

(Private)

Dear Sir,   Philadelphia July 21st 1793

I should have thanked you at an earlier period for your obliging letter of the 14th ulto, had it not come to my hands a day or two only before I set out for Mount Vernon; and at a time when I was much hurried, and indeed very much perplexed with the disputes, Memorials and what not, with which the Government were pestered by one or other of the petulant representatives of the Powers at War. And because, since my return to this City (nine days ago) I have been more than ever overwhelmed with their complaints. In a word, the trouble they give is hardly to be described.

My Journey to and from Mt Vernon was sudden & rapid, and as short as I could make it. It was occasioned by the unexpected death of Mr Whitting (my Manager) at a critical season for the business with which he was entrusted. Where to supply his place I know not; of course my concerns at Mt Vernon are left as a body without a head—but this bye the by.

The communications in your letter were pleasing and grateful. For although I have done no public Act with which my Mind upbraids me, yet it is highly satisfactory to learn that the things which I do (of an interesting tendency to the peace & happiness of this Country) are generally approved by my fellow Citizens. But were the case otherwise, I should not be less inclined to know the sense of the People upon every matter of great public concern; for as I have no wish superior to that of promoting the happiness & welfare of this Country, so, consequently, it is only for me to know the means, to accomplish the end, if it is within the compass of my Powers.

That there are in this, as in all other Countries, discontented characters, I well know; as also that these characters are actuated by very different views. Some good, from an opinion that the measures of the general Government are impure. Some bad, and (if I might be allowed to use so harsh an epithet) diabolical; inasmuch as they are not only meant to impede the measures of that Government generally, but more especially (as a great mean towards the accomplishment of it) to destroy the confidence which it is necessary for the People to place (until they have unequivocal proof of demerit) in their public Servants; for in this light I consider myself, whilst I am an occupant of Office; and if they were to go farther & call me there Slave (during this period) I would not dispute the point. But in what will this abuse terminate? The result, as it respects myself, I care not; for I have a consolation within that no earthly efforts can deprive me of—and, that is, that neither ambitious, nor interested motives have influenced my conduct. The arrows of malevolence therefore, however barbed & well pointed, never can reach the most valuable part of me; though, whilst I am *up* as a *mark*, they will be continually aimed. The publications in Freneau's and Beach's Papers are outrages on common decency; and they progress in that style, in proportion as their pieces are treated with contempt, & passed by in silence by those, at whom they are aimed. The tendency of them, however, is too obvious to be mistaken by men of cool & dispassionate minds; and, in my opinion, ought to alarm them; because it is difficult to prescribe bounds to the effect.

The light in which you endeavored to place the views and conduct of this Country to Mr G—t; and the sound policy thereof as it respected his own; was, unquestionably the true one; and such as a man of penetration, left to himself, would most certainly have viewed them in. but mum on this head. time may unfold more, than prudence ought to disclose at present.

As we are told that you have exchanged the rugged & dangerous field of Mars, for the soft and pleasurable bed of Venus, I do in this as I shall in every thing you may pursue like unto it good & laudable, wish you all imaginable success and happiness; being with much truth and regard Dear Sir, Your Affecte Servt

HAMILTON ON TRIAL

To Edmund Pendleton

My dear Sir, Mount Vernon Sep: 23d 1793
   With very sincere pleasure I received your private letter of the 11th instant. This pleasure was not a little enhanced by your reiterated assurance of my still holding that place in your estimation which, on more occasions than one, you have given me the most flattering testimony—highly gratifying to my mind. This assurance came opportunely, as I had begun to conceive (though unable to assign a cause) that some part of my public conduct—how ever well meant my endeavors—had appeared unfavorable in your eyes, for you will please to recollect that,

formerly you promised me, and I always expected, an annual letter from you. It is now (if my memory has not failed me) at least four years since I have had that pleasure.

Sequestered you say you are, from the World, and know little of what is transacting in it but from Newspapers. I regret this exceedingly. I wish you had more to do on the great theatre; and that your means of information were co-equal to your abilities, and the disposition I know you possess to judge properly of public measures. It would be better perhaps for that public it should be so; for be assured we have some infamous Papers—calculated for disturbing if not absolutely intended to disturb, the peace of the community.

With respect to the fiscal conduct of the S—t—y of the Tr—s—y I will say nothing; because an enquiry, more than probable, will be instituted next Session of Congress into some of the Alligations against him, which, eventually, may involve the whole; and because, if I mistake not, he will seek, rather than shrink from, an investigation. A fair opportunity will then be given to the impartial world to form a just estimate of his Acts, and probably of his motives. No one, I will venture to say, wishes more devoutly than I do that they may be probed to the bottom—be the result what it will.

With the most scrupulous truth I can assure you, that your free & unreserved opinion upon any public measure of importance will always be acceptable to me, whether it respects men, or measures—and on no man do I wish it to be expressed more fully than on myself; for as I can conscientiously declare that I have no object in view incompatible with the Constitution, and the obvious interests of this Country—nor no earthly desire *half* as strong as that of returning to the walks of private life, so, of consequence I only wish whilst I am a Servant of the public, to know the will of my masters, that I may govern myself accordingly.

You do me no more than justice when you suppose that from motives of respect to the Legislature (and I might add from my interpretation of the Constitution) I give my Signature to many Bills with which my judgment is at varience. In declaring this, however, I allude to no particular Act. From the nature of the Constitution, I must approve all the parts of a Bill, or reject it in toto. To do the latter can only be justified upon the clear and obvious ground of propriety; and I never had such confidence in my own faculty of judging as to be over tenacious of the opinions I may have embibed in doubtful cases.

Mrs Washington who enjoys tolerable good health joins me most cordially in best wishes for you and Mrs Pendleton. I wish you may live long—continue in good health—and end your days as you have been wearing them away, happily and respected. Always, and most affectionately, I am Your Obedt Servt

"IF WE DESIRE TO AVOID INSULT,
WE MUST BE ABLE TO REPEL IT"

Fifth Annual Message to Congress

Fellow Citizens of the Senate, and of the House of Representatives

Since the commencement of the term, for which I have been again called into office, no fit occasion has arisen for expressing to my fellow Citizens at large, the deep and respectful sense, which I feel, of the renewed testimony of public approbation. While on the one hand, it awakened my gratitude for all those instances of affectionate partiality, with which I have been honored by my Country; on the other, it could not prevent an earnest wish for that retirement, from which no private consideration should ever have torn me. But influenced by the belief, that my conduct would be estimated according to its real motives; and that the people, and the authorities derived from them, would support exertions, having nothing personal for their object, I have obeyed the suffrage which commanded me to resume the Executive power; and I humbly implore that Being, on whose Will the fate of Nations depends, to crown with success our mutual endeavours for the general happiness.

As soon as the War in Europe had embraced those Powers, with whom the United States have the most extensive relations; there was reason to apprehend that our intercourse with them might be interrupted, and our disposition for peace, drawn into question, by the suspicions, too often entertained by belligerent

Nations. It seemed therefore to be my duty, to admonish our Citizens of the consequences of a contraband trade, and of hostile Acts to any of the parties; and to obtain by a declaration of the existing legal state of things, an easier admission of our right to the immunities, belonging to our situation. Under these impressions the Proclamation, which will be laid before you, was issued.

In this posture of affairs, both new & delicate, I resolved to adopt general rules, which should conform to the Treaties, and assert the priviledges, of the United States. These were reduced into a system, which will be communicated to you. Although I have not thought myself at liberty to forbid the Sale of the prizes, permitted by our treaty of Commerce with France to be brought into our ports; I have not refused to cause them to be restored, when they were taken within the protection of our territory; or by vessels commissioned, or equipped in a warlike form within the limits of the United States.

It rests with the wisdom of Congress to correct, improve or enforce this plan of proceedure; and it will probably be found expedient, to extend the legal code, and the Jurisdiction of the Courts of the United States, to many cases which, though dependent on principles, already recognized, demand some further provisions.

Where individuals shall, within the United States, array themselves in hostility against any of the powers at war; or enter upon Military expeditions, or enterprizes within the jurisdiction of the United States; or usurp and exercise judicial authority within the United States; or where the penalties on violations of the law of Nations may have been indistinctly marked, or are inadequate; these offences cannot receive too early and close an attention, and require prompt and decisive remedies.

Whatsoever those remedies may be, they will be well administered by the Judiciary, who possess a long established course of investigation, effectual process, and Officers in the habit of executing it.

In like manner; as several of the Courts have *doubted*, under particular circumstances, their power to liberate the vessels of a Nation at peace, and even of a citizen of the United States, although siezed under a false colour of being hostile property;

and have *denied* their power to liberate certain captures within the protection of our territory; it would seem proper to regulate their jurisdiction in these points. But if the Executive is to be the resort in either of the two last mentioned cases, it is hoped, that he will be authorized by law, to have facts ascertained by the Courts, when, for his own information, he shall request it.

I cannot recommend to your notice measures for the fulfilment of *our* duties to the rest of the world, without again pressing upon you the necessity of placing ourselves in a condition of compleat defence, and of exacting from *them* the fulfilment of *their* duties towards *us.* The United States ought not to endulge a persuasion, that, contrary to the order of human events, they will for ever keep at a distance those painful appeals to arms, with which the history of every other nation abounds. There is a rank due to the United States among Nations, which will be withheld, if not absolutely lost, by the reputation of weakness. If we desire to avoid insult, we must be able to repel it; if we desire to secure peace, one of the most powerful instruments of our rising prosperity, it must be known, that we are at all times ready for War. The documents, which will be presented to you, will shew the amount, and kinds of Arms and Military stores now in our Magazines and Arsenals: and yet an addition even to these supplies cannot with prudence be neglected; as it would leave nothing to the uncertainty of procuring a warlike apparatus, in the moment of public danger.

Nor can such arrangements, with such objects, be exposed to the censure or jealousy of the warmest friends of Republican Government. They are incabable of abuse in the hands of the Militia, who ought to possess a pride in being the depositary of the force of the Republic, and may be trained to a degree of energy, equal to every military exigency of the United States. But it is an inquiry, which cannot be too solemnly pursued, whether the act "more effectually to provide for the national defence by establishing an uniform Militia throughout the United States" has organized them so as to produce their full effect; whether your own experience in the several States has not detected some imperfections in the scheme; and whether a material feature in an improvement of it, ought not to be, to

afford an opportunity for the study of those branches of the
Military art, which can scarcely ever be attained by practice
alone?

The connexion of the United States with Europe, has become extremely interesting. The occurrences, which relate to
it, and have passed under the knowledge of the Executive, will
be exhibited to Congress in a subsequent communication.

When we contemplate the war on our frontiers, it may be
truly affirmed, that every reasonable effort has been made to
adjust the causes of dissention with the Indians, North of the
Ohio. The Instructions given to the Commissioners evince a
moderation and equity, proceeding from a sincere love of
peace, and a liberality, having no restriction but the essential
interests and dignity of the United States. The attempt, however, of an amicable negotiation having been frustrated, the
troops have marched to act offensively. Although the proposed
treaty did not arrest the progress of Military preparation; it is
doubtful, how far the advance of the Season, before good faith
justified active movements, may retard them, during the remainder of the year. From the papers and intelligence, which
relate to this important subject, you will determine, whether
the deficiency in the number of Troops, granted by law, shall
be compensated by succours of Militia; or additional encouragements shall be proposed to recruits.

An anxiety has been also demonstrated by the Executive, for
peace with the Creeks and the Cherokees. The former have
been relieved with Corn and with clothing, and offensive measures against them prohibited during the recess of Congress.
To satisfy the complaints of the latter, prosecutions have been
instituted for the violences committed upon them. But the
papers, which will be delivered to you, disclose the critical footing on which we stand in regard to both those tribes; and it is
with Congress to pronounce, what shall be done.

After they shall have provided for the present emergency, it
will merit their most serious labours, to render tranquillity
with the Savages permanent, by creating ties of interest. Next
to a vigorous execution of justice on the violators of peace, the
establishment of commerce with the Indian nations in behalf
of the United States, is most likely to conciliate their attachment. But it ought to be conducted without fraud, without

extortion, with constant and plentiful supplies; with a ready market for the commodities of the Indians, and a stated price for what they give in payment, and receive in exchange. Individuals will not pursue such a traffic, unless they be allured by the hope of profit; but it will be enough for the United States to be reembursed only. Should this recommendation accord with the opinion of Congress, they will recollect, that it cannot be accomplished by any means yet in the hands of the Executive. Gentlemen of the House of Representatives

The Commissioners, charged with the settlement of Accounts between the United and Individual States, concluded their important functions, within the time limited by Law; and the balances, struck in their report, which will be laid before Congress, have been placed on the Books of the Treasury.

On the first day of June last, an instalment of one million of florins became payable on the loans of the United States in Holland. This was adjusted by a prolongation of the period of reimbursement, in nature of a new loan, at an interest of five per cent for the term of ten years; and the expences of this operation were a commission of three prCent.

The first instalment of the loan of two millions of dollars from the Bank of the United States, has been paid, as was directed by Law. For the second it is necessary, that provision should be made.

No pecuniary consideration is more urgent, than the regular redemption and discharge of the public debt: on none can delay be more injurious, or an œconomy of time more valuable.

The productiveness of the public revenues hitherto, has continued to equal the anticipations which were formed of it; but it is not expected to prove commensurate with all the objects, which have been suggested. Some auxiliary provisions will, therefore, it is presumed, be requisite; and it is hoped that these may be made, consistently with a due regard to the convenience of our Citizens, who cannot but be sensible of the true wisdom of encountering a small present addition to their contributions, to obviate a future accumulation of burthens.

But here, I cannot forbear to recommend a repeal of the tax on the transportation of public prints. There is no resource so firm for the Government of the United States, as the affections of the people guided by an enlightened policy; and to this primary good, nothing can conduce more, than a faithful representation of public proceedings, diffused, without restraint, throughout the United States.

An estimate of the appropriations, necessary for the current service of the ensuing year, and a statement of a purchase of Arms and Military stores, made during the recess, will be presented to Congress. Gentlemen of the Senate, and of the House of Representatives.

The several subjects, to which I have now referred, open a wide range to your deliberations; and involve some of the choicest interests of our common Country. Permit me to bring to your remembrance the magnitude of your task. Without an unprejudiced coolness, the welfare of the Government may be hazarded; without harmony, as far as consists with freedom of sentiment, its dignity may be lost. But, as the Legislative proceedings of the United States will never, I trust, be reproached for the want of temper or of candour; so shall not the public happiness languish, from the want of my strenuous and warmest co-operation.

December 3, 1793

CONFRONTING THE WHISKEY REBELLION

To Charles Mynn Thruston

(Private)

Philadelphia, August 10, 1794.

Dear Sir: Your favor of the 21st. of June came duly to hand. For the communications contained in it, I thank you; as I shall do for any other that is interesting to the Community and necessary for me to be informed of. That there should exist in this country such a spirit as you say pervades the people of Kentucky (and which I have also learnt through other channels) is, to me, matter of great wonder; and that it should prevail there, more than in any other part of the Union, is not less surprising to those who are acquainted with the exertions of the General government in their favor. But it will serve to evince whensoever, and to whomsoever facts are developed (and they are not unknown at this moment, to many of the principal characters in that State) that there must exist a predisposition among them to be dissatisfied under any circumstances, and under every exertion of government (short of a war with Spain, which must eventually involve one with Great Britain) to promote their welfare.

The protection they receive, and the unwearied endeavours of the General government to accomplish (by repeated and ardent remonstrances) what they seem to have most at heart, viz, the navigation of the Mississipi, obtain no credit with them, or what is full as likely, may be concealed from them or misrepresented by those Societies who under specious colourings are spreading mischief far and wide either from *real* ignorance of the measures pursuing by the government, or from a wish to bring it, as much as they are able, into discredit; for what purposes, every man is left to his own conjectures.

That similar attempts to discontent the public mind have been practiced with too much success in some of the Western Counties in this State you are, I am certain, not to learn. Actual rebellion against the Laws of the United States exist at this moment notwithstanding every lenient measure which could comport with the duties of the public Officers have been exercised to reconcile them to the collection of the taxes upon spirituous liquors and Stills. What may be the consequences of such violent and outrageous proceedings is painful in a high degree even in contemplation. But if the Laws are to be so trampled upon, with impunity, and a minority (a small one too) is to dictate to the majority there is an end put, at one stroke, to republican government; and nothing but anarchy and confusion is to be expected thereafter; for Some other man, or society, may dislike another Law and oppose it with equal propriety until all Laws are prostrate, and every one (the strongest I presume) will carve for himself. Yet, there will be found persons I have no doubt, who, although they may not be hardy enough to justify such open opposition to the Laws, will, nevertheless, be opposed to coercion even if the proclamation and the other temperate measures which are in train by the Executive to avert the dire necessity of a resort to arms, should fail. How far such people may extend their influence, and what may be the consequences thereof is not easy to decide; but this we know, that it is not difficult by concealment of some facts, and the exaggeration of others, (where there is an influence) to bias a well-meaning mind, at least for a time, truth will ultimately prevail where pains is taken to bring it to light.

I have a great regard for Genl. Morgan, and respect his military talents, and am persuaded if a fit occasion should occur no one would exert them with more zeal in the service of his country than he would. It is my ardent wish, however, that this Country should remain in Peace as long as the Interest, honour and dignity of it will permit, and its laws, enacted by the Representatives of the People freely chosen, shall obtain. With much esteem &c.

"THE FIRST *FORMIDABLE* FRUIT OF THE DEMOCRATIC SOCIETIES"

To Henry Lee

(Private)

German Town, August 26, 1794.

Dear Sir: Your favor of the 17th. came duly to hand, and I thank you for its communications. As the Insurgents in the western counties of this State are resolved (as far as we have yet been able to learn from the Commissioners, who have been sent among them) to persevere in their rebellious conduct untill what they call the excise Law is repealed, and acts of oblivion and amnesty are passed; it gives me sincere consolation amidst the regret with which I am filled, by such lawless and outrageous conduct, to find by your letter above mentioned, that it is held in general detestation by the good people of Virginia; and that you are disposed to lend your *personal* aid to subdue this spirit, and to bring those people to a proper sense of their duty.

On this latter point I shall refer you to letters from the War office; and to a private one from Colo. Hamilton (who in the absence of the Secretary of War, superintends the *military* duties of that department) for my sentiments on this occasion.

It is with equal pride and satisfaction I add, that as far as my information extends, this insurrection is viewed with universal indignation and abhorrence; except by those who have never missed an opportunity by side blows, or otherwise, to aim their shafts at the general government; and even among these there is not a Spirit hardy enough, yet, *openly* to justify the daring infractions of Law and order; but by palliatives are attempting to suspend all proceedings against the insurgents until Congress shall have decided on the case, thereby intending to gain time, and if possible to make the evil more extensive, more formidable, and of course more difficult to counteract and subdue.

I consider this insurrection as the first *formidable* fruit of the Democratic Societies; brought forth I believe too prematurely for their own views, which may contribute to the annihilation of them.

That these societies were instituted by the *artful* and *designing* members (many of their body I have no doubt mean well, but know little of the real plan,) primarily to sow the seeds of jealousy and distrust among the people, of the government, by destroying all confidence in the Administration of it; and that these doctrines have been budding and blowing ever since, is not new to any one, who is acquainted with the characters of their leaders, and has been attentive to their manœuvres. I early gave it as my opinion to the confidential characters around me, that, if these Societies were not counteracted (not by prosecutions, the ready way to make them grow stronger) or did not fall into disesteem from the knowledge of their origin, and the views with which they had been instituted by their father, Genet, for purposes well known to the Government; that they would shake the government to its foundation. Time and circumstances have confirmed me in this opinion, and I deeply regret the probable consequences, not as they will affect me personally, (for I have not long to act on this theatre, and sure I am that not a man amongst them can be more anxious to put me aside, than I am to sink into the profoundest retirement) but because I see, under a display of popular and fascinating guises, the most diabolical attempts to destroy the best fabric of human government and happiness, that has ever been presented for the acceptance of mankind.

A part of the plan for creating discord, is, I perceive, to make me say things of others, and others of me, wch. have no foundation in truth. The first, in many instances I *know* to be the case; and the second I believe to be so; but truth or falsehood is immaterial to them, provided their objects are promoted.

Under this head may be classed, I conceive, what it is reported I have said of Mr. Henry, and what Mr. Jefferson is reported to have said of me; on both of which, particularly the first, I mean to dilate a little. With solemn truth then I can declare, that I never expressed such sentiments of that Gentleman, as from your letter, he has been led to believe. I had heard, it is true, that he retained his enmity to the Constitution; but with very peculiar pleasure I learnt from Colo. Coles (who I am sure will recollect it) that Mr. Henry was acquiescent in his conduct, and that though he could not give up his opinions respecting the Constitution, yet, unless he should be called upon by official duty, he wd. express no sentiment unfriendly to the exercise of the powers of a government, which had been chosen by a majority of the people; or words to this effect.

Except intimating in this conversation (which to the best of my recollection was introduced by Colo. Coles) that report had made Mr. Henry speak a different language; and afterwards at Prince Edward Court house, where I saw Mr. Venable, and finding I was within eight or ten miles of Mr. Henry's seat, and expressing my regret at not seeing him, the conversation might be similar to that held with Colo. Coles; I say, except in these two instances, I do not recollect, nor do I believe, that in the course of the journey to and from the Southward I ever mentioned Mr. Henrys name in conjunction with the Constitution, or the government. It is evident therefore, that these reports are propagated with evil intentions, to create personal differences. On the question of the Constitution Mr. Henry and myself, it is well known, have been of different opinions; but personally, I have always respected and esteemed him; nay more, I have conceived myself under obligations to him for the friendly manner in which he transmitted to me some insidious anonymous writings that were sent to him in the close of the year

1777, with a view to embark him in the opposition that was forming against me at that time.

I well recollect the conversations you allude to in the winter preceeding the last; and I recollect also, that difficulties occurred which you, any more than myself, were not able to remove. 1st., though you believed, yet you would not undertake to *assert*, that Mr. Henry would be induced to accept *any appointment* under the General Government; in which case, and supposing him to be inemical to it, the wound the government would receive by his refusal, and the charge of attempting to silence his opposition by a place, would be great; 2d., because you were of opinion that *no* office which would make a residence at the Seat of government essential would comport with his disposition, or views; and 3dly., because if there was a vacancy in the supreme Judiciary at that time (of which I am not at this time certain) it could not be filled from Virginia without giving two Judges to that State, which would have excited unpleasant sensations in other States. Any thing short of one of the great Offices, it could not be presumed he would have accepted; nor would there (under any opinion he might entertain) have been propriety in offering it. What is it then, you have in contemplation, that you conceive would be relished? and ought there not to be a moral certainty of its acceptance? This being the case, there wd. not be wanting a disposition on my part; but strong inducements on public and private grounds, to invite Mr. Henry into any employment under the General Government to which his inclination might lead, and not opposed by those maxims which has been the invariable rule of my conduct.

With respect to the words said to have been uttered by Mr. Jefferson, they would be enigmatical to those who are acquainted with the characters about me, unless supposed to be spoken ironically; and in that case they are too injurious to me, and have too little foundation in truth, to be ascribed to him. There could not be the trace of doubt on his mind of predilection in mine, towards G. Britain or her politics, unless (which I do not believe) he has set me down as one of the most deceitful, and uncandid men living; because, not only in private conversations between ourselves, on this subject; but in my meetings with the confidential servants of the public, he has heard me often, when occasions presented themselves, express very different sentiments with an energy that could not be mistaken by *any one* present.

Having determined, as far as lay within the power of the Executive, to keep this country in a state of neutrality, I have made my public conduct accord with the system; and whilst so acting as a public character, consistency, and propriety as a private man, forbid those intemperate expressions in favor of one Nation, or to the prejudice of another, wch. many have indulged themselves in, and I will venture to add, to the embarrassment of government, without producing any good to the Country. With very great esteem &c.

ANGER AT GREAT BRITAIN

To John Jay

Philadelphia, August 30, 1794.

My dear Sir: Your letter of the 23d of June from London (and the duplicate) have both been received; and your safe arrival after so short a passage gave sincere pleasure, as well on private as on public account, to all your friends in this Country; and to none in a greater degree, I can venture to assure you, than it did to myself.

As you will receive letters from the Secretary of States Office giving an official account of the public occurrences as they have arisen, and progressed, it is unnecessary for me to retouch any of them: and yet, I cannot restrain myself from making some observations on the most recent of them, the communication of which was received this morning *only*. I mean the protest of the Govr. of Upper Canada (delivered by Lieutt. Sheaffe, against our occupying Lands far from any of the Posts which, long ago, they ought to have surrendered; and far within the known, *and until now*, the acknowledged limits of the United States.

On this irregular, and high handed proceeding of Mr. Simcoe, which is no longer *masked*, I would rather hear what the

Ministry of G. Britain will say, than pronounce my own sentimts. thereon. But can that government or will it attempt, after this *official* act of one of their governors, to hold out ideas of friendly intentions towds. the United States, and suffer such conduct to pass with impunity?

This may be considered as the most open and daring act of the British Agents in America, though it is not the most hostile or cruel; for there does not remain a doubt in the mind of any well informed person in this country (not shut against conviction) that all the difficulties we encounter with the Indians, their hostilities, the murders of helpless women and innocent children along our frontiers, results from the conduct of the Agents of Great Britain in this Country. In vain is it then for its Administration *in Britain* to disavow having given orders which will warrant such conduct, whilst their Agents go unpunished; whilst we have a thousand corroborating circumstances and indeed almost as many evidences (some of which cannot be brought forward) to prove that they are seducing from our alliances (endeavouring to remove over the line) tribes that have hitherto been kept in peace and friendship with us, at a heavy expence, and who have no cause of complaint except pretended ones, of their creating; whilst they keep in a state of irritation the tribes who are hostile to us, and are instigating those who know little of us, or we of them, to unite in the War against us; and whilst it is an undeniable fact that they are furnishing the whole with Arms, Ammunition, cloathing, and even provisions to carry on the war; I might go further, and if they are not much belied, add men also, in disguise.

Can it be expected I ask, so long as these things are known in the United States, or at least firmly believed, and suffered with impunity by G. Britain, that there ever will, or can be any cordiality between the two Countries? I answer NO! and I will undertake, without the gift of prophecy, to predict, that it will be impossible to keep this Country in a state of amity with G. Britain long if the Posts are not surrendered. A knowledge of these being *my* sentiments, would have little weight I am persuaded with the British Admn; nor perhaps with the Nation, in effecting the measure: but both may rest satisfied that if they want to be in Peace with this Country, and to enjoy the benefits of its trade &ca. to give up the Posts is the only road to it. withholding them, and the consequences we feel at present, continuing, war will be inevitably.

This letter is written to you in extreme haste, whilst the Papers respecting this subject I am writing on are copying at the Secretary of States Office to go by Express to New York, for a Vessel which we have just heard Sails tomorrow: you will readily perceive therefore I had no time for digesting, and as little for correcting it. I shall only add that you may be assured always of the sincere friendship and Affection of your &c.

THOUGHTS ON LOVE AND MARRIAGE

To Elizabeth Parke Custis

German Town, September 14, 1794.

My dear Betcy: Shall I, in answer to your letter of the 7th. instant say, when you are as near the *Pinnacle* of happiness as your sister Patcy conceives herself to be; or when your candour shines more conspicuously than it does in *that* letter, that I will *then*, comply with the request you have made, for my Picture?

No: I will grant it without either: for if the latter was to be a preliminary, it would be sometime I apprehend before *that* Picture would be found pendant *at* your breast; it not being within the bounds of probability that the contemplation of an inanimate thing, whatever might be the reflections arising from the possession of it, can be the *only* wish of your heart.

Respect may place it among the desirable objects of it, but there are emotions of a softer kind, to wch. the heart of a girl turned of eighteen, is susceptible, that must have generated much warmer ideas, although the fruition of them may, apparently, be more distant than those of your Sister's.

Having (by way of a hint) delivered a sentiment to Patty, which may be useful to her (if it be remembered after the change that is contemplated, is consummated) I will suggest another, more applicable to yourself.

Do not then in your contemplation of the marriage state, look for perfect felicity before you consent to wed. Nor conceive, from the fine tales the Poets and lovers of old have told us, of the transports of mutual love, that heaven has taken its abode on earth: Nor do not deceive yourself in supposing, that the only mean by which these are to be obtained, is to drink deep of the cup, and revel in an ocean of love. Love is a mighty pretty thing; but like all other delicious things, it is cloying; and when the first transports of the passion begins to subside, which it assuredly will do, and yield, oftentimes too late, to more sober reflections, it serves to evince, that love is too dainty a food to live upon *alone*, and ought not to be considered farther than as a necessary ingredient for that matrimonial happiness which results from a combination of causes; none of which are of greater importance, than that the object on whom it is placed, should possess good sense, good dispositions, and the means of supporting you in the way you have been brought up. Such qualifications cannot fail to attract (after marriage) your esteem and regard, into wch. or into disgust, sooner or later, love naturally resolves itself; and who at the sametime, has a claim to the respect, and esteem of the circle he moves in. Without these, whatever may be your first impressions of the man, they will end in disappointment; for be assured, and experience will convince you, that there is no truth more certain, than that all our enjoyments fall short of our expectations; and to none does it apply with more force, than to the gratification of the passions. You may believe me to be always, and sincerely Your Affectionate.

"MY FRIENDS ENTERTAIN A VERY ERRONEOUS IDEA OF MY PECUNIARY RESOURCES"

To Charles Carter, Jr.

Philadelphia, March 10, 1795.
Dear Sir: Your favor of the 23d ulto. came duly to hand. I wish, sincerely, it was in my power to comply with your request in behalf of your son; but it really is not, to the extent of it.

My friends entertain a very erroneous idea of my pecuniary resources, when they set me down for a money lender, or one who (now) has a command of it. You may believe me, when I assert that the Bonds which were due to me before the Revolution, were discharged during the progress of it, with a few exceptions in depreciated paper (in some instances as low as a shilling in the pound). That such has been the management of my estate, for many years past, especially since my absence from home, now six years, as scarcely to support itself. That my public allowance (whatever the world may think of it) is inadequate to the expence of living in this city; to such an extravagant height has the necessaries as well as the conveniences of life, arisen. And, moreover, that to keep myself out of debt; I have found it expedient, now and then, to sell lands, or something else to effect this purpose.

These are facts I have no inclination to publish to the world, nor should I have disclosed them on this occasion, had it not been due to friendship, to give you some explanation of my inability to comply with your request. If, however, by joining with nine others, the sum required can be obtained, notwithstanding my being under these circumstances, and notwithstanding the money will be withdrawn from another purpose, I will contribute one hundred pounds towards the accommodation of your sons wants, without any view to the receipt of interest therefrom. With very great esteem &c.

WEIGHING THE JAY TREATY

To Alexander Hamilton

(Private, & perfectly confidential)

My dear Sir,   Philadelphia 3d July 1795

The treaty of Amity, Commerce and Navigation, which has lately been before the Senate, has, as you will perceive, made its public entry into the Gazettes of this city. Of course the merits, & demerits of it will (especially in its unfinished state) be freely discussed.

It is not the opinions of *those* who were determined (before it was promulgated) to *support*, or *oppose* it, that I am sollicitous to obtain; for *these* I well know rarely do more than examine the side to which they lean; without giving the reverse the consideration it deserves; possibly without a wish to be apprised of the reasons, on which the objections are founded. My desire is to learn from dispassionate men, who have knowledge of the subject, and abilities to judge of it, the genuine opinion they entertain of *each* article of the instrument; and the *result* of it in the aggregate. In a word, placed on the footing the matter now stands, it is, more than ever, an incumbent duty on me, to do what propriety, and the true interest of this country shall appear to require at my hands on so important a subject, under such delicate circumstances.

You will be at no loss to perceive, from what I have already said, that my wishes are, to have the favorable, and unfavorable side of *each* article stated, and compared together; that I may see the bearing and tendency of them: and, ultimately, on which side the balance is to be found.

This treaty has, I am sensible, many relations, which, in deciding thereon, ought to be attended to; some of them too are of an important nature. I know also, that to judge with precision of its commercial arrangements, there ought likewise to be an intimate acquaintance with the various branches of commerce between this Country and Great Britain as it *now* stands; as it will be placed by the treaty; and as it may affect our present, or restrain our future treaties with other nations. All these things I am persuaded you have given as much attention to as most men; and I believe that your late employment under the General government afforded you more opportunities of deriving knowledge therein, than most of them who had not studied and practiced it scientifically, upon a large & comprehensive scale.

I do not know how you may be occupied at present; or how incompatible this request of mine may be to the business you have in hand. All I can say is, that however desirous I may be of availing myself of your sentiments on the points I have enumerated, and such others as are involved in the treaty, & the resolution of the Senate; (both of which I send you, lest they should not be at hand) it is not my intention to interrupt you in that business; or, if you are disinclined to go into the investigation I have requested, to press the matter upon you:

for of this you may be assured, that with the most unfeigned regard—and with every good wish for your health & prosperity I am Your Affecte friend and Obedient Servant

PS. Admitting that his B. Majesty will consent to the suspension of the 12th. article of the treaty, is it necessary that the treaty should again go to the Senate? or is the President authorized by the Resolution of that body to ratify it without?

"A CRISIS IS APPROACHING"

To Patrick Henry

Mount Vernon, October 9, 1795.

Dear Sir: Whatever may be the reception of this letter; truth and candour shall mark its steps. You doubtless know that the Office of State is vacant, and no one can be more sensible than yourself of the importance of filling it with a person of abilities, and one in whom the public would have confidence.

It would be uncandid not to inform you that this office has been offered to others, but it is as true that it was from a conviction in my mind that you would not accept it (until Tuesday last in a conversation with Genl. (late Governor,) Lee he dropped sentiments which made it less doubtful) that it was not offered first to you.

I need scarcely add, that if this appointment could be made to comport with your own inclination it would be as pleasing to me, as I believe it would be acceptable to the public. With this assurance, and under this belief I make you the offer of it. My first wish is, that you would accept it; the next is that you would be so good as to give me an answer as soon as you conveniently can, as the public business in that departt. is now suffering for want of a Secretary.

I persuade myself, Sir, it has not escaped your observation, that a crisis is approaching that must if it cannot be arrested soon decide whether order and good government shall be preserved or anarchy and confusion ensue. I can most religiously aver I have no wish, that is incompatible with the dignity, happiness and true interest of the people of this country. My ardent desire is, and my aim has been (as far as depended upon the Executive Department,) to comply strictly with *all* our engagemts. foreign and domestic; but to keep the U States free from *political* connexions with *every* other Country. To see that they *may be* independent of *all*, and under the influence of *none*. In a word, I want an *American* character, that the powers of Europe may be convinced we act for *ourselves* and not for *others*; this in my judgment, is the only way to be respected abroad and happy at home and not by becoming the partizans of Great Britain or France, create dissensions, disturb the public tranquillity, and destroy, perhaps for ever the cement wch. binds the Union.

I am satisfied these sentiments cannot be otherwise than congenial to your own; your aid therefore in carrying them into effect would be flattering and pleasing to Dr. Sir &c.

A QUESTION OF EXECUTIVE PRIVILEGE

To the Cabinet

Philadelphia, March 25, 1796.
Sir: The resolution moved in the House of Representatives, for the papers relative to the negotiation of the Treaty with G. Britain having passed in the affirmative, I request your opinion,

Whether that branch of Congress hath, or hath not a right, by the Constitution, to call for those papers?

Whether, if it does not possess the right, it would be expedient under the circumstances of this particular case, to furnish them?

And, in either case, in what terms would it be most proper to comply with, or to refuse the request of the House?

These opinions in writing, and your attendance, will be expected at ten o'Clock tomorrow.

"TO ADMIT . . . WOULD BE TO ESTABLISH A
DANGEROUS PRECEDENT"

To the House of Representatives

United States, March 30, 1796.

Gentlemen of the House of Representatives: With the utmost attention I have considered your resolution of the 24th. instant, requesting me to lay before your House, a copy of the instructions to the Minister of the United States who negotiated the Treaty with the King of Great Britain, together with the correspondence and other documents relative to that Treaty, excepting such of the said papers as any existing negotiation may render improper to be disclosed.

In deliberating upon this subject, it was impossible for me to lose sight of the principle which some have avowed in its discussion; or to avoid extending my views to the consequences which must flow from the admission of that principle.

I trust that no part of my conduct has ever indicated a disposition to withhold any information which the Constitution has enjoined upon the President as a duty to give, or which could be required of him by either House of Congress as a right; And with truth I affirm, that it has been, as it will continue to be, while I have the honor to preside in the Government, my constant endeavour to harmonize with the other branches thereof; so far as the trust delegated to me by the People of the United States, and my sense of the obligation it imposes to "preserve, protect and defend the Constitution" will permit.

The nature of foreign negotiations requires caution; and their success must often depend on secrecy: and even when brought to a conclusion, a full disclosure of all the measures, demands, or eventual concessions, which may have been proposed or contemplated, would be extremely impolitic: for this might have a pernicious influence on future negotiations; or produce immediate inconveniences, perhaps danger and mischief, in relation to other powers. The necessity of such caution and secrecy was one cogent reason for vesting the power of making Treaties in the President, with the advice and consent of the

Senate, the principle on which that body was formed confining it to a small number of Members.

To admit then a right in the House of Representatives to demand, and to have as a matter of course, all the Papers respecting a negotiation with a foreign power, would be to establish a dangerous precedent.

It does not occur that the inspection of the papers asked for, can be relative to any purpose under the cognizance of the House of Representatives, except that of an impeachment, which the resolution has not expressed. I repeat, that I have no disposition to withhold any information which the duty of my station will permit, or the public good shall require to be disclosed: and in fact, all the Papers affecting the negotiation with Great Britain were laid before the Senate, when the Treaty itself was communicated for their consideration and advice.

The course which the debate has taken, on the resolution of the House, leads to some observations on the mode of making treaties under the Constitution of the United States.

Having been a member of the General Convention, and knowing the principles on which the Constitution was formed, I have ever entertained but one opinion on this subject; and from the first establishment of the Government to this moment, my conduct has exemplified that opinion, that the power of making treaties is exclusively vested in the President, by and with the advice and consent of the Senate, provided two thirds of the Senators present concur, and that every treaty so made, and promulgated, thenceforward became the Law of the land. It is thus that the treaty making power has been understood by foreign Nations: and in all the treaties made with them, *we* have declared, and *they* have believed, that when ratified by the President with the advice and consent of the Senate, they became obligatory. In this construction of the Constitution every House of Representatives has heretofore acquiesced; and until the present time, not a doubt or suspicion has appeared to my knowledge that this construction was not the true one. Nay, they have more than acquiesced: for till now, without controverting the obligation of such treaties, they have made all the requisite provisions for carrying them into effect.

There is also reason to believe that this construction agrees with the opinions entertained by the State Conventions, when they were deliberating on the Constitution; especially by those who objected to it, because there was not required, in *commercial treaties*, the consent of two thirds of the whole number of the members of the Senate, instead of two thirds of the Senators present; and because in treaties respecting territorial and certain other rights and claims, the concurrence of three fourths of the whole number of the members of both houses respectively, was not made necessary.

It is a fact declared by the General Convention, and universally understood, that the Constitution of the United States was the result of a spirit of amity and mutual concession. And it is well known that under this influence the smaller States were admitted to an equal representation in the Senate with the larger States; and that this branch of the government was invested with great powers: for on the equal participation of those powers, the sovereignty and political safety of the smaller States were deemed essentially to depend.

If other proofs than these, and the plain letter of the Constitution itself, be necessary to ascertain the point under consideration, they may be found in the journals of the General Convention, which I have deposited in the office of the department of State. In these journals it will appear that a proposition was made, "that no Treaty should be binding on the United States which was not ratified by a Law"; and that the proposition was explicitly rejected.

As therefore it is perfectly clear to my understanding, that the assent of the House of Representatives is not necessary to the validity of a treaty: as the treaty with Great Britain exhibits in itself all the objects requiring legislative provision; And on these the papers called for can throw no light: And as it is essential to the due administration of the government, that the boundaries fixed by the constitution between the different departments should be preserved: A just regard to the Constitution and to the duty of my Office, under all the circumstances of this case, forbids a complyance with your request.

HAMILTON AS PRIVATE ADVISOR

To Alexander Hamilton

(Private)

My dear Sir,   Philadelphia 31st Mar: 1796
   I do not know how to thank you sufficiently, for the trouble you have taken to dilate on the request of the House of Representatives for the Papers relative to the British Treaty; or how to apologize for the trouble (much greater than I had any idea of giving) which you have taken to shew the impropriety of that request.
   From the first moment, and from the fullest conviction in my own mind, I had resolved to *resist the principle* wch. was evidently intended to be established by the call of the House of Representatives; and only deliberated on the manner, in which this could be done, with the least bad consequences.
   To effect this, three modes presented themselves to me—1. a denial of the Papers in toto, assigning concise, but cogent reasons for the denial; 2 to grant them in whole; or 3. in part; accompanied with a pointed protest against the rights of the House to controul Treaties, or to call for Papers without specifying their object; and against the compliance being drawn into precedent.
   I had as little hesitation in deciding that the first was the most tenable ground, but from the peculiar circumstances of *this case* It merited consideration, if the *principle* could be saved, whether facility in the provisions might not result from a compliance. An attentive examination however of the Papers and the subject, soon convinced me that to furnish *all* the Papers would be highly improper; and that a *partial* delivery of them would leave the door open for as much calumny as the entire refusal—perhaps more so—as it might, and I have no doubt would be said, that all such as were essential to the purposes of the House, were withheld.
   Under these impressions, I proceeded, with the heads of Departments and the Attorney General, to collect materials; & to prepare an answer, subject however to revision, & alteration,

according to circumstances. This answer was ready on Monday—and proposed to be sent in on Tuesday but it was delayed until I should receive what was expected; not doing it definitively on that day, the delivery of my answer was further postponed till the next; notwithstanding the anxious solicitude which was visible in all quarters, to learn the result of Executive decision.

Finding that the draft I had prepared, embraced most, if not all the principles which were detailed in the Paper I received yesterday; though not the reasonings—That it would take considerable time to copy the latter—and above all, having understood that if the Papers were refused a fresh demand, with strictures might be expected; I sent in the answer wch. was ready; reserving the other as a source for reasoning if my information proves true.

I could not be satisfied without giving you this concise acct. of the business. To express again my sincere thanks for the pains you have been at to investigate the subject, and to assure you, over & over, of the warmth of my friendship and of the affectionate regard with which

I am Your Affectionate

STAGING AN EXIT

To Alexander Hamilton

My dear Sir,   Mount Vernon 26th June 1796.

Your letter without date, came to my hands by Wednesdays Post; and by the first Post afterwards I communicated the purport of it (withholding the names) to the Secretary of State; with directions to bestow the closest attention to the subject, and if the application which had been made to the Minister of France, consequent of the Capture of the Ship Mount Vernon, had not produced such an answer as to supercede the necessity, then to endeavor to obtain such explanation of the views of the French government relatively to our Commerce with Great Britain, as the nature of the case appeared to require.

That the fact is, as has been represented to you, I have very little, if any doubt. Many, very many circumstances are continually happening in confirmation of it: among which, it is evident Bache's Paper, which *receives* and *gives* the hope, is endeavouring to prepare the Public mind for this event, by representing it as the *predicted*, and *natural* consequence of the Ratification of the Treaty with Great Britn.

Let me ask therefore.

Do you suppose that the Executive, in the recess of the Senate, has power in such a case as the one before us—especially if the measure should not be *avowed* by authority—to send a special character to Paris, as Envoy Extraordinary, to give, & receive explanations? And if there be a doubt, whether it is not probable—nay more than probable, that the French Directory would, in the present state of things, avail themselves of the unconstitutionallity of the measure, to decline receiving him? The policy of delay, to avoid explanations, would induce them to adopt any pretext to accomplish it. Their reliance upon a party in this country for support, would stimulate them to this conduct; and we may be assured they will not be deficient in the most minute details of every occurrence, and every opinion, worthy of communication. If then an Envoy cannot be sent to Paris without the Agency of the Senate, will the information you have received, admitting it should be realized, be sufficient ground for convening that body?

These are serious things; they may be productive of serious consequences; and therefore require very serious & cool deliberation. Admitting, however, that the Powers of the President during the recess, were adequate to such an appointment, where is the character who would go, that unites the proper qualifications for such a Mission; and would not be obnoxious to one party or the other? And what should be done with Mr. M—— in that case?

As the affairs of this country in their administration, receive great embarrassment from the conduct of characters among ourselves; and as every act of the Executive is mis-represented, and tortured with a view to make it appear odious, the aid of the friends to government is peculiarly necessary under such circumstances; and at such a crises as the present: It is unnecessary therefore to add, that I should be glad upon the present, and all other important occasions, to receive yours: and as I have great confidence in the abilities, and purity of Mr. Jays views, as well as in his experience, I should wish that his sentiments on the purport of this letter; and other interesting matters as they occur, may accompany yours; for having no other wish than to promote the true and permanent interests of this country, I am anxious, always, to compare the opinions of those in whom I confide with one another; and these again (without being bound by them) with my own, that I may extract all the good I can.

Having from a variety of reasons (among which a disinclination to be longer buffitted in the public prints by a set of infamous scribblers) taken my ultimate determination "to seek the Post of honor in a private Station" I regret exceedingly that I did not publish my valedictory address the day after the Adjournment of Congress. This would have preceeded the canvassing for Electors (wch. is commencing with warmth, in this State). It would have been announcing *publicly*, what seems to be very well understood, and is industriously propagated, *privately*. It would have removed doubts from the minds of *all*, and left the field clear for *all*: It would, by having preceeded any unfavorable change in our foreign relations (if any should happen) render my retreat less difficult and embarrassing. And it might have prevented the remarks which, more than probable will follow a late annunciation—namely—that I delayed it long enough to see, that the current was turned against me, before I declared my intention to decline. This is one of the reasons which makes me a little tenacious of the draught I furnished you with, to be modified & corrected.

Having passed, however, what *I now* conceive would have been the *precise* moment to have addressed my Constituents, let me ask your opinion (under a full conviction that nothing will shake my determination to withdraw) of the *next* best time, considering the present, and what may, probably, be the existing state of things at different periods previous to the Election; or rather, the middle of Octr, beyond which the promulgation of my intentions cannot be delayed. Let me hear from you as soon as it is convenient; and be assured always of the sincere esteem, and affecte. regard of

"IN SUCH EXAGGERATED AND INDECENT
TERMS AS COULD SCARCELY BE
APPLIED TO A NERO"

To Thomas Jefferson

Mount Vernon, July 6, 1796.

Dear Sir: When I inform you, that your letter of the 19th. Ulto. went to Philadelphia and returned to this place before it was received by me; it will be admitted, I am persuaded, as an apology for my not having acknowledged the receipt of it sooner.

If I had entertained any suspicions before, that the queries, which have been published in Bache's Paper, proceeded from you, the assurances you have given of the contrary, would have removed them; but the truth is, I harboured none. I am at no loss to *conjecture* from what source they flowed; through what channel they were conveyed; and for what purpose they and similar publications, appear. They were known to be in the hands of Mr. Parker, in the early part of the last Session of Congress; They were shown about by Mr. Giles during the Cession, and they made their public exhibition about the close of it.

Perceiving, and probably, hearing, that no abuse in the Gazettes would induce me to take notice of anonymous publications, against me; those who were disposed to do me *such friendly Offices*, have embraced without restraint every opportunity to weaken the confidence of the People; and, by having the *whole* game in their hands, they have scrupled not to publish things that do not, as well as those which do exist; and to mutilate the latter, so as to make them subserve the purposes which they have in view.

As you have mentioned the subject yourself, it would not be frank, candid, or friendly to conceal, that your conduct has been represented as derogatory from that opinion *I* had conceived you entertained of me. That to your particular friends and connextions you have described, and they have denounced me, as a person under a dangerous influence; and that, if I would listen *more* to some *other* opinions, all would be well. My answer invariably has been, that I had never discovered any thing in the conduct of Mr. Jefferson to raise suspicions, in my mind, of his insincerity; that if he would retrace my public conduct while he was in the Administration, abundant proofs would occur to him, that truth and right decisions, were the *sole* objects of my pursuit; that there were as many instances within his *own* knowledge of my having decided *against*, as in *favor of* the opinions of the person evidently alluded to; and moreover, that I was no believer in the infallibility of the politics, or measures of *any man living*. In short, that I was no party man myself, and the first wish of my heart was, if parties did exist, to reconcile them.

To this I may add, and very truly, that, until within the last year or two ago, I had no conception that Parties would, or even could go, the length I have been witness to; nor did I believe until lately, that it was within the bonds of probability; hardly within those of possibility, that, while I was using my utmost exertions to establish a national character of our own, independent, as far as our obligations, and justice would permit, of every nation of the earth; and wished, by steering a steady course, to preserve this Country from the horrors of a desolating war, that I should be accused of being the enemy of one Nation, and subject to the influence of another; and to prove it, that every act of my administration would be tortured, and the grossest, and most insidious mis-representations of them be made (by giving one side *only* of a subject, and that too in such exaggerated and indecent terms as could scarcely be applied to a Nero; a notorious defaulter; or even to a common pick-pocket). But enough of this; I have already gone farther in the expression of my feelings, than I intended.

The particulars of the case you mention (relative to the Little Sarah) is a good deal out of my recollection at present, and I have no public papers here to resort to. When I get back to Philadelphia (which, unless I am called there by something new, will not be 'till towards the last of August) I will examine my files.

It must be pleasing to a Cultivator, to possess Land which will yield Clover kindly; for it is certainly a great Desiderata in Husbandry. My Soil, without very good dressings, does not produce it well: owing, I believe, to its stiffness; hardness at bottom; and retention of Water. A farmer, in my opinion, need never despair of raising Wheat to advantage, upon a Clover lay; with a single ploughing, agreeably to the Norfolk and Suffolk prac- tice. By a misconception of my Manager last year, a field at one of my Farms which I intended shd. have been fallowed for Wheat, went untouched. Unwilling to have my crop of Wheat at that place so much reduced, as would have been occasioned by this omission, I directed, as soon as I returned from Phila- delphia (about the middle of September) another field, not in the usual rotation, which had lain out two years, and well covered with mixed grasses, principally white clover, to be turned over with a good Bar-share; and the Wheat to be sown, and harrowed in at the tail of the Plough. It was done so ac- cordingly, and was, by odds, the best Wheat I made this year. It exhibits an unequivocal proof to my mind, of the great advan- tage of Clover lay, for Wheat. Our Crops of this article, here- abouts, are more or less injured by what some call the Rot; others the Scab; occasioned, I believe, by high winds and beating rain when the grain is in blossom, and before the Farina has per- formed its duties.

Desirous of trying the field Peas of England, and the Winter Vetch, I sent last fall to Mr. Marray of Liverpool for 8 bushels of each sort. Of the Peas he sent me two kinds (a white and dark, but not having the letter by me, I am unable to give the names). They did not arrive until the latter end of April; when they ought to have been in the ground the beginning of March. They were sown however, but will yield no Seed; of course the experiment I intended to make, is lost. The Vetch is yet on hand for Autumn Seeding. That the Albany Peas will grow well with us, I know from my own experience: but they are subject to the same bug which perforates, and injures the Garden Peas, and will do the same, I fear, to the imported Peas, of any sort from England, in this climate, from the heat of it.

I do not know what is meant by, or to what uses the Caroline drill is applied. How does your Chicorium prosper? Four years since I exterminated all the Plants raised from Seed sent me by Mr. Young, and to get into it again, the seed I purchased in Philadelphia last Winter, and what has been sent me by Mr. Murray this Spring, has cost me upwards of twelve pounds Sterling. This, it may be observed, is a left handed way to make money; but the first was occasioned by the manager I then had, who pretended to know it well in England and pronounced it a noxious weed; the restoration of it, is indebted to Mr. Strickland and others (besides Mr. Young) who speak of it in exalted terms. I sowed mine broad-cast; some with and some without grain. It has come up well; but there seems to be a serious struggle between *it* and the grass and weeds; the issue of which (as I can afford no relief to the former) is doubtful at present, and may be useful to know.

If you can bring a moveable threshing Machine, constructed upon simple principles to perfection, it will be among the most valuable institutions in this Country; for nothing is more wanting, and to be wished for on our farms. Mrs. Washington begs you to accept her best wishes, and with very great esteem etc.

"'TIS OUR TRUE POLICY TO STEER CLEAR OF PERMANENT ALLIANCES"

Farewell Address

United States, September 19, 1796.

Friends, and Fellow-Citizens: The period for a new election of a Citizen, to Administer the Executive government of the United States, being not far distant, and the time actually arrived, when your thoughts must be employed in designating the person, who is to be cloathed with that important trust, it appears to me proper, especially as it may conduce to a more distinct expression of the public voice, that I should now apprise you of the resolution I have formed, to decline being considered among the number of those, out of whom a choice is to be made.

I beg you, at the same time, to do me the justice to be assured, that this resolution has not been taken, without a strict regard to all the considerations appertaining to the relation, which binds a dutiful citizen to his country, and that, in with drawing the tender of service which silence in my situation might imply, I am influenced by no diminution of zeal for your future interest, no deficiency of grateful respect for your past kindness; but am supported by a full conviction that the step is compatible with both.

The acceptance of, and continuance hitherto in, the office to which your Suffrages have twice called me, have been a uniform sacrifice of inclination to the opinion of duty, and to a deference for what appeared to be your desire. I constantly hoped, that it would have been much earlier in my power, consistently with motives, which I was not at liberty to disregard, to return to that retirement, from which I had been reluctantly drawn. The strength of my inclination to do this, previous to the last Election, had even led to the preparation of an address to declare it to you; but mature reflection on the then perplexed and critical posture of our Affairs with foreign Nations, and the unanimous advice of persons entitled to my confidence, impelled me to abandon the idea.

I rejoice, that the state of your concerns, external as well as internal, no longer renders the pursuit of inclination incompatible with the sentiment of duty, or propriety; and am persuaded whatever partiality may be retained for my services, that in the present circumstances of our country, you will not disapprove my determination to retire.

The impressions, with which I first undertook the arduous trust, were explained on the proper occasion. In the discharge of this trust, I will only say, that I have, with good intentions, contributed towards the Organization and Administration of the government, the best exertions of which a very fallible judgment was capable. Not unconscious, in the outset, of the inferiority of my qualifications, experience in my own eyes, perhaps still more in the eyes of others, has strengthened the motives to diffidence of myself; and every day the encreasing weight of years admonishes me more and more, that the shade of retirement is as necessary to me as it will be welcome. Satisfied that if any circumstances have given peculiar value to my services, they were temporary, I have the consolation to believe, that while choice and prudence invite me to quit the political scene, patriotism does not forbid it.

In looking forward to the moment, which is intended to terminate the career of my public life, my feelings do not permit me to suspend the deep acknowledgment of that debt of gratitude wch. I owe to my beloved country, for the many honors it has conferred upon me; still more for the stedfast confidence with which it has supported me; and for the opportunities I have thence enjoyed of manifesting my inviolable attachment, by services faithful and persevering, though in usefulness unequal to my zeal. If benefits have resulted to our country from these services, let it always be remembered to your praise, and as an instructive example in our annals, that, under circumstances in which the Passions agitated in every direction were liable to mislead, amidst appearances sometimes dubious, viscissitudes of fortune often discouraging, in situations in which not unfrequently want of Success has countenanced the spirit of criticism, the constancy of your support was the essential prop of the efforts, and a guarantee of the plans by which they were effected. Profoundly penetrated with this idea, I shall carry it with me to my grave, as a strong incitement to unceasing vows that Heaven may continue to you the choicest tokens of its beneficence; that your Union and brotherly affection may be perpetual; that the free constitution, which is the work of your hands, may be sacredly maintained; that its Administration in every department may be stamped with wisdom and Virtue; that, in fine, the happiness of the people of these States, under the auspices of liberty, may be made complete, by so careful a preservation and so prudent a use of this blessing as will acquire to them the glory of recommending it to the applause, the affection, and adoption of every nation which is yet a stranger to it.

Here, perhaps, I ought to stop. But a solicitude for your welfare, which cannot end but with my life, and the apprehension of danger, natural to that solicitude, urge me on an occasion like the present, to offer to your solemn contemplation, and to recommend to your frequent review, some sentiments; which are the result of much reflection, of no inconsiderable observation, and which appear to me all important to the permanency of your felicity as a People. These will be offered to you with the more freedom, as you can only see in them the disinterested warnings of a parting friend, who can possibly have no personal motive to biass his counsel. Nor can I forget, as an encouragement to it, your endulgent reception of my sentiments on a former and not dissimilar occasion

Interwoven as is the love of liberty with every ligament of your hearts, no recommendation of mine is necessary to fortify or confirm the attachment.

The Unity of Government which constitutes you one people is also now dear to you. It is justly so; for it is a main Pillar in the Edifice of your real independence, the support of your tranquility at home; your peace abroad; of your safety; of your prosperity; of that very Liberty which you so highly prize. But as it is easy to foresee, that from different causes and from different quarters, much pains will be taken, many artifices employed, to weaken in your minds the conviction of this truth; as this is the point in your political fortress against which the batteries of internal and external enemies will be most constantly and actively (though often covertly and insidiously) directed, it is of infinite moment, that you should properly estimate the immense value of your national Union to your collective and individual happiness; that you should cherish a cordial, habitual and immoveable attachment to it; accustoming yourselves to think and speak of it as of the Palladium of your political safety and prosperity; watching for its preservation with jealous anxiety; discountenancing whatever may suggest even a suspicion that it can in any event be abandoned, and indignantly frowning upon the first dawning of every attempt to alienate any portion of our Country from the rest, or to enfeeble the sacred ties which now link together the various parts.

For this you have every inducement of sympathy and interest. Citizens by birth or choice, of a common country, that country has a right to concentrate your affections. The name of AMERICAN, which belongs to you, in your national capacity, must always exalt the just pride of Patriotism, more than any appellation derived from local discriminations. With slight shades of difference, you have the same Religion, Manners, Habits and political Principles. You have in a common cause fought and triumphed together. The independence and liberty you possess are the work of joint councils, and joint efforts; of common dangers, sufferings and successes.

But these considerations, however powerfully they address themselves to your sensibility are greatly outweighed by those which apply more immediately to your Interest. Here every portion of our country finds the most commanding motives for carefully guarding and preserving the Union of the whole.

The *North*, in an unrestrained intercourse with the *South*, protected by the equal Laws of a common government, finds in the productions of the latter, great additional resources of Maratime and commercial enterprise and precious materials of manufacturing industry. The *South* in the same Intercourse, benefitting by the Agency of the *North*, sees its agriculture grow and its commerce expand. Turning partly into its own channels the seamen of the *North*, it finds its particular navigation envigorated; and while it contributes, in different ways, to nourish and increase the general mass of the National navigation, it looks forward to the protection of a Maratime strength, to which itself is unequally adapted. The *East*, in a like intercourse with the *West*, already finds, and in the progressive improvement of interior communications, by land and water, will more and more find a valuable vent for the commodities which it brings from abroad, or manufactures at home. The *West* derives from the *East* supplies requisite to its growth and comfort, and what is perhaps of still greater consequence, it must of necessity owe the *secure* enjoyment of indispensable *outlets* for its own productions to the weight, influence, and the future Maritime strength of the Atlantic side of the Union, directed by an indissoluble community of Interest as *one Nation*. Any other tenure by which the *West* can hold this essential advantage, whether derived from its own seperate strength, or from an apostate and unnatural connection with any foreign Power, must be intrinsically precarious.

While then every part of our country thus feels an immediate and particular Interest in Union, all the parts combined cannot fail to find in the united mass of means and efforts greater strength, greater resource, proportionably greater security from external danger, a less frequent interruption of their Peace by foreign Nations; and, what is of inestimable value! they must derive from Union an exemption from those broils and Wars between themselves, which so frequently afflict neighbouring countries, not tied together by the same government; which their own rivalships alone would be sufficient to produce, but which opposite foreign alliances, attachments and intriegues would stimulate and imbitter. Hence likewise they will avoid the necessity of those overgrown Military establish-ments, which under any form of Government are inauspicious to liberty, and which are to be regarded as particularly hostile to Republican Liberty: In this sense it is, that your Union ought to be considered as a main prop of your liberty, and that the love of the one ought to endear to you the preservation of the other.

These considerations speak a persuasive language to every reflecting and virtuous mind, and exhibit the continuance of the UNION as a primary object of Patriotic desire. Is there a doubt, whether a common government can embrace so large a sphere? Let experience solve it. To listen to mere speculation in such a case were criminal. We are authorized to hope that a proper organization of the whole, with the auxiliary agency of governments for the respective Sub divisions, will afford a happy issue to the experiment. 'Tis well worth a fair and full experiment With such powerful and obvious motives to Union, affecting all parts of our country, while experience shall not have demonstrated its impracticability, there will always be reason, to distrust the patriotism of those, who in any quarter may endeavor to weaken its bands.

In contemplating the causes wch. may disturb our Union, it occurs as matter of serious concern, that any ground should have been furnished for characterizing parties by *Geographical* discriminations: *Northern* and *Southern*; *Atlantic* and *Western*; whence designing men may endeavour to excite a belief that there is a real difference of local interests and views. One of the expedients of Party to acquire influence, within particular dis-tricts, is to misrepresent the opinions and aims of other Districts. You cannot shield yourselves too much against the jealousies and heart burnings which spring from these misrepresenta-tions. They tend to render Alien to each other those who ought to be bound together by fraternal affection. The Inhabitants of our Western country have lately had a useful lesson on this head. They have seen, in the Negociation by the Executive, and in the unanimous ratification by the Senate, of the Treaty with Spain, and in the universal satisfaction at that event, throughout the United States, a decisive proof how unfounded were the suspicions propagated among them of a policy in the General Government and in the Atlantic States unfriendly to

their Interests in regard to the MISSISSIPPI. They have been
witnesses to the formation of two Treaties, that with G: Britain
and that with Spain, which secure to them every thing they
could desire, in respect to our Foreign relations, towards con-
firming their prosperity. Will it not be their wisdom to rely for
the preservation of these advantages on the UNION by wch.
they were procured? Will they not henceforth be deaf to those
advisers, if such there are, who would sever them from their
Brethren and connect them with Aliens?

To the efficacy and permanency of Your Union, a Government for the whole is indispensable. No Alliances however strict
between the parts can be an adequate substitute. They must
inevitably experience the infractions and interruptions which
all Alliances in all times have experienced. Sensible of this momentous truth, you have improved upon your first essay, by
the adoption of a Constitution of Government, better calculated than your former for an intimate Union, and for the
efficacious management of your common concerns. This government, the offspring of our own choice uninfluenced and
unawed, adopted upon full investigation and mature deliberation, completely free in its principles, in the distribution of its
powers, uniting security with energy, and containing within
itself a provision for its own amendment, has a just claim to
your confidence and your support. Respect for its authority,
compliance with its Laws, acquiescence in its measures, are
duties enjoined by the fundamental maxims of true Liberty.
The basis of our political systems is the right of the people to
make and to alter their Constitutions of Government. But the
Constitution which at any time exists, 'till changed by an explicit and authentic act of the whole People, is sacredly obligatory upon all. The very idea of the power and the right of the
People to establish Government presupposes the duty of every
Individual to obey the established Government.

All obstructions to the execution of the Laws, all combinations and Associations, under whatever plausible character,
with the real design to direct, controul counteract, or awe the
regular deliberation and action of the Constituted authorities
are distructive of this fundamental principle and of fatal tendency. They serve to organize faction, to give it an artificial
and extraordinary force; to put in the place of the delegated

will of the Nation, the will of a party; often a small but artful and enterprizing minority of the Community; and, according to the alternate triumphs of different parties, to make the public administration the Mirror of the ill concerted and incongruous projects of faction, rather than the organ of consistent and wholesome plans digested by common councils and modefied by mutual interests. However combinations or Associations of the above description may now and then answer popular ends, they are likely, in the course of time and things, to become potent engines, by which cunning, ambitious and unprincipled men will be enabled to subvert the Power of the People, and to usurp for themselves the reins of Government; destroying afterwards the very engines which have lifted them to unjust dominion.

Towards the preservation of your Government and the permanency of your present happy state, it is requisite, not only that you steadily discountenance irregular oppositions to its acknowledged authority, but also that you resist with care the spirit of innovation upon its principles however specious the pretexts. one method of assault may be to effect, in the forms of the Constitution, alterations which will impair the energy of the system, and thus to undermine what cannot be directly overthrown. In all the changes to which you may be invited, remember that time and habit are at least as necessary to fix the true character of Governments, as of other human institutions; that experience is the surest standard, by which to test the real tendency of the existing Constitution of a country; that facility in changes upon the credit of mere hypotheses and opinion exposes to perpetual change, from the endless variety of hypotheses and opinion: and remember, especially, that for the efficient management of your common interests, in a country so extensive as ours, a Government of as much vigour as is consistent with the perfect security of Liberty is indispensable. Liberty itself will find in such a Government, with powers properly distributed and adjusted, its surest Guardian. It is indeed little else than a name, where the Government is too feeble to withstand the enterprises of faction, to confine each member of the Society within the limits prescribed by the laws and to maintain all in the secure and tranquil enjoyment of the rights of person and property.

I have already intimated to you the danger of Parties in the State, with particular reference to the founding of them on Geographical discriminations. Let me now take a more comprehensive view, and warn you in the most solemn manner against the baneful effects of the Spirit of Party, generally

This spirit, unfortunately, is inseperable from our nature, having its root in the strongest passions of the human Mind. It exists under different shapes in all Governments, more or less stifled, controuled, or repressed; but, in those of the popular form it is seen in its greatest rankness and is truly their worst enemy.

The alternate domination of one faction over another, sharpened by the spirit of revenge natural to party dissention, which in different ages and countries has perpetrated the most horrid enormities, is itself a frightful despotism. But this leads at length to a more formal and permanent despotism. The disorders and miseries, which result, gradually incline the minds of men to seek security and repose in the absolute power of an Individual: and sooner or later the chief of some prevailing faction more able or more fortunate than his competitors, turns this disposition to the purposes of his own elevation, on the ruins of Public Liberty.

Without looking forward to an extremity of this kind (which nevertheless ought not to be entirely out of sight) the common and continual mischiefs of the spirit of Party are sufficient to make it the interest and the duty of a wise People to discourage and restrain it.

It serves always to distract the Public Councils and enfeeble the Public administration. It agitates the Community with ill founded jealousies and false alarms, kindles the animosity of one part against another, foments occasionally riot and insurrection. It opens the door to foreign influence and corruption, which find a facilitated access to the government itself through the channels of party passions. Thus the policy and the will of one country, are subjected to the policy and will of another.

There is an opinion that parties in free countries are useful checks upon the Administration of the Government and serve to keep alive the spirit of Liberty. This within certain limits is probably true, and in Governments of a Monarchical cast Patriotism may look with endulgence, if not with favour, upon the spirit of party. But in those of the popular character, in Governments purely elective, it is a spirit not to be encouraged. From their natural tendency, it is certain there will always be enough of that spirit for every salutary purpose. And there being constant danger of excess, the effort ought to be, by force of public opinion, to mitigate and assuage it. A fire not to be quenched; it demands a uniform vigilance to prevent its bursting into a flame, lest instead of warming it should consume.

It is important, likewise, that the habits of thinking in a free Country should inspire caution in those entrusted with its administration, to confine themselves within their respective Constitutional spheres; avoiding in the exercise of the Powers of one department to encroach upon another. The spirit of encroachment tends to consolidate the powers of all the departments in one, and thus to create whatever the form of government, a real despotism. A just estimate of that love of power, and proneness to abuse it, which predominates in the human heart is sufficient to satisfy us of the truth of this position. The necessity of reciprocal checks in the exercise of political power; by dividing and distributing it into different depositories, and constituting each the Guardian of the Public Weal against invasions by the others, has been evinced by experiments ancient and modern; some of them in our country and under our own eyes. To preserve them must be as necessary as to institute them. If in the opinion of the People, the distribution or modification of the Constitutional powers be in any particular wrong, let it be corrected by an amendment in the way which the Constitution designates. But let there be no change by usurpation; for though this, in one instance, may be the instrument of good, it is the customary weapon by which free governments are destroyed. The precedent must always greatly overbalance in permanent evil any partial or transient benefit which the use can at any time yield.

Of all the dispositions and habits which lead to political prosperity, Religion and morality are indispensable supports. In vain would that man claim the tribute of Patriotism, who should labour to subvert these great Pillars of human happiness, these firmest props of the duties of Men and citizens. The mere Politician, equally with the pious man ought to respect and to cherish them. A volume could not trace all their connections with private and public felicity. Let it simply be asked where is the security for property, for reputation, for life, if the sense of religious obligation *desert* the oaths, which are the instruments of investigation in Courts of Justice? And let us with caution indulge the supposition, that morality can be maintained without religion. Whatever may be conceded to the influence of refined education on minds of peculiar structure, reason and experience both forbid us to expect that National morality can prevail in exclusion of religious principle.

'Tis substantially true, that virtue or morality is a necessary spring of popular government. The rule indeed extends with more or less force to every species of free Government. Who that is a sincere friend to it, can look with indifference upon attempts to shake the foundation of the fabric

Promote then as an object of primary importance, Institutions for the general diffusion of knowledge. In proportion as the structure of a government gives force to public opinion, it is essential that public opinion should be enlightened

As a very important source of strength and security, cherish public credit. One method of preserving it is to use it as sparingly as possible: avoiding occasions of expence by cultivating peace, but remembering also that timely disbursements to prepare for danger frequently prevent much greater disbursements to repel it; avoiding likewise the accumulation of debt, not only by shunning occasions of expence, but by vigorous exertions in time of Peace to discharge the Debts which unavoidable wars may have occasioned, not ungenerously throwing upon posterity the burthen which we ourselves ought to bear. The execution of these maxims belongs to your Representatives, but it is necessary that public opinion should cooperate. To facilitate to them the performance of their duty, it is essential that you should practically bear in mind, that towards the payment of debts there must be Revenue; that to have Revenue there must be taxes; that no taxes can be devised which are not more or less inconvenient and unpleasant; that the intrinsic embarrassment inseperable from the selection of the proper objects (which is always a choice of difficulties) ought to be a decisive motive for a candid construction of the Conduct of the Government in making it, and for a spirit of acquiescence in the measures for obtaining Revenue which the public exigencies may at any time dictate.

Observe good faith and justice towds. all Nations. Cultivate peace and harmony with all. Religion and morality enjoin this conduct; and can it be that good policy does not equally enjoin it? It will be worthy of a free, enlightened, and, at no distant period, a great Nation, to give to mankind the magnanimous and too novel example of a People always guided by an exalted justice and benevolence. Who can doubt that in the course of time and things the fruits of such a plan would richly repay any temporary advantages wch. might be lost by a steady adherence to it? Can it be, that Providence has not connected the permanent felicity of a Nation with its virtue? The experiment, at least, is recommended by every sentiment which ennobles human Nature. Alas! is it rendered impossible by its vices?

In the execution of such a plan nothing is more essential than that permanent, inveterate antipathies against particular Nations and passionate attachments for others should be excluded; and that in place of them just and amicable feelings towards all should be cultivated. The Nation, which indulges towards another an habitual hatred, or an habitual fondness, is in some degree a slave. It is a slave to its animosity or to its affection, either of which is sufficient to lead it astray from its duty and its interest. Antipathy in one Nation against another, disposes each more readily to offer insult and injury, to lay hold of slight causes of umbrage, and to be haughty and intractable, when accidental or trifling occasions of dispute occur. Hence frequent collisions, obstinate envenomed and bloody contests. The Nation, prompted by illwill and resentment sometimes impels to War the Government, contrary to the best calculations of policy. The Government sometimes participates in the national propensity, and adopts through passion what reason would reject; at other times, it makes the animosity of the Nation subservient to projects of hostility instigated by pride, ambition and other sinister and pernicious motives. The peace often, sometimes perhaps the Liberty, of Nations has been the victim.

So likewise, a passionate attachment of one Nation for another produces a variety of evils. Sympathy for the favourite nation, facilitating the illusion of an imaginary common interest, in cases where no real common interest exists, and infusing into one the enmities of the other, betrays the former into a participation in the quarrels and Wars of the latter, without adequate inducement or justification: It leads also to concessions to the favourite Nation of priviledges denied to others, which is apt doubly to injure the Nation making the concessions; by unnecessarily parting with what ought to have been retained; and by exciting jealousy, ill will, and a disposition to retaliate, in the parties from whom eql. priviledges are withheld: And it gives to ambitious, corrupted, or deluded citizens (who devote themselves to the favourite Nation) facility to betray, or sacrifice the interests of their own country, without odium, sometimes even with popularity; gilding with the appearances of a virtuous sense of obligation a commendable deference for public opinion, or a laudable zeal for public good, the base or foolish compliances of ambition corruption or infatuation.

As avenues to foreign influence in innumerable ways, such attachments are particularly alarming to the truly enlightened and independent Patriot. How many opportunities do they afford to tamper with domestic factions, to practice the arts of seduction, to mislead public opinion, to influence or awe the public Councils! Such an attachment of a small or weak, towards a great and powerful Nation, dooms the former to be the satellite of the latter.

Against the insidious wiles of foreign influence, (I conjure you to believe me fellow citizens) the jealousy of a free people ought to be *constantly* awake; since history and experience prove that foreign influence is one of the most baneful foes of Republican Government. But that jealousy to be useful must be impartial; else it becomes the instrument of the very influence to be avoided, instead of a defence against it. Excessive partiality for one foreign nation and excessive dislike of another, cause those whom they actuate to see danger only on one side, and serve to veil and even second the arts of influence on the other. Real Patriots, who may resist the intriegues of the favourite, are liable to become suspected and odious; while its tools and dupes usurp the applause and confidence of the people, to surrender their interests.

The Great rule of conduct for us, in regard to foreign Nations is in extending our commercial relations to have with them as little *political* connection as possible. So far as we have already formed engagements let them be fulfilled, with perfect good faith. Here let us stop.

Europe has a set of primary interests, which to us have none, or a very remote relation. Hence she must be engaged in frequent controversies, the causes of which are essentially foreign to our concerns. Hence therefore it must be unwise in us to implicate ourselves, by artificial ties, in the ordinary vicissitudes of her politics, or the ordinary combinations and collisions of her friendships, or enmities:

Our detached and distant situation invites and enables us to pursue a different course. If we remain one People, under an efficient government, the period is not far off, when we may defy material injury from external annoyance; when we may take such an attitude as will cause the neutrality we may at any time resolve upon to be scrupulously respected; when belligerent nations, under the impossibility of making acquisitions upon us, will not lightly hazard the giving us provocation; when we may choose peace or war, as our interest guided by our justice shall Counsel.

Why forego the advantages of so peculiar a situation? Why quit our own to stand upon foreign ground? Why, by interweaving our destiny with that of any part of Europe, entangle our peace and prosperity in the toils of European Ambition, Rivalship, Interest, Humour or Caprice?

'Tis our true policy to steer clear of permanent Alliances, with any portion of the foreign world. So far, I mean, as we are now at liberty to do it, for let me not be understood as capable of patronising infidility to existing engagements (I hold the maxim no less applicable to public than to private affairs, that honesty is always the best policy). I repeat it therefore, let those engagements be observed in their genuine sense. But in my opinion, it is unnecessary and would be unwise to extend them.

Taking care always to keep ourselves, by suitable establishments, on a respectably defensive posture, we may safely trust to temporary alliances for extraordinary emergencies.

Harmony, liberal intercourse with all Nations, are recommended by policy, humanity and interest. But even our Commercial policy should hold an equal and impartial hand: neither seeking nor granting exclusive favours or preferences; consulting the natural course of things; diffusing and deversifying by gentle means the streams of Commerce, but forcing nothing; establishing with Powers so disposed; in order to give to trade a stable course, to define the rights of our Merchants, and to enable the Government to support them; conventional rules of intercourse, the best that present circumstances and mutual opinion will permit, but temporary, and liable to be from time to time abandoned or varied, as experience and circumstances shall dictate; constantly keeping in view, that 'tis folly in one Nation to look for disinterested favors from another; that it must pay with a portion of its Independence for whatever it may accept under that character; that by such acceptance, it may place itself in the condition of having given equivalents for nominal favours and yet of being reproached with ingratitude for not giving more. There can be no greater error than to expect, or calculate upon real favours from Nation to Nation. 'Tis an illusion which experience must cure, which a just pride ought to discard.

In offering to you, my Countrymen these counsels of an old and affectionate friend, I dare not hope they will make the strong and lasting impression, I could wish; that they will controul the usual current of the passions, or prevent our Nation from running the course which has hitherto marked the Destiny of Nations: But if I may even flatter myself, that they may be productive of some partial benefit, some occasional good; that they may now and then recur to moderate the fury of party spirit, to warn against the mischiefs of foreign Intriegue, to guard against the Impostures of pretended patriotism; this hope will be a full recompence for the solicitude for your welfare, by which they have been dictated.

How far in the discharge of my Official duties, I have been guided by the principles which have been delineated, the public Records and other evidences of my conduct must Witness to You and to the world. To myself, the assurance of my own conscience is, that I have at least believed myself to be guided by them.

In relation to the still subsisting War in Europe, my Proclamation of the 22d. of April 1793 is the index to my Plan. Sanctioned by your approving voice and by that of Your Representatives in both Houses of Congress, the spirit of that measure has continually governed me; uninfluenced by any attempts to deter or divert me from it.

After deliberate examination with the aid of the best lights I could obtain I was well satisfied that our Country, under all the circumstances of the case, had a right to take, and was bound in duty and interest, to take a Neutral position. Having taken it, I determined, as far as should depend upon me, to maintain it, with moderation, perseverence and firmness.

The considerations, which respect the right to hold this conduct, it is not necessary on this occasion to detail. I will only observe, that according to my understanding of the matter, that right, so far from being denied by any of the Belligerent Powers has been virtually admitted by all.

The duty of holding a Neutral conduct may be inferred, without any thing more, from the obligation which justice and humanity impose on every Nation, in cases in which it is free to act, to maintain inviolate the relations of Peace and amity towards other Nations.

The inducements of interest for observing that conduct will best be referred to your own reflections and experience. With me, a predominant motive has been to endeavour to gain time to our country to settle and mature its yet recent institutions, and to progress without interruption, to that degree of strength and consistency, which is necessary to give it, humanly speaking, the command of its own fortunes.

Though in reviewing the incidents of my Administration, I am unconscious of intentional error, I am nevertheless too sensible of my defects not to think it probable that I may have committed many errors. Whatever they may be I fervently beseech the Almighty to avert or mitigate the evils to which they may tend. I shall also carry with me the hope that my Country will never cease to view them with indulgence; and that after forty five years of my life dedicated to its Service, with an upright zeal, the faults of incompetent abilities will be consigned to oblivion, as myself must soon be to the Mansions of rest.

Relying on its kindness in this as in other things, and actuated by that fervent love towards it, which is so natural to a Man, who views in it the native soil of himself and his progenitors for several Generations; I anticipate with pleasing expectation that retreat, in which I promise myself to realize, without alloy, the sweet enjoyment of partaking, in the midst of my fellow Citizens, the benign influence of good Laws under a free Government, the ever favourite object of my heart, and the happy reward, as I trust, of our mutual cares, labours and dangers.

TROUBLE WITH TEETH

To John Greenwood

Philadelphia, January 20, 1797.

Sir: I must again resort to you for assistance. The teeth herewith enclosed have, by degrees, worked loose and, at length, two or three of them have given way altogether. I send them to you to be repaired, if they are susceptible of it; if not, then for the purpose of substituting others. I would thank you for, returning them as soon as possible for although I now make use of another sett, they are both uneasy in the mouth and bulge my lips out in such a manner as to make them appear considerably swelled.

You will perceive at the first view, that one cause of these teeth giving way is for want of a proper socket for the root part of them to rest in, as well for the purpose of keeping them firm and in place at bottom, as to preserve them against the effect of the saliva, which softens the part that formerly was covered by the gums and afforded them nourishment. Whether this remedy can be applied to the present sett I know not; for nothing must be done to them which will, in the *least* degree force the lips out more than *now* do, as it does this too much already; but if both upper and lower teeth were to incline inwards more, it would shew the shape of the mouth better, and not be the worse in any other respect.

Send with the teeth, springs about a foot in length, but not cut; and about double that length of a tough gold wire, of the size you see with the teeth, for fastening the springs. Accompany the whole with your Account, and the amount shall be immediately sent by Post in a bank note. I am etc.

"BEFORE THE CURTAIN DROPS"

To Jonathan Trumbull, Jr.

Philadelphia, March 3, 1797.

My dear Sir: Before the curtain drops on my political life, which it will do this evening, I expect for ever; I shall acknowledge, although it be in a few hasty lines only, the receipt of your kind and affectionate letter of the 23d. of January last.

When I add, that according to custom, all the Acts of the Session; except two or three very unimportant Bills, have been presented to me within the last four days, *you* will not be surprised at the pressure under which I write at present; but it must astonish *others* who know that the Constitution allows the President ten days to deliberate on *each Bill* that is brought before him that he should be allowed by the Legislature less than half that time to consider *all* the business of the Session; and in some instances, scarcely an hour to revolve the most important. But as the scene is closing, with me, it is of little avail *now* to let it be with murmers.

I should be very unhappy if I thought my relinquishing the Reins of government wd. produce any of the consequences which your fears forebode. In all free governments, contention in elections will take place; and, whilst it is confined to our own citizens it is not to be regretted; but severely indeed ought it to be reprobated when occasioned by foreign machinations. I trust however, that the good sense of our Countrymen will guard the public weal against this, and every other innovation; and that, altho we may be a little wrong, now and then, we shall return to the right path, with more avidity. I can never believe that Providence, which has guided us so long, and through such a labirinth, will withdraw its protection at this Crisis.

Although I shall resign the chair of government without a single regret, or any desire to intermeddle in politics again, yet there are many of my compatriots (among whom be assured I place you) from whom I shall part sorrowing; because, unless I meet with them at Mount Vernon it is not likely that I shall ever see them more, as I do not expect that I shall ever be twenty miles from it after I am tranquilly settled there. To tell you how glad I should be to see you at that place is unnecessary; but this I will add, that it would not only give me pleasure, but pleasure also to Mrs. Washington, and others of the family with whom you are acquainted; and who all unite in every good wish for you, and yours, with Dear Sir, Your sincere friend and Affectionate Servant.

THE RHYTHM OF LIFE AT MOUNT VERNON

To James McHenry

Dear Sir,   Mount Vernon 29th May 1797

I am indebted to you for several unacknowledged letters, but ne'er mind that; go on, as if you had them. You are at the source of information & can find many things to relate, while I have nothing to say that could either inform, or amuse a Secretary of War in Philadelphia.

To tell him that I begin my diurnal course with the Sun; that if my hirelings are not in their places at that time I send them messages expressive of my sorrow for their indisposition—then having put these wheels in motion, I examine the state of things farther; and the more they are probed, the deeper I find the wounds are, which my buildings have sustained by an absence, and neglect of eight years. By the time I have accomplished these matters, breakfast (a little after seven oclock, about the time I presume you are taking leave of Mrs McHenry) is ready. This over, I mount my horse and ride round my farms, which employs me until it is time to dress for dinner; at which I rarely miss seeing strange faces—come, as they say, out of respect to me. Pray, would not the word curiosity answer as well? and how different this, from having a few social friends at a cheerful board? The usual time of sitting at Table—a walk—and Tea—brings me within the dawn of Candlelight; previous to which, if not prevented by company, I resolve, that as soon as the glimmering taper, supplies the place of the great luminary, I will retire to my writing Table and acknowledge the letters I have received; but when the lights are brought, I feel tired, and disinclined to engage in this work, conceiving that the next night will do as well; the next comes, and with it the same causes for postponement, & effect; and so on.

This will account for *your* letters remaining so long unacknowledged—and having given you the history of a day, it will serve for a year; and I am persuaded you will not require a second edition of it: but it may strike you, that in this detail no mention is made of any portion of time allotted for reading; the remark would be just, for I have not looked into a book since I came home, nor shall be able to do it until I have discharged my workmen; probably not before the nights grow longer; when, possibly, I may be looking in doomsday book.

On the score of the plated ware in your possession I will say something in a future letter. At present I shall only add that I am always and affectionately Yours

"THE DECLINE OF LIFE"

To Lawrence Lewis

Dear Sir,   Mount Vernon 4th Augt 1797.
Your letter of the 24th Ulto has been received, and I am sorry to hear of the loss of your Servant; but it is my opinion these elopements will be *much more*, before they are *less* frequent; and that the persons making them should never be retained, if they are recovered, as they are sure to contaminate and discontent others. I wish from my Soul that the Legislature of this State could see the policy of a gradual abolition of Slavery; It might prevt much future mischief.

Whenever it is convenient to you to make this place your home, I shall be glad to see you at it for that purpose; and that there may be no misunderstanding in the matter, I shall inform you before hand, that you, servant (if you bring one) and horses, will fare in all respects as We, & mine do; but that I shall expect no Services from you for which pecuniary compensation will be made. I have already as many on wages as are sufficient to carry on my business, and more indeed than I can find means to pay, conveniently. As both your Aunt and I are in the decline of life, and regular in our habits, especially in our hour of rising

& going to bed, I require some person (fit & Proper) to ease
me of the trouble of entertaining company; particularly of
Nights, as it is my inclination to retire (and unless prevented by
very particular company, always do retire) either to bed, or to
my study, soon after candle light. In taking these duties (which
hospitality obliges one to bestow on company) off my hands, it
would render me a very acceptable Service. And for a little time
only, to come, an hour in the day, now and then, devoted to the
recording of some Papers which time would not allow me to
complete before I left Philadelphia, would also be acceptable.
Besides these, I know nothing at present, that would require
any portion of your time, or attention: both of which, if you
have inclination for it, might be devoted to Reading, as I have
a great many instructive Books, on many subjects, as well as
amusing ones; or, they might be employed in sporting, there
being much game of all sorts here; or in riding, & viewing the
management of my farms, from whence something useful may
be drawn, as I think Mr Anderson in many things could give
you useful lessons and a better insight into husbandry than
your opportunities have, Hitherto, presented to you.

I do not mean however, that any of these things should restrain you from attending to your own affairs, or restrain you
from visiting your friends at pleasure; all I have in view by
making this communication is to guard against misconception
on either side. Your Aunt unites with me in best regards for
you, and I am your sincere friend and Affectionate Uncle

"THE URGENCY OF CIRCUMSTANCES"

To John Adams

Dear Sir,   Mount Vernon 13th July 1798
    I had the honour on the evening of the 11th instant to re-
ceive from the hands of the Secretary of War, your favour of
the 7th announcing that you had with the advice and consent
of the Senate appointed me "Lieutenant General and Commander in Chief of all the armies raised, or to be raised for the
Service of the U. S."

I cannot express how greatly affected I am at this New proof of public confidence, and the highly flattering manner in which you have been pleased to make the communication; at the same-time I must not conceal from you my earnest wish, that the choice had fallen upon a man less declined in years and better qualified to encounter the usual vicissitudes of War.

You know, Sir, what calculation I had made relative to the probable course of events, on my retiring from Office, and the determination I had consoled myself with, of closing the remnant of my days in my present peaceful abode; you will therefore be at no loss to conceive and appreciate, the Sensations I must have experienced, to bring my mind to any conclusion, that would pledge me, at so late a period of life, to leave Scenes I sincerely love, to enter upon the boundless field of public action—incessant trouble—and high responsibility.

It was not possible for me to remain ignorant of, or indifferent to, recent transactions. The conduct of the Directory of France towards our Country; their insiduous hostility to its Government; their various practices to withdraw the affections of the People from it; the evident tendency of their acts and those of their Agents to countenance and invigorate opposition; their disregard of solemn treaties and the laws of Nations; their war upon our defenceless Commerce; their treatment of our Ministers of Peace, and their demands amounting to tribute, could not fail to excite in me corresponding sentiments with those my countrymen have so generally expressed in their affectionate addresses to you. Believe me, Sir, no one can more cordially approve of the wise and prudent measures of your Administration. They ought to inspire universal confidence, and will no doubt, combined with the state of things call from Congress such laws & means as will enable you to meet the full force and extent of the Crisis.

Satisfied therefore, that you have sincerely wished and endeavoured to avert war, and exhausted to the last drop, the cup of reconciliation, we can with pure hearts appeal to Heaven for the justice of our cause, and may confidently trust the final result to that kind Providence who has heretofore, and so often, signally favoured the People of these United States.

Thinking in this manner, and feeling how incumbent it is upon every person, of every description, to contribute at all times to his Countrys welfare, and especially in a moment like the present, when every thing we hold dear & Sacred is so seriously threatned, I have finally determined to accept the Commission of Commander in Chief of the Armies of the United States, with the reserve only, that I shall not be called into the field until the Army is in a Situation to require my presence, or it becomes indispensible by the urgency of circumstances.

In making this reservation, I beg it to be understood that I do not mean to withhold any assistance to arrange and organise the Army, which you may think I can afford. I take the liberty also to mention, that I must decline having my acceptance considered as drawing after it any immediate charge upon the Public, or that I can receive any emoluments annexed to the appointment, before entering into a Situation to incur expence.

The Secretary of War being anxious to return, to the Seat of Government, I have detained him no longer than was necessary to a full communication upon the several points he had in charge. With very great respect and consideration I have the honor to be Dear Sir Your Most Obedt Hble Sert

A PRESIDENT AND A COMMANDER-IN-CHIEF

To John Adams

Sir,   Mount Vernon 25th Septr 1798.
    With all the respect which is due to your public station, and with the regard I entertain for your private character, the following representation is presented to your consideration. If in the course of it, any expression should escape me which may appear to be incompatible with either, let the purity of my intentions; the candour of my declarations; and a due respect for my own character, be received as an apology.

The subject on which I am about to address you, is not less delicate in its nature, than it is interesting to my feelings. It is the change which you have directed to be made in the relative rank of the Major Generals, which I had the honor of presenting to you, by the Secretary of War; the appointment of an Adjutant General *after* the first nomination was rejected; and the *prepared* state you are in to appoint a third, if the second should decline, without the least intimation of the matter to me.

It would have been unavailing, *after* the nomination and appointment of me to the Chief command of the Armies of the United States, (without any previous consultation of my sentiments) to have observed to you the delicate situation in which I was placed by that act. It was still less expedient, to have dwelt more than I did, on my sorrow at being drawn from my retirement; where I had fondly hoped to have spent the few remaining years which might be dispensed to me, if not in profound tranquillity, at least without public responsibility. But if you had been pleased, previously to the nomination, to have enquired into the train of my thoughts upon the occasion, I would have told you with the frankness & candour which I hope will ever mark my character, on what terms I would have consented to the nomination; you would then have been enabled to decide whether they were admissible, or not.

This opportunity was not afforded *before* I was brought to public view. To declare them *afterwards*, was all I could do; and this I did, in explicit language, to the Secretary of War, when he honoured me with your letter of the 7th of July; shewed me his powers; and presented the Commission. They were, that the General Officers, and General staff of the Army should not be appointed without my concurrence. I extended my stipulations no farther, but offered to give every information, and render every service in my power in selecting good officers for the Regiments.

It would be tedious to go into all the details which led to this determination; but before I conclude my letter, I shall take the liberty of troubling you with some of them. Previously to the doing of which, however, let me declare, and I do declare, in the most unequivocal manner, that I had nothing more in view in making this stipulation, than to insure the most eligable characters for these highly responsible offices; conceiving that my opportunities, both in the Civil & Military administration of the Affairs of this Country, had enabled me to form as correct an opinion of them as any other could do.

Neither the Secretary of War, nor myself, entertained any doubt, from your letters to me, and Instructions to him, that this was the meaning and object of his Mission. Unwilling, however, to let a matter of such serious importance to myself remain upon uncertain ground, I requested *that* Gentleman to declare this in *his official letter* to you (supposing, as was the case, that the one I should have the honor of writing to you, might be laid before the Public, and that to incumber it with stipulations of that sort, would be improper). Nay more, as the acceptance was conditional, & you might, or might not be disposed to accede to the terms, I requested him to take the Commission back, to be annulled, or restored, according to your conception of the propriety, or impropriety of them. His remark upon this occasion was, that it was unnecessary, inasmuch as, if you did not incline to accept my services upon the conditions they were offered, you would be under the necessity of declaring it; whilst, on the other hand, silence must be construed into acquiescence. This consideration, and believing that the latter mode would be most respectful, as the other might imply distrust of your intentions, arrested that measure.

This, Sir, is a true, candid & impartial statement of facts. It was the ground on which I *accepted* and *retained* the Commission; and was the authority on which I proceeded to the arrangement that was presented to you by the Secretary of War.

Having *no idea* that the General Officers for the Provisional army would be nominated at that time they were, I had not even contemplated characters for those appointments.

I will now, respectfully ask, in what manner these stipulations on my part, have been complied with?

In the arrangement made by me, with the Secretary of War, the three Major Generals stood—Hamilton, Pinckney, Knox. and in this order I expected their Commissions would have been dated. This, I conceive, must have been the understanding of the Senate. And certainly was the expectation of all those with whom I have conversed. But you have been pleased to order the last to be first, and the first to be last. Of four Brigadiers for the Provisional army, one I never heard of as a Military character, has been nominated and appointed; and another is so well known to all those who served with him, in the Revolution, as (for the appointment) to have given the greatest disgust, and will be the means of preventing many valuable Officers of that army from coming forward. One Adjutant General has been, & another is ready to be appointed in case of the

non-acceptance of Mr North, not only without any consultation with me, but without the least intimation of the intention;
although in the letter I had the honor to write you on the 4th
of July in acknowledgment of your favour of the 22d of June
preceeding, and still more strongly in one of the same date to
the Secretary of War, which (while here) his Clerk was, I know,
directed to lay before you, I endeavoured to shew, in a strong
point of view, how all important it was that this officer (besides
his other qualifications) should be agreeable to the Commander
in Chief, and possess his *entire* confidence. To increase the
Powers of the Commander in Chief—or to lessen those of the
President of the United States, I pray you to be persuaded, was
most foreign from my heart. To secure able Coadjutors in the
arduous task I was about to enter upon, was my *sole* aim. This
the public good demanded—and this must have been equally
the wish of us both. But to accomplish it, required an intimate
knowledge of the *componant* parts of the characters among us,
in the higher grades of the late army. and I hope (without incurring the charge of presumption) I may add, that the opportunities I have had to judge of these, are second to none. It
was too interesting to me, who had staked every thing which
was dear & valuable upon the issue, to trust more to chance
than could be avoided. It could not be supposed that I was
insensible to the risk I was about to run—knowing that the
chances of losing, was at least equal to those of encreasing, that
reputation which the partiality of the world had been pleased
to bestow on me. No one then, acquainted with these circumstances; the sacrafices I was about to make; and the impartiality
of my conduct in the various walks of life, could suppose that I
had any other object in view than to obtain the best aids the
country afforded, & my judgment could dictate.

If an Army had been in actual existence, and you had been
pleased to offer the command of it to me, my course would
have been plain: I should have examined the Constitution of
it; looked into its organization; and enquired into the character
of its Officers &ca—As the Army was to be raised, & the Officers
to be appointed, could it be expected (as I was no Candidate
for the Office) that I would be less cautious, or less attentive to
secure these advantages?

It was not difficult for me to perceive that if we entered into a Serious contest with France, that the character of the War would differ materially from the last we were engaged in. In the latter, time, caution, and worrying the enemy until we could be better provided with arms, & other means, and had better disciplined Troops to carry it on, was the plan for us. But if we should be engaged with the former, they ought to be attacked at every step, and, if possible, not suffered to make an establishment in the Country—acquiring thereby strength from the disaffected and the Slaves, whom I have no doubt they will arm—and for that purpose will commence their operations South of the Potomack.

Taking all these circumstances into view, you will not be surprised at my sollicitude to intrench myself as I did; nor is it to be supposed that I made the arrangement of the three Major Generals without an eye to possible consequences. I wished for time, it is true, to have effected it, hoping that an amicable adjustment might have taken place, & offered, at a very short summons, (inconvenient as it would have been) to proceed to Philadelphia for that purpose; but as no subsequent notice was taken thereof, I presumed there were operative reasons against the measure, and did not repeat it.

It is proper too I should add, that, from the information which I received from various quarters, & through different channels, I had no doubt in my mind that the current sentiment among the members of Congress, and particularly among those from New England, was in favor of Colonel Hamilton's being second in command—and this impression has been since confirmed in the most unequivocal manner by some respectable members of that body, whom I have myself seen & conversed with, on the subject.

But if no regard was intended to be had to the *order* of my arrangement, why was it not altered before it was submitted to the Senate? This would have placed matters upon Simple ground. It would then have been understood as it is at present, namely—that the Gentlemen would rank in the order they were named: but the change will contravene this, and excite much conversation, & unpleasant consequences.

I cannot lay my hand readily upon the resolves of the old Congress, relative to the settlement of Rank between Officers of the same grade, who had been in service & were disbanded,

while a part of the Army remained in existance; but if I have a
tolerable recollection of the matter, they are totally irrevelent
to the present case. Those resolves passed, if I am not mistaken, at a time when the proportion of Officers to men was so
unequal as to require a reduction of the former: or when the
Army was about to undergo a reduction in part, and the officers might be called upon again. But will a case of this sort
apply to Officers of an army which has ceased to exist for more
than fourteen years? I give it frankly as my opinion (if I have
not entirely forgotten the principle on which the Resolves took
place) that they will not: and I as frankly declare, that the only
motive I had for examining a list of the Officers of that army,
was to be reminded of names. If the rule contended for was to
obtain, what would be the consequences, & where would the
evil end? In all probability resort will be had to the field Officers of the Revolutionary army to fill similar grades in the
augmented, and Provisional Corps which are to be raised.
What then is to be done with General Dayton, who never ranked
higher than Captain? The principle will apply with equal force
in that case as in the case of Hamilton and Knox. The injury (if
it is one) of putting a junr over the head of a Senr Officer of
the last war, is not ameliorated by the nominations or appointments of them on different days. It is the act itself, not the
manner of doing it, that affects.

I have dwelt longer on this point than perhaps was necessary, in order to shew, that in my opinion, former rank in the
Revolutionary Army ought to have no influence in the present
case, farther than may be derived from superior experience,
brilliant exploits, or general celebrity of character. And that, as
the Armies about to be raised are commencing de novo, the
President has the right to make Officers of Citizens, or Soldiers, at his pleasure; and to arrange them in any manner he
shall deem most conducive to the public weal.

It is an invidious task, at all times, to draw comparisons; and
I shall avoid it as much as possible; but I have no hesitation in
declaring, that if the Public is to be deprived of the Services of
Coll Hamilton in the Military line, that the Post he was destined to fill will not be easily supplied; and that this is the sentiment of the Public, I think I can venture to pronounce.
Although Colo. Hamilton has never acted in the character of a

General Officer, yet his opportunities, as the principal & most confidential aid of the Commander in chief, afforded him the means of viewing every thing on a larger scale than those whose attentions were confined to Divisions or Brigades; who knew nothing of the correspondences of the Commander in Chief, or of the various orders to, or transactions with, the General Staff of the Army. These advantages, and his having served with usefulness in the Old Congress; in the General Convention; and having filled one of the most important departments of Government with acknowledged abilities and integrity, has placed him on high ground; and made him a conspicuous character in the United States, and even in Europe. To these, as a matter of no small consideration may be added, that as a lucrative practice in the line of his Profession is his *most certain* dependence, the inducement to relinquish it, must, in some degree, be commensurate. By some he is considered as an ambitious man, and therefore a dangerous one. That he is ambitious I shall readily grant, but it is of that laudable kind which prompts a man to excel in whatever he takes in hand. He is enterprising, quick in his perceptions, and his judgment intuitively great: qualities essential to a great military character, and therefore I repeat, that his loss will be irreparable.

With respect to General Knox, I can say with truth, there is no man in the United States with whom I have been in habits of greater intimacy; no one whom I have loved more sincerely; nor any for whom I have had a greater friendship. But, esteem, love & friendship, can have no influence on my mind when I conceive that the subjugation of our Government and Independence, are the objects aimed at by the enemies of our Peace; and when, possibly, our all is at stake.

In the first moments of leisure, after the Secretary of War had left this place I wrote a friendly letter to Genl Knox, stating my firm belief that if the French should invade this country, with a view to conquest, or to the division of it, that their operations would commence to the Southward, and endeavoured to shew him, in that case, how all important it was to engage General Pinckney, his numerous family, friends & influential acquaintance, *heartily* in the cause. Sending him, at the same time, a copy of the arrangement, which I supposed *to be final*; and in a subsequent letter, I gave him my opinion fully with respect to the relative situation of himself & Colo. Hamilton; not expecting, I confess, the difficulties which have occurred.

I will say but little, relatively to the appointment of the Brigadiers before alluded to; but I must not conceal, that after what had passed, and my understanding of the compact, that my feelings were not a little wounded by the appointment of any, much more such characters, with out my knowledge.

In giving these details, I have far exceeded the limits of a letter, but hope to be excused for the prolixity of it. My object has been, to give you a clear and distinct view of my understanding of the terms on which I received the Commission with which you were pleased to honor me.

Lengthy as this letter is, there is another subject, not less interesting to the Commander in Chief of the Armies (be him whom he may) than it is important to the United States, which I beg leave to bring respectfully to your view. We are now, near the end of September, and not a man recruited, nor a Battalion Officer appointed, that has come to my knowledge. The consequence is, that the spirit and enthusiasm which prevailed a month or two ago, and would have produced the *best* men in a short time, is evaporating *fast*, and a month or two hence, may induce but few, and those perhaps of the *worst* sort, to Inlist. Instead therefore of having the augmented force in a state of preparation, and under a course of discipline, it is now to be *raised*; and possibly may not be in existence when the Enemy is in the field: we shall then have to meet veteran Troops, inured to conquest, with Militia, or raw recruits; the consequence of which is not difficult to conceive, or to foretell.

I have addressed you, Sir, with openness & candour—and I hope with respect; requesting to be informed whether your determination to reverse the order of the three Major Generals is final—and whether you mean to appoint another Adjutant General without my concurrence. With the greatest respect & consideration I have the honor to be Sir, Your Most Obedient and Most Humble Servant

THOUGHTS ON THE ALIEN AND SEDITION ACTS

To Alexander Spotswood, Jr.

Dr Sir,   Philadelphia 22d Novr 1798

Your letter of the 13th instt enclosing a publication under the signature of Gracchus, on the Alien & Sedition Laws, found me at this place—deeply engaged in business.

You ask my opinion of these Laws, professing to place confidence in my judgment, for the compliment of which I thank you. But to give opinions unsupported by reasons might appear dogmatical, especially, as you have declared that, Gracchus has produced "thorough conviction in your mind of the unconstitutionality, and inexpediency of the acts above mentioned." To go into an explanation on these points I have neither leizure nor inclination; because it would occupy more time than I have to spare.

But I will take the liberty of advising such as are not "thoroughly convinced" and whose minds are yet open to conviction, to read the peices, and hear the arguments which have been adduced in favor of, as well as those against the Constitutionality and expediency of those Laws, before they decide. And consider to what lengths a certain description of men, in our Country, have already driven, and seem resolved further to drive matters; and then ask themselves, if it is not time & expedient to resort to protecting Laws against aliens (for Citizens you certainly know are not affected by that Law) who acknowledge *no allegiance* to this Country, and in many instances are sent among us (as there is the best circumstantial evidence) for the *express purpose* of poisoning the minds of our people; and to sow dissentions among them; in order to alienate *their* affections from the Government of their choice, thereby endeavouring to dissolve the Union; and of course, the fair and happy prospects which were unfolding to our View from the Revolution—But, as I have observed before, I have no time to enter the field of Politicks; and therefore shall only add my best respects to the good family at New Post—and the assurances of being Dr Sir Your Very Hble Servant

IN DEFENSE OF GOVERNMENT

To Patrick Henry

Confidential
Dear Sir   Mount Vernon 15th Jany 1799
    At the threshold of this letter, I ought to make an apology
for its contents; but if you will give me credit for my motives, I
will contend for no more, however erroneous my sentiments
may appear to you.

    It would be a waste of time, to attempt to bring to the view of
a person of your observation & discernment, the endeavors
of a certain party among us, to disquiet the Public mind with
unfounded alarms; to arraign every act of the Administration;
to set the People at varience with their Government; and to
embarrass all its measures. Equally useless would it be, to predict what must be the inevitable consequences of such policy,
if it cannot be arrested.

    Unfortunately, and extremely do I regret it, the State of
Virginia has taken the lead in this opposition. I have said the
State Because the conduct of its Legislature in the Eyes of the
World, will authorise the expression; because it is an incontro-
vertable fact, that the principle leaders of the opposition dwell
in it; and because no doubt is entertained, I believe, that with
the help of the Chiefs in other States, all the plans are arranged;
and systematically pursued by their followers in other parts of
the Union; though in no State except Kentucky (that I have
heard of) has Legislative countenance been obtained, beyond
Virginia.

    It has been said, that the great mass of the Citizens of this
State are well affected, notwithstanding, to the General Government, and the Union; and I am willing to believe it—nay
do believe it: but how is this to be reconciled with their suffrages at the Elections of Representatives; both to Congress &
their State Legislature; who are men opposed to the first, and
by the tendency of their measures would destroy the latter?
Some among us, have endeavored to account for this inconsistency and though convinced themselves, of its truth, they are

unable to convince others; who are unacquainted with the internal polity of the State.

One of the reasons assigned is, that the most respectable, & best qualified characters among us, will not come forward. Easy & happy in their circumstances at home, and believing themselves secure in their liberties & property, will not forsake them, or their occupations, and engage in the turmoil of public business; or expose themselves to the calumnies of their opponents, whose weapons are detraction.

But at such a crisis as this, when every thing dear & valuable to us is assailed; when this Party hang upon the Wheels of Government as a dead weight, opposing every measure that is calculated for defence & self preservation; abetting the nefarious views of another Nation, upon our Rights; prefering, as long as they durst contend openly against the spirit & resentment of the People, the interest of France to the Welfare of their own Country; justifying the first at the expence of the latter: When every Act of their own Government is tortured by constructions they will not bear, into attempts to infringe & trample upon the Constitution with a view to introduce Monarchy; When the most unceasing, & purest exertions were making, to maintain a Neutrality which had been proclaimed by the Executive, approved unequivocally by Congress, by the State Legislatures, nay by the People themselves, in various meetings; and to preserve the Country in Peace, are charged as a measure calculated to favor Great Britain at the expence of France, and all those who had any agency in it, are accused of being under the influence of the former, and her Pensioners; When measures are systematically, and pertenaciously pursued, which must eventually dissolve the Union or produce coertion. I say, when these things have become so obvious, ought characters who are best able to rescue their Country from the pending evil to remain at home? rather, ought they not to come forward, and by their talents and influence, stand in the breach wch such conduct has made on the Peace and happiness of this Country, and oppose the widening of it?

Vain will it be to look for Peace and happiness, or for the security of liberty or property, if Civil discord should ensue; and what else can result from the policy of those among us, who, by all the means in their power, are driving matters to extremity, if they cannot be counteracted effectually? The views of Men can only be known, or guessed at, by their words or actions. Can those of the *Leaders* of Opposition be mistaken then, if judged by this Rule? That they are *followed* by numbers who are unacquainted with their designs, and suspect as little, the tendency of their principles, I am fully persuaded—But, if their conduct is viewed with indifference; if there is activity and misrepresentation on one side, and supiness on the other; their numbers, accumulated by Intrieguing, and discontented foreigners under proscription, who were at war with their own governments, and the greater part of them with *all* Government, their numbers will encrease, & nothing, short of Omniscience, can foretel the consequences.

I come now, my good Sir, to the object of my letter—which is—to express a hope, and an earnest wish, that you wd come forward at the ensuing Elections (if not for Congress, which you may think would take you too long from home) as a candidate for representation, in the General Assembly of this Commonwealth.

There are, I have no doubt, very many sensible men who oppose themselves to the torrent that carries away others, who had rather swim with, than stem it, without an able Pilot to conduct them—but these are neither old in Legislation, nor well known in the Community. Your weight of character and influence in the Ho. of Representatives would be a bulwark against such dangerous Sentiments as are delivered there at present. It would be a rallying point for the timid, and an attraction of the wavering. In a word, I conceive it to be of immense importance at this Crisis that you should be there; and I would fain hope that all minor considerations will be made to yield to the measure.

If I have erroneously supposed that your sentiments on these subjects are in unison with mine; or if I have assumed a liberty which the occasion does not warrant, I must conclude as I began, with praying that my motives may be received as an apology; and that my fear, that the tranquillity of the Union, and of this State in particular, is hastening to an awful crisis, have extorted them from me. With great, and very sincere regard and respect, I am—Dear Sir Your Most Obedt & Very Hble Servt

MANUMISSION

Last Will and Testament

In the name of God amen I George Washington of Mount Vernon—a citizen of the United States, and lately President of the same, do make, ordain and declare this Instrument; which is written with my own hand and every page thereof subscribed with my name, to be my last Will & Testament, revoking all others.

Imprimus.　All my debts, of which there are but few, and none of magnitude, are to be punctually and speedily paid—and the Legacies hereinafter bequeathed, are to be discharged as soon as circumstances will permit, and in the manner directed.

Item.　To my dearly beloved wife Martha Washington I give and bequeath the use, profit and benefit of my whole Estate, real and personal, for the term of her natural life—except such parts thereof as are specifically disposed of hereafter: My improved lot in the Town of Alexandria, situated on Pitt & Cameron streets, I give to her and her heirs forever; as I also do my household & Kitchen furniture of every sort & kind, with the liquors and groceries which may be on hand at the time of my decease; to be used & disposed of as she may think proper.

Item　Upon the decease of my wife, it is my Will & desire that all the Slaves which I hold in my *own right*, shall receive their freedom. To emancipate them during her life, would, tho' earnestly wished by me, be attended with such insuperable difficulties on account of their intermixture by Marriages with the dower Negroes, as to excite the most painful sensations, if not disagreeable consequences from the latter, while both descriptions are in the occupancy of the same Proprietor; it not being in my power, under the tenure by which the Dower Negroes are held, to manumit them. And whereas among those who will recieve freedom according to this devise, there may be some, who from old age or bodily infirmities, and others who on account of their infancy, that will be unable to support themselves; it is my Will and desire that all who come under the first & second description shall be comfortably cloathed & fed by my heirs while they live; and that such of the latter description as have no parents living, or if living are unable, or unwilling to provide for them, shall be bound by the Court until they shall arrive at the age of twenty five years; and in cases where no record can be produced, whereby their ages can be ascertained, the judgment of the Court, upon its own view of the subject, shall be adequate and final. The Negros thus bound, are (by their Masters or Mistresses) to be taught to read & write; and to be brought up to some useful occupation, agreeably to the Laws of the Commonwealth of Virginia, providing for the support of Orphan and other poor Children. and I do hereby expressly forbid the Sale, or transportation out of the said Commonwealth, of any Slave I may die possessed of, under any pretence whatsoever. And I do moreover most pointedly, and most solemnly enjoin it upon my Executors hereafter named, or the Survivors of them, to see that *this* clause respecting Slaves, and every part thereof be religiously fulfilled at the Epoch at which it is directed to take place; without evasion, neglect or delay, after the Crops which may then be on the ground are harvested, particularly as it respects the aged and infirm; seeing that a regular and permanent fund be established for their support so long as there are subjects requiring it; not trusting to the uncertain provision to be made by individuals. And to my Mulatto man William (calling himself William Lee) I give immediate freedom; or if he should prefer it (on account of the accidents which have befallen him, and which have rendered him incapable of walking or of any active employment) to remain in the situation he now is, it shall be optional in him to do so: In either case however, I allow him an annuity of thirty dollars during his natural life, which shall be independent of the victuals and cloaths he has been accustomed to receive, if he chuses the last alternative; but in full, with his freedom, if he prefers the first; & this I give him as a testimony of my sense of his attachment to me, and for his faithful services during the Revolutionary War.

Item. To the Trustees (Governors, or by whatsoever other name they may be designated) of the Academy in the Town of Alexandria, I give and bequeath, in Trust, four thousand dollars, or in other words twenty of the shares which I hold in the

Bank of Alexandria, towards the support of a Free school established at, and annexed to, the said Academy; for the purpose
of Educating such Orphan children, or the children of such
other poor and indigent persons as are unable to accomplish it
with their own means; and who, in the judgment of the Trustees of the said Seminary, are best entitled to the benefit of this
donation. The aforesaid twenty shares I give & bequeath in
perpetuity; the dividends only of which are to be drawn for,
and applied by the said Trustees for the time being, for the uses
above mentioned; the stock to remain entire and untouched;
unless indications of a failure of the said Bank should be so
apparent, or a discontinuance thereof should render a removal
of this fund necessary; in either of these cases, the amount of
the Stock here devised, is to be vested in some other Bank or
public Institution, whereby the interest may with regularity &
certainty be drawn, and applied as above. And to prevent misconception, my meaning is, and is hereby declared to be, that
these twenty shares are in lieu of, and not in addition to, the
thousand pounds given by a missive letter some years ago; in
consequence whereof an annuity of fifty pounds has since been
paid towards the support of this Institution.

Item.   Whereas by a Law of the Commonwealth of Virginia,
enacted in the year 1785, the Legislature thereof was pleased
(as an evidence of Its approbation of the services I had rendered the Public during the Revolution—and partly, I believe,
in consideration of my having suggested the vast advantages
which the Community would derive from the extensions of its
Inland Navigation, under Legislative patronage) to present me
with one hundred shares of one hundred dollars each, in the
incorporated company established for the purpose of extending the navigation of James River from tide water to the Mountains: and also with fifty shares of one hundred pounds Sterling
each, in the Corporation of another company, likewise established for the similar purpose of opening the Navigation of the
River Potomac from tide water to Fort Cumberland, the acceptance of which, although the offer was highly honourable,
and grateful to my feelings, was refused, as inconsistent with a
principle which I had adopted, and had never departed from—
namely—not to receive pecuniary compensation for any services I could render my country in its arduous struggle with

great Britain, for its Rights; and because I had evaded similar propositions from other States in the Union; adding to this refusal, however, an intimation that, if it should be the pleasure of the Legislature to permit me to appropriate the said shares to *public uses*, I would receive them on those terms with due sensibility; and this it having consented to, in flattering terms, as will appear by a subsequent Law, and sundry resolutions, in the most ample and honourable manner, I proceed after this recital, for the more correct understanding of the case, to declare—

That as it has always been a source of serious regret with me, to see the youth of these United States sent to foreign Countries for the purpose of Education, often before their minds were formed, or they had imbibed any adequate ideas of the happiness of their own; contracting, too frequently, not only habits of dissipation & extravagence, but principles unfriendly to Republican Governmt and to the true & genuine liberties of Mankind; which, thereafter are rarely overcome. For these reasons, it has been my ardent wish to see a plan devised on a liberal scale, which would have a tendency to sprd systemactic ideas through all parts of this rising Empire, thereby to do away local attachments and State prejudices, as far as the nature of things would, or indeed ought to admit, from our National Councils. Looking anxiously forward to the accomplishment of so desirable an object as this is (in my estimation) my mind has not been able to contemplate any plan more likely to effect the measure than the establishment of a UNIVERSITY in a central part of the United States, to which the youth of fortune and talents from all parts thereof might be sent for the completion of their Education in all the branches of polite literature; in arts and Sciences, in acquiring knowledge in the principles of Politics & good Government; and (as a matter of infinite Importance in my judgment) by associating with each other, and forming friendships in Juvenile years, be enabled to free themselves in a proper degree from those local prejudices & habitual jealousies which have just been mentioned; and which, when carried to excess, are never failing sources of disquietude to the Public mind, and pregnant of mischievous consequences to this Country: Under these impressions, so fully dilated,

Item   I give and bequeath in perpetuity the fifty shares

which I hold in the Potomac Company (under the aforesaid Acts of the Legislature of Virginia) towards the endowment of a UNIVERSITY to be established within the limits of the District of Columbia, under the auspices of the General Government, if that government should incline to extend a fostering hand towards it; and until such Seminary is established, and the funds arising on these shares shall be required for its support, my further Will & desire is that the profit accruing therefrom shall, whenever the dividends are made, be laid out in purchasing Stock in the Bank of Columbia, or some other Bank, at the discretion of my Executors; or by the Treasurer of the United States for the time being under the direction of Congress; provided that Honourable body should Patronize the measure, and the Dividends proceeding from the purchase of such Stock is to be vested in more stock, and so on, until a sum adequate to the accomplishment of the object is obtained, of which I have not the smallest doubt, before many years passes away; even if no aid or encouraged is given by Legislative authority, or from any other source.

Item   The hundred shares which I held in the James River Company, I have given, and now confirm in perpetuity to, and for the use & benefit of Liberty-Hall Academy, in the County of Rockbridge, in the Commonwealth of Virga.

Item   I release exonerate and discharge, the Estate of my deceased brother Samuel Washington, from the payment of the money which is due to me for the Land I sold to Philip Pendleton (lying in the County of Berkeley) who assigned the same to him the said Samuel; who, by agreement was to pay me therefor. And whereas by some contract (the purport of which was never communicated to me) between the said Samuel and his son Thornton Washington, the latter became possessed of the aforesaid Land, without any conveyance having passed from me, either to the said Pendleton, the said Samuel, or the said Thornton, and without any consideration having been made, by which neglect neither the legal nor equitable title has been alienated; it rests therefore with me to declare my intentions concerning the Premises—and these are, to give & bequeath the said land to whomsoever the said Thornton Washington (who is also dead) devised the same; or to his heirs forever if he died Intestate: Exonerating the estate of the said

Thornton, equally with that of the said Samuel from payment of the purchase money; which, with Interest; agreeably to the original contract with the said Pendleton, would amount to more than a thousand pounds. And whereas two other Sons of my said deceased brother Samuel—namely, George Steptoe Washington and Lawrence Augustine Washington, were, by the decease of those to whose care they were committed, brought under my protection, and in conseqe have occasioned advances on my part for their Education at College, and other Schools, for their board—cloathing—and other incidental expences, to the amount of near five thousand dollars over and above the Sums furnished by their Estate wch Sum may be inconvenient for them, or their fathers Estate to refund. I do for these reasons acquit them, and the said estate, from the payment thereof. My intention being, that all accounts between them and me, and their fathers estate and me shall stand balanced.

Item   The balance due to me from the Estate of Bartholomew Dandridge deceased (my wife's brother) and which amounted on the first day of October 1795 to four hundred and twenty five pounds (as will appear by an account rendered by his deceased son John Dandridge, who was the acting Exr of his fathers Will) I release & acquit from the payment thereof. And the Negros, then thirty three in number) formerly belonging to the said estate, who were taken in execution—sold —and purchased in on my account in the year   and ever since have remained in the possession, and to the use of Mary, Widow of the said Bartholomew Dandridge, with their increase, it is my Will & desire shall continue, & be in her possession, without paying hire, or making compensation for the same for the time past or to come, during her natural life; at the expiration of which, I direct that all of them who are forty years old & upwards, shall receive their freedom; all under that age and above sixteen, shall serve seven years and no longer; and all under sixteen years, shall serve until they are twenty five years of age, and then be free. And to avoid disputes respecting the ages of any of these Negros, they are to be taken to the Court of the County in which they reside, and the judgment thereof, in this relation shall be final; and a record thereof made; which may be adduced as evidence at any time thereafter, if disputes should arise concerning the same. And I further direct, that the heirs of the said Bartholomew Dandridge shall, equally, share the benefits arising from the services of the said negros according to the tenor of this devise, upon the decease of their Mother.

Item If Charles Carter who intermarried with my niece Betty Lewis is not sufficiently secured in the title to the lots he had of me in the Town of Fredericksburgh, it is my will & desire that my Executors shall make such conveyances of them as the Law requires, to render it perfect.

Item To my Nephew William Augustine Washington and his heirs (if he should conceive them to be objects worth prosecuting) and to his heirs, a lot in the Town of Manchester (opposite to Richmond) No. 265—drawn on my sole account, and also the tenth of one or two, hundred acre lots, and two or three half acre lots in the City, and vicinity of Richmond, drawn in partnership with nine others, all in the lottery of the deceased William Byrd are given—as is also a lot which I purchased of John Hood, conveyed by William Willie and Samuel Gordon Trustees of the said John Hood, numbered 139 in the Town of Edinburgh, in the County of Prince George, State of Virginia.

Item To my Nephew Bushrod Washington, I give and bequeath all the Papers in my possession, which relate to my Civel and Military Administration of the affairs of this Country; I leave to him also, such of my private Papers as are worth preserving; and at the decease of wife, and before—if she is not inclined to retain them, I give and bequeath my library of Books and Pamphlets of every kind.

Item Having sold Lands which I possessed in the State of Pennsylvania, and part of a tract held in equal right with George Clinton, late Governor of New York, in the State of New York; my share of land, & interest, in the Great Dismal Swamp, and a tract of land which I owned in the County of Gloucester; withholding the legal titles thereto, until the consideration money should be paid. And having moreover leased, & conditionally sold (as will appear by the tenor of the said leases) all my lands upon the Great Kanhawa, and a tract upon Difficult Run, in the county of Loudoun, it is my Will and direction, that whensoever the Contracts are fully, & respectively complied with, according to the spirit; true intent & meaning thereof, on the part of the purchasers, their heirs or Assigns, that then, and in that case, Conveyances are to be made, agreeably to the terms of the said Contracts; and the money arising therefrom, when paid, to be vested in Bank stock; the dividends whereof, as of that also wch is already vested therein, is to inure to my said Wife during her life—but the Stock itself is to remain, & be subject to the general distribution hereafter directed.

Item   To the Earl of Buchan I recommit "the box made of the Oak that sheltered the Great Sir William Wallace after the battle of Falkirk" presented to me by his Lordship, in terms too flattering for me to repeat, with a request "to pass it, on the event of my decease, to the man in my country, who should appear to merit it best, upon the same conditions that have induced him to send it to me." Whether easy, or not, to select *the man* who might comport with his Lordships opinion in this respect, is not for me to say; but conceiving that no disposition of this valuable curiosity can be more eligable than the re-commitment of it to his own Cabinet, agreeably to the original design of the Goldsmiths Company of Edenburgh, who presented it to him, and at his request, consented that is should be transferred to me; I do give & bequeath the same to his Lordship, and in case of his decease, to his heir with my grateful thanks for the distinguished honour of presenting it to me; and more especially for the favourable sentiments with which he accompanied it.

Item   To my brother Charles Washington I give & bequeath the gold headed Cane left me by Doctr Franklin in his Will. I add nothing to it, because of the ample provision I have made for his Issue. To the acquaintances and friends of my Juvenile years, Lawrence Washington & Robert Washington of Chotanck, I give my other two gold headed Canes, having my Arms engraved on them; and to each (as they will be useful where they live) I leave one of the Spy-glasses which constituted part of my equipage during the late War. To my compatriot in arms, and old & intimate friend Doctr Craik, I give my Bureau (or as the Cabinet makers call it, Tambour Secretary) and the circular chair—an appendage of my Study. To Doctor David Stuart I give my large shaving & dressing Table, and my

Telescope. To the Reverend, now Bryan, Lord Fairfax, I give a
Bible in three large folio volumes, with notes, presented to me
by the Right reverend Thomas Wilson, Bishop of Sodor &
Man. To General de la Fayette I give a pair of finely wrought
steel Pistols, taken from the enemy in the Revolutionary War.
To my Sisters in law Hannah Washington & Mildred Washington; to my friends Eleanor Stuart, Hannah Washington of
Fairfield, and Elizabeth Washington of Hayfield, I give, each, a
mourning Ring of the value of one hundred dollars. These
bequests are not made for the intrinsic value of them, but as
mementos of my esteem & regard. To Tobias Lear, I give the
use of the Farm which he now holds, in virtue of a Lease from
me to him and his deceased wife (for and during their natural
lives) free from Rent, during his life; at the expiration of which,
it is to be disposed as is hereinafter directed. To Sally B. Haynie
(a distant relation of mine) I give and bequeath three hundred
dollars. To Sarah Green daughter of the deceased Thomas
Bishop, & to Ann Walker daughter of Jno. Alton, also deceased, I give, each—one hundred dollars, in consideration of
the attachment of their fathers to me; each of whom having
lived nearly forty years in my family. To each of my Nephews,
William Augustine Washington, George Lewis, George Steptoe Washington, Bushrod Washington and Samuel Washington, I give one of the Swords or Cutteaux of which I may die
possessed; and they are to chuse in the order they are named.
These Swords are accompanied with an injunction not to un-
sheath them for the purpose of shedding blood, except it be
for self defence, or in defence of their Country and its rights;
and in the latter case, to keep them unsheathed, and prefer
falling with them in their hands, to the relinquishment thereof.

*   *   *   *

In witness of all, and of each of the things herein contained,
I have set my hand and Seal, this ninth day of July, in the year
One thousand seven hundred and ninety nine and of the Inde-
pendence of the United States the twenty fourth.

"LET THAT PARTY SET UP A BROOMSTICK,
AND CALL IT A TRUE SON OF LIBERTY . . .
AND IT COMMAND THEIR VOTES IN TOTO!"

To Jonathan Trumbull, Jr.

My dear Sir, Mount Vernon 21st July 1799

Your favour of the 22d Ulto got to my hands yesterday, *only*. It came safe, and without any apparent marks of violence; but whence the length of its passage, I am unable to inform you.

To you, and to your brother Colo. Jno. Trumbull, I feel much indebted for the full, frank, and interesting communication of the political sentiments contained in both your letters.

The project of the latter is vast—and under any circumstances would require very mature consideration; but in its extent, and an eye being had to the disorganizing Party in the United States, I am sure it would be impracticable in the present order of things.

Not being able to convey my ideas to you, on this subject, in more concise terms than I have already done to your brother, in answer to the letter he informs you he had written to me, I shall take the liberty of giving you an extract thereof—as follow.

"For the Political information contained in it (that is his letter) I feel grateful, as I always shall for the free, & unreserved communication of your sentiments upon subjects so important in their nature, and tendency. No well informed, and unprejudiced man, who has viewed with attention the conduct of the French Government since the Revolution in that Country, can mistake its objects, or the tendency of the ambitious projects it is pursuing. Yet, strange as it may seem, a party, and a powerful one too, among us, affect to believe that the measures of it are dictated by a principle of self preservation; that the outrages of which the Directory are guilty, proceed from dire necessity; that it wishes to be upon the most friendly & amicable terms with the United States; that it will be the fault of the latter if this is not the case; that the defensive measures which this Country have adopted, are not only unnecessary & expensive, but have a tendency to produce the evil which, to deprecate, is mere pretence in the Government; because War with France they say, is its wish; that on the Militia we shd rest our security; and that it is time enough to call upon these, when the danger is imminent, & apparent.

"With these, and such like ideas, attempted to be inculcated upon the public mind (aided by prejudices not yet eradicated) and with art, and Sophistry, which regard neither truth nor decency; attacking every character, without respect to persons —public or Private, who happen to differ from themselves in Politics, I leave you to decide on the probability of carrying such an extensive plan of defence as you have suggested in your last letter, into operation; and in the short period which you suppose may be allowed to accomplish it in."

I come now, my dear Sir, to pay particular attention to that part of Your Letter which respects myself.

I remember well, the conversation which you allude to, and have not forgot the answer I gave you. In my judgment it applies with as much force *now*, as *then*; nay more, because at that time the line between Parties was not so clearly drawn, and the views of the opposition, so clearly developed as they are at present; of course, allowing your observation (as it respects myself) to be founded, personal influence would be of no avail.

Let that party set up a broomstick, and call it a true son of Liberty, a Democrat, or give it any other epithet that will suit their purpose, and it will command their votes in toto! Will not the Federalists meet, or rather defend their cause, on the opposite ground? Surely they must, or they will discover a want of Policy, indicative of weakness, & pregnant of mischief; which cannot be admitted. Wherein then would lye the difference between the present Gentleman in Office, & myself?

It would be matter of sore regret to me, if I could believe that a serious thot was turned towards me as his successor; not only as it respects my ardent wishes to pass through the vale of life in retiremt, undisturbed in the remnant of the days I have to sojourn here, unless called upon to defend my Country (which every citizen is bound to do)—but on Public ground also; for although I have abundant cause to be thankful for the good health with whh I am blessed, yet I am not insensible to my declination in other respects. It would be criminal therefore in me, although it should be the wish of my Country men, and I could be elected, to accept an Office under this conviction, which another would discharge with more ability; and this too at a time when I am thoroughly convinced I should not draw a *single* vote from the Anti-federal side; and of course, should stand upon no stronger ground than any other Federal character well supported; & when I should become a mark for the shafts of envenomed malice, and the basest calumny to fire at; when I should be charged not only with irresolution, but with concealed ambition, which wants only an occasion to blaze out; and, in short, with dotage and imbicility.

All this I grant, ought to be like dust in the balance, when put in competition with a *great* public good, when the accomplishment of it is apparent. But as no problem is better defined in my mind than that principle, not men, is now, and will be, the object of contention; and that I could not obtain a *solitary* vote from that Party; that any other respectable Federal character would receive the same suffrages that I should; that at my time of life, (verging towards three score & ten) I should expose myself without rendering any essential service to my Country, or answering the end contemplated: Prudence on my part must arrest any attempt at the well meant, but mistaken views of my friends, to introduce me again into the Chair of Government.

Lengthy as this letter is, I cannot conclude it without expressing an *earnest* wish that, some intimate & confidential friend of the Presidents would give him to understand that, his long absence from the Seat of Government in the present critical conjuncture, affords matter for severe animadversion by the friends of government; who speak of it with much disappobation; while the other Party chuckle at and set it down as a favourable omen for themselves. It has been suggested to me to make this Communication, but I have declined it, conceiving that it would be better received from a private character—more in the habits of social intercourse and friendship. With the most sincere friendship, and Affectionate regard, I am always, Your Obedient Servant

ON THE ESTABLISHMENT OF
A MILITARY ACADEMY

To Alexander Hamilton

Sir,   Mount Vernon, December 12th 1799.
    I have duly received your letter of the 28th ultimo, enclosing
a Copy of what you had written to the Secretary of War, on the
subject of a Military Academy.

    The Establishment of an Institution of this kind, upon a re-
spectable and extensive basis, has ever been considered by me
as an Object of primary importance to this Country; and while
I was in the Chair of Government, I omitted no proper opportunity of recommending it, in my public Speeches, and
otherways, to the attention of the Legislature: But I never undertook to go into a *detail* of the organization of such an Academy; leaving this task to others, whose pursuits in the paths of
Science, and attention to the Arrangements of such Institutions, had better qualified them for the execution of it.

    For the same reason I must now decline making any obser-
vations on the details of your plan; and as it has already been
submitted to the Secretary of War, through whom it would
naturally be laid before Congress, it might be too late for alterations, if any should be suggested.

    I sincerely hope that the subject will meet with due atten-
tion, and that the reasons for its establishment, which you have
so clearly pointed out in your letter to the Secretary, will prevail
upon the Legislature to place it upon a permanent and respectable footing. With very great esteem & regard I am, Sir, Your
most Obedt Servt

THE LAST LETTER

To James Anderson

Mr Anderson,   Mount Vernon 13th Decr 1799

I did not know that you were here yesterday morning until I had mounted my horse, otherwise I should have given you what I now send.

As Mr Rawlins was going to the Union Farm, to lay off the Clover lots, I sent by him the Duplicate for that Farm to his brother—and as I was going to River Farm myself, I carried a copy for that Farm to Dowdal—Both of them have been directed to consider them attentively, & to be prepared to give you their ideas of the mode of arrangeing the Work when they are called upon.

Such a Pen as I saw yesterday at Union Farm, would, if the Cattle were kept in it one Week, destroy the whole of them. They would be infinitely more comfortable in this, or any other weather, in the open fields—Dogue run Farm Pen may be in the same condition—It did not occur to me as I passed through the yard of the Barn to look into it. I am Your friend &ca

CHRONOLOGY

NOTE ON THE TEXTS

NOTES

INDEX

.

Chronology

1732 Born February 22 (February 11, Old Style) on plantation on Potomac River between Bridges Creek and Popes Creek in Westmoreland County, Virginia, first child of Mary Ball and Augustine Washington. (Great-grandfather John Washington immigrated to Virginia from England in 1657. Father, born 1694, married Jane Butler in 1715; they had three surviving children—Lawrence, Augustine, and Jane —before her death in 1729. In 1731 father married Mary Ball, born c. 1708.) Father is a planter, land speculator, part owner of an ironworks located near Fredericksburg, Virginia, and county justice of the peace.

1733 Sister Betty born.

1734 Brother Samuel born.

1735 Half sister Jane dies. Family moves to Epsewasson, plantation on the Potomac near Little Hunting Creek in Stafford County (Fairfax County after 1742).

1736 Brother John Augustine born.

1738 Brother Charles born.

1739 Family moves to Ferry Farm on Rappahannock River in King George County, near Fredericksburg. Washington begins schooling. Sister Mildred born.

1740 Half brother Lawrence (born c. 1718) serves as officer with Virginia troops in the Caribbean during unsuccessful British attempt to capture Cartagena from the Spanish. Sister Mildred dies.

1743 Father dies on April 12, leaving estate of 10,000 acres and 50 slaves. Largest portion is bequeathed to Lawrence; at age 21, Washington is to receive 260-acre Ferry Farm, four other tracts of land, and ten slaves. On July 19 Lawrence marries Ann Fairfax, daughter of William Fairfax, cousin and land agent of Thomas, Lord Fairfax, proprietor of the Northern Neck, a tract of over five million acres in northern Virginia.

1744–45   Lives with mother at Ferry Farm, with half brother Augustine at Westmoreland County plantation, and with Lawrence at Mount Vernon (Epsewasson plantation, now renamed in honor of Admiral Edward Vernon, commander of the Cartagena expedition). Lawrence becomes Washington's mentor and introduces him to the influential Fairfax family, whose house, Belvoir, is four miles from Mount Vernon. Washington studies mathematics, surveying, and geography along with legal forms and accounting methods used in plantation business.

1746–47   Considers joining the Royal Navy, but mother's opposition forces him to abandon the idea. Becomes proficient surveyor. Ends formal education.

1748   Joins George William Fairfax, son of William Fairfax, on surveying expedition of Fairfax lands in the Shenandoah Valley, March–April. Meets frontier settlers and Indians.

1749   With help from Fairfax family, Washington becomes surveyor of Culpeper County on July 20 (holds position until summer of 1750). Performs over 190 professional surveys between July 1749 and October 1752, mostly of Fairfax lands in the Shenandoah Valley.

1750   Buys total of 1,459 acres in Shenandoah Valley, first of many western land acquisitions.

1751   Sails to Barbados in September with Lawrence, who is suffering from chronic lung illness (probably tuberculosis). Arrives in November and is stricken with smallpox, but recovers by early December and gains lifelong immunity to the disease, a major cause of death in 18th-century army camps. Leaves Barbados in late December.

1752   Returns to Virginia in January. Lawrence Washington dies at Mount Vernon July 26, leaving the bulk of his estate to his wife, Ann, and infant daughter, Sarah. Washington joins Fredericksburg Masonic Lodge. On November 6 Virginia Council appoints him adjutant of militia for the Southern District, with rank of major.

1753   Volunteers to carry ultimatum demanding French withdrawal from the Ohio Valley from Lieutenant Governor Robert Dinwiddie (the highest-ranking British official residing in Virginia) to the commander of the French forces in the Valley. Receives orders from Dinwiddie to assess

French strength and intentions and confer with leaders of the Iroquois Six Nations. Leaves Williamsburg on October 31 and travels to the Forks of the Ohio (now Pittsburgh). Meets with Iroquois chiefs at Logstown on the Ohio, then goes to Fort Le Boeuf, French outpost near shore of Lake Erie. Delivers ultimatum on December 12 to Le Gardeur de Saint-Pierre, French commander in the Ohio Valley, who declines to comply. Begins return to Williamsburg on December 16.

1754   Reaches Williamsburg on January 16. Writes account of his journey, published in Williamsburg as *The Journal of Major George Washington* and reprinted in Maryland and Massachusetts newspapers and in London as a pamphlet. Commissioned lieutenant colonel of militia and adjutant of the Northern Neck District. Ordered to occupy Forks of the Ohio; sets out from Winchester on April 18 with force of 160 men. Learns that the French have seized the Forks of the Ohio. Surprises and defeats small French force on May 28 near present-day Uniontown, Pennsylvania, in first skirmish of what becomes the French and Indian War (1754–1763). Among the ten French dead is Ensign de Jumonville, the force's commander; although captured survivors insist de Jumonville was on a diplomatic mission to deliver ultimatum demanding British evacuation of Ohio country, Washington informs Dinwiddie that French were engaged in a military reconnaissance. Writes in letter to brother John Augustine: "I heard Bullets whistle and believe me there was something charming in the sound." (When letter is printed in the London press, George II reportedly remarks: "He would not say so, if he had been used to hear many.") Builds Fort Necessity at Great Meadows, Pennsylvania. French and Indians attack fort on July 3; after several hours of fighting, Washington surrenders on terms allowing the garrison to withdraw to Virginia. Signs capitulation document written in French, which he cannot read, containing admission that de Jumonville had been "assassinated." (French capture Washington's diary of the 1754 campaign; it is published in France in 1756 and in England and the colonies in 1757, though Washington will dispute the accuracy of the printed English text.) Returns to Williamsburg on July 17. Resigns commission in October rather than accept reduction in rank to captain brought about by Dinwiddie's reorganization of the Virginia militia.

Leases Mount Vernon from Ann Fairfax Lee, Lawrence's widow (now remarried), on December 17.

1755   Volunteers in spring to serve as aide, without rank or pay, to General Edward Braddock, commander in chief of British forces in North America. Despite severe attacks of illness (probably dysentery), accompanies expedition of British regulars and colonial militia against Fort Duquesne at the Forks of the Ohio. On July 9 Braddock's advance force of 1,450 men is attacked and defeated by 900 French and Indians after crossing the Monongahela seven miles from the fort. Although two horses are shot from under him and four bullets pierce his clothing, Washington is not wounded during the battle and helps command the withdrawal of surviving troops after Braddock is mortally wounded. Buries Braddock in secret grave along the retreat route on July 14. Commissioned as colonel and commander of the Virginia Regiment on August 14 with orders to defend frontier, left exposed to attack by Braddock's defeat and the withdrawal of surviving British regulars to Pennsylvania. Entered as candidate in December election for seat in House of Burgesses from Frederick County, possibly without his knowledge, but is defeated.

1756   Travels to Boston in February to confer with Massachusetts governor William Shirley, the acting British commander in chief in North America. Seeks royal commissions for himself and his officers and resolution of disputes concerning seniority of royal and colonial commissions. Returns to Virginia in March without royal commission. Struggles to defend 350 miles of frontier with inadequate resources and undisciplined militiamen.

1757   Travels to Philadelphia in February to see Lord Loudoun, new British commander in chief. Advocates mounting a new expedition against Fort Duquesne and unsuccessfully seeks royal commission. Returns to Virginia in April. Defeated again in election for House of Burgesses from Frederick County. Forced by severe dysentery to return to Mount Vernon in November for prolonged convalescence.

1758   Returns to active duty in March. Proposes marriage to Martha Dandridge Custis (b. 1731), wealthy widow of Daniel Parke Custis and mother of two young children, John Parke Custis (b. 1754) and Martha Parke Custis (b. 1756). Elected to House of Burgesses from Frederick

County on July 24 (will be reelected through 1774, after 1765 from Fairfax, his home county). Commands Virginia troops in expedition against Fort Duquesne led by British brigadier John Forbes. Argues with Forbes over route expedition should use in advance to the Forks of the Ohio. Writes love letter to Sally Cary Fairfax, wife of his friend George William Fairfax. Nearly killed on November 12 when two lines of Virginia troops mistakenly exchange musket fire. British and colonial forces occupy Forks of the Ohio on November 25 after French burn and abandon Fort Duquesne. Resigns commission in December.

1759 Marries Martha Custis on January 6; Custis estate includes thousands of acres and hundreds of slaves. Attends his first session of Virginia Assembly in Williamsburg. Expands Mount Vernon estate, buying more land and slaves and enlarging mansion house; imports luxury goods from England. Orders books on agriculture and farm management. Engages in active social life, visiting and entertaining neighbors; enjoys riding, shooting, fox-hunting, and playing cards.

1761 Inherits Mount Vernon after death of Ann Fairfax Lee, Lawrence's widow (Lawrence's daughter Sarah had died in 1754).

1762 Becomes vestryman of Anglican church for Truro Parish.

1763 French and Indian War ends with Britain in possession of Canada but burdened with heavy war debt. Washington joins company of investors in plan to drain Great Dismal Swamp on Virginia–North Carolina border.

1764–67 Washington's debt to British merchants increases due to high spending on imported goods and continued difficulty in growing tobacco profitably in poor Mount Vernon soil. Plants more wheat and corn and experiments with growing hemp and flax. Makes wheat his main crop in 1767 and stops planting tobacco on his Potomac farms, though he continues to receive tobacco from tenants as rent. Stamp Act, passed by British Parliament in 1765, is repealed in 1766 after meeting with widespread colonial resistance, but in 1767 Parliament passes Townshend Acts, levying new taxes on the American colonies.

1768 Stepdaughter suffers first in series of epileptic seizures.

Washington becomes a justice of the Fairfax County Court.

1769   Joins in growing colonial opposition to the Townshend Acts. Writes privately to neighbor George Mason that he would use arms as a last resort to defend American freedom. Mason drafts plan for boycott of imported British goods which Washington circulates among members of the Assembly in Williamsburg. Washington votes for resolutions asserting rights of Virginia colonists, including the right of self-taxation. When Governor Botetourt responds by dissolving the Assembly on May 17, delegates hold extralegal session in tavern. Washington serves on committee that drafts Nonimportation Association, which is adopted by majority of the burgesses on May 18. (Parliament repeals Townshend Acts, except for tax on tea, in 1770, and Virginia Association is dissolved in 1771.) Enlarges frontier land holdings by patenting land in western Pennsylvania and by campaigning for fulfillment of proclamation promising 200,000 acres of bounty land in Ohio Valley to members of the Virginia Regiment who participated in the 1754 campaign against the French. Takes leading role in securing fulfillment of proclamation and directs selection, surveying, and division of land among eligible officers and men. Receives 15,000 acres as a field officer; buys up rights of others (will gain title by 1773 to 24,000 acres on Ohio and Kanawha rivers in western Virginia).

1770   Joins Maryland attorney Thomas Johnson in promoting plan for improving navigation on the upper Potomac. Travels in the autumn by canoe down the Ohio from Pittsburgh to the mouth of the Kanawha River in search of land to claim under proclamation of 1754.

1771   Opens commercial flour mill at Mount Vernon; other plantation ventures designed to reduce debt owed to British merchants include weaving and commercial fishing.

1772   Has portrait painted by Charles Willson Peale at Mount Vernon in May; poses wearing uniform of colonel of the Virginia Regiment.

1773   Travels to New York City in May to enroll stepson John Parke Custis at King's College (now Columbia University). Stepdaughter Martha Parke Custis dies during epileptic seizure on June 19. Martha Washington inherits £8,000 from her daughter's share of Custis estate, which Washington uses to pay British debts.

1774   Learns while attending Assembly in May that Parliament has closed Boston harbor in retaliation for the Boston Tea Party. Votes for resolution calling for day of prayer and fasting to protest Boston Port Act. After Governor Dunmore responds by dissolving the Assembly on May 26, joins other delegates in adopting resolution calling for the appointment of delegates to a "general congress" of "the several Colonies of British America." Presides at Fairfax County meeting on July 18 that adopts "Fairfax Resolves," influential series of resolutions drafted by George Mason asserting colonial right of self-government and calling for a boycott of British trade. Attends Virginia Convention, extralegal session of Assembly held in Williamsburg, and is elected as one of seven Virginia delegates to the First Continental Congress. Travels to Philadelphia to attend Congress in September. Supports measures adopted by the Congress, including resolution declaring that colonial legislatures have an "exclusive power of legislation . . . in all cases of taxation and internal policy" in the colonies; a boycott of British imports; and a call for delegates to be elected to a Second Continental Congress. Returns to Mount Vernon at the end of October.

1775   Elected as one of seven Virginia delegates to Second Continental Congress at Virginia Convention, held in Richmond March 20–27. Revolutionary War begins with fighting between Massachusetts militia and British army at Lexington and Concord, April 19. New England forces besiege British in Boston. Washington is chosen as field commander of five independent Virginia militia companies. Leaves Mount Vernon for Philadelphia on May 4 (will not see his home again until 1781). Attends sessions of Congress in Philadelphia wearing buff and blue militia uniform. Congress creates Continental Army on June 14; seeking to unite colonies by appointing a southerner to command predominately New England army, Massachusetts delegate John Adams nominates Washington to be commander in chief. Receives unanimous vote of Congress on June 15 and accepts commission on June 16; declines salary but asks for reimbursement of expenses. Takes command of Continental Army, numbering about 14,000 men, at Cambridge, Massachusetts, on July 3. Works to equip, train, and reorganize army; is dismayed by lack of discipline among New England troops and inability of their elected officers to exercise authority. Dispatches 1,000 men under command of Benedict Arnold to join with American forces in northern New York in attack on Quebec (invasion of Canada ends in American defeat in June 1776). Martha Washington arrives in Cambridge on December 11 (she will continue to share winter quarters with Washington throughout the war). Enlistments of most Continental soldiers expire in December; although many reenlist, strength of army falls to 10,000 men by end of year.

1776   Washington becomes convinced by British policy and by reading Thomas Paine's pamphlet *Common Sense* that American independence is inevitable. Holds council of war on February 16 and proposes launching assault on Boston, but abandons plan when it is unanimously opposed by his generals. Moves artillery brought from Fort Ticonderoga onto Dorchester Heights overlooking the city on March 4. British evacuate Boston on March 17 and sail to Nova Scotia. Washington marches Continental Army to New York City in April in anticipation of British attack. British fleet anchors off New York on June 29 and begins landing troops on Staten Island on July 3. Washington orders Declaration of Independence read to entire army on July 9. By mid-August Washington has 19,000 inexperienced Continental soldiers and state militia under his command at New York, facing 32,000 regular troops under command of General William Howe (the largest expeditionary force in British history). British begin landing at western end of Long Island, August 22, and defeat Americans in battle of Long Island, August 27. Washington withdraws army from Brooklyn Heights to Manhattan on August 30. Howe lands troops at Kip's Bay on east side of Manhattan on September 15, forcing Americans to retreat northward to Harlem Heights. Washington evacuates Harlem Heights on October 18 and moves army to White Plains. British attack at White Plains, October 28, forcing Americans to withdraw several miles further north. Washington divides Continental Army between New Jersey and New York banks of Hudson River and considers evacuating Fort Washington, remaining American outpost in Manhattan. British capture Fort Washington and take 2,800 prisoners on November 16, then cross Hudson on November 20 and force evacuation of Fort Lee. Washington retreats Continental Army across New Jersey and crosses Delaware River into Pennsylvania on December 8. Fears army will dissolve when enlistments of most soldiers expire at end of year. Howe abandons attempts to capture Philadelphia and disperses his army into garrisons across New Jersey. Washington leads 2,400 men across Delaware on night of December 25 and defeats Hessian garrison at Trenton, New Jersey, on morning of December 26, capturing over 900 prisoners. On December 27 Congress grants Washington extraordinary powers for six-month period, including authority to raise troops, appoint officers, requisition supplies, and arrest disloyal persons.

1777   Orders attack on British force at Princeton, New Jersey, on January 3; during battle Washington rides within 30 yards of the enemy line while leading successful assault. Victories at Trenton and Princeton strengthen American morale. Continental Army goes into winter quarters at Morristown, New Jersey, on January 6. Howe evacuates most British garrisons from New Jersey and takes his army into winter quarters in New York City. Washington pardons New Jersey citizens who swore loyalty to the crown during British advance in late 1776 on condition that they now declare allegiance to the United States. Alexander Hamilton joins Washington's military "family" (staff) in March and becomes trusted aide. By late May army at Morristown numbers 9,000 men, now equipped with arms covertly supplied by France. British and American armies maneuver inconclusively in New Jersey during June. Howe decides to attack Philadelphia rather than move up Hudson Valley to meet British army advancing south from Canada and sails from New York with 18,000 men on July 23. British begin disembarking at Head of Elk, Maryland, on August 25 as Washington moves to defend Philadelphia. British defeat Continental Army at Brandywine Creek, Pennsylvania, September 11, and occupy Philadelphia on September 26 as Congress flees to York, Pennsylvania. Washington attacks British at Germantown, Pennsylvania, on October 4 but is forced to retreat after initial success. After series of defeats, General John Burgoyne surrenders army of 5,700 men to Americans under General Horatio Gates at Saratoga, New York, on October 17, ending British attempt to split New England off from other colonies by seizing Hudson Valley.

Washington becomes alarmed by rumors of "Conway Cabal," alleged plot by General Thomas Conway to have Gates replace him as commander of the Continental Army. Congress submits proposed Articles of Confederation to states for ratification on November 15 (ratification is not completed until March 1, 1781). Washington takes army into winter quarters at Valley Forge, Pennsylvania, on December 21.

1778 Appeals to Congress for money and supplies as army suffers through winter at Valley Forge. France and the United States sign treaties of alliance and commerce in Paris on February 6; under their terms, France recognizes the independence of the United States and pledges to fight until American independence is won if the treaties lead to war between France and Britain. (News of French alliance reaches Washington at Valley Forge on May 3.) Washington wins renewed support of leaders in Congress; has army trained and drilled by Friedrich Steuben, a former Prussian officer. Sir Henry Clinton replaces Howe as British commander in chief in May. Anticipating arrival of French fleet in Delaware Bay, Clinton evacuates Philadelphia on June 18 and begins withdrawing army to New York City. Washington attacks British at Monmouth Court House, New Jersey, on June 28; battle is intense but inconclusive, and British complete march to New York. Continental Army moves to White Plains. French fleet with expeditionary force of 4,000 men under Comte d'Estaing arrives off Delaware Bay on July 8. Combined French and American attack on Newport, Rhode Island, in August fails, in part due to poor coordination between d'Estaing and American commander, General John Sullivan; failure causes mistrust between new allies. French fleet sails for West Indies on November 11. Washington establishes winter headquarters at Middlebrook, New Jersey, on December 11. British capture Savannah, Georgia, on December 29.

1779 Continues to appeal to Congress for support of army. Discouraged by desertion, rapid depreciation of Continental currency, corruption, and failure to sustain army with new enlistments ("too many melancholy proofs of the decay of public virtue"). Spain concludes alliance with France and declares war on Britain on June 21, but does not recognize American independence. Washington orders daring night attack led by General Anthony Wayne that recaptures Stony Point, New York, and takes 500 British prisoners on July 16, raising American morale and halting attempt by Clinton to extend British outposts up the Hudson Valley. Principal armies in north remain largely inactive through campaigning season while fighting continues in Georgia and South Carolina. Washington dispatches strong force under Sullivan on punitive mission against the Six Nations, British allies who have been raiding frontier settlements; expedition burns dozens of Iroquois villages in central New York. Takes army into winter quarters at Morristown, New Jersey, on December 1. Leaving garrison of 10,000 men to hold New York City, Clinton sails for South Carolina with army of 8,500 on December 26.

1780   Massachusetts troops at West Point briefly mutiny over terms of enlistment, January 1. Army at Morristown suffers from severe cold and hunger. Clinton captures Charleston, South Carolina, with over 5,000 prisoners on May 12, inflicting worst American defeat of Revolutionary War. Connecticut troops at Morristown mutiny over pay and rations, May 25, but are persuaded to return to duty. Clinton returns to New York in June, leaving behind 8,000 men under Lord Charles Cornwallis to continue campaign in the South. French expeditionary force of 5,500 men under Comte de Rochambeau lands at Newport, Rhode Island, on July 10. Cornwallis routs American army in South commanded by General Horatio Gates at Camden, South Carolina, on August 16. Washington meets with Rochambeau at Hartford, Connecticut, September 20, to discuss strategy; conference is inconclusive. Discovers treachery of General Benedict Arnold on September 25 while inspecting West Point, New York, key Hudson River fortress that Arnold has been conspiring to surrender to the British (Arnold escapes). Appoints General Nathanael Greene to succeed Gates as American commander in the South and advises him on strategy (Greene will successfully command troops in the Carolinas during 1781 campaign). Establishes winter headquarters at New Windsor, New York.

1781   Over 2,000 Pennsylvania soldiers at Morristown mutiny on January 1 and begin marching on Philadelphia. Mutiny ends January 8 after Congress makes concessions regarding pay and terms of enlistments. When New Jersey troops at Pompton mutiny on January 20, Washington sends troops from West Point to suppress mutiny by force; two ringleaders are summarily executed by firing squad on January 27. Cornwallis begins major campaign in Virginia on May 20. Washington and Rochambeau meet at Wethersfield, Connecticut, May 21–22, to plan attack on New York City. Clinton orders Cornwallis to establish strong base on Chesapeake Bay, and Cornwallis occupies Yorktown, Virginia, on August 2. American and French armies are concentrated outside New York when news arrives on August 14 that powerful French fleet under Admiral de Grasse is on its way from the West Indies to Chesapeake Bay. Washington perceives opportunity "to strike the enemy in the most vulnerable quarter" and orders march on Virginia while feinting attack on Staten Island. Directs rapid movement of more than 7,000 men, with stores and equipment, over 450 miles by land and water to Yorktown. (While traveling south with Rochambeau, Washington stops at Mount Vernon for three days in September, his first visit home since 1775.) French victory in naval battle of Chesapeake Capes on September 5 deprives Cornwallis of hope of reinforcement or evacuation by sea. Washington begins siege of Yorktown on September 30, commanding army of 9,000 American and 7,800 French soldiers. Cornwallis asks for terms on October 17; his army of 7,250 men marches out and surrenders on October 19. Cornwallis declines to attend surrender ceremony and sends a subordinate; Washington declines to accept subordinate's sword. Yorktown surrender ends British hopes of winning decisive military victory in America and brings an end to major fighting in the Revolutionary War. Stepson John Parke Custis joins staff during Yorktown siege; stricken with "camp fever," he dies November 5, leaving a widow and four young children (the two youngest will be raised by the Washingtons at Mount Vernon). Travels to Philadelphia to confer with Congress, arriving on November 26; remains for four months, while Continental Army goes into winter quarters at Newburgh, New York.

1782   Rejoins Continental Army at Newburgh on March 31. British open peace negotiations with Americans in April. Washington is outraged by May 22 letter from Colonel Lewis Nicola recommending that the army overthrow Congress and establish military rule with Washington serving as king. Orders Nicola never to speak of scheme again.

American peace commissioners in Paris sign preliminary treaty with Britain on November 30.

1783   Britain, France, and Spain sign preliminary peace treaty on January 20. Anonymous papers circulated among officers at Newburgh, March 10–12, condemn Congress and exhort officers to rebel if their demands for pay are not met (discontented officers may have been working in collusion with Congressional proponents of stronger national government). Washington fears officers are "wavering on a tremendous precipice" above "a gulph of Civil horror" that threatens to "deluge our rising Empire in Blood." In dramatic meeting of March 15, wins over officers, who declare subordination to civil authority. Sets April 19, eighth anniversary of battles of Lexington and Concord, as official date for end of hostilities. Sends lengthy farewell address to state governors and legislatures on June 8, announcing intention to retire and calling for "indissoluble Union of the States under one federal Head." Elected president of Society of the Cincinnati, a fraternal organization of former Continental and French officers, on June 19. Final peace treaty is signed in Paris on September 3. British evacuate New York on November 25, and Washington leads army into city later that day. Bids emotional farewell to his officers on December 4. In carefully arranged ceremony, appears before Congress in Annapolis, Maryland, on December 23 and declares that he will never again hold public office, then hands over commission as commander in chief given him in Philadelphia in June 1775. Returns to Mount Vernon as a private citizen on December 24.

1784   Finds Mount Vernon run down after his eight-year absence. Persuaded by Thomas Jefferson and others that Society of the Cincinnati, with hereditary membership suggestive of European aristocracy, has anti-republican tendencies. Attends general meeting of the Society in May and urges abolition of hereditary membership; thereafter tries to distance himself from the organization. Revives project of improving Potomac navigation. Travels across Alleghenies in September to inspect his western lands and scout route for canals and roads designed to link tributaries of the Ohio with the Potomac.

1785   Serves as host for conference held at Mount Vernon, March 25–28, by commissioners appointed by Virginia and

Maryland legislatures to resolve disputes regarding trade and navigation of common waterways. (Success of Mount Vernon conference leads to call for a general meeting of the states to discuss interstate trade.) Named president on May 17 of Potomac Navigation Company, chartered by Virginia and Maryland to build canal and road system joining Potomac and Ohio. Advocates opening of navigation as means to bind Ohio Valley settlements politically to United States. Begins correspondence with leading English agronomists, hires English agricultural workers, and imports seeds, plants, agricultural equipment, and livestock, including a Spanish jackass used to breed mules.

1786   Conducts census of 216 slaves living on Mount Vernon farms in February; about half belong to him, others to Custis estates. Declares privately that it is "among my first wishes to see some plan adopted, by which slavery in this country may be abolished by slow, sure, and imperceptible degrees." Grows increasingly concerned that weakness of Congress, state rivalries, and local unrest may sink American experiment in republican self-government into anarchy or despotism. Annapolis Convention meets September 11–14 to continue negotiations on interstate trade; delegates approve resolution calling for meeting of representatives from all states in Philadelphia on May 14, 1787, "to devise such further provisions as shall appear to them necessary to render the constitution of the Federal Government adequate to the exigencies of the Union." Washington is dismayed by reports of "Shays' Rebellion," outbreak of civil unrest by debt-burdened farmers in Massachusetts. Initially declines election by Virginia legislature on December 4 as delegate to Philadelphia convention, believing acceptance would violate 1783 pledge not to hold public office; is also wary of expending prestige on a potentially unsuccessful attempt to establish stronger national government.

1787   Urged by James Madison and Virginia governor Edmund Randolph to attend convention. Reluctantly agrees on March 28 to join Virginia delegation. Arrives in Philadelphia May 13. Unanimously elected president of the convention when quorum is reached on May 25. As presiding officer, does not take part in debates, but exerts influence by his presence (South Carolina delegate Pierce Butler later writes: "many of the members cast their eyes towards

General Washington as President; and shaped their Ideas of the Powers to be given to a President, by their opinions of his Virtue"). During recess from July 26 to August 6, goes fishing and visits site of Continental Army's wartime encampment at Valley Forge. Observes local agricultural practices, poses for portraits, and visits William Bartram's botanical garden and Charles Willson Peale's museum. Convention votes September 15 to adopt Constitution. Document is presented for signing on September 17, final day of the convention. When three delegates propose changing apportionment of the House of Representatives so that the number of representatives not exceed one for every 30,000 persons instead of the 40,000 previously agreed upon, Washington speaks in debate for the first time, supporting the change in the hope that it will remove a possible objection to the Constitution. Change is adopted without opposition, and convention votes to deposit its official records in Washington's custody. Constitution is then signed by 39 delegates and forwarded to Congress and the states. Washington returns home on September 22. Closely follows ratification struggle from Mount Vernon (ratification by nine states is necessary to put Constitution into effect). Constitution is ratified in Delaware, December 7; Pennsylvania, December 12; New Jersey, December 18; and Georgia, December 31.

1788 Ratification is approved in Connecticut, January 9; Massachusetts, February 6; Maryland, April 26; and South Carolina, May 23. New Hampshire becomes ninth state to ratify, June 21, and is followed by key states of Virginia, June 27, and New York, July 26, ensuring that Constitution will go into effect. Washington remains reluctant to return to public life, but indicates in private correspondence that he would accept election to the presidency. Faced with chronic shortage of cash, tries unsuccessfully to sell or rent his Ohio lands.

1789 Presidential electors meet on February 4 and vote for two candidates in balloting for president. Washington receives votes from all 69 electors and is unanimously elected president; John Adams, with 34 votes, is elected vice-president. First Federal Congress achieves quorum in New York City on April 6, and electoral votes are officially counted. Washington is notified of his election at Mount Vernon on April 14. Borrows £600 to pay debts and for trip to New York.

Greeted with pageantry and public acclaim along route. Takes oath of office at Federal Hall in New York on April 30. Offers to serve without pay, but Congress approves presidential salary of $25,000 a year. Lives in lavish style in rented New York mansion, staging elaborate weekly receptions criticized by some as monarchical in tone. Stricken in June with painful carbuncle on left leg, accompanied by high fever; recovers slowly after abscess is incised. Appears in person before the Senate on August 22 and August 24 to seek its "advice and consent" on treaty negotiations with Creek Indians; finds experience frustrating, and never again appears before the Senate to seek its advice (a precedent followed by all subsequent presidents). Mother Mary Ball Washington dies, August 25. Congress creates executive departments of State, War, and Treasury, and Washington appoints Alexander Hamilton as secretary of the treasury, Henry Knox as secretary of war, and Thomas Jefferson as secretary of state. Judiciary Act, creating federal court system and office of the attorney general, becomes law on September 24; Senate confirms appointments of Chief Justice John Jay, five associate Supreme Court justices, and Attorney General Edmund Randolph on September 26. Washington makes presidential tour of Connecticut, Massachusetts, and New Hampshire in October and November.

1790   Delivers first annual message to Congress on January 8. Hamilton submits report on public credit to Congress on January 14. Plan provides for funding of national debt of $54 million dollars through taxes and new borrowing, and for federal assumption of $25 million of debt incurred by the states during the Revolutionary War. James Madison leads successful opposition in the House to federal assumption of state debts, arguing that it unfairly discriminates against states, such as Virginia, that have already paid much of their war debt. Washington falls seriously ill with pneumonia in May; predicts after his recovery that another serious illness will kill him. Jefferson, Hamilton, and Madison agree in late June that in exchange for southern support of the assumption measure, northern members of Congress will support moving the capital to Philadelphia for ten years and then permanently establishing it along the Potomac in 1800. In November Washington arrives in Philadelphia, where the house of wealthy financier Robert

Morris has been rented as presidential mansion. Hamilton submits plan to Congress on December 14 calling for chartering a national bank.

1791 Washington chooses ten-mile square area on the Potomac near Mount Vernon as site for national capital (new city is officially named "Washington" in September). Bank bill passes Congress but is opposed as unconstitutional by Madison, who urges Washington to veto it. Unsure of its constitutionality, Washington asks Randolph, Jefferson, and Hamilton for advisory opinions. Jefferson and Randolph also oppose measure as unconstitutional, but after reading Hamilton's opinion, Washington signs bill into law on February 25. Makes presidential tour of Virginia, North Carolina, South Carolina, and Georgia, April–June. Sends expedition under General Arthur St. Clair against hostile Indians in the Northwest Territory, and cautions him against being taken by surprise. Angered when St. Clair's army is routed in surprise attack on November 4 and suffers over 900 casualties. (Indians resisting American settlement in the Northwest are supplied and encouraged by the British, who continue to occupy forts in territory ceded to the United States in the 1783 peace treaty.) Washington begins meeting with Jefferson, Hamilton, Knox, and Randolph to discuss policy (term "cabinet" comes into use by 1793).

1792 Uses presidential veto power for the first time, April 5, disapproving a bill apportioning representatives on the grounds that it unconstitutionally gives some states more than one representative for every 30,000 persons; Congress sustains veto. (Washington believes veto should be used only against legislation president considers unconstitutional.) Appoints General Anthony Wayne to replace St. Clair as military commander on the Northwest frontier. Tired of public life and certain that age is diminishing his powers, intends to retire when term ends in 1793. Prepares draft of farewell address and on May 20 asks Madison to put it in final form. Madison, Jefferson, Randolph, Hamilton, Knox, and others urge him to serve another term. Dismayed by deepening personal bitterness between Hamilton and Jefferson and growing discord within the cabinet, Congress, and press as two political parties emerge—Federalists, who support Hamilton and his fiscal policies, and Republicans, whose leadership includes Jefferson and Madison. Attempts unsuccessfully to reconcile Hamilton and Jefferson. Persuaded that he must remain in office, does not announce intention to retire. Receives votes of all 132 presidential electors on December 5 and is unanimously reelected; Adams receives 77 votes and is reelected vice-president.

1793   Inaugurated for second term on March 4. When news that France has declared war on Britain arrives in April, holds cabinet meetings at which Hamilton and Jefferson disagree over proper response. Issues proclamation of neutrality on April 22 while maintaining 1778 treaty of alliance with France (action establishes important precedent regarding presidential power to make foreign policy decisions without consulting Congress). Controversy regarding relations with France increases bitterness between Republicans, who sympathize with revolutionary French republic, and Federalists, many of whom admire British constitutional monarchy. Becomes alarmed by enthusiastic public reception given to Edmond Genêt, new French minister to the United States, and rise of Democratic Societies formed by supporters of France. Refuses to allow outfitting of French privateers in American ports and asks French government to recall Genêt (will later grant Genêt asylum in the United States during the Jacobin terror). Growing repugnance for slavery results in plan to rent Mount Vernon to capable farmers and then free his slaves, who could stay on as hired hands. Searches without success for suitable tenants. Jefferson resigns as secretary of state December 31.

1794   Names Edmund Randolph secretary of state, January 2; William Bradford becomes attorney general. Resists demands for commercial retaliation against Britain in response to British seizures of American ships trading with the French West Indies. Appoints Chief Justice John Jay, a leading New York Federalist, as special envoy to Britain on April 16 in effort to avert Anglo-American war. Wayne defeats Indian coalition at Battle of Fallen Timbers on August 20 (Indians will be forced to yield much of Ohio territory in 1795 treaty). Farmers in western Pennsylvania violently resist collection of federal excise tax on distilled spirits adopted in 1791 as part of Hamilton's plan for funding the national debt. Washington issues proclamation on August 7 calling for the insurgents to disperse and summoning 15,000 militia into service, then issues a second proclamation on September 25, calling for suppression of the insurrection.

"Whiskey Rebellion" collapses without further bloodshed when Washington leads 12,000 troops into region in October (later pardons two men convicted of treason for their role in disorders). Creates controversy by accusing Democratic Societies of having fomented Whiskey Rebellion. Finds buyer for Pennsylvania frontier land (will realize $50,000 from sales of western tracts over next five years).

1795   Appoints Timothy Pickering as secretary of war and Oliver Wolcott, Jr., as secretary of the treasury after Knox and Hamilton resign in January; Hamilton continues to serve as his principal adviser. Receives on March 7 text of treaty signed by Jay in London on November 19, 1794. Treaty provides for evacuation of British garrisons from frontier posts in the Northwest but contains few British concessions regarding neutral maritime rights or terms of Anglo-American commerce. Senate ratifies treaty on June 24 after secret debate. Treaty is published on July 1 and is furiously attacked for failing to secure American rights. Despite his serious misgivings about its terms, Washington signs treaty on August 18. Forces Randolph to resign on August 19 after intercepted French diplomatic dispatch causes him to suspect Randolph of having solicited a bribe from the French. Names Pickering as secretary of state and James McHenry as secretary of war, making cabinet entirely Federalist. Appoints Charles Lee as attorney general after death of Bradford.

1796   Submits for Senate ratification treaty with Spain granting right of Mississippi River navigation to Americans; Senate ratifies treaty on March 3. House of Representatives votes on March 24 to request secret papers relating to Jay Treaty. Washington replies on March 30, withholding the papers on the grounds that the House has no constitutional role in ratifying treaties and asserting an executive right to maintain the confidentiality of diplomatic correspondence. After an intense debate, House narrowly votes on April 30 to appropriate money for implementation of Jay Treaty. Distressed by continuing attacks on his character and competence in the Republican press. Drafts farewell address and sends it to Hamilton in May for his revision. Makes public decision to retire on September 19, when farewell address is published in *American Daily Advertiser*, a Philadelphia newspaper. Delivers last annual message to Congress on December 7. In the presidential election,

Federalist candidate John Adams receives 71 electoral votes and is elected president, while Jefferson, the Republican candidate, receives 68 electoral votes and becomes vice-president.

1797   Adams is inaugurated on March 4. Washington returns to Mount Vernon on March 15, gratefully taking up routine on his farms. Allows some of his household slaves to remain behind in Philadelphia, thereby giving them their freedom. Finds mansion house at Mount Vernon in need of repair. Plans new building "for the accomadation & security of my Military, Civil & private Papers." Continues revision of his French and Indian War correspondence, a task he had begun in the 1780s.

1798   Congress votes to expand army as relations with France worsen. President Adams commissions Washington as lieutenant general and commander in chief of the army on July 4. Washington insists on naming Hamilton as his second-in-command, and Adams reluctantly agrees. Travels to Philadelphia in November to direct planning of new army; returns to Mount Vernon on December 19.

1799   Supports diplomatic initiative by Adams that splits Federalist party but succeeds in preventing a full-scale war with France. Dismisses renewed suggestions that he seek third term. Drafts lengthy will in July, with detailed provisions for emancipating his slaves after Martha's death. Stipulates that his heirs provide pensions for freed slaves who are aged or infirm, and that freed slave children without parents capable of caring for them be apprenticed, taught to read and write, and "be brought up to some useful occupation" in accordance with the Virginia laws for poor white children and orphans. In schedule of property appended to will, inventories his 50,000 acres and calculates net worth at $530,000. Chilled by rain and snow during customary five-hour horseback inspection of Mount Vernon farms on December 12. Stricken with suffocating respiratory infection in early morning hours of December 14, and is treated by three physicians, who administer copious bleedings. Attended by Martha and his secretary Tobias Lear, dies while taking his own pulse sometime after 10 P.M. on the night of December 14. Buried in family vault at Mount Vernon on December 18.

Note on the Texts

Drawn from *George Washington: Writings* (John Rhodehamel, editor), volume 91 in the Library of America series, this Library of America Paperback Classic presents the texts of 169 documents—official and private letters, military orders, addresses, proclamations, memoranda, and diary entries—that were written by George Washington, or written at his direction, between 1754 and 1799. Most of these documents were not written for publication, and almost all of them existed only in manuscript form at the time of Washington's death in 1799.

For over forty years Washington carefully attended to the organization, copying, and preservation of his papers. He began making copies of his outgoing correspondence in letter books while serving as a Virginia military officer during the French and Indian War in the 1750s and continued keeping letter-book copies of both personal and business letters while living at Mount Vernon in the 1760s and early 1770s. As commander of the Continental Army, Washington wrote many letters in his own hand, but he also used the secretaries and aides who served in his military "family," including Joseph Reed, Thomas Mifflin, Robert Hanson Harrison, Tench Tilghman, Alexander Hamilton, John Laurens, and Jonathan Trumbull, Jr., to help him conduct his official correspondence. Typically Washington would give a written memorandum or an oral directive to an aide regarding the particular letter or order to be written. The aide would then prepare a draft, which Washington would review and often revise. A fair copy would be made for Washington's signature and then sent, and the revised draft would be retained at headquarters as a copy; in cases where no changes were made to the draft, it was often signed and sent after a copy was made from it. (At the beginning of the war a separate letter-book copy was often made in addition to the retained draft, but in 1776 this procedure became increasingly impracticable and fell into disuse.) In 1781–83 Washington ordered Lieutenant Colonel Richard Varick to arrange the records at Continental Army headquarters systematically; while doing so, Varick had a new transcription made of Washington's wartime correspondence, which eventually filled forty-four volumes. Thus there are often three extant forms of a Washington letter sent between 1775 and 1783: the signed copy sent to the recipient; the draft retained at Continental Army headquarters; and the copy made for the Varick transcripts. (In some cases there is also a contemporary letter-book copy and in a few instances, such as letters received by the Continental Congress, a copy made by the recipient.)

At the close of the Revolutionary War Washington moved his Continental Army papers into the office wing at Mount Vernon. Sometime during the 1780s, possibly in 1786–87, he began to make revisions in letter-book copies of the letters and orders he wrote during the French and Indian War, apparently intending to improve their clarity and diction. Washington appears not to have finished making these revisions until after his retirement from the presidency in 1797; once done, he then had the revised texts copied, possibly by his nephew Lawrence Lewis, into a new set of letter books. Only two of the original letter books from the French and Indian War, covering March 2–August 14, 1755, and June 14–September 12, 1758, are known to be extant.

During his presidency Washington continued to have copies of his correspondence and official papers recorded in letter books. At times he would ask his advisers, including Alexander Hamilton and, in his first term, James Madison and Thomas Jefferson, for assistance in drafting official papers. In his will Washington bequeathed his official and private papers to his nephew, Supreme Court justice Bushrod Washington. After Bushrod Washington's death in 1829, possession of the papers passed to Bushrod's nephew and heir, George Corbin Washington, who sold them in two lots to the United States government in 1834 and 1849 for the sum of $45,000. In 1903 the Washington papers were moved from the custody of the Department of State to the Library of Congress.

Three major editions of Washington's writings have appeared: *The Writings of George Washington*, edited by Jared Sparks (12 volumes, 1833–37); *The Writings of George Washington*, edited by Worthington Chauncey Ford (14 volumes, 1889–93); and *The Writings of George Washington from the Original Manuscript Sources, 1745–1799*, edited by John C. Fitzpatrick (39 volumes, 1931–44). A fourth edition, *The Papers of George Washington*, edited by W. W. Abbot, Dorothy Twohig, and others, is ongoing, with sixty-two volumes having been published since 1976, all of which are also available in an online digital edition. When this edition is complete it will be the most comprehensive edition so far.

Sparks began work on his edition in 1827 with the cooperation of Bushrod Washington and eventually included approximately 2,500 documents in it. He freely revised texts, correcting spelling and grammar, altering phrasing, omitting material he thought inconsequential, and in some instances rewriting passages. During the several years in which Sparks had custody of the Washington papers, he also mutilated or dispersed many manuscripts in order to produce souvenir autographs. Much of this material has not been subsequently located and either has never been printed or has been printed only in the form in which it appeared in the Sparks edition. Worthington Chauncey Ford exercised greater editorial restraint in preparing his edition, but he added only about 500 documents to those already published by Sparks.

The most complete edition to date is *The Writings of George Washington from the Original Manuscript Sources, 1745–1799*, edited by John C. Fitzpatrick of the Library of Congress and published under the auspices of the United States George Washington Bicentennial Commission. It contains the texts of some 17,000 Washington documents, mostly taken from the Washington papers in the Library of Congress, although in some cases Fitzpatrick was able to use the recipient's copy of a Washington letter as his text. In presenting these documents, Fitzpatrick frequently altered punctuation and paragraphing and in some instances regularized spelling, often by spelling out words that Washington had written in contracted form (e.g., printing "about" for "abt"). Fitzpatrick also printed in abbreviated form the formal closings Washington habitually used in his correspondence; for example, the closing "I have the honor to be With great respect & esteem Your Excellency's Most Obedt Humble Servt" appears in the Fitzpatrick edition as "I have the honor etc."

In 1969 work began on *The Papers of George Washington*, a new edition sponsored by the Mount Vernon Ladies' Association of the Union and the University of Virginia and published by the University Press of Virginia. The editors of *The Papers of George Washington* initiated a worldwide search for manuscript material, including both documents sent by and received by Washington, and have located, catalogued, and transcribed over 100,000 documents. Under the editorship of W. W. Abbot, Donald Jackson, Dorothy Twohig, and others, publication of *The Papers of George Washington* has proceeded in six series, of which two are still ongoing: *The Diaries of George Washington* (6 vols., 1976–79), *Colonial Series* (10 vols., 1983–95), *Revolutionary War Series* (20 vols. to date, 1985–2010), *Confederation Series* (6 vols., 1992–97), *Presidential Series* (16 vols. to date, 1987–2011), and *Retirement Series* (4 vols., 1998–99). All of these series are collected in *The Papers of George Washington Digital Edition* (http://gwpapers.virginia.edu/index.html). Whenever possible, *The Papers of George Washington* prints the recipient's copy of a Washington letter. Documents are transcribed and printed without alteration in their spelling, capitalization, paragraphing, and punctuation, except for the omission of dashes in instances where a dash appears together with another mark of punctuation.

The present volume prints 125 documents from *The Papers of George Washington*, its preferred source of texts. The texts for another six documents not yet included in *The Papers of George Washington* are drawn from *The Papers of Alexander Hamilton*, a modern edition that, like the on-going Virginia edition, presents texts with fewer editorial alterations than are present in the Fitzpatrick edition. The remaining thirty-eight documents are taken from the Fitzpatrick edition.

This volume presents texts as they appeared in these sources, but with a few alterations in editorial procedure. Bracketed editorial conjectural readings in the source texts, in cases where the original manuscript was damaged or difficult to read, are accepted without brackets in this volume when that reading seems to be the only possible one; but when it does not, or when the editor has made no conjecture, the missing words are indicated by a bracketed space, i.e., [ ]. Where the editors of a source text use a bracketed space to indicate a space left blank in the manuscript, this volume uses a blank two-em space without brackets. Bracketed editorial insertions used in the source texts to expand contractions, abbreviations, or place names have been deleted in this volume. The editorial *sic* used in the Fitzpatrick edition after repeated words has been omitted in this volume and the indicated correction accepted. In his edition, Fitzpatrick also used brackets to indicate which portions of a document were in Washington's handwriting, as opposed to that of an aide or secretary; this volume omits the brackets. In cases where the draft of a letter in Washington's handwriting contains alternate wordings supplied by an aide seeking to improve Washington's diction, Fitzpatrick printed the aide's emendations within brackets. This volume does not print these emendations and presents Washington's original version as its text. *The Papers of George Washington* presents documents from the French and Indian War letter book covering the period March 2–August 14, 1755, in texts in which material deleted by Washington while making his revisions in the 1780s and 1790s is printed with lines through it, and material added by Washington during his revisions is printed in the form of interlinear interpolations. This volume prints the deleted words without cancellations and omits the revisions printed as interpolations, presenting a clear text of the document as it was written by Washington in 1755.

The following is a list of the documents included in this volume, in the order of their appearance, giving the source of each text. The most common sources are indicated by these abbreviations:

Writings	*The Writings of George Washington from the Origi-nal Manuscript Sources, 1745–1799*, edited by John C. Fitzpatrick (39 vols., Washington: United States Government Printing Office, 1931–44).
PGW: *Diaries*	*The Diaries of George Washington* (6 vols., Charlottesville: University Press of Virginia, 1976–79). Volume I, edited by Donald Jackson (1976); Volume III, edited by Donald Jackson (1978), Volume V, edited by Donald Jackson and Dorothy Twohig (1979). Copyright © 1976, 1978, 1979 by the Rectors and Visitors of the University of Virginia. Reprinted courtesy of the University Press of Virginia.
PGW: *Colonial*	*The Papers of George Washington: Colonial Series*, vols. 1–6, edited by W. W. Abbot, vols. 7–9, edited by W. W. Abbot and Dorothy Twohig, vol. 10, edited by Beverly H. Runge (10 vols., Charlottesville: University Press of Virginia, 1983–95). Volumes 1, 2 (1983), Volumes 3, 4 (1984), Volumes 5, 6 (1988), Volume 7 (1990), Volume 8 (1993), Volume 9 (1994), Volume 10 (1995). Copyright © 1983, 1984, 1988, 1990, 1993, 1994, 1995 by the Rectors and Visitors of the University of Virginia. Reprinted courtesy of the University Press of Virginia.
PGW: *Revolutionary*	*The Papers of George Washington: Revolutionary War Series*, vols. 1–5, 7, 9, 17 edited by Philander D. Chase, vol. 6, edited by Philander D. Chase and Frank E. Grizzard, Jr., vols. 8, 10 edited by Frank E. Grizzard, Jr., vol. 11, edited by Philander D. Chase and Edward G. Lengel, vol. 12, edited by Frank E. Grizzard, Jr. and David R. Hoth, vols. 13, 15, 18, 20, edited by Edward G. Lengel, vols. 14, 16, edited by David R. Hoth, vol. 19, edited by Philander D. Chase and William M. Ferraro (20 vols. to date, Charlottesville: University Press of Virginia, 1985–2010). Volume 1 (1985), Volume 2 (1987), Volume 3 (1988), Volume 4 (1991), Volume 5 (1993), Volume 6 (1994), Volume 7 (1997), Volume 8 (1998), Volume 9 (1999), Volume 10 (2000), Volume 11 (2001), Volume 12 (2002), Volume 13 (2003), Volume 14 (2004), Volumes 15, 16 (2006), Volumes 17, 18 (2008), Volume 19 (2009), Volume 20 (2010). Copyright © 1985, 1987, 1988, 1991, 1993, 1994, 1997, 1998, 1999, 2000, 2001,

2002, 2003, 2004, 2006, 2008, 2009, 2010 by the Rectors and Visitors of the University of Virginia. Reprinted courtesy of the University Press of Virginia.

PGW:
Confederation

The Papers of George Washington: Confederation Series, edited by W. W. Abbot (6 vols., Charlottesville: University Press of Virginia, 1992–97). Volumes 1, 2 (1992), Volume 3 (1994), Volume 4 (1995), Volumes 5, 6 (1997). Copyright © 1992, 1994, 1995, 1997 by the Rectors and Visitors of the University of Virginia. Reprinted courtesy of the University Press of Virginia.

PGW:
Presidential

The Papers of George Washington: Presidential Series, vols. 1–4, edited by Dorothy Twohig, vol. 5, edited by Dorothy Twohig, Mark A. Mastromarino, and Jack D. Warren, vols. 6, 8, edited by Mark A. Mastromarino, vol. 7, edited by Jack D. Warren, Jr., vol. 9, edited by Mark A. Mastromarino and Jack D. Warren, vol. 10, edited by Robert F. Haggard and Mark A. Mastromarino, vols. 11, 13, 15, edited by Christine S. Patrick, vol. 12, edited by Christine S. Patrick and John C. Pinheiro, vol. 14, edited by David R. Hoth, vol. 16, edited by David R. Hoth and Carol S. Ebel (16 vols. to date, Charlottesville: University Press of Virginia, 1987–2011). Volumes 1, 2 (1987), Volume 3 (1989), Volume 4 (1993), Volumes 5, 6 (1996), Volume 7 (1998), Volume 8 (1999), Volume 9 (2000), Volumes 10, 11 (2002), Volume 12 (2005), Volume 13 (2007), Volume 14 (2008), Volume 15 (2009), Volume 16 (2011). Copyright © 1987, 1989, 1993, 1996, 1998, 1999, 2000, 2002, 2005, 2007, 2008, 2009, 2011 by the Rectors and Visitors of the University of Virginia. Reprinted courtesy of the University Press of Virginia.

PGW:
Retirement

The Papers of George Washington: Retirement Series, vols. 1–4, edited by W. W. Abbot (4 vols., Charlottesville: University Press of Virginia, 1998–99). Volumes 1, 2 (1998), Volumes 3, 4 (1999). Copyright © 1998, 1999 by the Rectors and Visitors of the University of Virginia. Reprinted courtesy of the University Press of Virginia.

PGW: Digital	*The Papers of George Washington Digital Edition.* Edited by Theodore J. Crackel (Charlottesville: University Press of Virginia, Rotunda 2007–). Copyright © 2008 by the Rector and Visitors of the University of Virginia. Printed with permission of the University Press of Virginia.
PAH	*The Papers of Alexander Hamilton* (27 vols., New York: Columbia University Press, 1961–81). Volume 3 (1962) edited by Harold C. Syrett and Jacob Ernest Cooke, Volume 18 (1973), Volume 20 (1974) edited by Harold C. Syrett. Copyright © 1962, 1973, 1974 by Columbia University Press. Reprinted with permission of the publisher.

Journey to the French Commandant, January 16–17, 1754. *PGW Diaries*, vol. 1, 130–60.

To Richard Corbin, January 28, 1754. *PGW: Colonial*, vol. 1, 70.

To Robert Dinwiddie, April 25, 1754. *PGW: Colonial*, vol. 1, 87–90.

To Robert Dinwiddie, May 18, 1754. *PGW: Colonial*, vol. 1, 98–100.

To Robert Dinwiddie, May 29, 1754. *PGW: Colonial*, vol. 1, 107–13.

To John Augustine Washington, May 31, 1754. *PGW: Colonial*, vol. 1, 118.

To John Augustine Washington, June 28–July 2, 1755. *PGW: Colonial*, vol. 1, 319–24.

To Robert Dinwiddie, July 18, 1755. *PGW: Colonial*, vol. 1, 339–40.

To John Augustine Washington, July 18, 1755. *PGW: Colonial*, vol. 1, 343.

To Robert Dinwiddie, October 11–14, 1755. *PGW: Colonial*, vol. 2, 101–7.

To Robert Dinwiddie, March 10, 1757. *PGW: Colonial*, vol. 4, 112–15.

Farewell Address to the Virginia Regiment, January 10, 1759. *PGW: Colonial*, vol. 6, 186–87.

To Robert Cary & Company, May 1, 1759. *PGW: Colonial*, vol. 6, 315–16.

Diary Entry, May 22, 1760. *PGW Diaries*, vol. 1, 283.

Reward for Runaway Slaves, August 11, 1761. *PGW: Colonial*, vol. 7, 65–66.

To Robert Cary & Company, September 20, 1765. *PGW: Colonial*, vol. 7, 398–402.

To Joseph Thompson, July 2, 1766. *PGW: Colonial*, vol. 7, 453–54.

To George Mason, April 5, 1769. *PGW: Colonial*, vol. 8, 177–80.

To Bryan Fairfax, July 4, 1774. *PGW: Colonial*, vol. 10, 109–10.

To Robert McKenzie, October 9, 1774. *PGW: Colonial*, vol. 10, 171–72.

To George William Fairfax, May 31, 1775. *PGW: Colonial*, vol. 10, 367–68.

Address to the Continental Congress, June 16, 1775. *PGW: Revolutionary*, vol. 1, 1.

To Martha Washington, June 18, 1775. *PGW: Revolutionary*, vol. 1, 3–5.

To John Augustine Washington, June 20, 1775. *PGW: Revolutionary*, vol. 1, 19–20.

To Martha Washington, June 23, 1775. *PGW: Revolutionary*, vol. 1, 27.

General Orders, July 4, 1775. *PGW: Revolutionary*, vol. 1, 54–56.

To Richard Henry Lee, July 10, 1775. *PGW: Revolutionary*, vol. 1, 98–100.

To Thomas Gage, August 11, 1775. *PGW: Revolutionary*, vol. 1, 289–90.

To Thomas Gage, August 19, 1775. *PGW: Revolutionary*, vol. 1, 326–27.

To Lund Washington, August 20, 1775. *PGW: Revolutionary*, vol. 1, 334–37.

To the Inhabitants of Canada, c. September 14, 1775. *PGW: Revolutionary*, vol. 1, 461–62.

To Benedict Arnold, December 5, 1775. *PGW: Revolutionary*, vol. 2, 493–94.

General Orders, January 1, 1776. *PGW: Revolutionary*, vol. 3, 1–3.

To Joseph Reed, January 4, 1776. *PGW: Revolutionary*, vol. 3, 23–25.

To John Hancock, February 9, 1776. *PGW: Revolutionary*, vol. 3, 274–76.

To Phillis Wheatley, February 28, 1776. *PGW: Revolutionary*, vol. 3, 387.

To John Hancock, March 19, 1776. *PGW: Revolutionary*, vol. 3, 489–91.

To John Augustine Washington, March 31, 1776. *PGW: Revolutionary*, vol. 3, 566–70.

General Orders, July 9, 1776. *PGW: Revolutionary*, vol. 5, 245–47.

To John Hancock, September 8, 1776. *PGW: Revolutionary*, vol. 6, 248–52.

To John Augustine Washington, November 6, 1776. *PGW: Revolutionary*, vol. 7, 102–5.

To John Hancock, December 5, 1776. *PGW: Revolutionary*, vol. 7, 262–64.

To John Hancock, December 27, 1776. *PGW: Revolutionary*, vol. 7, 454–56.

To the Executive Committee of the Continental Congress, January 1, 1777. *PGW: Digital* (*Revolutionary*, vol. 7). http://rotunda.upress.virginia.edu/founders/GEWN-03-07-02-0395.

To John Hancock, January 5, 1777. *PGW: Digital* (*Revolutionary*, vol. 7). http://rotunda.upress.virginia.edu/founders/GEWN-03-07-02-0411.

Proclamation Concerning Loyalists, January 25, 1777. *PGW: Digital* (*Revolutionary*, vol. 8). http://rotunda.upress.virginia.edu/founders/GEWN-03-08-02-0160.

To Benedict Arnold, April 2, 1777. *PGW: Digital* (*Revolutionary*, vol. 9). http://rotunda.upress.virginia.edu/founders/GEWN-03-09-02-0044.

To John Hancock, September 11, 1777. *PGW: Digital* (*Revolutionary*, vol. 11). http://rotunda.upress.virginia.edu/founders/GEWN-03-11-02-0190-0009.

To Richard Henry Lee, October 16, 1777. *PGW: Digital* (*Revolutionary*, vol. 11). http://rotunda.upress.virginia.edu/founders/GEWN-03-11-02-0538.

To John Augustine Washington, October 18, 1777. *PGW: Digital* (*Revolutionary*, vol. 11). http://rotunda.upress.virginia.edu/founders/GEWN-03-11-02-0561.

To Henry Laurens, December 23, 1777. *PGW: Digital* (*Revolutionary*, vol. 12). http://rotunda.upress.virginia.edu/founders/GEWN-03-12-02-0629.

To Henry Laurens, January 2, 1778. *PGW: Digital* (*Revolutionary*, vol. 13). http://rotunda.upress.virginia.edu/founders/GEWN-03-13-02-0100.

To Horatio Gates, January 4, 1778. *PGW: Digital* (*Revolutionary*, vol. 13). http://rotunda.upress.virginia.edu/founders/GEWN-03-13-02-0113.

To William Gordon, February 15, 1778. *PGW: Digital* (*Revolutionary*, vol. 13). http://rotunda.upress.virginia.edu/founders/GEWN-03-13-02-0459.

To Bryan Fairfax, March 1, 1778. *PGW: Digital* (*Revolutionary*, vol. 14). http://rotunda.upress.virginia.edu/founders/GEWN-03-14-02-0009.

To John Augustine Washington, May 1778. *PGW: Digital* (*Revolutionary*, vol. 15). http://rotunda.upress.virginia.edu/founders/GEWN-03-15-02-0296.

To Henry Laurens, July 1, 1778. *PGW: Digital* (*Revolutionary*, vol. 16). http://rotunda.upress.virginia.edu/founders/GEWN-03-16-02-0003.

To Thomas Nelson, Jr., August 20, 1778. *PGW: Digital* (*Revolutionary*, vol. 16). http://rotunda.upress.virginia.edu/founders/GEWN-03-16-02-0373.

To Gouverneur Morris, October 4, 1778. *PGW: Digital* (*Revolutionary*, vol. 17). http://rotunda.upress.virginia.edu/founders/GEWN-03-17-02-0265.

To Henry Laurens, November 14, 1778. *PGW: Digital* (*Revolutionary*, vol. 18). http://rotunda.upress.virginia.edu/founders/GEWN-03-18-02-0147.

To Lund Washington, February 24, 1779. *Writings*, vol. 14, 147–94.

To Henry Laurens, March 20, 1779. *Writings*, vol. 14, 263–64.

Speech to the Delaware Chiefs, May 12, 1779. *Writings*, vol. 15, 53–56.

To Marquis de Lafayette, September 30, 1779. *Writings*, vol. 16, 368–76.

To Robert Howe, November 20, 1779. *Writings*, vol. 17, 144–46.

To Benedict Arnold, August 3, 1780. *Writings*, vol. 19, 309–11.

To Samuel Huntington, September 26, 1780. *Writings*, vol. 20, 91–93.

Instructions to Spies Going into New York, c. September 1780. *Writings*, vol. 20, 104–5.

To John Cadwalader, October 5, 1780. *Writings*, vol. 20, 121–23.

To John Laurens, October 13, 1780. *Writings*, vol. 20, 172–74.

Circular to New England State Governments, January 5, 1781. *Writings*, vol. 21, 61–63.

To Robert Howe, January 22, 1781. *Writings*, vol. 21, 128–29.

General Orders, January 30, 1781. *Writings*, vol. 21, 158–60.

To Lund Washington, April 30, 1781. *Writings*, vol. 22, 14–15.

An excerpt from the Journal of the Yorktown Campaign, August 14–October 19, 1781. *PGW Diaries*, vol. 3, 409–33.

To Lewis Nicola, May 22, 1782. *Writings*, vol. 24, 272–73.

To Benjamin Lincoln, October 2, 1782. *Writings*, vol. 25, 226–29.

To Benjamin Franklin, October 18, 1782. *Writings*, vol. 25, 272–73.

To Nathanael Greene, February 6, 1783. *Writings*, vol. 26, 103–5.

To Lund Washington, February 12, 1783. *Writings*, vol. 26, 126–27.

To Alexander Hamilton, March 4, 1783. *PAH*, vol. 3, 277–79.

General Orders, March 11, 1783. *Writings*, vol. 26, 208–9.

To Alexander Hamilton, March 12, 1783. *PAH*, vol. 3, 286–88.

Speech to the Officers of the Army, March 15, 1783. *Writings*, vol. 26, 222–27.

To Nathanael Greene, March 31, 1783. *Writings*, vol. 26, 275.

To Alexander Hamilton, March 31, 1783. *PAH*, vol. 3, 309–11.

Circular to State Governments, June 8, 1783. *Writings*, vol. 26, 483–96.

To James Duane, September 7, 1783. *Writings*, vol. 27, 133–40.

Farewell Address to the Armies of the United States, November 2, 1783. *Writings*, vol. 27, 222–27.

Address to Congress on Resigning Commission, December 23, 1783. *Writings*, vol. 27, 284–85.

To Benjamin Harrison, January 18, 1784. *PGW: Confederation*, vol. 1, 56–57.

To Marquis de Lafayette, February 1, 1784. *PGW: Confederation*, vol. 1, 87–89.

To Tench Tilghman, March 24, 1784. *PGW: Confederation*, vol. 1, 232.

To Richard Henry Lee, December 14, 1784. *PGW: Confederation*, vol. 2, 181–3.

To William Gordon, December 20, 1784. *PGW: Confederation*, vol. 2, 196–97.

To Benjamin Harrison, January 22, 1785. *PGW: Confederation*, vol. 1, 282–84.

To David Humphreys, July 25, 1785. *PGW: Confederation*, vol. 3, 148–51.

To Robert Morris, April 12, 1786. *PGW: Confederation*, vol. 4, 15–16.

To John Jay, May 18, 1786. *PGW: Confederation*, vol. 4, 55–56.

To Thomas Jefferson, August 1, 1786. *PGW: Confederation*, vol. 4, 183–85.

To John Jay, August 15, 1786. *PGW: Confederation*, vol. 4, 212–13.

To James Madison, November 18, 1786. *PGW: Confederation*, vol. 4, 382–83.

To David Humphreys, December 26, 1786. *PGW: Confederation*, vol. 4, 477–80.

To Mary Ball Washington, February 15, 1787. *PGW: Confederation*, vol. 5, 33–36.

To Edmund Randolph, March 28, 1787. *PGW: Confederation*, vol. 5, 112–14.

To Alexander Hamilton, July 10, 1787. *PGW: Digital* (*Confederation*, vol. 5). http://rotunda.upress.virginia.edu/founders/GEWN-04-05-02-0236.

Diary Entry, September 17, 1787. *PGW Diaries*, vol. 5, 185.

To Henry Knox, October 15, 1787. *PGW: Confederation*, vol. 5, 375–76.

To Bushrod Washington, November 9, 1787. *PGW: Confederation*, vol. 5, 421–24.

To Marquis de Lafayette, April 28–May 1, 1788. *PGW: Digital* (*Confederation*, vol. 6). http://rotunda.upress.virginia.edu/founders/GEWN-04-06-02-0211.

To Marquis de Lafayette, June 18, 1788. *PGW: Digital* (*Confederation*, vol. 6). http://rotunda.upress.virginia.edu/founders/GEWN-04-06-02-0301.

To Richard Henderson, June 19, 1788. *PGW: Digital* (*Confederation*, vol. 6). http://rotunda.upress.virginia.edu/founders/GEWN-04-06-02-0304.

To Alexander Hamilton, August 28, 1788. *PGW: Digital* (*Confederation*, vol. 6). http://rotunda.upress.virginia.edu/founders/GEWN-04-06-02-0432.

To Alexander Hamilton, October 3, 1788. *PGW: Presidential*, vol. 1, 31–33.

To Marquis de Lafayette, January 29, 1789. *PGW: Presidential*, vol. 1, 262–64.

To Henry Knox, April 1, 1789. *PGW: Presidential*, vol. 2, 2.

Diary Entries, April 16 and 23, 1789. *PGW Diaries*, vol. 5, 445–47.

First Inaugural Address, April 30, 1789. *PGW: Presidential*, vol. 2, 173–77.

To James Madison, May 5, 1789. *PGW: Presidential*, vol. 2, 216–17.

To John Adams, May 10, 1789. *PGW: Presidential*, vol. 2, 245–47.

To Gouverneur Morris, October 13, 1789. *PGW: Presidential*, vol. 4, 176–79.

First Annual Message to Congress, January 8, 1790. *PGW: Presidential*, vol. 4, 543–46.

To Thomas Jefferson, January 21, 1790. *PGW: Presidential*, vol. 5, 29–31.

To David Stuart, March 28, 1790. *PGW: Presidential*, vol. 5, 286–87.

To the Hebrew Congregation in Newport, Rhode Island, August 18, 1790. *PGW: Presidential*, vol. 6, 284–86.

Second Annual Message to Congress, December 8, 1790. *PGW: Digital* (*Presidential*, vol. 7). http://rotunda.upress.virginia.edu/founders/GEWN-05 -07-02-0024.

To the Chiefs of the Seneca Nation, December 29, 1790. *PGW: Digital* (*Presidential*, vol. 7). http://rotunda.upress.virginia.edu/founders/GEWN-05 -07-02-0080.

To Marquis de Lafayette, July 28, 1791. *PGW: Digital* (*Presidential*, vol. 8). http://rotunda.upress.virginia.edu/founders/GEWN-05-08-02-0260.

To Jean Baptiste Ternant, September 24, 1791. *PGW: Digital* (*Presidential*, vol. 9). http://rotunda.upress.virginia.edu/founders/GEWN-05-09-02-0005.

To Gouverneur Morris, January 28, 1792. *PGW: Digital* (*Presidential*, vol. 9). http://rotunda.upress.virginia.edu/founders/GEWN-05-09-02-0303.

To James Madison, May 20, 1792. *PGW: Digital* (*Presidential*, vol. 10). http://rotunda.upress.virginia.edu/founders/GEWN-05-10-02-0260.

To Thomas Jefferson, July 17, 1792. *PGW: Digital* (*Presidential*, vol. 10). http://rotunda.upress.virginia.edu/founders/GEWN-05-10-02-0381.

To Alexander Hamilton, July 29, 1792. *PGW: Digital* (*Presidential*, vol. 10). http://rotunda.upress.virginia.edu/founders/GEWN-05-10-02-0401.

To Thomas Jefferson, August 23, 1792. *PGW: Digital* (*Presidential*, vol. 11). http://rotunda.upress.virginia.edu/founders/GEWN-05-11-02-0009.

To Alexander Hamilton, August 26, 1792. *PGW: Digital* (*Presidential*, vol. 11). http://rotunda.upress.virginia.edu/founders/GEWN-05-11-02-0015.

To Edmund Randolph, August 26, 1792. *PGW: Digital* (*Presidential*, vol. 11). http://rotunda.upress.virginia.edu/founders/GEWN-05-11-02-0018.

To John Francis Mercer, September 26, 1792. *PGW: Digital* (*Presidential*, vol. 11). http://rotunda.upress.virginia.edu/founders/GEWN-05-11-02-0083.

To Thomas Jefferson, October 18, 1792. *PGW: Digital* (*Presidential*, vol. 11). http://rotunda.upress.virginia.edu/founders/GEWN-05-11-02-0126.

Second Inaugural Address, March 4, 1793. *PGW: Digital* (*Presidential*, vol. 12). http://rotunda.upress.virginia.edu/founders/GEWN-05-12-02-0200.

To Gouverneur Morris, March 25, 1793. *PGW: Digital* (*Presidential*, vol. 12). http://rotunda.upress.virginia.edu/founders/GEWN-05-12-02-0302.

To Thomas Jefferson, April 12, 1793. *PGW: Digital* (*Presidential*, vol. 12). http://rotunda.upress.virginia.edu/founders/GEWN-05-12-02-0353.

To Henry Lee, July 21, 1793. *PGW: Digital* (*Presidential*, vol. 13). http://rotunda.upress.virginia.edu/founders/GEWN-05-13-02-0176.

To Edmund Pendleton, September 23, 1793. *PGW: Digital* (*Presidential*, vol. 14). http://rotunda.upress.virginia.edu/founders/GEWN-05-14-02-0084.

Fifth Annual Message to Congress, December 3, 1793. *PGW: Digital* (*Presidential*, vol. 14). http://rotunda.upress.virginia.edu/founders/GEWN-05 -14-02-0306.

To Charles Mynn Thruston, August 10, 1794. *Writings*, vol. 33, 464–66.

To Henry Lee, August 26, 1794. *Writings*, vol. 33, 474–79.

To John Jay, August 30, 1794. *Writings*, vol. 33, 483–85.

To Elizabeth Parke Custis, September 14, 1794. *Writings*, vol. 33, 500–1.

To Charles Carter, Jr., March 10, 1795. *Writings*, vol. 34, 139–40.

To Alexander Hamilton, July 3, 1795. *PAH*, vol. 18, 398–400.

To Patrick Henry, October 9, 1795. *Writings*, vol. 34, 334–35.

To the Cabinet, March 25, 1796. *Writings*, vol. 34, 505.

To the House of Representatives, March 30, 1796. *Writings*, vol. 35, 2–5.

To Alexander Hamilton, March 31, 1796. *PAH*, vol. 20, 103–5.

To Alexander Hamilton, June 26, 1796. *PAH*, vol. 20, 237–40.

To Thomas Jefferson, July 6, 1796. *Writings*, vol. 35, 118–2.

Farewell Address, September 19, 1796. *Writings*, vol. 35, 214–38.

To John Greenwood, January 20, 1797. *Writings*, vol. 35, 370–71.

To Jonathan Trumbull, Jr., March 3, 1797. *Writings*, vol. 35, 411–12.

To James McHenry, May 29, 1797. *PGW: Digital* (*Retirement*, vol. 1).
http://rotunda.upress.virginia.edu/founders/GEWN-06-01-02-0128.

To Lawrence Lewis, August 4, 1797. *PGW: Digital* (*Retirement*, vol. 1).
http://rotunda.upress.virginia.edu/founders/GEWN-06-01-02-0245.

To John Adams, July 13, 1798. *PGW: Digital* (*Retirement*, vol. 2).
http://rotunda.upress.virginia.edu/founders/GEWN-06-02-02-0314.

To John Adams, September 25, 1798. *PGW: Digital* (*Retirement*, vol. 3).
http://rotunda.upress.virginia.edu/founders/GEWN-06-03-02-0015.

To Alexander Spotswood, Jr., November 22, 1798. *PGW: Digital* (*Retirement*,
vol. 3). http://rotunda.upress.virginia.edu/founders/GEWN-06-03-02-
0157.

To Patrick Henry, January 15, 1799. *PGW: Digital* (*Retirement*, vol. 3).
http://rotunda.upress.virginia.edu/founders/GEWN-06-03-02-0225.

An excerpt from the Last Will and Testament, July 9, 1799. *PGW: Digital* (*Retirement*, vol. 4). http://rotunda.upress.virginia.edu/founders/GEWN-06-04
-02-0404-0001.

To Jonathan Trumbull, Jr., July 21, 1799. *PGW: Digital* (*Retirement*, vol. 4).
http://rotunda.upress.virginia.edu/founders/GEWN-06-04-02-0165.

To Alexander Hamilton, December 12, 1799. *PGW: Digital* (*Retirement*, vol.
4). http://rotunda.upress.virginia.edu/founders/GEWN-06-04-02-0402.

To James Anderson, December 13, 1799. *PGW: Digital* (*Retirement*, vol. 4).
http://rotunda.upress.virginia.edu/founders/GEWN-06-04-02-0403
-0001.

This volume presents the texts of the editions chosen as sources here but does not attempt to reproduce features of their typographic design. Some headings have been changed and George Washington's name at the end of the letters has been omitted. The texts are printed without alteration except for the changes previously discussed and for the correction of typographical errors. Spelling, punctuation, and capitalization were often used as expressive features in the eighteenth century, and they are not altered here, even when inconsistent or irregular. The following is a list of typographical errors corrected, cited by page and line number: 19.25, or our; 38.7, sumbitted; 81.5, porvide; 84.17, strenght; 117.11, Heard-Quarters,; 153.21, Brethen; 191.16, whole; 195.9, conincides; 214.8, (who; 257.22, willfind; 279.2, though; 300.20, frontrier; 339.5, for the the; 350.20, be to be; 357.23, was to; 365.29, strengthned; 365.36, patriotim; 368.27, foregin; 386.2, it so; 400.16, certain; 404.18, Bryd.

Notes

In the notes below, reference numbers denote page and line of this volume (the line count includes headings). Names and designations mentioned by Washington are identified only when they are essential to an understanding of the text; if not clear from context, notes are provided to identify each correspondent, his or her relation to Washington at the time of the correspondence, and, during his years of wartime service, the location from which Washington is writing. For further biographical background, references to other studies, and more detailed notes, see Ron Chernow, *Washington: A Life* (New York: The Penguin Press, 2010) and *The Papers of George Washington* (Charlottesville: University Press of Virginia), which is comprised of six series: *The Diaries of George Washington* (6 vols., 1976–79); *Colonial Series* (10 vols., 1983–95); *Revolutionary War Series* (20 vols. to date, 1985–2010); *Confederation Series* (6 vols., 1992–97); *Presidential Series* (16 vols. to date, 1987–2011); and *Retirement Series* (4 vols., 1998–99). All of these series are collected in *The Papers of George Washington Digital Edition* (http://gwpapers.virginia.edu/index.html).

xv. 32   "Indian walking Dress"]   See page 15, lines 28–29 in this volume.

xv.34–36   "a Constitution . . . severe tryals."]   24.25–27.

xvi.9–11   "I heard . . . sound."]   30.30–31.

xvi.11–12   "application . . . study"]   18.18.

xvi.14–15   "Insolence . . . of the Officers."]   38.30–31.

xvi.18–20   "We cant . . . to preferment"]   44.4–6.

xvii.2–3   "a Rogue & Runaway"]   55.26.

xvii.12   "direful attack"]   54.8.

xvii.14–15   "our lordly Masters . . . American freedom."]   56.15–17.

xvii.18–21   "that a Brother's . . . Sad alternative!"]   64.16–19.

xvii.31–32   "all Distinctions . . . animate the whole"]   69.35–70.1.

xvii.33–34   "profane cursing . . . drunkeness"]   70.12–13.

xviii.2   "an exceeding . . . people."]   78.1–2.

1.3   Commission'd] Washington's commission from Virginia Lieutenant Governor Robert Dinwiddie (1693–1770), dated Williamsburg, October 30, 1753, ordered him to deliver Dinwiddie's letter to the French commandant and wait no more than a week for an answer before returning to Virginia. The letter, dated the same day, declared all the Ohio country the "Property of the

Crown of Great Britain" and demanded the "peaceable Departure" of all French forces therein.

1.9   Jacob Vanbraam]   Dutch-born Jacob Van Braam (b. 1729) would later be responsible for the faulty translation of the Fort Necessity surrender document, July 3, 1754, in which Washington unwittingly admitted to having "assassinated" a French officer.

1.14   Mr. Gist]   Christopher Gist (c. 1706–59) made several early surveying explorations of the Ohio region.

1.23   the General's Death]   Montreal native Pierre Paul de la Malgue, sieur de Marin (1692–1753), was the leader of the French expedition into the Ohio that had aroused Dinwiddie's protest. He had died on October 29.

2.27   Half King]   English name for the Seneca leader Tanacharison. Allied with the British, he would also accompany Washington during the Fort Necessity campaign in 1754.

3.14   Black Islands]   A mistranslation of Illinois (as "Iles noires"), probably referring here to the Illinois River.

3.22   Obaish]   The Wabash River.

3.34   Venango]   A trading post located at the confluence of the Allegheny River and French Creek, near present-day Franklin, Pennsylvania.

4.14   Morail]   Montreal.

5.15   Lead was the Man]   A somewhat obscure construction that appears to refer to René-Robert Cavelier, sieur de La Salle (1643–87), who had explored the Ohio, Illinois, and Mississippi Valleys in search of a water passage to the east. He claimed the territory for Louis XIV, naming it Louisiana in his honor.

5.34   Goal]   Jail.

8.15   Joncaire]   Captain Philippe Thomas de Joncaire, sieur de Chabert (1707–c. 1766), captain of marines in the French army and an experienced Indian negotiator.

9.40   La Sol]   La Salle.

11.4   Commandant]   Canadian-born Jacques Legardeur, sieur de Saint-Pierre (1701–55), became commandant of the French forces in the Ohio country after the death of Marin.

12.2   Monsieur Riparti]   Louis Le Gardeur de Repentigny (1721–86), also a native of Canada, was a veteran of frontier conflict.

17.24   Belvoir]   Plantation of Colonel William Fairfax on the Potomac, four miles downstream from Mount Vernon. Washington's brother Lawrence had married William's daughter Ann in 1743, and Washington was close friends with Ann's brother George William and his wife Sally.

18.2   *Richard Corbin*] A member of the Virginia governor's council, Richard Corbin (1708–90) served as the colony's receiver general from 1754 to 1776.

18.4   Green Spring] Plantation of Philip Ludwell (1716–76), who, like Corbin, was a councilor active in the management of Virginia's frontier.

18.27   Forks of the Monongehele] The Forks of the Ohio, where the Allegheny and Monongahela come together to form the Ohio River. The French seized the forks on April 17, 1754, and built Fort Duquesne on the site. It fell to the British in November 1758 and was renamed Fort Pitt. Now Pittsburgh, Pennsylvania.

20.11   Connotaucarious] Meaning "town taker" or "devourer of villages," the Indian name given to Washington's great-grandfather John Washington and applied by the Half King to Washington himself.

22.6   Committee's resolves] The pay of officers engaged in the expedition to the Ohio had been set by a committee of the Virginia House of Burgesses. This letter had presumably covered a list of complaints drawn up by Washington's officers.

24.15   Belhaven] Alexandria, Virginia.

25.25–26   Regimentals] Uniforms.

25.32   curry] Currency.

27.15   Monsieur De Jumonville] Leading a force of thirty-five, French officer Joseph Coulon de Villiers, sieur de Jumonville (1718–54), had left Fort Duquesne on May 23, 1754, to carry to the British a message demanding their withdrawal from the Ohio.

30.2   *John Augustine Washington*] Often called Jack, John Augustine Washington (1736–87) was one of Washington's younger brothers.

30.32   something charming . . . sound] A version of this letter was published in the *London Magazine* for August 1754. Horace Walpole wrote that British king George II remarked: "He would not say so, if he had been used to hear many."

31.5   C. at Geors. Ck] Camp at Georges Creek, approximately eight miles northwest of Cumberland, Maryland.

31.9   Doctr Jas Powder] In 1746 Londoner Dr. Robert James (1705–76) took out a patent on his popular fever remedy, composed principally of phosphate of lime and oxide of antimony.

31.10   W] World.

32.29   Lt Colo. Gage] Thomas Gage (c. 1719–87), lieutenant colonel of the 44th Regiment. Gage and Washington were friendly for many years following the Braddock expedition, but became adversaries with the coming of the Revolution, when Gage, as commander in chief of the British army in North America (1763–75) and the last royal governor of Massachusetts (1774–75), faced off against his former comrade at the siege of Boston. See Washington's letters to Gage, pages 74–76.

34.9   Gt xing on the Yaughe] Great Crossing on the Youghiogheny River, in Pennsylvania, a few miles north of the Maryland border.

34.31–32   our late Engagemt] "Braddock's Defeat," July 9, 1755. Scottish-born major general Edward Braddock (1695–1755) led the ill-fated expedition against Fort Duquesne in July 1755. His force of 1400 was routed by a smaller force of 900 French and Indians, suffering nearly 1000 casualties and the loss of 53 of 86 officers, including Braddock himself.

41.1   Rects] Recruits.

43.6   March 10th 1757] Washington had arrived in Philadelphia in late February for a meeting of the governors of the southern colonies with the commander in chief of British forces in North America, John Campbell, 4th Earl of Loudoun.

46.9   10th Janry 1759] Washington wrote this letter just four days after marrying wealthy widow Martha Dandridge Custis.

47.28   Robert Cary & Company] A London firm trading with Virginia, the company had managed the Custis accounts; after his marriage Washington gave most of his business to the firm.

49.13   Dogue Run] One of the five working farms on Washington's eight-thousand acre Mount Vernon estate.

50.33   Hhds of Master Custis's Tobo] Washington served as custodian on the estate of his young stepson, John Parke Custis (1754–81). Here he expresses concern to his London factor about receipts on the sale of his and his stepson's tobacco, which had been transported to England in large casks, or hogsheads, weighing roughly 1000 pounds each. Through his factor, Washington used the proceeds from the sale of tobacco, and later wheat and other commodities, to purchase consumer goods in the London market.

53.32–33   Hemp . . . Act of Parliament] The British government provided incentives for the production of hemp, essential for the manufacture of naval stores.

54.5   Stamp Act] Passed by Parliament on March 22, 1765, the Stamp Act imposed a direct tax in the colonies on the paper used in formally written and printed documents, including newspapers, almanacs, broadsides, pamphlets, diplomas, and legal and commercial papers. It provoked widespread protest from American colonists, many of whom believed that taxation without the consent of the taxed was unconstitutional. The act proved unenforceable and was repealed on March 18, 1766.

55.15   *Joseph Thompson*] Thompson was the captain of the schooner *Swift*, which sailed from Alexandria to St. Christopher's in July 1766.

56.10   a letter and sundry papers] In early April 1769 Washington had received a packet from Dr. David Ross, a merchant in Blandensburg, Maryland, bringing news of associations set up in Philadelphia and Annapolis to boycott British goods in response to Parliament's passage in July 1767 of the Townshend Revenue Act, which imposed duties on lead, glass, paper, tea, and other goods imported by the colonies. The packet included an unsigned plan for a similar association in Virginia, which as it happened was the work of George Mason (1725–92), Washington's friend and neighbor to whom he now unknowingly directed it. In his first major initiative as a legislator, Washington later presented the plan to the House of Burgesses and served on the committee that drafted the Nonimportation Association adopted on May 18 in the Apollo Room of the Raleigh Tavern in Williamsburg, whence the Burgesses had adjourned after the governor had formally dissolved them the day before.

59.3   *Bryan Fairfax*] Fairfax (1737–1802) was half brother of George William Fairfax (see note 17.24).

60.31   *Robert McKenzie*] McKenzie had served under Washington as a captain in the Virginia Regiment before receiving a commission in the British army in 1761. On September 13, 1774, now a lieutenant in the 43rd Regiment of Foot stationed at "Boston Camp," he had addressed a letter to Washington highly critical of the people of Massachusetts, their "rebellious and numerous meetings" and "scandalous and ungenerous Attacks upon the best Characters in the Province."

63.27–28   the engagement in the Massachusetts Bay] The fighting on April 19, 1775 at Lexington, Concord, and along the road to Boston resulted in the deaths of seventy-three British soldiers and forty-nine Americans.

64.26   The President] John Hancock (1737–93) of Massachusetts served as president of the Second Continental Congress from May 1775 to October 1777. Like his successors Henry Laurens, John Jay, and Samuel Huntington, he was as president the recipient of Washington's wartime reports to Congress.

65.17   *To Martha Washington*] This letter and the letter dated June 23, 1775 (pages 68–69) are the only letters from Washington to his wife known to be extant. Martha Washington is believed to have burned all of the other letters sometime after Washington's death in 1799.

69.4   Jack & Nelly] John Parke Custis, Washington's stepson, and his wife Eleanor Calvert Custis.

71.27   *Richard Henry Lee*] A signer of the Declaration of Independence and a member of the famous family of Lees that included his brothers Arthur, Thomas Ludwell, Francis Lightfoot, and William, Richard Henry Lee (1732–94) was later president of Congress from November 1784 to November 1785 (see page 232).

72.2–3   I arrivd here . . . week]   Washington had arrived in Cambridge on July 2, 1775. He formally took command of the Continental Army, numbering about 14,000 men, at the Cambridge Common on the following day.

74.2   *Thomas Gage*]   See note 32.29.

76.5–6   to despise all Rank . . . your own]   Replying on August 13 to Washington's letter, Gage admitted that he treated captured American officers and soldiers indiscriminately, "for I acknowledge no Rank that is not derived from the King." Gage also took the opportunity to lecture his rebellious former comrade: "Be temperate in political disquisition, give free Operation to truth, and punish those who deceive and misrepresent, and not only the effects, but the Causes of this unhappy Conflict will be removed."

76.21–22   If your Officers . . . to shew them]   On August 14, Washington had indeed ordered that captured British officers, previously given special consideration owing to their rank, be placed in a common jail in Northampton, Massachusetts. But he thought better of it the next day, allowing British officers to continue to remain at liberty after pledging not to try to escape.

76.26   *Lund Washington*]   Lund Washington (1737–96) was a distant cousin. He managed Mount Vernon during the Revolutionary War.

81.18   *Benedict Arnold*]   Washington had received encouraging reports, dated November 8 and 13, 1775, from Colonel Benedict Arnold (1741–1801), who had led an expeditionary force through the Maine wilderness and had arrived at Lévis, across the St. Lawrence River from Quebec. On the same day he wrote this reply to Arnold, Washington praised him in another letter to Major General Philip Schuyler: "The Merit of this Gentleman is certainly great and I heartily wish that Fortune may distinguish him as one of her Favorites."

82.23   the new-army]   Enlistments in the old army expired with the year 1775; by December 31 only 9,650 men had enlisted in the new army, less than half the 20,000 authorized by Congress. Fearing the British in Boston would perceive the vulnerability of the American positions during the transition, Washington called out militia reinforcements and appealed to departing soldiers to stay on until replacements could be enlisted.

84.27   *Joseph Reed*]   Reed (1741–85) had been Washington's secretary (see page 69.27) before taking a leave of absence to tend to his law practice in Philadelphia on October 30, 1775.

85.3–4   his Majesty's . . . Speech]   Copies of George III's speech of October 26, 1775, in which he declared his determination to crush the American rebellion, had arrived at Cambridge on January 3, 1776. The king had formally proclaimed the colonies to be in rebellion on August 23, 1775.

90.3   *Phillis Wheatley*]   In 1761, when she was seven or eight years old, Phillis Wheatley (c. 1753–84) was kidnapped from her home in the Senegambian region of West Africa and brought to Boston where she was purchased by

John Wheatley, a prosperous tailor, as a servant for his wife, Susanna. Taught to read, Phillis soon demonstrated a prodigious mastery of scripture and began to write verse. Her 42-line poem in praise of Washington was published in *The Pennsylvania Magazine: or, American Monthly Museum* in April 1776.

90.30   the 17th Instant] March 17, or Evacuation Day, was observed as an official state holiday in Massachusetts's Suffolk County, which includes Boston, as well as in the cities of Cambridge and Somerville, from 1941 until 2010.

96.27   General Lee] English-born Major General Charles Lee (1731–84) had served in the British Army in America during the French and Indian War and later as a mercenary in Portugal and Poland before returning to the colonies in 1773. He was retired as a major on half-pay from the British army when at Washington's request he was appointed a major general in the Continental Army.

96.33   Lewis] Andrew Lewis (1720–81) had served as a captain under Washington at Fort Necessity and was later a major in Washington's Virginia Regiment. In 1774 he led the Regiment against Indians at the Battle of Point Pleasant, near the mouth of the Kanawha River, and was afterwards accused of cowardice. He was nonetheless appointed brigadier general in the Continental Army on March 1, 1777.

96.37   Colo. Mercer] Dr. Hugh Mercer (c. 1725–77), a colonel of the 3d Virginia Regiment, became a brigadier general in the Continental Army of June 5, 1776. Washington notes his death from wounds suffered at the Battle of Princeton in a January 5, 1777 letter to Congress on page 115.

96.39   Bullet] Thomas Bullitt (1730–78) had also served in Washington's Virginia Regiment; on March 6, 1776, Congress appointed him deputy adjutant general for the Southern Department, with the rank of a lieutenant colonel.

103.17   White plains] In New York, approximately thirty-three miles northeast of New York City.

106.37–38   vine, & fig Tree.] Cf. 1 Kings 4:25.

111.28–29   *the Executive Committee of the Continental Congress*] Comprised of Robert Morris and George Clymer of Pennsylvania and George Walton of Georgia.

113.3–4   powers . . . unlimited in extent] On December 27, 1776, Congress voted Washington extraordinary powers for six months to sustain the Continental Army, including the power to raise troops, gather provisions, and "to arrest and confine Persons who refuse to take the Continental Currency, or are otherwise disaffected to the American cause."

113.22   Pluckamin] Pluckemin, New Jersey, approximately twenty-three miles north of Princeton.

114.13–14   Sanpink Creek]   Assunpink Creek.

116.3–4   the best cover I can]   Washington remained in winter quarters at Morristown, twelve miles northeast of Pluckemin, until May 1777.

116.12–13   a Proclamation . . . by Lord and General Howe]   When British Admiral Lord Richard Howe and his brother General William Howe assumed command, respectively, of British naval and land forces in North America in 1775 they were empowered to open negotiations with colonial representatives and to make offers of amnesty to Americans prepared to swear a loyalty oath to the Crown.

118.12   Chester]   On the Delaware River in Pennsylvania, approximately fifteen miles southwest of Philadelphia.

119.18   Matuchen Hills]   Washington had established his headquarters in the home of Peter Wentz, on Methacton Hill, in Worcester, Pennsylvania, approximately twenty-four miles northwest of Philadelphia.

121.22–23   Potomack Run, Aquia]   Potomac and Aquia creeks are tributaries of the Potomac River in Stafford County, Virginia, midway between Mount Vernon and John Augustine Washington's home at Bushfield.

123.9–10   the change in your Family]   Referring to the union of John Augustine's daughter Jane (1759–91) and William Augustine Washington (1757–1810), son of George Washington's half brother Augustine.

123.17–18   Important and glorious News]   Washington here copied a dispatch describing the surrender of British General John Burgoyne's army of 5,000 men to American forces under Horatio Gates at Saratoga, New York, on October 17.

123.22   *Henry Laurens*]   South Carolina merchant-planter Henry Laurens (1724–92) was president of the Continental Congress from November 1777 to December 1778.

128.11   Genl Conway]   Over Washington's objections, Congress appointed Major General Thomas Conway (1735–c. 1800) inspector-general of the army in December 1777. That winter, Conway was allegedly involved in an effort, sometimes called the "Conway Cabal," to elevate Horatio Gates, victor at Saratoga, to the command of the Continental Army in Washington's place. The effort to oust Washington owed its beginnings to the dissatisfaction of some delegates in Congress with his leadership, but his detractors repeatedly blundered and the plot, if there was one, collapsed when General William Alexander informed Washington of a damaging statement contained in a letter from General Conway to General Gates. In letters to both men, Washington confronted them directly with the statement. (See his letter to Gates on page 129). Completely discredited, Conway resigned in April 1778.

129.5   *Horatio Gates*]   A British officer who served in America in the Seven Years War and returned to the colonies in 1772, Horatio Gates (1729–1806) was drawn to the American cause by his contempt for the English caste system. Relations between Washington and Major General Gates were strained when the latter failed to inform his commander directly of his victory at Saratoga and then balked at sending troop reinforcements south as Washington requested.

131.2   *William Gordon*]   Massachusetts clergyman William Gordon (1728–1807) was collecting material for a history of the American Revolution. It was published in 1788 as *The History of the Rise, Progress, and Establishment of the Independence of the United States of America.*

132.36   his late speech]   On November 18, 1777, Charles Pratt, Baron Camden (1714–94) spoke in Parliament in support of an amendment calling for "an immediate cessation of hostilities" in America. Washington here embraces Camden's assertion that the conflict in America resulted from a determined effort by the British ministers to drive the colonists into rebellion.

134.4   indisposition of Miss Fairfax]   Sally Cary Fairfax (1760–1778), Bryan Fairfax's daughter, died on March 29.

134.16   forged Letters]   A series of letters purportedly written by Washington was published in London in 1776 in a pamphlet titled *Letters of General Washington to several of his Friends in the year 1776*; by 1778 the spurious letters had been reprinted in America. The aim of the deception was to discredit Washington's leadership by depicting him as an opponent of independence and a critic of those who favored the break with England.

136.12   English Town]   In New Jersey, approximately twenty-five miles northeast of Trenton.

136.30   General Clinton]   The son of a British admiral who was the royal governor of New York from 1740–51, Henry Clinton (1730–95) joined the New York militia in 1745, rising to the rank of lieutenant. He went to London in 1749 and was commissioned in the British army in 1751. Wounded in the Seven Years' War in Europe and promoted to major general in 1772, he returned to North America in 1775, shortly becoming second-in-command to William Howe, after the latter replaced Thomas Gage as commander in chief. In May 1778, he in turn replaced Howe.

137.10   Brigadier General Wayne]   Anthony Wayne (1745–96). His zealous, bloodthirsty fighting style earned him the sobriquet "Mad" Anthony Wayne.

137.34   Chasseurs]   French for "hunters"; riflemen.

141.7   The peculiar Situation of General Lee at this time]   A court martial convened on July 2 to try Lee for disobeying orders, misbehavior before the enemy, and showing disrespect to the commander in chief in two letters he wrote to Washington after the battle. On August 12, 1778, Lee was found guilty of all three charges and suspended from command for a year. Congress approved the sentence on December 5, 1778, and dismissed Lee from the army for good on January 10, 1780.

141.27   *Thomas Nelson, Jr.*]   A signer of the Declaration of Independence and later governor of Virginia, Thomas Nelson, Jr., (1738–89) had given Washington a fine horse which Washington named Nelson and which he rode during much of the Revolutionary War. Washington returned the horse after the war ended.

142.5   discontinuance of your Corps]   Nelson had raised a troop of volunteer Virginia cavalry that Congress subsequently declined to authorize.

142.25   Count D'Estaign]   Charles Hector Théodat, Comte d'Estaing (1729–94) was the commander of the French navy in America until 1780. His fleet carrying an expeditionary force of 4,000 men arrived off Delaware Bay on July 8, 1778 and participated in an unsuccessful Franco-American attack on the British garrison at Newport, Rhode Island from July 29 to August 31, 1778.

143.20   the Secretary]   Thomas Nelson Sr. (c.1716–82), known as "Secretary Nelson" because of his thirty-year service as secretary of the governor's council. Thomas Nelson, Jr., was his nephew.

143.30   *Gouverneur Morris*]   A member of Congress from New York and a scion of that state's landed aristocracy, Gouverneur Morris (1752–1816) had visited the Continental camp at Valley Forge in the dark winter of 1778 and come away with a lasting admiration for its commander.

143.34   on that head]   In two letters dated October 3, 1778, Washington had communicated to Henry Laurens his rationale for moving his headquarters to Fishkill, approximately seventy-five miles north of New York City, in order to be better positioned to protect the vital garrison at West Point against a British assault up the Hudson.

145.13   a memorial]   Officers at White Plains issued their grievances to Congress in a memorial dated September 13, 1778; Congress read the remonstrance on October 20 and promptly tabled it.

145.24   Fredericksburg in N. Yk]   Now several villages in New York's Dutchess and Putnam counties; Washington's encampment was in present-day Patterson, New York, approximately twenty miles east of Fishkill.

148.26   Middle Brook]   In central New Jersey, approximately thrity-six miles southwest of New York City.

151.7   arming Slaves]   Though he was himself a substantial slaveholder with plantations in South Carolina and Georgia, Henry Laurens had written to Washington on March 16, 1779 to propose arming slaves: "had we Arms for 3000 such black Men, as I could select in Carolina I should have no doubt of success in driving the British out of Georgia."

151.23   Mr. Laurens]   Lieutenant colonel John Laurens (1754–82), son of Henry Laurens, served on Washington's staff. He was an ardent proponent of offering slaves emancipation in exchange for military service.

151.29   *Speech to the Delaware Chiefs*]   On May 12, 1779, Washington welcomed a delegation of six Delaware Indian chieftains to his camp at Middle Brook in hopes of enlisting their support for the American cause.

154.5   *Marquis de Lafayette*]   Young French aristocrat Marie Joseph Paul Yves Roch Gilbert du Motier, Marquis de Lafayette (1757–1834) had been commissioned a major general in the Continental army in 1777; he became Washington's surrogate son and the most famous foreigner to fight on behalf of the American cause.

155.16–17   Swords . . . pruning hook]   Cf. Isaiah 2:4.

157.9   declaration of Spain]   Allied with France, Spain had declared war on Britain on June 21, 1779.

158.24   G.]   Garrison.

160.19   *Robert Howe*]   North Carolinian Robert Howe (1732–86), a major general in the Continental Army, had been in command of the Continental Army's Southern Department from October 1777 to April 1779.

160.21–22   Mr. Pulteney's lucubrations]   William Pulteney, *Thoughts on the Present State of Affairs with America, and the Means of Conciliation* (London, 1778).

162.10   Peekskill]   In New York, on the eastern side of the Hudson River, approximately ten miles south of West Point.

163.21   *Samuel Huntington*]   Connecticut signer Samuel Huntington (1731–96) was president of Congress from September 1779 to July 1781.

166.3   *John Cadwalader*]   Cadwalader (1742–86) was a brigadier general in the Pennsylvania militia.

166.4   Tappan]   Washington kept his headquarters at the DeWint House in Tappan, New York, just north of the border with New Jersey and some twenty-seven miles north of New York City, from September 28–October 7 while observing the trial of British spy Major John André, who had conspired with Arnold to compromise West Point.

167.36   a member of my family]   A member of Washington's staff.

168.6   Passaic Falls]   In Paterson, New Jersey, some twenty-one miles northwest of New York City.

168.9   Baron de Steuben]   Retired Prussian officer Friedrich Wilhelm Augustus von Steuben (1730–94) had travelled to America in 1777 with a letter of introduction to Washington from Benjamin Franklin, whom Steuben had met in Paris. After introducing new standards of military discipline and drilling acumen to the Continental Army at Valley Forge, he became, in May of 1778, its inspector general.

169.15   New Windsor]   In October, Washington established winter quarters for his army of 7,500 men in New Windsor, New York, some ten miles north of West Point.

169.20–21   mutiny . . . Pennsylvania Line]   The mutiny by enlisted men of General Anthony Wayne's Pennsylvania Line broke out at winter quarters in Morristown, New Jersey, on January 1, 1781. The mutineers marched under arms to Princeton, where they presented their grievances over back pay, terms of enlistment, and supplies to representatives of Congress. Washington, who took no part in the negotiations, feared that mutiny would spread through the Continental Army's main winter encampment at New Windsor. On January 8, Joseph Reed, formerly Washington's military secretary and now president of the Pennsylvania executive council, negotiated a settlement that made significant concessions to the mutineers.

174.8–13   that you should go on board . . . Plantation in ruins]   A British warship (probably the armed sloop *Actaeon*) had threatened Mount Vernon while on a raid up the Potomac. Lund Washington's letter describing the incident is not known to be extant; in a letter of April 23, 1781, Lafayette wrote: "Mr Lund Washington Went on Board the Ennemy's vessels and Consented to give them provisions. This Being done By the Gentleman who in Some Measure Represents you at your House will certainly Have a Bad effect, and Contrasts with Spirited Answers from Some Neighbors that Had their Houses Burnt Accordingly."

175.2   my Negroes]   Eighteen Mount Vernon slaves escaped to the British vessel; seven were eventually recaptured.

175.19   *Journal of the Yorktown Campaign*]   On or about May 1, 1781, Washington began "a concise Journal of Military transactions &ca." He regretted "not having attempted it from the commencement of the War, in aid of my memory and wish the multiplicity of matter which continually surround me and the embarrassed State of our affairs which is momently calling the attention to perplexities of one kind or another, may not defeat altogether or so interrupt my present intention, & plan, as to render it of little avail." The current selection from the Journal commences on August 14, 1781, when Washington, still in New York, learns that a substantial French fleet under Admiral François Joseph Paul, Comte de Grasse (1722–88), was on its way from the West Indies to the Chesapeake.

176.13   Cornwallis]   British General Charles Cornwallis (1738–1805), second in command to Henry Clinton, had begun a major campaign in Virginia in May 1781. On August 2 he established a strong base at Yorktown, on the York River, a tributary of Chesapeake Bay.

180.19–20   Barras had done before]   A page, or pages, perhaps containing entries for September 23 and 24, 1781, may be missing from the journal at this point.

180.23   remr.]   Remainder.

182.17 French opened a battery] According to a contemporary account, "his Excellency General Washington put the match to the first gun, and a furious discharge of cannon and mortars immediately followed, and Earl Cornwallis has received his first salutation."

183.26 royals] A royal was a small mortar that fired an explosive shell.

186.26 *Lewis Nicola*] Born in France and educated in Ireland, Lewis Nicola (1717–1807) came to Philadelphia in 1766 and with the Revolution became a colonel in the Continental Army.

186.29 Sentiments you have submitted] In his letter of May 22, 1782, Nicola wrote: "This war must have shewn to all, but to military men in particular the weakness of republicks, & the exertions the army has been able to make by being under a proper head, therefore, I little doubt, when the benefits of a mixed government are pointed out & duly considered, but such will be readily adopted; in this case it will, I believe, be uncontroverted that the same abilities which have led us, through difficulties apparently unsurmountable by human power, to victory & glory, those qualities that have merited & obtained the universal esteem & veneration of an army, would be most likely to conduct & direct us in the smoother paths of peace." He continued: "Some people have so connected the ideas of tyranny & monarchy as to find it very difficult to separate them, it may therefore be requisite to give the head of such a constitution as I propose some title apparently more moderate, but if all other things were once adjusted I believe strong arguments might be produced for admitting the title of king, which I conceive would be attended with some material advantages. . . ."

187.20 *Benjamin Lincoln*] Massachusetts farmer Benjamin Lincoln (1733–1810) rose through the ranks of the militia to become a major general and in February 1777, at Washington's recommendation, Congress appointed him a major general in the Continental Army. He was appointed commander of the Southern Department in September 1778 and, after surrendering Charleston to the British on May 12, 1780 and enduring six months on parole, he was on hand for Cornwallis's surrender at Yorktown. On October 30, 1781, Lincoln was named the first secretary of war, or secretary at war, under the Articles of Confederation, in which capacity he received this letter.

189.32 *Benjamin Franklin*] At the time of this exchange of letters, Benjamin Franklin (1706–1790) was minister plenipotentiary to France and a commissioner to negotiate peace with Britain.

191.3 *Nathanael Greene*] Rhode Islander Nathanael Greene (1742–86) was commissioned brigadier general in the Continental Army in June 1775; in August 1776 he became a major general. He served as quartermaster general of the army from February 1778 to August 1780, when he succeeded Arnold as commander in the Hudson Highlands. Shortly thereafter, on October 14, 1780, Washington tapped him to take over command of the southern department, in which capacity he received this letter at his headquarters in Charleston.

196.12   the Newbuilding]   A meeting house built at the Continental Army's Newburgh, New York, cantonment for the use of the officers; it was also called the "Temple of Virtue."

196.12–13   paper . . . circulated yesterday]   The anonymous paper circulated on March 10, 1783, was written by Continental Army officer John Armstrong (1758–1843), later secretary of war (1813–1814) during the War of 1812. In his address, Armstrong described himself as "A fellow soldier whose interest and affection bind him strongly to you, whose past sufferings, have been as great & whose future fortune may be as desperate as yours" who until recently had "believed in the Justice of his Country." Armstrong concluded: "After a pursuit of seven long Years, the object for which we set out, is at length brot within our reach—Yes, my friends, that suffering Courage of yours, was active once, it has conducted the United States of America, thro' a doubt-full and bloody War—it has placed her in the Chair of Independancy—and peace returns again to bless—Whom? a Country willing to redress your wrongs? cherish your worth—and reward your Services—a Country courting your return to private life, with Tears of gratitude & smiles of Admiration—longing to divide with you, that Independancy, which Your Gallantry has given, and those riches which your wounds have preserved. Is this the case? or is it rather a Country that tramples upon your rights, disdains your Cries—& insults your distresses? have you not more than once suggested your wishes—and made known your wants to Congress (wants and wishes, which gratitude and policy should have anticipated, rather than evaded)—and have you not lately, in the meek language of intreating Memorials, begged from their Justice, what you would no longer expect from their favor. How have you been answered? let the Letter which you are called to consider tomorrow, make reply, If this then be your treatment while the swords you wear are necessary for the Defence of America, what have you to expect from peace; when your voice shall sink, and your strength dissipate by division—when those very swords, the Instruments and Companions of your Glory, shall be taken from your sides—and no remaining mark of Military distincion left, but your wants, infirmities & Scars— can you then consent to be the only sufferers by this revolution—and retiring from the field, grow old in poverty, wretchedness, and Contempt; can you consent, to wade thro' the vile mire of dependency, and owe the miserable remnant of that life to Charity, which has hitherto been spent in honor? If you can—Go—and carry with you the jest of Tories, & the Scorn of Whigs—the ridicule—and what is worse—the pity of the world—go—Starve and be forgotten. But if your spirits should revolt at this—if you have sense enough to discover, and spirit enough to oppose Tyranny, under whatever Garb it may assume—whether it be the plain Coat of Republicanism—or the splendid Robe of Royalty—if you have yet learned to discriminate between a people and a Cause—between men & principles—Awake—attend to your Situation

& redress yourselves; If the present moment be lost, every future Effort, is in vain—and your threats then, will be as empty, as your entreaties now—I would advise you therefore, to come to some final opinion, upon what you can bear —and what you will suffer—If your determination be in any proportion to your wrongs—carry your appeal from the Justice to the fears of government— Change the Milk & Water stile of your last Memorial—assume a bolder Tone, decent, but lively, spirited and determined—And suspect the man, who would advise to more moderation, and longer forbearance. Let two or three Men, who can feel as well as write, be appointed to draw up your last Remonstrance (for I would no longer give it the sueing, soft, unsuccessful Epithet of Memorial) Let it be represented in language that will neither dishonor you by its Rudeness, nor betray you by its fears—what has been promised by Congress and what has been performed—how long and how patiently you have suffered —how little you have asked, and how much of that little, have been denied— Tell them, that tho' you were the first, and would wish to be the last to encounter Danger—tho' dispair itself can never drive you into dishonor, it may drive you from the field—That the wound often irritated and never healed, may at length become incurable—and that the slightest mark of indignity from Congress now, must operate like the Grace, and part you forever—That in any political Event, the Army has its alternative—if peace, that nothing shall seperate you from your Arms but Death—If War—that courting the Auspicies, and inviting the direction of your Illustrous Leader, you will retire to some unsettled Country, Smile in your Turn, and 'mock when their fear cometh on' [cf. Proverbs 1:26]—But let it represent also, that should they comply with the request of your late Memorial, it would make you more happy; and them more respectable—That while War should continue, you would follow their standard into the field, and When it came to an End, you would withdraw into the shade of private Life—and give the World another subject of Wonder & applause, An Army victorious over its Enemies, Victorious over itself."

197.3 *Alexander Hamilton*] At the time of this exchange of letters, Alexander Hamilton (1755–1804), formerly a member of Washington's military family who had left the army after leading a successful assault at Yorktown, was a delegate to Congress from New York. He had written to Washington in February 1783 suggesting that the growing discontent in the army be used to pressure Congress into adopting new revenue measures. Hamilton would resume his close working relationship with Washington while serving as the first secretary of the treasury, 1789–95.

197.7 a certain Gentleman] Walter Stewart (c. 1756–96), a colonel of the Pennsylvania Line.

199.7 second address] This address of March 12, 1783, also written by John Armstrong, asserted that Washington's general orders of March 11 (see page 196) demonstrated that the commander in chief sympathized with the aims and methods of the disaffected officers.

199.16   *Speech to the Officers of the Army*]   In the meeting with the disgruntled officers held in the Temple of Virtue on March 15, 1783, Washington first read this speech and then began to read a letter from congressional delegate Joseph Jones promising justice to the army. Washington paused, produced a pair of spectacles—which very few of the officers had ever seen him wear—and said: "Gentlemen, you must pardon me. I have grown gray in your service and now find myself growing blind." (This remark has also been reported: "Gentleman, you will permit me to put on my spectacles, for I have grown not only gray, but almost blind, in the service of my country.") Some of the formerly rebellious officers were moved to tears. Washington then left the building and major generals Henry Knox and Israel Putnam introduced and carried a resolution strongly repudiating the anonymous address of March 10 and pledging the army's continued obedience to civil authority.

201.12–13   Emissary . . . from New York]   From the British high command (New York City remained under British occupation until November 1783).

203.29   General Peace]   Britain, France, and Spain had signed a preliminary peace agreement on January 20, 1783.

216.2   *James Duane*]   Conservative jurist James Duane (1733–1797) was a New York delegate to Congress.

216.3   Rocky Hill]   In central New Jersey, approximately five miles north of Princeton.

217.18   Compn.]   Compassion.

220.22   The author]   John Baker Holroyd, Earl of Sheffield (1735–1821).

227.26   *Benjamin Harrison*]   Virginian Benjamin Harrison (1726–1791) was a signer of the Declaration of Independence and from December 1781 to December 1784 the fifth governor of his state. (His son, William Henry Harrison, would become the ninth president of the United States.)

231.8   the bust]   In 1782 the Virginia house of delegates had commissioned a bust of Lafayette by Jean-Antoine Houdoun in gratitude for the Marquis's service to the American cause, a gesture that, Washington wrote when first informing his young friend of the news, "fills my Heart With a pleasing Sense of pride."

231.28   *Tench Tilghman*]   Washington's military secretary from 1776 to 1783, Tench Tilghman (1744–1786) went into business in Baltimore with financier Robert Morris after the war.

232.19–20   treaty . . . Fort Stanwix]   The Six Nations of the Iroquois Confederacy ceded all claims to the Ohio country to the United States in the Treaty of Fort Stanwix, October 22, 1784.

233.14   repealed . . . British debts]   In 1782 the Virginia Assembly passed a law forbidding British citizens to sue for the recovery of debts contracted before April 19, 1775. The repeal measure introduced during the 1784 session did not pass.

235.6   Colo. Ward] Formerly commissary general of prisoners during the war, Joseph Ward was forty-seven years old at the time of his marriage.

235.18   Miss Custis] Martha Washington's granddaughter Eleanor (Nelly) Parke Custis (1779–1852) was raised by the Washingtons.

237.28   Fanny Bassett] Frances Bassett Washington (1767–96) was a niece of Martha Washington who began living at Mount Vernon in 1784. In 1785 she married George Augustine Washington (1763–93), son of Washington's brother Charles and manager of Mount Vernon from 1785 until his death. In 1795 Fanny married Tobias Lear (1762–1816), George Washington's private secretary.

238.3   *David Humphreys*] From June 1780 to the war's end, David Humphreys (1752–1818) served as an aide-de-camp to Washington. After the war, Humphreys served as secretary to the commission established by Congress to negotiate treaties of commerce with European nations. (The commissioners included John Adams, Thomas Jefferson, and Benjamin Franklin.)

239.30   an Ordinance] The Land Ordinance of 1785, adopted by Congress on May 20, provided for the surveying and sale of the Ohio lands. It was the basis for the Northwest Ordinance of 1787.

241.2   *Robert Morris*] A signer of the Declaration of Independence and principal financier of the American war effort, Robert Morris (1734–1806) had served from 1781 to 1784 as Congress's superintendant of finance.

241.6   law-suit . . . slave] Philip Dalby of Alexandria, Virginia, had traveled to Philadelphia in February 1785 with his servant, a young slave named Frank. According to Dalby, a committee of Quakers approached Frank, persuaded him to seek his freedom, and brought a writ of habeas corpus on his behalf. Dalby won the case and returned to Virginia with Frank, who then ran away early in 1787.

242.15   *John Jay*] At the time of this exchange John Jay (1745–1829) was secretary for foreign affairs for the Confederation Congress, a post he held from June 1784, when he returned to America after signing the Treaty of Paris ending the war with Britain, to March 22, 1790, when he was relieved by Thomas Jefferson, the first secretary of state under the new Federal Constitution.

243.25   *Thomas Jefferson*] At the time of this exchange Thomas Jefferson (1743–1826) was American minister to France.

243.30–31   the Statue in question] The state of Virginia commissioned Jean-Antoine Houdoun to create the statue of Washington that still stands in the Virginia State Capitol in Richmond. Houdoun had come to Mount Vernon in October 1785 to model his subject from life. As Washington suggested, the finished statue was garbed in modern dress.

244.6   Mr West]   Benjamin West (1738–1820), the celebrated American-born artist who left for Italy in 1760, and from there to Britain in 1763, where he eventually became history painter to the king.

244.19   Majr L'Enfant]   Pierre Charles L'Enfant (1754–1825), a native of France, was a Continental Army major and designer of the master plan for the city of Washington, D.C.

245.9   Genl McDougall]   A radical patriot in prewar New York and a major general in the Continental Army, Alexander McDougall (1732–1786) was a member of the New York senate at the time of his death.

247.16   last legacy]   Washington is referring to his June 8, 1783, valedictory Circular to State Governments, see pages 205–215.

247.22   *James Madison*]   At the time of this exchange James Madison (1751–1836), formerly a delegate to Congress, was a member of the Virginia Assembly.

247.35   the Convention at Annapolis]   Commissioners from five states met at Annapolis, Maryland, September 11–14, 1786, to discuss interstate commercial regulations. They adopted a report calling for a convention of delegates from all thirteen states to meet in Philadelphia on May 14, 1787, to "devise such further provisions as shall appear to them necessary to render the constitution of the Federal Government adequate to the exigencies of the Union." On December 4, 1786, the Virginia Assembly elected Madison as one of the state's seven delegates to the Philadelphia convention.

248.31–34   Colo. Lee. . . . new choice]   The Virginia Assembly had declined to reelect Henry "Light-Horse Harry" Lee (1756–1818) as a delegate to Congress. Madison was reelected.

249.10–11   your publication . . . Captn Asgill]   "The Conduct of General Washington Respecting the Confinement of Captain Asgill," published in the November 16, 1786, edition of the *New-Haven Gazette and Connecticut Magazine*. After Loyalists hanged an American prisoner, militia captain Joshua Huddy, in New Jersey in April 1782, Washington had ordered the selection of a British officer for possible retaliation. Captain Charles Asgill (c. 1762–1823), who had surrendered at Yorktown, was chosen by lot in May 1782. On August 19, 1782, Washington referred the matter to Congress with the recommendation that Asgill not be hanged. Congress ordered his release on November 7, 1782, after learning that Asgill's mother had appealed to the king and queen of France.

249.32   old frd of yours]   The old friend was Washington himself: Humphreys had warned in his letter of November 1, 1786, that "in case of civil discord . . . you could not remain neuter—and that you would be obliged, in self-defence, to take part on one side or the other: or withdraw from this Continent."

252.16   *Mary Ball Washington*]   Mary Ball Washington (1708–89), Washington's mother, with whom he had a cool relationship.

252.18–19   to George Washington]   George Augustine Washington, Washington's nephew and Mount Vernon's manager.

255.30   *Edmund Randolph*]   Governor of Virginia from 1786 to 1788, Edmund Randolph (1753–1813) would later serve as President Washington's attorney general (1789–94) and secretary of state (1794–95).

257.5–6   *attending* delegates]   The Virginia delegates to the Convention were George Washington, George Mason, James Madison, George Wythe, Edmund Randolph, John Blair, and James McClurg. McClurg was chosen after Patrick Henry, Thomas Nelson, and Richard Henry Lee declined to serve.

257.24–25   proceedings of the Convention]   Shortly after Hamilton left Philadelphia on June 29, 1787, the Convention was stymied over the question of representation in Congress and the delegates referred the matter to a "grand committee" consisting of one member from each state. A week later, as Washington wrote this letter, the delegates were still engaged in a contentious debate about representation in the lower house.

258.26   *Henry Knox*]   A Boston bookseller who made a special study of military science and engineering and became Washington's commander of artillery during the war, Henry Knox (1750–1806) was secretary of war for the Confederation Congress, a post he retained under the new federal constitution.

260.6   *Bushrod Washington*]   Son of Washington's brother John Augustine, Bushrod Washington (1762–1829) would inherit both Mount Vernon and Washington's papers. He was appointed associate justice of the Supreme Court by President Adams in 1798, and he served on the Marshall court for three decades.

261.25–26   nine other States]   Article VII of the Constitution stipulated: "The Ratification of the Conventions of nine States, shall be sufficient for the Establishment of this Constitution between the States so ratifying the Same."

265.6   Arret]   Decree.

266.29   explained by Mr Wilson]   This probably refers to an October 6, 1787, speech by Pennsylvanian James Wilson (1742–98), which was widely printed.

271.21   *Richard Henderson*]   Henderson was a resident of Bladensburg, Maryland, who operated an ironworks near Antietam Creek.

273.17–20   Abbe Raynale . . . Mr Morse of New Haven]   Guillaume Thomas François, Abbé Raynal, *A Philosophical and Political History of the British Settlements and Trade in North America* (Edinburgh, 1779); William Guthrie, *New Geographical, Historical and Commercial Grammar* (London,

1777); Jedidiah Morse, *The American Geography; or, a View of the Present Situation of the United States of America* (1789).

273.24   of books at present existing] At his death Washington's library included a copy of the second edition (1794) of Thomas Jefferson's *Notes on the State of Virginia* (1785). In 1787 Washington received from Michel-Guillaume Jean de Crèvecoeur a copy of the three-volume French edition of *Letters from an American Farmer*; Washington had read the English edition of 1782.

279.34–35   Hartford fabric] In an endorsement of domestic manufactures, Washington wore a suit of this material at his inauguration on April 30, 1789.

284.17–18   Fifth article of the Constitution] The article providing for amendment. Madison, now a leader in the House of Representatives, opened debate on amendments on June 8, 1789, and Congress proposed twelve amendments to the states on September 25, 1789. Ratification of ten of the amendments —the "Bill of Rights"—was completed on December 15, 1791.

284.39   pecuniary compensation] Washington requested that he receive no presidential salary; as during the Revolutionary War, he asked only that his expenses be reimbursed. Congress, however, voted him an annual salary of $25,000.

285.27   short reply . . . Address] Madison had composed the address of the House of Representatives to the new president and would also draft Washington's May 8 reply to that address.

286.2   *John Adams*] After spending most of the war on diplomatic missions in Europe, John Adams (1735–1826) returned to the United States in June 1788 and on February 4, 1789 was elected vice president. Having queried Adams and others about protocol, Washington settled on one levee a week, on Tuesday afternoons.

287.11   tour of the United States] Washington made presidential tours to New England, October–November 1789, and to the South, April–June 1791.

294.22   your Office abroad] Jefferson had been American minister to France since 1785.

296.3   *David Stuart*] In 1783, Eleanor (Nellie) Custis, widow of Washington's stepson John Parke Custis, married Dr. David Stuart (1753–1814) of Alexandria, a physician trained in Edinburgh.

296.8   such jealousies] Stuart had written: "A spirit of jealousy which may be dangerous to the Union, towards the Eastern States, seems to be growing fast among us. It is represented, that the Northern phalanx is so firmly united, as to bear down all opposition, while Virginia is unsupported."

297.33   Mr Madison . . . discrimination] During the debate in Congress

over Secretary of the Treasury Alexander Hamilton's plan for funding the national debt, Madison had proposed making a distinction in the rates of repay-
ment between the original holders of Continental securities and the speculators
who had bought up the securities at reduced prices. The House voted against
discrimination, 36–13, on February 22, 1790.

297.39   Memorial of the Quakers] Stuart had written that the "late applications to Congress, respecting the slaves, will certainly tend to promote"
Southern suspicions. He added: "It gives particular umbrage, that the Quakers
should be so busy in this business." On February 11, 1790, Quakers had presented a petition to the House calling for Congress to take action against the
slave trade, notwithstanding the prohibition in the Constitution against abolition of the slave trade before 1808. The House considered the petition and
eventually adopted a report declaring that Congress could not prohibit the
importation of slaves before 1808 or interfere with the treatment of slaves
within the states.

307.11–12   your letters are far from quieting] Lafayette's letter of May 3,
1791, from Paris, which enclosed a copy of his April 22 speech to the Paris
commune and national guard, reads: "My dear General I Wish it Was in My
power to Give You an Assurance that our troubles are at an End, and our
Constitution totally Established—But altho dark clouds are Still Before us, We
Came So far as to foresee the Moment When a Legislative Corps Will Succeed
this Convention, and, Unless Foreign Powers interfere, I Hope that Within
four Month Your friend Will Have Reassumed the life of a Private and Quiete
Citizen. The Rage of Parties, Even Among the Patriots, is Gone as far as it is
Possible, Short of Blood shed—But Altho' Hatreds Are far from Subsiding,
Matters don't Appear So Ill disposed as they formerly were towards a Coalition
Among the Supporters of the Popular Cause—I Myself am Exposed to the
Envy and Attacks of all parties for this Simple Reason, that Who Ever acts or
Means wrong finds me an insuperable obstacle, and there Appears a kind of
phœnomenen in My Situation, all Parties Against me, and Yet a National
Popularity Which in Spite of Every effort Has Been Unshakable—a proof of
this I Had lately when disobeïed By the Guard, And Unsupported By the
Administrative Powers Who Had Sent me, Unnoticed By the National As-
sembly Who Had taken fright, the King I do not Mention, as He Could do
But little in the Affair, and Yet the little He did Was Against me, Given up to
all the Madnesses of licence, faction, and Popular Rage, I Stood alone in de-
fense of the law, and turned the tide Up into the Constitutional Channel—I
Hope this lesson Will Serve My Country, and Help towards Establishing the
Principles of Good order—But Before I Could Bring My fellow Citizens to a
Sense of legal Subordination I Must Have Conducted them through the fear
to loose the Man they love—inclosed is the Speech I delivered on the occasion—I send it Not for Any Merit of it, But on Account of the Great Effect it
Had on the Minds of the People, and the discipline of an Army of five and
forty thousand Men, Upwards of thirty of Whom are Volunteers, and Who
to a Man are Exposed to all the Suggestions of a dozen of Parties, and the

Corruptions of all kinds of pleasures and Allurements. The Commitee of Revision is Going to distinguish in our Immense Materials Every Article that deserves to Be Constitutional, and as I Hope to Convene in a tolerable State of
Union the Members of that Committee, as their Votes Will in the House influence the popular Part of the Assembly, I Hope that Besides the Restoration of
all Natural Rights, the destruction of all the Abuses, We May Present to the
Nation Some Very Good institutions of Governement, and organïse it so as to
Ensure to the people the Principal Consequences, and Enjoïements of a free
Constitution, leaving the Remainder to the legislative Corps to Mend into
well digested Bills, and Waïting Untill Experience Has fitted us for a More
Enlightened, and less Agitated National Convention. in the Mean While our
Principles of liberty and Equality are invading all Europe, and Popular Revolu-
tions Ripening Every Where. Should foreign Powers Employ this Summer
with Attaks Against our Constitution, there Will Be Great Blood shed, But
our liberty Cannot fail us—we Have done Every thing for the General Class of
the Country people, and in Case the Cities Were frightened into Submission,
Yet the peasants Would Swarm Round me, and fight to death, Rather than
Give up their Rights. Adieu, My Beloved General, My Best Respects Wait on
Mrs Washington—Remember me to Hamilton, jay, jefferson, Knox, and all
friends."

309.14   *Jean Baptiste Ternant*]   Ternant was French minister to the United
States.

312.2–3   subject . . . conversed upon]   Madison prepared memoranda
recording his conversations with Washington on May 5 and 9, 1792, regarding
the President's hope to retire from office in 1793. Madison had urged Washington to stay on, insisting "that in the great point of conciliating and uniting
all parties under a Govt which had excited such violent controversies & divisions, it was well known that his services had been in a manner essential."

314.26   furnish me with them]   Madison responded on June 20, 1792,
enclosing a draft of a brief valedictory speech. Washington consulted Madison's draft in 1796 and incorporated it into the draft of the Farewell Address
that he sent to Hamilton on May 15, 1796; for the final version of the address,
see pages 364–380 in this volume.

315.3   Returning]   Jefferson did visit Mount Vernon briefly on his journey to
Monticello and on his return trip to Philadelphia.

315.22   quandom friend Colo. M.]   Washington here refers to his once and
former friend George Mason.

315.24   the following heads]   The enumerated points that follow were
copied almost verbatim from a letter Thomas Jefferson had written to Washington on May 23, 1792.

319.7   as soon as you can make it convenient]   On August 11, 1792, Hamilton promised to send Washington his reply by the "next Monday's Post," that is August 13, but he did not mail his lengthy response until August 18.

319.27   Mr Carmichael]   On January 24, 1792, the Senate approved the appointment of William Carmichael and William Short as joint commissioners plenipotentiary to negotiate with Spain for free navigation rights on the Mississippi River. Carmichael was already in Madrid serving as the American chargé d'affaires. Short did not arrive in Spain until February 1793. Their efforts would result in the Treaty of San Lorenzo, or Pinckney's Treaty, Thomas Pinckney having stepped in to complete the negotiations after Carmichael's death in 1795.

325.1   the interesting subject]   In his letter of August 5, 1792, Randolph had urged Washington to continue to serve as president for another term.

325.6   health of my Nephew]   George Augustine Washington was ill with tuberculosis. He died on February 5, 1793.

326.2   *John Francis Mercer*]   An aide-de-camp to General Charles Lee during the Revolutionary War and a dissenting member of the Constitutional Convention, John Francis Mercer (1759–1821) was a U.S. congressman from Maryland, 1792–1794.

329.8   *Second Inaugural Address*]   This speech remains the shortest inaugural address ever delivered by an American president.

331.26   *Henry Lee*]   Henry "Light-Horse Harry" Lee (1756–1818) was governor of Virginia from 1792 to 1794. (His son, Robert E. Lee, was commanding general of Confederate forces in the Civil War.)

333.4   Freneau's and Beach's]   Philip Freneau's *National Gazette* and Benjamin Franklin Bache's *General Advertiser* were two pro-French Philadelphia newspapers that regularly attacked administration policy, often at the direction, or at least with the support, of the Secretary of State.

333.12   Mr G—t]   Edmond Charles Genêt (1763–1834) arrived in Philadelphia in May 1793 as the first minister to the United States from the new French republic. His refusal to respect American neutrality in the Anglo-French war led the Washington administration to ask for his recall in August 1793, and he was replaced in February 1794.

333.25   *Edmund Pendleton*]   Virginia jurist and patriot leader Edmund Pendleton (1721–1803) was the president of his state's Supreme Court of Appeals from 1779 until his death.

334.14   an enquiry]   Alexander Hamilton's actions as secretary of the treasury had been investigated by Congress in early 1793. However, criticism of that investigation led Hamilton to request in December "that a new Inquiry may be without delay instituted, in some mode most effectual for an accurate and thorough investigation." That inquiry culminated with a report on the "Condition of the Treasury Department" submitted to the House on May 22,

1794. The committee found that Hamilton had not "either directly or indirectly . . . procured any discount or credit" from the banks "upon the basis
of any public moneys which . . . have been deposited therein under his direction," and that "no moneys of the United States . . . have ever been . . .
used for, or applied to any purposes, but those of the Government, *except*, so
far as all moneys deposited in a bank are concerned in the general operations
thereof."

338.1–3   study of those branches . . . practice alone?] This would seem a
subtle call for a national military academy, for which Washington would advocate to the end of his life (see page 410.)

339.38   public prints] Newspapers.

340.22   *Charles Mynn Thruston*] Thruston (1738–1812) was an Anglican
minister who had served as a lieutenant in the Virginia militia during the
French and Indian War.

340.29–30   the people of Kentucky] Thruston had written "there is
existing at Kentuckey a powerful faction for placing that Country under the
protection of the British Government, & of seperating from the Union of the
States."

341.13   those Societies] Democratic Societies. Inspired by the French
Revolution, and championing the cause of the French republic in its war with
monarchical Britain, at least eleven Democratic Societies were founded in the
United States in 1793, and approximately twenty-four more were organized in
1794.

342.7   Genl. Morgan] In his letter to Washington, Thruston had recommended that former Continental general Daniel Morgan (1736–1802) be entrusted with the defense of the frontier in the event of a British or Spanish
invasion.

344.9–10   Mr. Henry . . . have said of me] Lee had written that Patrick
Henry believed that Washington considered him, Henry, to be "a factious se-
ditious character." Lee also reported that Jefferson, when recently asked if
Washington has attached himself to Britain and was being "governed by British influence," had replied "'that there was no danger of your being biassed by
consideration of that sort so long as you was influenced by the wise advisers or
advice which you at present had.'"

345.1–2   opposition . . . against me] The so-called "Conway Cabal."
See note 128.11.

346.17–18   your safe arrival] Washington had nominated Jay, then chief
justice of the Supreme Court, as a special envoy to Britain on April 16, 1794,
in an effort to avoid an Anglo-American war. Jay sailed on May 12 and landed
June 8. His instructions, largely drafted by Hamilton, directed him to seek a
commercial treaty with Britain and to secure the evacuation of British posts
still held in the Northwest Territory, compensation for captured American

shipping, and compensation for the slaves liberated by the British during the Revolution.

346.33–34   Mr. Simcoe] John Graves Simcoe (1752–1806), lieutenant governor of Canada from 1792 to 1794.

348.12   *Elizabeth Parke Custis*] Martha Washington's granddaughter Elizabeth Custis (1776–1834) would marry Thomas Law in 1796.

348.16   your sister Patcy] Martha Washington's granddaughter Martha Parke Custis (1777–1854) had become engaged to Thomas Peter; they married on January 16, 1795.

349.29   *Charles Carter, Jr.*] Charles Carter, Jr., (1733–96) had asked Washington for a loan of $1,000 to help his son, William Carter, whose carriage-making business had fallen on hard times.

350.28–30   treaty of Amity . . . Gazettes] Jay had signed a treaty with Britain in London on November 19, 1794, and a copy had reached Washington on March 7, 1795. Although he had yet to decide whether to sign the treaty, Washington submitted it to the Senate, which ratified it on June 24 after a secret debate. Republican journalist Benjamin Franklin Bache obtained the text of the treaty and published it in his *Philadelphia Aurora* on July 1, 1795, arousing intense public controversy.

351.33   this request of mine] Hamilton responded to Washington's request for a review of the Jay Treaty on July 11, 1795, with a fifty-three-page commentary, concluding with the recommendation that the president sign the treaty.

351.37   resolution of the Senate] The Senate had ratified the Jay treaty with the provision that its 12th article, limiting the size of American merchant ships trading in the British West Indies to 70 tons, be suspended.

352.9   *Patrick Henry*] Perhaps the most famous orator of the Revolution and twice the governor of Virginia (1776–79 and 1784–86), Patrick Henry (1736–1799) declined Washington's offer to become secretary of state, as he would again three months later when Washington asked him to become chief justice of the Supreme Court. These offers signified a rapprochement between Washington and Henry, who had been a leading Anti-Federalist critic of the Constitution during the ratification debates but whose Republican views had been shaken by the radicalism of the French Revolution.

352.17   offered to others] Following the forced resignation of Edmund Randolph on August 19, 1795, Washington offered the position of secretary of state to William Paterson, Thomas Johnson, and Charles Cotesworth Pinckney; all three declined.

353.22   papers relative . . . the Treaty] The House resolution requesting the papers had passed on March 24, 1796. All of Washington's cabinet had responded to this note by March 26, and all advised against complying with Congress's request.

355.19   the General Convention]   The Constitutional Convention of 1787.

358.25   letter without date]   In a letter probably written on June 16, 1796, Hamilton told Washington that a French merchant in New York had informed him of a French plan to seize American ships trading with British ports.

358.30   the Ship Mount Vernon]   The American ship *Mount Vernon* was seized by a French privateer off the coast of Delaware on June 9, 1796.

359.31–32   Mr. M——]   James Monroe (1758–1831), the future president, was from May 1794 to September 1796 the American minister to France.

361.12   Bache's Paper]   The questions concerning American neutrality that Washington had submitted in writing to his cabinet on April 18, 1793, had been obtained surreptitiously and published by Benjamin Franklin Bache.

362.7   the person evidently alluded to]   Alexander Hamilton.

362.30–31   the Little Sarah]   In July 1793 French envoy Genêt had outfitted a captured British merchant ship, the *Little Sarah*, in Philadelphia and sent it to sea as a privateer in defiance of the Washington administration's neutrality policy.

364.16   *Farewell Address*]   Never given by Washington as a speech, the Farewell Address first appeared in the September 19, 1796, edition of the Philadelphia newspaper *American Daily Advertiser*, published by David C. Claypoole.

380.8   *John Greenwood*]   Greenwood was a New York City dentist who constructed several sets of false teeth for Washington.

381.2   *Jonathan Trumbull, Jr.*]   Washington's military secretary from June 1781 to December 1783, Jonathan Trumbull, Jr., (1740–1809) was the deputy governor of Connecticut at the time of this exchange.

381.20–21   consequences . . . fears forebode]   On January 23, 1797, Trumbull had written: "Some of the consequences while I have heretofore ventured to present to your View in contemplation, have already been experienced, in the late hardly contested Election for your Successor. Would to Heaven! that this might be the only Evil we shall have to encounter in this Event—circumstances however, almost forbid us the Hope."

382.8   *James McHenry*]   A native of Ireland who served as an aide to both Washington and Lafayette during the Revolutionary War and was a Maryland delegate to the Constitutional Convention, James McHenry (1753–1816) became Washington's secretary of war in January 1796. He retained the post in the Adams administration before being forced to resign in May 1800.

383.16   *Lawrence Lewis*]   The son of Washington's sister Betty Washington

Lewis, Lawrence Lewis (1767–1839) had agreed to serve as his uncle's secretary. On Washington's last birthday, February 22, 1799, Lewis married Nelly Custis, Martha Washington's granddaughter.

383.19   the loss of your Servant] Lewis had written that his departure for Mount Vernon had been delayed by the escape of a slave.

384.31   the Secretary of War] James McHenry.

385.24–25   demands amounting to tribute] Presidential electors met on December 7, 1796, and with seventy-one electoral votes Adams was elected to succeed Washington. (Thomas Jefferson received sixty-eight votes and became vice president.) The focus of the Adams administration was promptly directed toward U.S. relations with the French Directory, which by the time of this exchange had deteriorated significantly. Shortly after assuming the presidency, Adams had learned that the Directory has ordered Charles Cotesworth Pinckney, who had been appointed as minister to France by Washington in 1796, to leave the country. On May 16, 1797, addressing a special session of Congress, Adams announced that a new diplomatic mission, comprised of Pinckney, John Marshall, and Elbridge Gerry, would be sent to France. These new American envoys had a brief informal meeting with Talleyrand, the French foreign minister, on October 8, before being approached by three of Talleyrand's agents, who solicited $240,000 bribe as precondition for further negotiations; the agents also demanded that the Americans agree to loan France $12 million and repudiate critical remarks about French policy made by Adams in his May 16 address to Congress. The American commissioners refused to pay, and described their reception in dispatches sent to Secretary of State Timothy Pickering on October 22 and November 8. Pickering received the coded dispatches from the envoys on March 4, 1798, along with an uncoded letter reporting that the Directory had closed French ports to neutral shipping and made all ships carrying British products subject to capture. After the dispatches were decoded, Adams consulted with his cabinet, which divided over whether to seek a declaration of war. Adams sent a message to Congress on March 19 announcing failure of the peace mission and requesting the adoption of defensive measures. In response to a request from the House of Representatives, Adams submitted the dispatches to Congress on April 3, and they were quickly published, with Talleyrand's agents referred to as X, Y, and Z. Revelation of the "XYZ" affair caused popular furor against France, helping to bring the two countries into the state of quasi-war that forced Washington once more, and for the last time, to answer his nation's call.

394.2   *Alexander Spotswood*] Continental Army veteran Alexander Spotswood, Jr., (1751–1818) was married to Elizabeth Washington, daughter of Washington's half brother Augustine.

394.4–5   letter of the 13th . . . Sedition Laws] On December 9, 1798, Spotswood wrote Washington to protest that the letter "dated the 13th, bearing my signature, is an infamous forgery . . ." In June and July 1798 the

Federalist Congress had passed, and President Adams signed into law, three acts bearing on foreign aliens and one bearing on sedition. The alien acts extended the period required for naturalization from five to fourteen years and gave the president the power to expel or, in time of declared war, to imprison dangerous aliens. (No one was formally expelled under the law, though many French aliens left voluntarily). The sedition act made the publication of "false, scandalous, and malicious writing" attacking the federal government, the president, or the Congress a crime punishable by up to two years in prison and a fine not exceeding $2,000. (Ten Republican editors and printers were convicted under the Sedition Act during the Adams administration.)

397.18   candidate . . . General Assembly]   Henry agreed to become a candidate for the Virginia House of Delegates and was elected, but his death in June 1799 prevented his taking office.

398.25   Slaves which I hold]   In the summer of 1799, Washington drew up a detailed census of the Mount Vernon slaves, a document he titled "Negroes Belonging to George Washington in his own right and by Marriage." The census listed 317 slaves on the five Mount Vernon farms. Washington owned 124 of these people, 40 were leased from another owner, and the remaining 153 "Dower" slaves were the property of the Custis estate. The Custis slaves could not be freed by Washington or his wife; they were to be inherited by Martha Washington's grandchildren after her death. At the time of Washington's death, there were 314 slaves at Mount Vernon; 122 of them were freed by the terms of his will. The executors of Washington's estate continued to support the freed people who chose to remain as pensioners at Mount Vernon after the death of Martha Washington. The last pensioner died in 1833.

399.26   William Lee]   Washington had purchased his personal servant Billy, or William Lee, in 1768 from Mrs. Mary Lee, widow of Col. John Lee of Westmoreland Country, Virginia, for 68 15s. He served Washington throughout the Revolutionary War, during which time he took as his wife "one of his own colour a free woman" from Philadelphia, named Margaret Thomas, who was, Washington wrote, "also of my family." By 1799 William Lee, who had broken both knees, was crippled and employed as a shoemaker at Mansion House farm. He died at Mount Vernon in 1810.

400.22–29   Whereas by a Law . . . one hundred shares]   On January 6, 1785, Virginia Governor Benjamin Harrison had written Washington that "the assembly yesterday without a discenting voice complimented you with fifty shares in the potowmack company and one hundred in the James River company." Having committed himself to foregoing any public salary, Washington agonized about whether he should accept the shares. In the end he induced the legislature to provide that the future profit from stock should go not to him personally but instead "stand appropriated to such objects of a public nature, in such manner, and under such distributions, as the said George Washington, esq. by deed during his life, or by his last will and testament, shall direct and appoint."

402.22   Liberty-Hall Academy] Now Washington and Lee University.

408.17   the answer I gave you] In his letter of June 22, 1799, Trumbull had urged Washington to enter the presidential election of 1800. Washington continued to refuse to consider the suggestion.

408.31   present Gentleman in Office] President John Adams.

411.2   *James Anderson*] Anderson was farm manager and operator of the distillery at Mount Vernon. Washington enclosed detailed plans for the management of lands and labor at each of the Mount Vernon farms.

Index

478

The Library of America Paperback Classics Series

American Speeches: Political Oratory from Patrick Henry to Barack Obama (various authors)
Edited and with an introduction by Ted Widmer
ISBN: 978-1-59853-094-0

The Education of Henry Adams by Henry Adams
With an introduction by Leon Wieseltier
ISBN: 978-1-59853-060-5

The Red Badge of Courage by Stephen Crane
With an introduction by Robert Stone
ISBN: 978-1-59853-061-2

The Souls of Black Folk by W.E.B. Du Bois
With an introduction by John Edgar Wideman
ISBN: 978-1-59853-054-4

Essays: First and Second Series by Ralph Waldo Emerson
With an introduction by Douglas Crase
ISBN: 978-1-59853-084-1

The Autobiography by Benjamin Franklin
With an introduction by Daniel Aaron
ISBN: 978-1-59853-095-7

The Scarlet Letter by Nathaniel Hawthorne
With an introduction by Harold Bloom
ISBN: 978-1-59853-112-1

The Varieties of Religious Experience by William James
With an introduction by Jaroslav Pelikan
ISBN: 978-1-59853-062-9

Selected Writings by Thomas Jefferson
With an introduction by Tom Wicker
ISBN: 978-1-59853-096-4

The Autobiography of an Ex-Colored Man by James Weldon Johnson
With an introduction by Charles R. Johnson
ISBN: 978-1-59853-113-8

Selected Speeches and Writings by Abraham Lincoln
With an introduction by Gore Vidal
ISBN: 978-1-59853-053-7

The Call of the Wild by Jack London
With an introduction by E. L. Doctorow
ISBN: 978-1-59853-058-2

Moby-Dick by Herman Melville
With an introduction by Edward Said
ISBN: 978-1-59853-085-8

My First Summer in the Sierra and Selected Essays by John Muir
Edited with an introduction by Bill McKibben
ISBN: 978-1-59853-111-4

Selected Tales, with The Narrative of Arthur Gordon Pym
by Edgar Allan Poe
With an introduction by Diane Johnson
ISBN: 978-1-59853-056-8

Uncle Tom's Cabin by Harriet Beecher Stowe
With an introduction by James M. McPherson
ISBN: 978-1-59853-086-5

Walden by Henry David Thoreau
With an introduction by Edward Hoagland
ISBN: 978-1-59853-063-6

The Adventures of Tom Sawyer by Mark Twain
With an introduction by Russell Baker
ISBN: 978-1-59853-087-2

Life on the Mississippi by Mark Twain
With an introduction by Jonathan Raban
ISBN: 978-1-59853-057-5

Selected Writings by George Washington
With an introduction by Ron Chernow
ISBN: 978-1-59853-110-7

The House of Mirth by Edith Wharton
With an introduction by Mary Gordon
ISBN: 978-1-59853-055-1

Leaves of Grass, The Complete 1855 and 1891–92 Editions
by Walt Whitman
With an introduction by John Hollander
ISBN: 978-1-59853-097-1

For more information, please visit www.loa.org/paperbackclassics/

The contents of this Paperback Classic are drawn from *George Washington: Writings* (John Rhodehamel, editor), volume number 91 in the Library of America series, which collects over 440 letters, orders, addresses, and other documents.

Created with seed funding from the National Endowment for the Humanities and the Ford Foundation, The Library of America is a nonprofit cultural institution that preserves our nation's literary heritage by publishing, and keeping permanently in print, authoritative editions of America's best and most significant writing. Hailed as "the most important book-publishing project in the nation's history" (*Newsweek*), this award-winning series maintains America's most treasured writers in "the finest-looking, longest-lasting edition ever made" (*The New Republic*).

Since 1982, over 220 hardcover volumes have been published in the Library of America series, each containing up to 1600 pages and including a number of works. In many cases, the complete works of a writer are collected in as few as three compact volumes. New volumes are added each year to make all the essential writings of America's foremost novelists, historians, poets, essayists, philosophers, playwrights, journalists, and statesmen part of The Library of America.

Each volume features: authoritative, unabridged texts • a chronology of the author's life, helpful notes, and a brief textual essay • a handsomely designed, easy-to-read page • high-quality, acid-free paper, bound in a cloth cover and sewn to lie flat when opened • a ribbon marker and printed end papers.

For more information, a complete list of titles, tables of contents, and to request a catalogue, please visit www.loa.org.